Rapture

David B. Currie

Rapture

The End-Times Error That
Leaves the Bible Behind

SOPHIA INSTITUTE PRESS®
Manchester, New Hampshire

Cover design by Theodore Schluenderfritz

Sophia Institute Press®
Box 5284, Manchester, NH 03108
1-800-888-9344
www.sophiainstitute.com

Library of Congress Cataloging-in-Publication Data

Currie, David B.
    Rapture : the end-times error that leaves the Bible behind /
    David B. Currie.
        p. cm.
    Includes bibliographical references.
    ISBN 1-928832-72-5 (pbk. : alk. paper)
    1. Rapture (Christian eschatology) 2. Eschatology —
    Biblical teaching. 3. Catholic Church — Doctrines.
    I. Title.
BT887.C87 2003
236′.9 — dc21   2003006717

03 04 05 06 07 08 09 10 9 8 7 6 5 4 3 2

Contents

Dedicated to

Colleen and our children:
Jonathan, Kathleen, Matthew,
Benjamin, Stephen, Alison,
Elisabeth, Daniel, and Mary:
Without their patience and love,
life would be so gray.

While I take full responsibility
for any omissions or errors,
I gratefully acknowledge the
assistance of the following people:

Matthew and Benjamin Currie:
Their cheerful assistance
helped eliminate errors.

Thomas Howard:
His timely encouragement
enabled me to persevere.

Todd Aglialoro:
His able editing
proved invaluable.

Foreword

By Scott Hahn

David Currie has written something remarkable here. *Rapture* is much more than its title suggests. It's more than a topical treatment of a Fundamentalist fad. It's more than a book of apologetics. It's more than the refutation of an interpretive error.

I'm tempted to describe it as a virtual summa of apocalyptic texts and prophetic positions. In *Rapture*, Currie gives us a comprehensive collection of the biblical texts that Fundamentalist Protestants have commonly interpreted as end-times predictions. He subjects each passage to sane and sober analysis, correcting errors along the way, and establishing a range of reasonable interpretations, all in harmony with the Catholic Church's living Tradition (see CCC, pars. 111-114; see bibliography for publication details and for a list of abbreviations for works cited in this book).

If Currie had done no more than survey all these texts, he would have performed an invaluable service. Not only does he treat well-known passages from the Book of Revelation, but he also considers many lesser-known important texts from both the Old and New Testaments. The compilation itself encourages a contextual reading.

The Church interprets any scriptural text in its proper context, which is the entire Bible. The New Testament writers had a deep knowledge of the Old Testament books, and they assumed the same in their readers. Thus, Catholics have always found the Old Testament revealed in the New, and the New Testament concealed in the Old. This is why we hear readings from both Testaments every time we go to Mass. This is known as "typology" (see CCC, pars. 128-130). The Pontifical Biblical Commission describes how the Church's Liturgy makes this work: "By regularly associating a text of the Old Testament with the text of the Gospel, the cycle often suggests a scriptural interpretation moving in the direction of typology" (*The Interpretation of the Bible in the Church*, IV, C, 1).

The Fundamentalist tendency, however, is to read each biblical text in isolation from other texts and from the larger context of Sacred Tradition, including the ancient Israelite prophetic traditions. The problem, of course, is that the texts themselves were not written to be read this way. The biblical authors assumed that their readers would all share a common life, liturgical worship, and awareness of history. For all these things were catholic (that is, universal) and held in common. Yet these are precisely the things — sacraments, Liturgy, and Tradition — that modern movements such as Fundamentalism have rejected. Lacking these interpretive keys, they end up groping and guessing at what's behind the locked doors of apocalyptic passages.

Currie applies sound Catholic principles to the many and various scriptural texts, treating them in their canonical order — and a wonderful thing happens along the way. Gradually, we realize that these texts are more than prophetic bursts of surreal images and shocking announcements. They actually present a unified, coherent interpretation of salvation history.

The sacred authors saw history in covenantal terms. The covenant revealed a consistent pattern of how God would deal with His people in every age. Through the covenants, Israel was established as God's family, first as a nation (Moses) and then as a kingdom

(David). Accordingly, the fatherly terms of each covenant included rewards as well as punishments: "I set before you this day a blessing and a curse: the blessing, if you obey the commandments . . . and the curse, if you do not" (Deut. 11:26-28). The covenant, then, is what helped make sense of the events, both pleasant and painful, that befell Israel and their surrounding gentile neighbors.

From age to age, God's dealings with His people follow a consistent covenantal pattern of fatherly faithfulness, judgment, and mercy. That is why the prophets of ancient Israel could discern and describe God's future acts of deliverance in terms that reflected and amplified His saving acts in Israel's past. For example, God's future restoration of the Davidic kingdom is announced in terms of a New Exodus, by several prophets (Isaiah, Jeremiah, Ezekiel, and Hosea). As Jean Cardinal Danielou once stated, "Prophecy is the typological interpretation of history."

The biblical writers did indeed use cataclysmic imagery and cosmic figures to express world-ending events. For the world will surely end one day. But before the definitive end of the world, many worlds will come to an end. The Babylonian world came to an end, as did the world of the Pharaohs. The Israelite world came to an end, as did the world of the Second Temple Jews.

Indeed, the same pattern appears to continue on into the New Testament age. For the Roman world, the Byzantine world, the North African world — all these great worlds, great civilizations, came to an end, as will our own little world someday. Human history itself will eventually come to an end; we know neither the day nor the hour. But, until the absolute and plenary End, it will end many times over, as it were, on the installment plan. Thus the biblical apocalypses are timely for every age, and not just the last.

This is an important principle for us to understand, because the Bible's authority grows weak without it. Critics of the Scriptures like to point out that Jesus and the Apostles seemed to expect things on earth to come to a hasty conclusion. Before a generation had time to pass from the scene, the world was supposed to pass away and make room for the Kingdom of God.

Currie shows us that a world did indeed come to an end, and indeed it was forty years (exactly one *genea,* or generation) after Jesus had made His prediction. For in 70 A.D., Jerusalem was destroyed, and with it the Temple, which had been God's dwelling on earth. An end did come; it just wasn't *the* end that so many Fundamentalists project onto the biblical writers.

The New Testament writers and their first-century Christian readers were not Fundamentalists, and neither were the Jews who lived in the centuries before Christ. Our ancient ancestors expected a world to end, and their expectation was fulfilled. They took Jesus at His word, and He kept His word.

The destruction that God brought down on the Temple was a fulfillment of prophecy, but it was also itself a prophecy. The Temple was a piece of sacramental architecture that embodied the world as a microcosm. The destruction of the Temple was a prophetic event that pointed to the cosmic Temple's destruction at the end of history. And the judgment of Jerusalem is an object lesson for all other worlds until then.

Currie makes these difficult matters abundantly clear. His treatment is ambitious in that he always strives for a complete picture. He tries to present every text and consider every interpretation. Yet the book is, at the same time, modest to an almost miraculous degree. Although Currie has pondered the various interpretations as deeply as anyone has — and although he obviously has his favorites — he never puts forth his readings as the only interpretive possibilities. He recognizes that the Church permits plenty of liberty in this area. Put another way: Currie is dogmatic in the best sense. He respects the authority of defined dogma, but he never claims dogmatic status for mere interpretive opinions.

It is the same combination of holy ambition and intelligent modesty that gives this book its air of calm. I must say that this quality is unusual in books that discuss apocalyptic texts, which tend themselves to be fevered and passionate. But such calm is especially unusual in these troubled times, when the daily news serves only to feed apocalyptic hysteria.

Currie keeps a steady, charitable, clear voice through it all. There is nothing defensive about this book. Currie is not out to pick a fight or accept a dare; he's out to speak the truth. Nor does he hold Fundamentalists in contempt, for he once counted himself among their number. Instead, like St. Paul, he affirms "whatever is true, whatever is honorable, whatever is just, whatever is pure, whatever is lovely, whatever is gracious" (Phil. 4:8) in his opponents, even as he shows them where they go astray.

We can all learn much from David Currie, not only from what he says, which is wise, but from how he says it, which is Catholic and Christian.

Preface

The purpose of this book is to answer a simple question: "Is it possible that at any moment a secret rapture could occur that will take believing Christians to Heaven, while plunging the rest of the world into an inescapable Great Tribulation for seven horrendous years?" The answer is important, because if this rapture is about to happen, you might be among those left behind!

This is a simple question, but it requires a thorough answer. We must touch all the relevant bases. We must look under every rock and behind every door. For the answer should affect how you and I live our lives.

This book is unapologetically apologetic. I intend unequivocally to defend the historical teaching of the Church as it relates to the last things. Yet it is also a "no holds barred" search for the truth. I will admit any and all evidence that bears on the subject; the stakes are too high to do any less.

I have endeavored to be fair in my discussions of others' beliefs. If I am able to disagree with a group's propositional teachings without disparaging the personal faith of its members, I will have succeeded. You be my judge.

Although the groups that believe in a future rapture distinct from the second coming are diverse in almost every other conceivable way, for the sake of convenience I have chosen to name all those who hold to that particular belief "rapturists." This is a useful, descriptive term that avoids problems some other labels might have caused. For example, about half of these people would accept the designation "dispensationalist," but the other half would vehemently repudiate it. Another adequate term, Darbyites, is rejected as pejorative by all rapturist theologians.

For efficiency of language, I have also grouped Fundamentalists with other Protestants. Strictly speaking, many of them do not consider themselves to be Protestants. Protestantism began with Luther and Calvin in the sixteenth century, whereas Fundamentalists trace their lineage to the original Apostles. They believe that they had to "go underground" in the fourth century, only to emerge in modern times. Although Fundamentalists may dislike being called Protestants, I have been careful not to allow my use of this term to distort my descriptions.

Sections of this book deal with an extremely difficult and unique period of history. In the first century we will encounter Romans who were evil, and Jews who were scoundrels. We will encounter Roman Caesars who were not patriotic, and Jewish priests who were not devout. But it would be ludicrous to let the events that happened hundreds of years ago affect our relationships with groups of people alive today. Particularly in relation to Israel, we will do well to remember the words of G. K. Chesterton: "It is true . . . humanly speaking, that the world owes God to the Jews" (TEM). Nothing in this book should be taken as an indictment, however minuscule, of any modern person, nation, or race.

This manuscript is an outgrowth of a series of talks I gave in 1998 in Libertyville, Illinois. Like many Christians, I was sure that there would be an upswing in interest in the second coming of Christ as the previous millennium ended and the new began. Unlike some of my friends, however, I did not believe that this interest would disappear just because Christ did not return to rapture away believers when the clock chimed midnight on January 1, 2000.

No, there are powerful religious groups that will continue persuading people that the rapture is only a heartbeat away. They will continue to teach their interpretive view of Scripture well into the next century. Even though many Catholics have unwittingly been influenced by this teaching, its perspective on the second coming is not a Catholic one. In this book, I will attempt to show why, using the Bible as our authority. I will also reference the beliefs of the early Christians.

My own experience cannot help but influence this book. I was raised in a devout Protestant home, the only son of a Fundamentalist pastor. Many of the leaders of the "pre-mill, pre-trib" movement were close family friends. I attended Trinity College and Trinity Evangelical Divinity School in Deerfield, Illinois. While still a believer in a pretribulation rapture, I team-taught a college class on prophecy and preached it from many pulpits. Although I had no natural inclination toward Catholicism, I finally reconciled with the Church in my forties. The rationale behind that life-changing decision can be found in my book *Born Fundamentalist, Born Again Catholic*.

Before we get too far, I should let you know what this book is *not* about. We will not be examining in depth any of the prophecies not contained in the Bible — for example, any of the Marian apparitions or the prophecies of Nostradamus. These fall outside the focus of this book, and also outside the limits of my expertise. Others more qualified than I have already done excellent work in this area.

No, I want primarily to examine the Bible's teachings regarding the last things. I firmly believe Scripture remains a completely reliable authority for faith and practice.

I have written specifically for the lay reader acquainted with the Bible and its overall message, whether Catholic or Protestant. My goal is to help the average interested Christian understand the issues as presented in Scripture and make a reasonable, informed decision. Rather than being the last word on this topic, I hope to be for some readers the first word.

Where appropriate and practical, I have noted my sources in parentheses. In a few cases, because my research was done for personal reasons decades ago, I might have forgotten where the seed of my thinking originated. If I have failed to give credit where due, it is certainly unintentional.

I would be seriously remiss, however, if I did not mention two Masters' theses that were very helpful to me when I was rethinking these issues a decade ago as a mid-life Protestant. They are unfortunately unpublished, but are well worth a trip to the Trinity Evangelical Divinity School library for reading. They were individually researched and written by Richard White and David Palm. Both of these committed Protestant men later reconciled with the Church.

All quotations from the Bible use the Revised Standard Version, Catholic Edition, unless otherwise noted. I will refer to the last book of the Bible as The Apocalypse instead of as Revelation, so as to avoid confusion with the general concept of God's revelation of Himself to His people.

Please allow me to add one last word of caution: fight the temptation to skip ahead to the end for quick answers. Each chapter of this book, indeed each section, builds on the understanding forged in the sections that preceded it. The Apocalypse will make much better sense after we have understood the message of Daniel and Christ's Olivet Discourse.

True Stories

Something was amiss. David was used to his mother greeting him from the kitchen when he arrived home from school. Being ten years old, he knew his responsibility: find Mom and let her know he got home okay. Then he was free to play outside. After checking for her downstairs, he checked the bedrooms upstairs, poking his head into every room and calling, "Mom?"

"Where is she?" he wondered aloud. He rushed down the winding stairs to the laundry and storage rooms in the basement. But Mom never answered his calls. He charged outside to check the yard, but she was nowhere to be seen.

All of a sudden, a horrible thought popped into his mind. "I've been left behind!" Panic was right on the heels of that thought. He knew what *that* meant.

He had been taught in church that there would come a moment in the near future when the true believers in Christ would silently, mysteriously, and unexpectedly disappear in an instant. This was called the "rapture," and it would be followed immediately by seven years of "great tribulation." As David raced back into the house, he tried to reassure himself that he was, in fact, a true believer. But his ten-year-old mind found reasons to doubt his salvation.

Suddenly it struck him that even his sisters were nowhere to be found. They should have been home from school as well! He was truly alone in the house. The entire family had disappeared without a trace!

"I can call Dad at work," he reasoned in the midst of his panic. But he knew that would be pointless. Dad was a true believer just like his mother and sisters. Dad would have been raptured along with the rest of the family.

No, he was left behind in the rapture, and it was his own fault. He had come to his senses *too late*.

⌒

The elderly missionary spent many a night weeping on her pillow. It had come as such a shock when the Chinese communists overran China. She had spent most of her life in China attempting to explain the gospel of Christ to the Chinese people. She had helped start a small Protestant church for fellowship. But she was weeping not just because of the abruptness of her departure from her Chinese friends. She was mourning her message. Because she had been taught in Bible school that Christ would return at any moment and rapture His true believers away from the Great Tribulation, she had never prepared her new converts for substantial persecution. No need to prepare for trouble; Christ had suffered on the Cross to save us from both earthly suffering and God's wrath.

With agonizing clarity, she saw how wrong she had been. Although her Chinese converts may not have been living through the Great Tribulation, it made little difference to their daily experience. They were being systematically hunted down and persecuted by a godless government intent on breaking their faith. For many of them, this tribulation was their own personal great and final one.

Now she could do nothing for her friends to correct the errors she had so meticulously taught them earlier. She regularly wept in her pillow because she knew that it was *too late*.

⌒

Mitch and his wife, Linda, converted to Evangelical Christianity when they were in college. She had been raised a Catholic, and he had been raised a Lutheran. But neither of them had taken their faith seriously as a child. Of course, neither did anyone else in their families. When they got "saved" in college, spiritual things became fascinating to them. Like so many other converts, they were taught about the "end times." After they were married, Linda stayed home with the children, and Mitch did very well in his profession.

When the opportunity to move presented itself, they decided not to buy a house. After all, they had been taught in church that Christ could come back at any moment, probably within the next few years at the very latest. They knew that it had been almost a generation since Israel had been established in 1948. They had been taught that, according to the prophecy of Jesus in the Olivet Discourse, the rapture must occur within a generation of that event. They were the "generation of the fig tree." Their rapture would surprise the world at any moment. The Great Tribulation would immediately follow the rapture for the next seven years, but they would be safely taken up out of the carnage by Jesus Himself.

If the end was imminent, why invest in a house? So they moved in with Linda's mother. It might put a strain on their family, but better to give more to their church, in the hope that more people would hear the gospel before it was *too late*.

⌒

Don and Rose, too, had been taught that the rapture was about to occur at any moment. So they decided to stop having children. They already had three boys whose care took a great deal of time. They reasoned that if they had any more children, it would distract them from their ministry. Wouldn't it be better to use any extra time to try to win souls for Heaven before the rapture? After all, once that event occurred, the world would be thrown into chaos and sin by the antichrist, and for those left behind, it would already be *too late*.

☞

Dave's college grade-point average qualified him to enter any seminary he chose. But the older ministers whom Dave respected told him to not worry about getting a higher degree: "Jesus is coming. There is not much time before the rapture. Better to get involved in winning souls right now and take only those courses you feel are necessary for that ministry." So Dave made the decision to enter full-time Christian service, while enrolling in a nearby seminary on a part-time basis. A degree seemed so unimportant, almost selfish, in the light of the imminent return of Christ. He certainly did not want to be the reason even one person did not hear the gospel until after the rapture, when it would be *too late*.

☞

Ann believed that abortion was fundamentally irreconcilable with her Fundamentalist Christian convictions. She did not know whether she would be very good at it, but she wanted to get involved in the effort to reverse *Roe v. Wade*. Her Christian friends, however, counseled against it. "Why polish the brass on a sinking ship?" they asked. "Why not spend your time evangelizing your neighbors? Jesus is coming back to rapture the true believers at any moment. Abortion is wrong, but evangelizing the lost is more important. Share the gospel with unbelievers before it is *too late*."

☞

The year was 1950. Stephen and his wife, Beth, had always wanted to spend their lives serving God. But now they became aware of the significance of the year 1948, when Israel had been re-established as a sovereign state. Theologian friends convinced Stephen that this meant they were living in the end times. Based on the words of Jesus in the Olivet Discourse, this young couple was taught that they were in the final generation before Christ would rapture His Church. They decided to attend seminary. They built their lives around promulgating this message to anyone who would listen. It became the issue that defined them and their ministry. No sacrifice was too great when it came to getting the message out before it was *too late*.

In the late nineteenth century, William E. Blackstone wrote about the rapture in the book *Jesus Is Coming*. It became a bestseller and was one of the first books in the United States to herald this new view of Christ's return. A successful Chicago businessman, Blackstone used his influence to lobby President Harrison in favor of a Jewish homeland in Palestine. He believed that a Jewish homeland and a rebuilt Temple in Jerusalem were necessary prerequisites for Jesus' return after the rapture.

Blackstone put his money where his mouth was. He bought hundreds of Bibles and placed them in caves throughout Palestine. He believed that after the rapture, Jewish people would flee into the Judean hills during the persecution of the Great Tribulation and would be forced to hide in the caves to survive. Once there, Blackstone hoped they would discover his hidden Bibles. After reading them, these Jews in the middle of the Great Tribulation would come to realize the truth of Jesus' claims. Blackstone spent enormous amounts of money to store these Bibles safely in remote caves before it was *too late*.

General Orde Wingate's name is memorialized in Israel on street signs and historical markers. Knowledgeable Israelis know this Scottish military leader who trained much of the original Israeli guerrilla forces as the "gentle Gentile." Some of his students, such as Moshe Dayan and Yigal Allon, would become legendary through the use of Wingate's guerrilla tactics. It is generally agreed that Israel would not exist today without the commitment he made to share his unique abilities with those men.

But what motivated Wingate to embrace a people who were scorned as troublemakers by his fellow British officers? Many do not know that it was his Christian Fundamentalist upbringing, including a firm belief in premillennialism. He believed that an ethic Jewish nation would once again become the focus of God's spiritual program here on earth for precisely one thousand years. But he believed that this would not — indeed could not — occur until the modern state of Israel was founded. For Christ to return for His Church in the rapture, the Jews must first win the guerrilla warfare of the 1940s and reinhabit their ancient land. Wingate knew that this window of opportunity would not last forever, so he taught what he knew best, guerrilla warfare, before it was *too late*.

Peter grew up in a devout Catholic family. In college, he encountered a group of very persuasive Protestant students, led by a dynamic young Evangelical couple. They loaned him a novel, *The Late Great Planet Earth* — destined to become the biggest religious seller of all time, excepting only the Bible. The book was interesting, but, more important to Peter, it was very scary. It predicted the coming of an antichrist, a secret rapture of born-again believers, a Great Tribulation, and a final battle between Christ and Satan.

Peter was frightened at the prospect of suffering through the Great Tribulation, because he did not know for certain that he was born again. According to these Evangelical Protestants, the Rapture could occur momentarily. Although the Temple might be rebuilt first, and the antichrist might appear on the world scene at any time, there was nothing to prevent the secret rapture from occurring without warning. Peter prayed the prayer of salvation, was rebaptized, and started to fellowship with these dynamic Evangelicals.

He eventually married one of the nice young Protestant girls he met in the group, and they started a family. For years he was thankful that he had heard about the rapture and Great Tribulation, giving him the opportunity to get saved before it was *too late*.

IS THIS ISSUE IMPORTANT?

These are true stories about real people. I have known every one of them (except for William Blackstone and General Orde Wingate, both dead, but I have met Blackstone's descendants and Wingate's son, Colonel Orde Wingate). And yes, I am the little boy in the first story (I eventually did find Mom, who was at the neighbor's house).

These stories illustrate how this popular theology is of more than just academic significance. Every one of these individuals made decisions — some drastically life-changing — based on their belief in an imminent, secret rapture. But is this rapture theology a truly biblical way of interpreting the relevant Scripture texts? Catholics should further wonder how this theology squares with Church teaching.

The stakes are high. If the rapturists are correct, then those who count themselves as Christian, but are not Evangelical or Fundamentalist, are in for a very difficult time of seven years, a tribulation that could start at any moment without any warning. But if the rapturists are wrong, then people are making decisions based on skewed priorities, and some of those decisions have the potential to ruin their lives. What we believe makes a difference in how we live.

Rapture

Having grown up in the rapturist movement, I can assure you that it makes a monumental difference in the way the world is viewed. Most of the people in this movement believe that they, or at the very least their children or grandchildren, will see the end of the world. They feel certain that history will not extend so long that they might be forgotten before Christ returns. As a Catholic, I now understand that even my grandchildren's grandchildren may easily be dead before Christ returns. I now know that there is no reason that history will not continue until the very memory of my name and my family's name are entirely forgotten. That is a very different mindset.

But more important than any one person's life, truth is at stake. Either the rapture, the Great Tribulation, the Millennium, and eternity will unfold as rapturists claim, or they will not. Although no human can peer into the future to give us absolute certainty, we can and should study the teachings of divine revelation to determine what is really revealed there.

Further, truth is vitally important when raising children. Untold thousands of young Catholics have left the Faith after being exposed to rapturist ideas about the end times. Knowing the *truth* about biblical prophecy will enable parents and children to be prepared for the rapturist challenge when it comes. And it will come. The frenzy over the end times is running hot, and — if the success of the *Left Behind* books is any indication — it looks to continue for some time.

Rapture

"Study to show thyself approved unto God,
a workman that needeth not to be ashamed,
rightly dividing the word of truth."

Paul
2 Timothy 2:15 (KJV), first century

"What, pray, can be more sacred than
this sacred mystery of the Scriptures? . . .
What honey can be sweeter than to
learn of God's wise plan . . . and gaze
on the mind of the Creator?
Let the others, if they will, have their
wealth, and . . . bask in popular applause. . . .
Our delight shall be to meditate on the
Law of the Lord day and night,
to knock at His door when it is not open,
to receive the bread of the Trinity."

Jerome
Epistle 30 to Paula, fourth century

"Study. Study in earnest.
If you are to be salt and light,
you need knowledge.
Or do you imagine that an idle
and lazy life will entitle you to
receive infused knowledge?"

Josemaría Escrivá
The Way, twentieth century

Part I

What Is the Rapture?

Chapter One

A Short History

Is this fascination with the end of the world unique to our times? You may be surprised to find that it is not. In fact, the modern fascination with the end of the world is actually very unmodern. Join me in a short stroll through history that will illustrate that the end of the world has always been upon us.

MONTANIS'S MILLENNIUM

In 156 A.D., a charismatic leader named Montanis surfaced in Papuza, in what is now Turkey. He convinced many of the Christians in that part of Phrygia that a private revelation had predicted that Christ would return at any moment. They sought to bring the Church back to its "original simplicity" under the direct guidance of the Holy Spirit. Montanis's followers came to believe that they were the spiritual elite of the millennial kingdom that Christ would set up at His return. Christ would rule on earth for a thousand years, with Papuza as His seat of government. Because of their stubborn misuse of The Apocalypse, the Church in the East found herself questioning the canonicity of the last book of the Bible. Perhaps most disturbing, Montanis taught that the ecstatic utterances of their prophets (private revelation) were more authoritative than the teachings of the Apostles (general revelation). This led to the Montanists' splitting from the Church. Eventually

Montanis's followers became radically heretical, and the movement died out by the sixth century, but not before they became the blueprint for a multitude of later schismatic movements based on the promise of an imminent corporeal Millennium here on earth.

IRENAEUS: GODFATHER OF RAPTURISM

Almost all variants of the modern rapturist position cite the writings of St. Irenaeus as early evidence for their belief system. In 177 A.D., he was appointed bishop of Lyons. His life work was to combat the Gnostics. In that role, he began to teach that there would be a thousand-year earthly Kingdom of Christ immediately following the second coming. (This is called millenarianism, premillennialism, and chiliasm. But by any and all names, it was strongly and repeatedly rejected by the other leaders of the early Church.)

Irenaeus predicted that the world would end six thousand years after it had begun. He based his calculations on the Bible verse that says that a thousand years is as a day with God (2 Pet. 3:8). "For in as many days as this world was made, in so many thousand years shall it be concluded. . . . In six days created things were completed: it is evident, therefore, that they will come to an end at the sixth thousand year" (*AH*, V:28:3). This means the end of the world would have been around 1000 A.D., although some now claim he meant 2000 A.D. Either way, he was wrong.

A student of Irenaeus, the priest Hippolytus, also did what would be repeated throughout history as a logical conclusion of millenarianism. Around the end of the second century, he predicted that the world would end soon, and he set a specific date. Based on the size of Noah's ark, he determined the date to be 500 A.D.

Around the same time, Julius Africanus (b. 160) also wrote that the second coming would occur six thousand years after the Creation. He calculated that by the time of Christ's Passion, the earth had already been in existence for 5,531 years. As a result, he agreed with Hippolytus that the second coming would occur no later than 500 A.D. Irenaeus, Hippolytus, and Julius Africanus ended up like so many other men who have made these predictions: with egg on their faces.

TERTULLIAN'S RESURRECTED ANTICHRIST

In Carthage, around 200 A.D., Tertullian developed a scenario for the end times that now seems rather provincial. He wrote that "the Goths will conquer Rome and redeem the Christians; but then Nero [come back from the dead] will appear as the heathen Antichrist, reconquer Rome, and rage against the Christians three years and a half. He will then be conquered in turn by the Jewish and real Antichrist from the East, who . . . will return to Judea, perform false miracles, and be worshiped by the Jews. At last Christ appears, that is, God Himself with the lost Twelve Tribes as His army, which had lived beyond Persia in happy simplicity and virtue. Under astounding phenomena of nature He will conquer Antichrist and his host, convert all nations, and take possession of the holy city of Jerusalem" (*WQT*, III).

St. Martin of Tours (316-397) believed the end was so near that the antichrist was already alive. "There is no doubt that the antichrist has already been born. Firmly established already in his early years, he will, after reaching maturity, achieve supreme power" (*ETV*, 119). Of course, this would necessitate the end of the world within sixty or seventy years at the most.

The next six centuries saw somewhat less speculation about the end of the world. Perhaps it was the bracing influence of St. Augustine, who explained prophetic texts in understandable and irrefutable language. But there were still a few speculators. At the end of the eighth century, Beatus, Abbot of Liebana, announced that the world would end on Easter eve of 796. Around the same time, St. Gregory of Tours speculated that the end would occur sometime between 799 A.D. and 806 A.D.

FIRST-MILLENNIUM MADNESS

Toward the end of the tenth century, Bernard of Thuringia calculated that 992 A.D. would mark the end of the world. Around the end of the first millennium, the Archbishop of York preached a message of repentance linked to the imminent Day of Judgment that the turn of the century would bring. Even the German Kaiser Otto III proclaimed, "The last year of the thousand years is here, and now I go out in the desert to await, with fasting, prayer, and penance, the day of the Lord and the coming of my Redeemer."

These men were evidence of the phenomenal interest in the end of the world that arose around the end of the first millennium. Many followed Irenaeus in believing that a thousand years was literally "as a day" to the Lord. Since they reasoned that there had been six thousand years before Christ's first advent, they expected the seventh day to come to a close one thousand years after Christ's birth. They taught that the Millennium of The Apocalypse was going to be completed at the end of that millennium.

There was intense anxiety as the last day of the millennium arrived. Many people were worshiping in church, preparing themselves for the end. When Christ did not return, however, some teachers recalculated the thousand years to begin with Christ's Ascension, rather than with His birth. This meant that the end of the thousand years would be in 1033 A.D.

THE ROLLING
END OF THE WORLD

I hope I need not remind you that nothing of significance happened in 1033 A.D. But a new technique had been born, one that would serve end-times speculators for ten centuries: When a prediction concerning the second coming does not materialize, simply rework the calculations to move the date back a few years! I call this the "rolling end of the world." Just as stock analysts will update a fifty-day or two-hundred-day average by dropping the oldest date, doomsayers update their calculations every time a pro-phetic fulfillment fails to arrive on schedule.

The thirteenth century was a very difficult and discouraging time to be a Christian. The Muslim soldier Saladin had conquered Jerusalem, wresting control of it away from the Christians. Into this situation stepped Joachim Fiore, who popularized (some say invented) the historicist view of The Apocalypse.

THE APOCALYPSE AS HISTORY

Fiore took The Apocalypse as a description of all the events that had been occurring since the first advent of Christ. He placed the letters to the seven churches and the visions in chronological order and tagged them to various centuries in history. He was also the first "dispensationalist" in that he split the New Covenant in half. He believed in three ages: from creation to Christ was the age of the Father; from Christ to Fiore's time was the age of the Son; and from Fiore to the final judgment was the age of the Spirit.

When Fiore discovered the mention of 1,260 days in Apoca-lypse 12:6, he jumped to a conclusion that seemed logical to him. He modified Irenaeus's system, based on the notion that "a thou-sand years equals a day," and determined that the second coming could not come later than 1260 A.D. Until his death in 1250, many believed that Emperor Frederick II would be the one to usher in Christ's Kingdom as Fiore had predicted. Even after his death, many expected the emperor to reappear in time to start the Messianic age.

Obviously, nothing of note occurred in the year 1260. Fiore had died in 1201, so he did not live to witness his error. But his faulty exegesis of The Apocalypse caused a crisis of faith for many. Fra Salimbene of Parma wrote, "After . . . the year 1260 passed [without event] . . . I am disposed henceforth to believe nothing save what I see." Unfortunately, eventual loss of faith frequently accompanies belief in the end-times frenzy.

In 1501, the famous explorer and discoverer Christopher Columbus wrote *The Book of Prophecies,* in which he predicted that within 155 years, Christians would have converted all of mankind. Christ would then return, and the world would end. The date he calculated for the end was no later than 1656. As of this writing, that date is three and a half centuries off the mark, and counting.

THE REFORMATION ACCELERATES
MILLENNIAL SPECULATION

Something huge did occur shortly after Columbus's book was published, but it was not the final victory of Christ's Church. It was the splintering of that Church in the upheavals in Europe caused by the emergence of the Protestants. The more anarchistic Protestants, such as the Anabaptists, made an imminent Millennium a centerpiece of their theology, taking their cue from the radical Taborites and Hussites of a century earlier.

When the Anabaptists took over Munster, Germany, in 1534, they immediately proclaimed that it would be the center of the millennial kingdom. They preached forebodingly that those outside the city of Munster were in danger of Christ's condemnation upon His return. Catholic Mass was prohibited, and many Anabaptists flocked into the city. But the situation was far from stable. Even Protestant leaders of the day were alarmed at the developments. Polygamy was endorsed. Eventually even one of the three wives of the Protestant leader "King of Justice, the King of New Jerusalem Buckhold" was publicly executed by her husband because she resisted the teaching that all property must be shared — including wives.

In 1546 Martin Luther wrote, "All the signs which are to precede the last days [have] already appeared. . . . The day of judgment is not far off. . . . [It] will not be absent three hundred years longer" (*BET,* 25). Like Irenaeus, Hippolytus, Columbus, and Fiore, Luther fell into the trap of trying to generate enthusiasm by predicting a quick end of the world. Yet Luther was canny enough to predict the end a good distance off; no later than the mid 1800s. Need I say it again? Nothing happened.

IN SEARCH OF THE REAL ANTICHRIST

The emerging Protestants picked up on Fiore's discredited idea, but added a slight twist. They claimed that 1260 A.D. marked the start of the Great Tribulation rather than of the second advent. They reasoned, rather conveniently, that if the Church had been in the Great Tribulation for three centuries, then antichrist must have been on the scene since 1260 A.D. They did not look too long before settling on the Pope as the most likely candidate. This meant that the overthrow of the papacy was necessary for the millennial kingdom of God to come. Unfortunately, much of the Church's activities during this period gave credence to this theory by resembling those of a "beast" and a "harlot."

But the Pope was not alone. The Anabaptists believed that *Luther* was the antichrist. (Many Catholics of the time agreed with this one teaching of the Anabaptists.) A little later, the Puritans thought King George III was the antichrist. Down through history, the list of those tagged for the role of the final antichrist has been long. It includes Attila the Hun, King Charles I, Oliver Cromwell, Stalin, Franklin Delano Roosevelt, Mussolini, Hitler, Henry Kissinger, Mikhail Gorbachev, and Ronald Reagan, to name a few.

Even in modern America, many rapturists believe that "somewhere, at this very moment, on planet Earth, the antichrist is certainly alive — biding his time, awaiting his cue. Already a mature man, he is probably active in politics, perhaps even an admired world leader whose name is almost daily on everyone's lips" (GPR). Rapturists postulate that "at all times Satan has had to have one or more antichrist candidates waiting in the wings, lest the rapture come suddenly, and find him unprepared. That is why so many malevolent world leaders have had names whose letters added up to 666 when combined in certain ways" (ATF). Presumably if you want your child to grow up to be a good world leader rather than an evil one, it is essential to pick his name very carefully!

PREDICTIONS GALORE IN ENGLAND

In 1593, John Napier of Merchiston published a book predicting the time of the Day of Judgment. Napier was no ignoramus. He is credited with the invention of mathematical logarithms. He approached his subject as a math problem that could be solved with sufficient study. He determined that the Bible predicted the end of the world within the century, sometime between 1688 and 1700.

In the mid-seventeenth century, the Fifth Monarchy Men arose in England. They believed that the four kingdoms of Daniel were about to be replaced by the fifth kingdom of Daniel — Christ's Millennium. They sought to bring about Christ's return through "fire and sword" and set up a supreme council called the "Synhedrin" (CSP, III, 479). Christ was to be declared the only King of England, and the only law was to be that found in the Bible.

These men sounded strikingly similar to rapturists of today. They pointed to current events as signs of the end times. "All the teetering and tumbling affairs on earth now, which is universally shaking into a new Creation, are a history of Christ's coming to reign" (FMM, 26).

The Fifth Monarchy Men used the prophecies of Daniel, combined with the "thousand years for a day" proposal of Irenaeus, to determine that the end would be between 1650 and 1700. In preparation, they sought to begin the Kingdom of Christ by force in England and then "to go on to France, Spain, Germany, and Rome, to destroy the beast and whore, to burn her flesh with fire, to throw her down with violence as a millstone into the sea"

(*ADH*). They were convinced that the monarchies of Europe were the ten evil kingdoms of Daniel and The Apocalypse.

In 1694, the rector of Water Stratford in Buckinghamshire, John Mason, gathered a group of Englishmen who believed Christ would return on Easter Sunday, April 16. When nothing visible occurred that day, he convinced his flock that Christ had returned to begin His reign and would eventually become visible to all who were in Water Stratford. He died before that event occurred, but his followers continued to await Christ's appearance for another sixteen years.

In 1733, Sir Isaac Newton's study of the end was published posthumously. Although he set no definite date, of one fact Newton was quite certain: the blasphemous "little horn" of Daniel 7:8 was undoubtedly the papacy.

AMERICAN SECTS JOIN THE END-TIMES GAME

About a century later, Joseph Smith founded The Church of Jesus Christ of the Latter Day Saints, also known as the Mormons. In 1832 Smith proclaimed that he was sure that he was in the final generation. He stated that "fifty-six years should wind up the scene" (*BET*, 25). Some readers may perhaps agree with me when I claim that this was not the only teaching of Smith that was dead wrong.

In the early nineteenth century, William Miller predicted that Christ would return in the twelve months preceding March 21, 1844. He then extended the deadline to October 22, 1844. Many Millerites lost all faith when even this attempt at a rolling end of the world failed. Other followers coalesced into what is now known as the Seventh Day Adventists.

The Jehovah's Witnesses took "rolling end of the world" to a completely new level. On different occasions, they have set the date for Christ's return in the years 1874, 1914, 1918, 1920, 1925, 1941, 1975, and 1994. Amazingly, to this day they refuse to admit they were ever mistaken. Following the cue of John Mason, they teach that Christ really *did* return on these dates. Of course, any objective observer might point out that nothing visibly significant happened on any of them.

ENTER DARBY

The nineteenth century was a hotbed of end-times speculation. Into this environment stepped a man who would change the Protestant movement in America. John Nelson Darby (1800-1882) was an ex-Anglican priest who founded the Plymouth Brethren movement, and his apocalyptic view appealed to a young nation that was just recovering from the trauma of the Civil War. Christians who adhere to his theology are known in some circles as the Darbyites, although they dislike this name.

Around 1830, Darby met fifteen-year-old Margaret Mac-Donald, who claimed to have had a private revelation of a secret rapture that would occur shortly. Not all Christians would be included in this rapture, however. Only certain especially faithful believers would be rescued.

From this beginning, Darby and his followers developed a system that taught that all true believers would be rescued in a secret rapture that was distinct from the second coming of Christ. Although they never state it in this manner, this amounts to two future comings of Christ, or at the very least, two stages of the second coming. They justified this novel doctrine by claiming that, in the first stage, which was the secret rapture of only believers, Christ would not actually set foot on earth. Believers would "meet Him in the clouds" and go back to Heaven with Him before He touched down. There would be a "judgment" of Christians' works at that time.

Darbyites taught that the rapture would usher in Daniel's seventieth week: a seven-year Great Tribulation that would end with the defeat of the antichrist and the judgment of his followers.

Then the Millennium could begin: a thousand-year earthly reign of Christ for the benefit of ethnic Jews. After the Millennium, Gog and Magog would battle Christ one last time, and the final judgment would commence. This made for two to four judgments, along with a two-stage understanding of the second coming. Truly an innovative scheme!

DARBYISM NECESSITATES A SPLIT COVENANT

Although it is questionable whether Darby himself was even aware of the full ramifications of his theology, his Millennium also forced his followers into a new view of the Church. It meant that the Church was not God's main plan of redemption, but a parenthetical time — dubbed the "Church age" — that would eventually give way to God's *primary* plan: a corporeal reign of the Messiah over the Jews. Jews who came to God in the Millennium would never become a part of the Church. They would be part of redeemed Israel, which would remain forever distinct from Christ's Bride.

J. Dwight Pentecost wrote extensively from this perspective in the mid-twentieth century: "There are two new covenants presented in the New Testament: the first with Israel in reaffirmation of the covenant promised in Jeremiah 31 and the second made with the church in this age. This . . . would divide the references to the new covenant in the New Testament into two groups" (*TTC*, 124).

This idea, when developed, lays the foundation for the rapturist belief that *most of the teachings of Jesus do not apply to present-day Christians!* Clarence Lakin assured his readers that the Sermon on the Mount has "no application to the Christian, but only to those who are under the Law"; that is, those Jews who will come back to God during the Tribulation and the Millennium (*DT*, 26). Although this is gospel to rapturists, to many other Christians it sounds dangerously close to blasphemy.

DARBY'S IDEAS TAKE HOLD

While Darby's ideas were originally taught by the Plymouth Brethren, they were spread in the United States by various means. Edward Irving introduced these ideas to the Pentecostal churches in the early nineteenth century. In 1883, the Niagara Bible Conference movement aggressively spread his teachings. W. E. Blackstone, Charles Erdman, C. I. Scofield, and J. Hudson Taylor were all involved, and any knowledgeable rapturist will recognize their names. Moody Bible Institute, Dallas Theological Seminary, and Talbot Seminary all trained new pastors and supplied Bible study materials that promoted the belief that this imminent rapture was at the very core of the gospel message.

During this time, the Scofield Reference Bible was becoming the most influential study Bible in America, and its notes always explained passages from the rapturist perspective. Scofield himself had claimed that World War I was the beginning of the Armageddon he saw predicted in The Apocalypse (*BET*, 6). Oswald J. Smith predicted that "the Battle of Armageddon must take place before the year 1933" (*IAH*). Blackstone wrote that the rapture might very well be in 1934 or 1935 (*TWE*, May 13). Regardless of any failed predictions, however, by the mid-twentieth century, rapturists could be found in virtually every Protestant denomination in America. With the spread of Darby's ideas, Protestantism in America changed dramatically as end-times frenzy took America by storm again and again with the help of rapturists in the Protestant pulpit.

A CENTURY OF WAR AND
END-TIMES PREDICTIONS

The 1940s saw World War II and more predictions of the end. America was assured "that we are nearing the great battle of Armageddon" (*PE*). The evil army of the north was the Soviet Union. "Stalin is now in the process of building the very Empire outlined in Ezekiel 38-39" (RLP). After World War II failed to usher in the Great Tribulation, many rapturists saw the Cold War as the trigger mechanism for Armageddon.

Even someone of the reputation of Billy Graham has fallen prey to this fever. In a 1950 issue of *U.S. News and World Report*, Graham is quoted as claiming, "Two years and it's all going to be over." Granted there was tremendous world intrigue during that period, but we are well past 1952 and still counting. Much later, in April 1984, Graham proclaimed, "Anybody who's anybody believes that global war is imminent." Even as late as 1995, he wrote, "Each day, as we read our newspapers or watch the news on television, we are reminded of some of the signs Jesus told us to look for. . . . When will the end be? We don't know. . . . But every indication is that it will be sooner than we think" (DM, September 1995).

In 1970, Hal Lindsey's book *The Late Great Planet Earth* broke upon the American scene. Its entire message centered on the prediction that the rapture was due before the end of the 1980s. Its bestseller status revealed how widespread rapturist ideas had become.

In 1976, the United States elected its first avowedly Evangelical president. Rapturists rallied with more pronouncements of the impending end. In 1978, Chuck Smith, the pastor of a huge California Evangelical church, wrote, "The Lord is coming for His church before the end of 1981" (FS).

THE RAPTURE DATES COME . . . AND GO

In a 1978 edition of the influential Evangelical periodical *Christianity Today*, rapturist Gary Wilburn wrote, "The world must end within one generation from the birth of the state of Israel. Any opinion of world affairs that does not dovetail with this prophecy is dismissed." This is a reference to the "generation of the olive tree" which we will examine in the Olivet Discourse.

Rapturists claimed that this means the rapture must occur within forty years of the founding Israel in 1948.

The crucial year 1988 came and went. In the midst of this anxiety-ridden year for Evangelicals, Edgar C. Whisenant published and distributed his pamphlet 88 *Reasons Why the Rapture Will Be in 1988*. He specified September as the month in which Christ would return. The pamphlet sold an incredible 4.5 million copies before the year was out.

Believe it or not, when the rapture did not occur in 1988, Whisenant wrote 89 *Reasons Why the Rapture Will Be in 1989!* He claimed he had previously forgotten to include the extra year in 0 A.D. and confidently asserted, "It's going to be in September 1989." (He sold substantially fewer than 4.5 million copies of this second pamphlet.)

It is interesting to peruse the library at a seminary such as Trinity Evangelical Divinity School. Before 1988, there were plenty of Masters' theses being written about the rapture and its imminent arrival. After 1988, that choice of topic dropped off sharply.

NEW THEORIES BUY TIME FOR RAPTURISTS

To account for this failed prediction, rapturists have adopted the "rolling end of the world" technique used with such success by the Jehovah's Witnesses. Now rapturists claim that perhaps the year that Jerusalem was reunified, 1967, is the proper beginning of the forty-year "olive tree generation." Others are proposing that 1993 might be the key year because of the Peace Accords. These proposals would give rapturists until either 2007 or 2033 to continue teaching their system without accountability.

In a 1993 interview for the television show *This Week in Bible Prophecy*, Lindsey reaffirmed his belief that we are at the very end of history (while implicitly admitting he was wrong about the 1980s): "I have believed from the beginning that the generation of the fig tree in Matthew 24 was the generation that would see all the signs come together, and that would see the return of Christ. I haven't changed. This is the generation that will see the coming of the Lord in the rapture." By 1994 he was warning again about making any plans for the future: "I wouldn't make any long-term earthly plans. . . . The end times are almost here" *(PEW)*.

"LAST DAYS" PROPHETS CONTINUE UNABASHED

In the pews of Protestant churches after 1988, the frenzy continued. In 1989, the prominent Fundamentalist Jerry Falwell sent out a mass mailing to raise money from his supporters. It stated, "In just a few days we will enter what may very well be . . . the final decade! . . . Jesus is coming soon. . . . I want you to be ready" *(BET,* 11).

On October 14, 1990, readers of the *Chicago Tribune* were informed that there were close to fifty million Americans who believed the "end is near." A few years later, on December 19, 1994, *U.S. News and World Report* confirmed this number: almost one in five Americans believed the world would end within a few years.

As recently as the Persian Gulf War, fifteen percent of all Americans were sure that the conflict between Kuwait and Iraq was the start of Armageddon. In the midst of this speculation, Charles Dyer of Dallas Seminary fanned the flames of Armageddon Fever with the 1991 book *The Rise of Babylon: Sign of the End Time*. He argued that Iraq would successfully rebuild Babylon as a great city to have her ready for destruction as described in The Apocalypse.

In 1993, David Koresh appeared on the national scene. His Branch Davidian cult in Waco, Texas, had calculated that Armageddon would occur in 1995. This final worldwide battle was to start at their compound in Waco, dubbed "Ranch Apocalypse." A battle *did* occur: seventy-six souls perished on April 10, 1993 in the fire that suddenly engulfed their buildings during a raid by federal law-enforcement officials.

People continued to assure us that we were on the cusp of destruction. Harold Camping confidently declared, "When September 6, 1994 arrives, no one else can become saved; the end will have come" (*NNF*, 533).

Well-known televangelist Paul Crouch predicted on February 22, 1994 that the world cannot "go beyond 2005 or 2010."

Televangelist Pat Robertson urged viewers of *The 700 Club* on May 12, 1994, "We are possibly talking about the final age of humankind, right now. Let's work together while we have a chance. Please call and make a pledge." Unfortunately, this was not an isolated incident. The next year, he pleaded, "All signs point to the end of the world and the end of life as we have known it. . . . Nobody knows the day or the hour. . . . We're coming up on the time of the end. . . . Now the time is urgent to bolster the resources of the Christian Broadcasting Network. . . . The worst is yet to come. . . . Now is the lull before the storm. . . . Your dollars may not do any good in five years or so." It is now more than five years later, and I am quite sure that Robertson is still asking for financial support.

As the end of the millennium drew nearer, the frenzy intensified. Jack Van Impe is a well-known radio preacher on the largest Evangelical television program about the end times. On June 22, 1994, he unequivocally stated during his television show *On the Edge of Eternity* that the rapture would occur around the year 2000. Without Christians on earth, "by the year 2001, there will be global chaos." A few years later, on February 5, 1997, he started rolling the end of the world by announcing that "everything is winding up within the next ten years" and that the end would surely come somewhere between 2001 and 2012.

LEFT BEHIND BRINGS
RAPTURISM TO THE MASSES

In 1995, Tyndale House published a series of books about the rapture and the Great Tribulation, beginning with *Left Behind: A*

Novel of the Earth's Last Days. The series' theological assumptions are similar to those of *The Late Great Planet Earth*. Each new book in the series is also an instant bestseller. It seems as if almost everyone has read a book from this series, even otherwise sensible Catholics.

Left Behind author Tim LaHaye wants to convince America that the rapture "could be any time: today, tomorrow, next week" (CT), while protecting his flanks with the "rolling end of the world" strategy. He will not compromise on the fact that we are in the final generation. In his book *Are We Living in the End Times?* he writes that either the 1948 or 1967 date (for the beginning of the generation that will see the end) works just fine. But he goes on to add that a generation is no longer forty years, as rapturists have always assured us, but could be as long as eighty or ninety years. This, of course, gives him almost until the middle of the twenty-first century, most likely long after his own death. Only then will the truth of his interpretation of prophecy be determined. Of course, he will sell a lot of *Left Behind* books in the meantime.

In the 1997 *Prophecy Study Bible*, John Hagee also teaches that our generation is the final one. That is not a new statement. But his rolling end of the world has discovered a new start to the forty-year generation: the November 4, 1995 assassination of Israeli Prime Minister Yitzhak Rabin. That would give rapturists until 2035 to publish more books.

Perhaps the silliest proposal leading up to the new millennium was made by Michael Drosmin in *The Bible Code*, published in 1997. This book contended that computers have unlocked the Hebrew text of the Pentateuch to predict that the "time of the end" began in September 1996 and that Armageddon will be fought in 2000. Now that we are past that year, I suppose we can all rest easier. But don't get too comfortable. According to *The Bible Code*, all life is in danger of being wiped out when a comet crashes into the earth in 2012.

SOME GROUPS TRY TO
HASTEN GOD'S TIMETABLE

One of the scarier groups in the end-times frenzy is the Concerned Christians. Eight of their American members entered Israel with the intent of causing a deadly shoot-out with Jerusalem police on the eve of the new millennium. This violence was supposed to trigger Christ's return. There were also dozens of nonviolent Christians who settled in Israel in 1999 in hopes of getting a bird's-eye view of Jesus' return to the Mount of Olives.

Christian groups have reportedly raised more than five million dollars to assist in the rebuilding of the Temple in Jerusalem. Although this rebuilding need not start before the rapture occurs, they believe that the rapture cannot occur later than its completion. Therefore, the start of construction on the Temple would force the rapture to come quickly. Of course, the appearance of a completely red heifer for the Temple's cleansing is seen as a sign of the impending rapture as well.

SEPTEMBER 11: A PORTENT OF THE END?

The war on terrorism that followed the attacks of September 11, 2001 quickly became another reason for rapturists to declare the end was imminent. I had two friends contact me within days. One reminded me that The Apocalypse predicted that "Babylon would be burned up in a single day." This person saw a direct fulfillment in the tragedy in New York. The other stated that this was an event of biblical import, because Matthew tells us of "wars and rumors of wars" (Matt. 24:6) that would occur just before the end.

Rapturist preachers have certainly tried to connect September 11 to the prophecies of the Bible. Grant Jeffrey, a Pentecostal author and speaker, called this event a "part of the distress of the Last Days" (CT). Bishop G. E. Patterson, head of the Church of God in Christ, wrote that this "could very well be the beginning of the countdown that will usher in the final world conflict which will usher in the return of our Lord and Savior Jesus Christ" *(CT)*. Baptist Bishop Alden Gaines of Philadelphia has stated that the fulfillment of biblical prophecy "is happening right now. . . . I believe that's going to set the stage for this particular antichrist to step forward. . . . I see it all fitting in" *(CT)*.

Although the events of September 11, 2001 were momentous and horrible, there is no more reason to believe that they were prophesied in the Bible than was the sacking of Rome or the Communist revolution in Russia. (Come to think of it, some contemporaries *did* say the sacking of Rome was foretold in the Bible.) But the fact that this war on terrorism will be at least partially waged in the Middle East is seen by rapturists as confirmation that it is probably the beginning of the end. Anything touching on Jerusalem in Israel or Babylon in Iraq strikes a raw nerve with them.

SORTING THROUGH THE PREDICTIONS

Let me assure you: I do not doubt that Jesus is coming again! He said He would, and I certainly do not doubt His word. But there is something horribly wrong with the history we have just briefly surveyed. All these predictions, from the Montanists to the *Left Behind* series, fail for lack of fulfillment. Perhaps those who have made such predictions are misinterpreting Scripture. Perhaps if we examine the biblical data carefully, we will be able to ascertain its teaching while avoiding predictions that necessitate another rolling end of the world.

But first, we need to delineate exactly what rapturists believe. And so in this next section, I will attempt to explain and defend the "pretribulational scheme" of rapturist thought. (There are two others, the midtribulational and posttribulational. These two systems, however, have very few adherents.) We must first thoroughly understand this system if we are to decide for ourselves whether the Bible supports it.

Chapter Two

In Defense of the Rapture

In light of the embarrassing miscalculations of prominent rap-turists, why do people, particularly twenty-first-century Ameri-can Christians, still find the rapture and its related topics so fascinating? Is the biblical evidence for the rapture really that compelling?

It shouldn't surprise you to hear that I do not believe that the Bible teaches there will be a rapture distinct from the second com-ing. What *might* surprise you is that the leading living theological proponent of the rapturist system seems to agree with me.

For many years, Dr. John Walvoord was president of Dallas Theological Seminary, an institution that has become synonymous with an unwavering allegiance to the rapturist system I described earlier (pretribulationalism). Along with Dr. Charles Feinberg of Talbot Seminary, Walvoord has done more than any other in his generation to provide this system of theology with an intellectual foundation. Both men were family friends, and I have many fond memories of them at our family dinner table.

In the first edition of his 1957 book, *The Rapture Question*, Walvoord wrote, "The rapture question is determined more by ecclesiology [theology of the Church] than eschatology [theology of future events, specifically the last things]. *Neither posttribula-tionalism nor pretribulationalism is an explicit teaching of Scripture.*

Rapture

The Bible does not in so many words state it" (*TRQ*, foreword; emphasis added). Let me remind you that this is from a theologian whose commitment to *sola Scriptura* ("Scripture alone": the belief that Scripture alone is the primary and absolute source of authority for all Christian doctrine and practice) is unwavering!

This admission — that the believer's rapture is not a clear and concise teaching of the Bible — was so explosive that in all future editions of this book it was deleted. Lack of clear biblical support is the elephant in the living room that all educated rapturists know exists, but never discuss. But there it is: nowhere does one passage of the Bible speak of both the rapture and the second coming. Nowhere does one passage of the Bible lay out the time scheme that rapturists must justify by piecing one verse here with another verse there.

If an ardent proponent of a believer's rapture states that the teaching is nowhere in Scripture, what makes so many people think it is taught there?

Let me try to answer that question by giving a biblical case for the rapture. I will argue as I would have twenty-five years ago, when I was a convinced rapturist trying to justify this system of theology to students in class.

THE ANTICHRIST

All through history, Christians have believed that the world will see a terrible persecution just before the second coming of Christ. This persecution is tied inextricably to one person, the "antichrist." He is also known as the "man of sin," the "son of perdition," and the "man of lawlessness."

This man is spoken of repeatedly by the New Testament writers. John the beloved wrote, "You have heard that antichrist is coming, so now many antichrists have come. . . . This is the antichrist, he who denies the Father and the Son" (1 John 2:18, 22; cf. 2 John 7).

THE SECOND COMING

The most important passage in this regard, however, is 2 Thessalonians 2:1-12. First, the apostle Paul makes clear that his topic is the moment when Christ comes for His Church by writing, "now, concerning the coming of our Lord Jesus Christ and our assembling to meet Him" (2:1). This is speaking of the second coming of Jesus Christ, not the rapture.

Then Paul corrects those Christians who thought the second coming had already occurred, and that they had been forgotten. "We beg you, brethren, not to be quickly shaken in mind . . . by letter purporting to be from us, to the effect that the day of the Lord has come" (2:1-2).

The Lord could not already have come, says Paul, because the antichrist must come first. Paul warns not to let anyone "deceive you in any way; for that day will not come, unless the rebellion comes first, and the man of lawlessness is revealed, the son of perdition" (2:3).

Moreover, we need not worry about who the victor in the final analysis will be. Later in the same passage, Paul tells us, "And then the lawless one will be revealed, and the Lord Jesus will slay him with the breath of His mouth and destroy him by His appearing and His coming" (2:8).

It will not be a long, drawn-out battle once Christ appears. Christ will win. The prophet Daniel likens Christ's victory to a "stone . . . cut out by no human hand" that crushes the statue of this world's governments. They become "like the chaff of the summer threshing floors" (Dan. 2:34-35).

THE GREAT TRIBULATION

Yet Paul tells us that before this final victory, "the son of perdition, who opposes and exalts himself against every so-called god or object of worship, [will take] his seat in the Temple of God, proclaiming himself to be God" (2 Thess. 2:3-4). The antichrist wants to be declared God in God's Temple. This is the Temple in Jerusalem, the only temple God has ever inhabited.

This scenario described by Paul presupposes two realities. One has come to pass; the other has not — yet. First, the Jews must be in control of Jerusalem. That occurred partially in 1948 and completely in 1967. This is tremendously important for us to understand. We are living in the last days, and the fact that the Jews have come back into control of their land after almost nineteen centuries of exile is nothing short of miraculous. Only God could have made this possible. He is obviously preparing the world for its final trial.

The second reality concerns the Jewish Temple. It must be rebuilt. Otherwise how could the son of perdition proclaim himself to be God from a seat within that Temple? In fact, the prophet Zechariah informs us that "all the nations . . . shall go up . . . to worship. . . . All who sacrifice may come" (Zech. 14:16, 21). The Old Covenant animal sacrifices will be reinstated in the Temple, and it will once again become the center of God's worship here on earth. This is why the antichrist will choose to desecrate God's Temple in blasphemy.

Actually, there is one passage in the Bible more important than any other for understanding the end times. It is Daniel's "vision of the seventy weeks," found in Daniel 9:24-27. There Daniel also predicts that the antichrist will desecrate the rebuilt Temple.

THE CRITICAL VISION OF SEVENTY WEEKS

Daniel relates a vision of future events he has been shown. First, he informs us that within a certain length of time, "seventy weeks," there will be six blessings bestowed. It is decreed that these seventy weeks will be enough time "to finish the transgression, to put an end to sin, and to atone for iniquity, to bring in everlasting righteousness, to seal both vision and prophet, and to anoint a most holy place" (9:24). Rather than spend a great deal of time determining what the seventy weeks signify, let us draw a simple conclusion. Since sin is still in the world, and everlasting righteousness is not yet realized, these seventy weeks are *not yet accomplished*. This means that at least some of the seventy weeks must still be future.

All of the early Church understood this passage to be Christological. From his perspective in the sixth century B.C., Daniel saw that the "anointed one," the Messiah, would come. As Christians, we know that He did. Daniel also understood that Jerusalem and its sanctuary, or Temple, "shall be built again with squares and moat, but in a troubled time" (9:25). That, too, occurred. Jerusalem and its Temple were rebuilt, always under the threat or actuality of war. By about 10 B.C., the city and its Temple had finally been rebuilt and were in a state of relative peace under Herod.

Then Daniel's prophecy, which started out with such hope and promise, turns dour. Sometime after Jerusalem and its Temple are completed, Daniel understood that the Messiah would be "cut off," or killed. Sometime toward the end of the first sixty-nine weeks, "an anointed one shall be cut off, and shall have nothing" (9:26). This is an obvious reference to the Passion of our Lord. This has always been the most common Christian understanding of this vision. The Temple was to be rebuilt, and then the Messiah was to come and be killed. All of these events occurred in the first sixty-nine weeks of Daniel's prophecy. This left only one week, the seventieth week.

THE CHURCH AGE

But at this point, the time frame of Daniel's vision shifts. There is a parenthesis inserted into Daniel's vision of which Daniel is unaware. It is almost as if he were standing on a mountain, looking at two distant peaks. He sees both peaks clearly, but because of his perspective, he does not understand that there is a tremendous valley of hundreds of miles (thousands of years) between the two peaks. After Daniel sees the Passion of our Lord, he misses the parenthetical "Church age" that stretches between Christ's first and second advents.

THE ANTICHRIST'S ABOMINATIONS

So, after the death of Christ, the next event Daniel sees is more than two thousand years later. He sees a prince who shall come and destroy the Temple, but is unaware that this occurs in the middle of the Great Tribulation, still in the future even to us. "The people of the prince who is to come shall destroy the city and the sanctuary. Its end shall come with a flood, and to the end there shall be war; desolations are decreed" (9:26). This is a description of the antichrist and his attack on Jerusalem after the rapture.

How do we know? Because Daniel tells us that this prince shall desolate the Temple, "upon the wing of abominations" (9:27). What could be more abominable to the Jews than what Paul has already told us the future antichrist will do? The man of sin will enter the rebuilt Temple in Jerusalem, sit down, and proclaim himself to be God. To any devout Jew, this would certainly be an abomination and desolation.

THE LAST WEEK BEGINS

Now that we know that Daniel is describing the future antichrist, we can learn other events that will surround this son of perdition. He will make a covenant with the Jewish people at the beginning of the one week. "He shall make a strong covenant with many for one week." The one week is Daniel's last week, the seventieth week, which is best understood as seven years. This is how we know that the Great Tribulation will be for seven years. Daniel told us almost three millennia ago!

The strong covenant of the antichrist is a Middle East peace treaty (for which anyone who reads the newspaper today can understand the urgent need). He will establish peace between Israel and its neighbors at the beginning of these seven years. He will be internationally acclaimed as a peacemaker, and his power and influence will be unprecedented.

Then halfway through the seven years, the man of sin will break the covenant with the Jews and desecrate the Temple with his blasphemy. "For half of the week [three and a half seasons] he shall cause sacrifice and offering to cease" (9:27). This is the same event that is mentioned in Thessalonians. For the remaining three and a half years of the Great Tribulation, the antichrist will seek to destroy the Temple and Jerusalem after his abomination of desolation.

This antichrist will gather all nations together to destroy Jerusalem and its Temple. God predicts in Zechariah, "All nations of the earth will come together against [Jerusalem]. . . . I will gather all the nations against Jerusalem to battle, and the city shall be taken and the houses plundered. . . . Then the Lord shall go forth and fight against those nations as when He fights on a day of battle. On that day His feet shall stand on the Mount of Olives which lies before Jerusalem. . . . Then the Lord your God will come, and all the holy ones with Him" (Zech. 12:3; 14:2-5).

Daniel, too, assures us that the antichrist will be defeated in the end. "The decreed end is [to be] poured out on the desolator" (9:27). This refers to the second coming of Christ that we already learned about from Paul. When Christ comes at the end of these seven years, he will utterly defeat the antichrist and all his forces.

THE FINAL BATTLE AND FIRST RESURRECTION

This battle in which Christ will defeat the antichrist and his false prophet is called "Armageddon" in The Apocalypse: "I saw the beast and the kings of the earth with their armies gathered to make war against Him who sits upon the horse [Christ] and against His army. And the beast was captured, and with it the false prophet. . . . These two were thrown alive into the lake of fire that burns with brimstone. And the rest were slain by the sword of Him who sits upon the horse" (Apoc. 19:19-21). Such is the fate of all those who disobey Christ. Every evil person from the Great Tribulation will be killed in this battle with Christ.

Then the first resurrection occurs. This is the resurrection of all the righteous who died under the Old Covenantal system. This system was operational for the centuries before Christ's first advent and again during the seven-year Great Tribulation. While speaking to the Jews before offering the world His Church, Jesus said, "You will be repaid [for your good deeds] at the resurrection of the just" (Luke 14:14). This was in reference to those righteous people who lived under the Old Covenant, and so never made it into His Church.

We see this resurrection described in The Apocalypse: "I saw the souls of those who had been beheaded for their testimony to Jesus and for the word of God, and who had not worshiped the beast or its image and had not received its mark on their foreheads or their hands [during the Great Tribulation]. They came to life, and reigned with Christ a thousand years. The rest of the dead did not come to life until the thousand years were ended. This is the first resurrection" (Apoc. 20:4-5).

Those raised in the first resurrection are judged along with the Gentiles who survived the Great Tribulation. "Many of those who sleep in the dust of the earth shall awake, some to everlasting life, and some to shame and everlasting contempt" (Dan. 12:2). This is called the second future judgment (we will return to the first judgment in a moment). These souls will be judged according to their good deeds, particularly in their treatment of Israel. Jesus taught that those who practiced the corporal works of mercy would be shown mercy at this judgment. "You gave me food. . . . You gave me drink. . . . You clothed me. . . . In prison you came to me" (Matt. 25:31-46). Since people are judged by their works, and not according to their faith in Christ's finished work on the Cross, it is obvious that no Christian will be judged at this time. I repeat, *this is not how or when Christians will be judged.*

At this time, Israel will be judged as a nation in regard to its loyalty to the Old Covenant Law. "I will enter into judgment with you, says the Lord God. I will make you pass under the rod, and I will let you go in by number. I will purge out the rebels from among you, and those who transgress against me; I will bring them out of the land where they sojourn, but they shall not enter the land of Israel. Then you will know that I am the Lord" (Ezek. 20:36-38). This third judgment happens at the same time as the second judgment.

ANOTHER CHANCE FOR THE
JEWS TO RECOGNIZE THEIR MESSIAH

The third judgment makes clear the purpose of the Great Tribulation. During this seven-year period of trial, God will return to the Old Covenant. The first time the Jewish Messiah came, He was rejected and crucified. This seven-year period gives Israel a second chance to recognize Jesus as its Messiah. This time, because of the antichrist's persecution, the Jewish nation will finally recognize Jesus as their Messiah and call on Him for help in their need. Zechariah tells us that "the inhabitants of Jerusalem" will finally recognize Jesus as Messiah and repent of their rejection of Him. "When they [Israel] look on Him whom they have pierced, they shall mourn for Him" (Zech. 12:10). When the Jews call upon Christ at the end of the seven-year Great Tribulation, He will return in the glory of His second advent.

THE RAPTURE

"But wait," you may ask. "In all this, where is the Church? All of these events relate to ethnic Israel and the Gentiles. Nowhere have you mentioned Christians even once." There is actually a very good reason for that. During the seven-year Great

Rapture

Tribulation in which the antichrist rules the world, Christians will not be here on earth. They will have been raptured!

Just before the seven years start, all true believers will be taken out of harm's way by Christ. This rapture is imminent; it can occur at any moment, perhaps even before you finish this paragraph. There is nothing else in history that must occur before it.

Paul writes to the Thessalonian Christians about the end times more than once. They seem to have been quite confused and were concerned that those who had died as Christians might not be raptured with the living Christians. Paul assures them this is not so. In doing so, he gives us the clearest description in the Bible of the secret rapture of believers: "But we would not have you ignorant, brethren, concerning those who are asleep [dead]. . . . We who are alive, who are left until the coming of the Lord, shall not precede those who have fallen asleep. For the Lord Himself will descend from Heaven with a cry of command, with the archangel's call, and with the sound of the trumpet of God. And the dead in Christ will rise first; then we who are alive, who are left, shall be caught up together with them *in the clouds to meet the Lord in the air*; and so we shall always be with the Lord" (1 Thess. 4:13-17).

Notice that Christ will not actually touch earth at the rapture. We will meet Him "in the air." This indicates that this is not a prediction of the second coming, but a promise of the rapture of true Christians. This is the "blessed hope": the promise of Christ to spare believers from the wrath of God in the Great Tribulation. "[We are] awaiting our blessed hope, the appearing of the glory of our great God and Savior Jesus Christ" (Titus 2:13).

Only those who have accepted Jesus as their Savior — true believers; those who have been born again — will be taken. "Except a man be born again, he cannot see the Kingdom of God" (John 3:3, KJV). These believers may attend Baptist, Bible, Methodist, Presbyterian, or Catholic churches, but they are saved because they place their faith in the cross of Christ *alone*. "Believe in the

Lord Jesus, and you will be saved" (Acts 16:31). There can be no admixture of dependence on good works or on the spiritual benefits gained for them by others. "For by grace you have been saved through faith; and this is not your own doing; it is the gift of God — not because of works, lest any man should boast" (Eph. 2:8-9; cf. Rom. 1:16).

No one will expect these believers suddenly to disappear. Jesus told His disciples that when He raptures His believers into Heaven, the world will be in a completely normal situation. "As were the days of Noah, so will be the coming of the Son of man. For as in those days before the flood, they were eating and drinking, marrying and giving in marriage, until the day when Noah entered the ark, and they did not know until the flood came and swept them all away, so will be the coming of the Son of man" (Matt. 24:37-39).

When the rapture occurs, friends will be separated from each other for all eternity: one will be taken up in the rapture, while the other one will be left behind. "Two men will be in the field; one is taken and one is left. Two women will be grinding at the mill; one is taken and one is left. Watch, therefore, for you do not know on what day your Lord is coming" (Matt. 24:40-42). The rapture could occur today.

For those believers taken safely to Heaven in the rapture, there will be an immediate judgment of their works. Rewards will be given to each believer based on his faithfulness during his life. This is the first future judgment, and the only judgment of true believers. Some do not even call this a "judgment," saying that only rewards are involved. But 2 Corinthians 5:10 says that at the judgment, "each one may receive good or evil, according to what he has done in the body."

But in the meantime, do not forget what unbelievers will be left behind to experience here on earth: the seven-year Great Tribulation in which the antichrist reigns. The first three and a half years will be a time of peace for the world that will result from the treaty the antichrist initiates in the Middle East. During this time, the world will be at peace, and only those who resist the antichrist's plans will be persecuted. The persecution of anyone who sides with Christ will be immediate and intense. Only the latter three and a half years will be unbearable for Jews as well. "Then there will be great tribulation, such as has not been from the beginning of the world until now, no, and never will be. And if those days had not been shortened, no human being would be saved." (Matt. 24:21-22, cf. Dan. 9:27; Apoc. 7:14).

During the present time, the current Church age, Satan is not able to influence events unhindered. However, at the time of the rapture, the restraints will be removed from him: "You know what is restraining him now. For the mystery of lawlessness is already at work; only he who now restrains it will do so until he is out of the way." (2 Thess. 2:6-7). This restrainer is the Holy Spirit, present in the hearts of true believers. When the rapture occurs, the influence of the Holy Spirit will be removed along with the Church.

With Satan free to work his terror, things will be much worse than we can possibly imagine. The Apocalypse describes this time of trouble. There are seven seals, seven trumpets, three woes, and seven bowls. Their description of the future is enough to make the blood run cold. There will be famine, death, martyrdom, anarchy, a scorpion army, a red dragon, a sea-beast, a land-beast, painful sores, undrinkable water supplies, heavenly disturbances, darkness, frogs, earthquakes, monstrous hail, and destruction. All this awaits those left behind when the rapture occurs.

Jesus gave His disciples a series of signs to be passed down to the unfortunate unbelievers who were left behind to endure the Great Tribulation. These signs, along with the descriptions in The Apocalypse, will enable those left behind to recognize world events for what they were and come to believe that the Messiah will come again at the end of the Great Tribulation. By standing against the antichrist, and refusing to wear his blasphemous sign on their hands and foreheads, they would be spared at the second judgment mentioned above.

These signs that Jesus mentions include "wars and rumors of wars . . . famines and earthquakes . . . tribulation. . . . Many will fall away, and betray one another, and hate one another. And many false prophets will arise and lead many astray. . . . Most men's love will grow cold. . . . And this gospel of the Kingdom will be preached throughout the whole world. . . . So when you see the desolating sacrilege spoken of by the prophet Daniel, standing in the holy place . . . then let those who are in Judea flee to the mountains. . . . Then there will be great tribulation. . . . the sun will be darkened, and the moon will not give its light, and the stars will fall from heaven, and the powers of the heavens will be shaken" (Matt. 24:6-29). Obviously, at no point in history have these signs been fulfilled. These are all signs pointing to the second coming, which will be recognized by those left behind. Remember, the second coming will occur seven years after the rapture.

But beware! The fact that we see the beginnings of these signs already occurring should warn us. The rapture and Great Tribulation cannot be too far away when the signs that were promised to appear after the rapture have already begun to appear.

The generation that sees the beginning of these signs is the "generation of the fig tree." "From the fig tree learn its lesson: as soon as its branch becomes tender . . . you know that summer is near. So also, when you see all these things, you know that He is near, at the very gates. Truly, I say to you, this generation will not pass away till all these things take place" (Matt. 24:32-34).

We are the generation of the fig tree. We have already witnessed the return of God's chosen people, the Jews, back to Israel. This enables them to rebuild the Temple of God there. As we noted above, all of these passages about the end times presuppose the presence of the Jewish people in Jerusalem. For nineteen centuries, it was impossible even to imagine a Jewish state centered in Jerusalem. In our generation, it has become reality.

THE MILLENNIUM

As we mentioned, at the end of this seven years of Great Tribulation, Christ will return to earth to save the Jewish people from extinction. This is the second advent, at which He will set foot again on the Mount of Olives. Zechariah tells us that Christ's "feet shall stand on the Mount of Olives, which lies before Jerusalem on the east, and the Mount of Olives shall be split in two" (14:4). He will defeat the antichrist and throw Satan into the bottomless pit. "An angel . . . seized . . . Satan, and bound him for a thousand years, and threw him into the pit, and shut it and sealed it over him" (Apoc. 20:1-3).

This will be the beginning of the thousand-year reign of Christ on earth. "And the Lord will become king over all the earth" (Zech. 14:9).

Daniel informs us that the setting up of the millennial government will take about seventy-five days. The Bible repeatedly mentions the last three and a half years that make up the last half of the Great Tribulation as a time of 1,260 days. Daniel says, "There shall be a thousand two hundred and ninety days" (12:11). Although rapturists understand this differently, most agree that this extra thirty days spoken of by Daniel is the time needed to complete the second and third judgment at the end of the Great Tribulation.

Then Daniel speaks of another forty-five days: "Blessed is he who waits and comes to the thousand three hundred and thirty-five days" (12:12). This is a month-and-a-half period that follows immediately upon the judgments, yet precedes the Millennium. Although Daniel does not tell us the purpose of this additional period, it is most logically the time that it will take Christ to set up His government for the thousand-year reign. Governmental positions would be assigned immediately after the judgment to ensure peace on earth for a thousand years. Being "blessed" would signify that you successfully endured the judgment of Christ and would be assigned a role in the government of the Millennium.

The Millennium Kingdom set up by Christ will be a literal kingdom here on earth, centered in Jerusalem. All nations of earth will be subject to the Davidic King, Jesus Christ. Christians who were raptured seven years earlier will reign from Heaven, while those who followed Christ during the Great Tribulation will reign in the earthly Kingdom of Christ. "I saw the souls of those . . . who had not worshiped the beast or its image and had not received its mark. . . . They came to life, and reigned with Christ a thousand years" (Apoc. 20:4).

Finally, God's promises to Abraham and David will be fulfilled. King David had been promised, "Your kingdom shall be made sure forever before me; your throne shall be established forever" (2 Sam. 7:16). Jesus will rule as the child of Abraham and the son of David, and the entire Millennium will be a time of peace.

AT THE END OF THE
MILLENNIUM, ONE FINAL BATTLE

However, during the Millennium, people will be born, live normal lives, and die. Some of those born during the Millennium will not realize how good Christ's reign is. At the end of this Millennium, Satan will be loosed one more time to lead one last rebellion against Christ. "When the thousand years are ended, Satan will be loosed from his prison and will come out to deceive the nations . . . that is, Gog and Magog, to gather them for battle" (Apoc. 20:7-8).

Once again the focus of Satan's hatred will be the Jews in Jerusalem. Satan's forces "surrounded the camp of the saints and the beloved city" (Apoc. 20:9). All to no avail: this rebellion will also be crushed. "Fire came down from Heaven and consumed them, and the Devil . . . was thrown into the lake of fire" (Apoc. 20:9-10).

After this final defeat of evil, the "great white throne" commences (Apoc. 20:11). At this time, all unresurrected people of history will be brought for judgment. "And I saw the dead, great and small, standing before the throne, and books were opened" (Apoc. 20:12).

Since all Old and New Covenant saints have already been resurrected and judged in the first, second, and third judgments, this fourth judgment will deal only with the wicked. "If anyone's name was not found written in the book of life, he was thrown into the lake of fire" (Apoc. 20:11-15). The severity of their eternal punishment will reflect their opportunities for good and their knowledge of truth. "But he who did not know, and did what deserved a beating, shall receive a light beating. Every one to whom much is given, of him will much be required" (Luke 12:47-48).

After this fourth judgment, time ends and eternity dawns. The Church enjoys God in the new Heaven, while the redeemed of Israel enjoy the eternal kingdom of David's Son here on the new earth (Apoc. 21:1-22:5).

DON'T BE LEFT BEHIND!

It is essential that you understand your choice. Do you want to accept Jesus as your Lord and Savior now, and enter eternity by being raptured to Heaven before the Great Tribulation? You will spend those seven years in Heaven, and then return with Christ to defeat Satan and reign during the Millennium. After the Millennium, you will experience the joys of Heaven for all eternity.

Or if you prefer, you could wait. But delay one moment too long, and the rapture will intervene, and you will be left behind. The best you can hope for then is to endure the horrors that will unfold during the Great Tribulation. For the sake of your soul, it will be necessary to stand up to the beast and resist his power. Most people will not be able to endure without succumbing and receiving the mark of the beast. That mark will then condemn you to an eternity in Hell.

It is your choice. Only you can determine your eternal destiny. When the rapture comes, it will be too late. You will have already been left behind.

Part II

Terms and Ground Rules

Chapter Three

Surveying the Present Landscape

The competing predictions about the end times can be so confusing that the average person is tempted to throw up his hands in
dismay. To help avoid this sense of hopelessness, I would like to
proceed by simplifying and comparing the three major systems.
Please understand that this might appear to be something of an
*over*simplification. However, it is beyond our scope to investigate
every minor permutation and nuance of these systems.

Let us begin with premillennialism, which includes rapturism
(or pretribulational dispensationalism), and then examine postmillennialism and amillennialism. After this short survey, we will
prepare to dive headlong into our examination of the biblical
data.

In eschatology, the major point of contention revolves around
one issue: the meaning and timing of the Millennium. All Christians agree that the Bible describes a thousand-year reign of Christ.
But when does it occur? What is the nature of this reign, corporeal
or spiritual? How literal is the thousand years?

PREMILLENNIALISM

Premillennialists are those who expect Christ's second advent
to *precede* the Millennium. Most of them expect Christ's supernatural return soon. Upon His return, He will set up an earthly,

corporeal kingdom here on earth for a thousand years, centered in Jerusalem.

Premillennialism adopts a pessimistic view of mankind. Its adherents believe that man is so inherently evil and totally depraved that it will be a steady downward slope for civilization until Christ's return rescues us. They believe the present world is a sinking ship.

This rampant pessimism is certainly not hard to document. In Dallas Seminary's journal, *Bibliotheca Sacra,* Lehman Strauss wrote that our only hope is the rapture. This is because "we are witnessing in this twentieth century the collapse of civilization. It is obvious that we are advancing toward the end of the age. Science can offer no hope. . . . Doom is certain. I can see no bright prospects, through the efforts of man, for the earth and its inhabitants" ("Our Only Hope," *BS* [April 1963]:154).

The pessimism of premillennialists assumes that if America falls, so must Christianity. Perhaps it should come as no surprise that premillennialism is basically an American phenomenon.

Another prominent characteristic of premillennialism is found in its treatment of the Bible. Unlike postmillennialism, it truly seeks faithfully to answer to the biblical data. Although they tend to be literalists, premillennialists have a reverence for the Bible's message that strikes a chord with Christians of all faith traditions. If you read your Bible daily and try to understand God's message to you, there is a good chance you lean toward premillennialism.

PROBLEMS WITH PREMILLENNIALISM

The Millennium is mentioned only once in the Bible, in a very symbolic book, The Apocalypse. Its mention immediately follows a description of "the great supper of God," in which "the flesh of kings, the flesh of captains, the flesh of mighty men, the flesh of horses and their riders, and the flesh of all men, both free and slave, both small and great" is eaten (Apoc. 19:18). Critics believe that the premillennialist places too much emphasis on a literal interpretation of what certainly seems figurative.

This system — also called millenarianism, millennialism, and chiliasm by its critics — appeared quite early in the Church, but was never the majority position. The response of the eastern part of the early Church to what they viewed as a serious error was to question the authority of The Apocalypse. The western part of the early Church accepted the canonicity of The Apocalypse, while holding that the Millennium passage was symbolic. What is significant, however, is that neither East nor West accepted premillennialism as consistent with the original teaching of Jesus and His Apostles.

A second problem with premillennialists has to do with their vision of the Kingdom of God. Is it spiritual or physical? The premillennialist would claim it must be a corporeal reign of Christ here on earth. Critics would counter that this completely misunderstands the message of the major prophets of the Old Testament (Isaiah, Jeremiah, Ezekiel, and Daniel), not to mention the message of the entire New Testament.

The premillennial rapturist position is the focus of this book. It is the theology underlying the *Left Behind* series and *The Late Great Planet Earth*. As the Protestant Dr. Wells has aptly pointed out, rapturists are the most consistent of the premillennialists, although not all premillennialists are rapturists (*TSS*). We will return to a critique of premillennial rapturist thought when we examine the individual Bible passages.

POSTMILLENNIALISM

Postmillennialists believe that the second advent of Christ will *follow* the Millennium of peace and justice — the opposite of what the premillennialists believe. Postmillennialists teach that it is the duty of the Christian community to improve the world to such a point that Christ deems it ready for His return. They believe man can establish the "utopian kingdom" on earth. Unlike the pessimistic premillennialist, the postmillennialist espouses a very optimistic view of man.

For a modern rationalist, this idea is much easier to believe than an imminent supernatural second advent. It found fertile ground in the rationalistic mindset that enveloped Europe in the nineteenth and twentieth centuries and still appeals to those whose theology is of a modernist, antisupernaturalist bent. In postmillennialism, any supernatural invasion of our world by a victorious Christ is roughly a thousand years away.

PROBLEMS WITH POSTMILLENNIALISM

The violence and suffering of our modern world has made the rosy outlook of postmillennialists more difficult to swallow. In this country, World War II was a watershed. After the devastation and inhumanity of that conflict, preceded as it was by the suffering of the worldwide depression of the 1930s, the appeal of postmillennialism waned. It has a relatively small following now.

In addition, postmillennialism does not deal adequately with the scriptural data. Some would say it does not even try. As a result, we will not spend much of this book discussing it. The Catholic Church's view of this system has always been clear. "The kingdom will be fulfilled . . . not by a historic triumph of the Church through a progressive ascendancy, but only by God's victory over the final unleashing of evil, which will cause his Bride to come down from Heaven. God's triumph over the revolt of evil will take the form of the Last Judgment after the final cosmic upheaval of this passing world" (CCC, par. 677).

AMILLENNIALISM

The third view, amillennialism, is the one held by the vast majority of Christians, whether Catholic, Orthodox, or Protestant. It is the only acceptable option for the Protestant who claims to stand in the tradition of Luther or Calvin and for the Catholic who seeks to remain faithful to the teaching of the Church.

Amillennialists agree with historical premillennialists in believing that Christ's return can occur during any generation. This is what they mean by saying that the return of Christ is "imminent." However, they do not believe that there will be a corporeal reign of the risen Christ on earth after that second advent.

Amillennialists agree with postmillennialists in teaching that Christ's return will come *after* the Millennium and immediately before eternity. But unlike the postmillennialists, they believe the Millennium is a *spiritual* reign of Christ that has been present in the Church since Pentecost. In other words, the Millennium is an ecclesiastical kingdom, founded at Pentecost.

I was a convinced premillennialist for most of my life. Yet even then I knew that the bulk of the biblical data is rather clearly in the amillennial corner. The Bible continually uses the terms *Kingdom of God, Kingdom of Heaven, Messianic Kingdom,* and *Church* interchangeably (Matt. 7:21, 9:35, 16:13-20; Luke 11:20; John 3:15). As one of my premillennial professors at Trinity Evangelical Divinity School (full professors there must certify their belief in premillennialism) once stated, "There are only six verses that make me a premillennialist: Revelation 20:1-6. All the rest of the Bible is amillennial."

Some have claimed that the majority position of the early Church was the premillennial, but this is highly debatable. Indeed, early Christian writers could have talked about a thousand-year reign of Christ and still have been amillennial. In 200 or 300 A.D., the thousand years spoken of in The Apocalypse were still stretching into the future further than any human eye could see.

The crucial issue in understanding the early Church Fathers is their view of when the kingdom *started*. Were kingdom benefits already available? A premillennialist would have declared that millennial benefits were still unavailable, whereas an amillennialist would have believed he was already in the spiritual kingdom of God and its blessings had already arrived. Epiphanius of Salamis makes clear that the majority of the early Church were amillennialists (HE, 77:26). This includes even Justin Martyr. (DJT, LXXX; FA, XXXIX).

We will later determine why the amillennialist believes that while the thousand years is a long time, the biblical evidence does not necessitate a Church age of precisely 365,250 days. Amillennialists believe that the thousand years spoken of in The Apocalypse must be understood within its figurative context.

PROBLEMS WITH AMILLENNIALISM

I attended a premillennial seminary and taught premillennialism in both classroom and pulpit. During this time, it seemed to me that amillennialists did not take the teaching of Revelation 20:1-6 seriously. I never encountered an interpretation of that passage that I found true to Scripture.

A good part of the reason was that the purported kingdom of the amillennialist did not match the reality of the Church that I experienced. To my way of thinking, the contention of any Protestant that Christ's Kingdom was already established spiritually here on earth bordered on the ludicrous. I wondered where they saw it. The Presbyterian, Reformed, and Lutheran denominations were not worldwide, nor did they have an institutional unity that even remotely resembled a Kingdom of Christ. Nor were they ancient enough!

Not until many years later would I consider the Catholic Church as a possible embodiment of Christ's Kingdom here on earth.

Chapter Four

Biblical Ground Rules

The fairest way to decide the merits of any Christian belief system is to examine carefully the Bible passages that are said to support it. It was a thorough examination of just that sort that led me, a convinced rapturist Fundamentalist, to reconcile with the Roman Catholic Church almost a decade ago. (My book *Born Fundamentalist, Born Again Catholic* provides details of the journey.)

While the Catholic appeals to Scripture, Tradition, and the teaching authority, or Magisterium, of the Church to guide his beliefs, rapturists claim to rely exclusively on the ostensibly clear and self-interpreting text of the Bible. So it is fair to ask whether the rapturist belief system is the best way to understand the relevant Scripture passages, considered apart from other authoritative voices. Of course, as Catholics, we would say this approach removes two legs of the three-legged stool of truth. But discounting for our purposes Sacred Tradition and the Magisterium, can the rapture theory really do justice to what the Bible teaches?

HOW WE WILL PROCEED

To be thorough and fair, I will attempt to survey all of the relevant passages, looking at the common rapturist interpretation of each and trying to determine whether it is the best understanding. I will then offer my own conclusions from a Catholic perspective.

Keep in mind, however, that it is not possible for anyone to claim that his understanding of a passage is *the* Catholic one if the Church herself has been silent on the issue. "There are but few texts whose sense has been defined by the authority of the Church" (*DAS*). The passages we will examine most closely do not fall within those few texts. Yet we will at all times endeavor to stay within the parameters set by the Church, mindful that there can be a multitude of valid Catholic opinions about most passages.

Indeed, it is very probable that some good Catholics will disagree with my treatment of some of these passages. Your pastor may give a homily based on one of these passages that takes a different understanding from the one this book presents. There is nothing wrong or unusual about this, as long as he does not claim that everyone must agree with *his* perspective. My purpose is not to review the entire scope of Catholic possibilities, but to show that there exists at least one consistent Catholic perspective on each given passage that is truer to the text and to history than the rapturist perspective is.

OUR BIBLICAL METHOD

In our exegesis, we will be ever mindful of our goal. As St. Jerome said, "The office of a commentator is to set forth, not what he himself would prefer, but what his author says." I believe it is fair to state that this is how the early Church handled Scripture.

We will also honor the traditional Christian view of Scripture's reliability: that the texts as originally written are without error in all that they intend to teach. The Church has clearly stated that Scripture is fundamentally a revelation of God Himself, culminating in the deeds and words of our Lord Jesus Christ. As Vatican II stated, "The books of both the Old and New Testaments in their entirety, with all their parts, are written under the inspiration of the Holy Spirit; they have God as their author. . . . Therefore, since *everything asserted* . . . must be held to be asserted by the

Holy Spirit, it follows that the books of Scripture must be acknowledged as teaching solidly, faithfully, and *without error* that truth which God wanted put into sacred writings for the sake of salvation" (*DV*, 11).

As a former Protestant preacher, I think I can say that most rapturists would have no trouble agreeing with Church teaching regarding Scripture. (Granted, more than a few would have trouble with the source!)

APOCALYPTIC LITERATURE

Fortunately for us, there are not many passages of Scripture that bear on the discussion at hand. We will spend most of our efforts examining passages in three books of the Bible: Daniel, Matthew, and The Apocalypse. We will take brief excursions into a handful of other passages as well.

Perhaps unfortunately, these three books contain literature of the genre called "apocalyptic." This is unfortunate in that this type of writing is rather foreign to the twenty-first-century reader. Because the imagery is vivid and symbolic, apocalyptic literature can lead rather easily to misunderstandings.

In this type of writing, special rules apply. Apocalyptic literature must be interpreted with the full awareness of *how it was intended to be understood when it was written*. This is a basic rule of hermeneutics (rules for interpreting the Bible). Poetry should be understood as poetry, history as history, and apocalyptic writings should be understood in the larger framework of apocalyptic literature.

Moreover, apocalyptic text in the Bible does more than use vivid, symbolic imagery. It also purports supernaturally to inform readers about future events. In this sense, apocalyptic literature in the Bible is different from any secular literature of the apocalyptic genre. The best term I have encountered to describe this biblical literature is "prophetic-apocalyptic" (*ZPE*, I, 204).

NINE GROUND RULES

It will be much easier to navigate the apocalyptic passages touching on the rapture and second coming of Christ if we have first clarified certain principles. These ground rules can be discerned from Scripture itself, so that a fair-minded Protestant should be able to agree with them.

After laying the foundation of these ground rules, we will take the passages in their turn, examining them on their own merits. We will discuss the passages in the order they appear in the Bible, in order to keep them in approximate chronological order. That is how God revealed these truths to His people. First Daniel and Zechariah were available. Much in these books was difficult to understand until Jesus taught more truth in the Olivet Discourse (Matthew) about six hundred years later. At least three more decades transpired before the Church was finally given the perspective of The Apocalypse.

By following the order of God's unfolding revelation, we can learn from the earlier passages before we attempt to discern the meaning of the later ones. It is essential to remember that the later books presuppose a familiarity with the earlier books. If I follow this general scheme properly, at the end of Daniel you will have been introduced to some concepts of which you are not yet fully convinced. By the end of The Apocalypse, however, we should be able to look back in awe at the wondrous revelation of God through the ages.

GROUND RULE 1

"PROPHECY HAPPENS"

*Prophecy inspired by God can foretell events
in advance of any possible human foresight*

Like most people, I have vivid childhood memories of Christmas. One of my family's traditions was the reading of the Nativity story every Christmas morning before we opened any of our presents (which made us very willing to sit still so as not to create any delay!).

One of the passages giving us the details of Christ's birth can be found in the first two chapters of Matthew's Gospel. We read that after the birth of Jesus, "wise men from the East came to Jerusalem" (2:1) inquiring about the location of the new baby King.

This inquiry certainly piqued the interest of the reigning ruler in Judea at that time, Herod. King Herod was not a Jew, but an Edomite. He had been recently installed on the Jewish throne by the Romans, at the expense of the Jewish Hasmonean dynasty. It is quite certain that he knew of the prophecy of Balaam, recorded in Numbers 24:17-18, which foretold the ascendancy of Jacob's star (a Jewish King) at the expense of the Edomites: "A star shall come forth out of Jacob, and a scepter shall rise out of Israel; it shall crush the forehead of Moab. . . . *Edom* shall be dispossessed."

Herod was so troubled that, "assembling all the chief priests and scribes of the people, he inquired of them where the Christ was to be born. They told him, 'In Bethlehem of Judea; for so it is written by the prophet: "And you, O Bethlehem . . . from you shall come a ruler who will govern my people Israel" ' " (Matt. 2:4-6). In answering Herod's question, the leaders of Israel referenced Micah 5:2.

In this exchange, we can ascertain Ground Rule 1: *Prophecy inspired by God can foretell events in advance of any possible human foresight* (GR1). Modernist objections notwithstanding, Scripture is sprinkled liberally with prophecy that has been fulfilled in a way that no human being could have foreseen. It has been estimated that about one-quarter of the Bible was prophetic when penned.

Some 150 years before his birth, the Persian king Cyrus was named and described in Isaiah 41:25-45:4. He merited this mention because he paved the way for the Messiah when he decreed the rebuilding of Jerusalem. In 1 Kings 13:1-3, the name and actions of King Josiah are predicted almost three centuries before his birth. He stands as an important type of Jesus the Messiah as the reforming king, killed by Egypt. While modernist Catholic commentators refer to these as later glosses, added after the events, able Evangelical scholars have proven them wrong. These truly were prophecies, uttered before the fact.

This principle stands in direct opposition to a basic assumption of modern higher criticism, as adopted first by Islamic scholars, then by Protestants, and then by Catholics. Many laymen are not aware of the roots of modernist theology as it relates to New Testament studies, much of which can be traced to a Lutheran scholar by the name of Rudolf Bultmann.

One of Bultmann's basic assumptions was his total rejection of the supernatural. All miracles are automatically ruled out as impossible, whether they are found in the Old Testament or the New. The stories of the Old Testament about Noah, Moses, and Elijah are reinterpreted to fit the prejudices of a modern, rationalistic mindset. Likewise, the New Testament accounts of the Virgin Birth, the feeding of the five thousand, the raising of Lazarus, and the Resurrection of Jesus are explained, or rather, explained away, in modern rationalistic terms.

Since looking into the future and predicting it with an accuracy that human foresight cannot explain is certainly a miracle, true prophecy is impossible according to modernist theologians. This is an *a priori* article of faith for them. A favorite approach to any text containing a prophecy that was fulfilled is to strive to re-date its authorship to a time after the event occurred. Scholars call this "antedating" the authorship of Scripture. This makes it possible to explain away the prophecy. In their view, it is really history written in the style of prophecy.

This, however, is extremely difficult for them to do with the prophecy of Micah, quoted by the chief priests to Herod in Matthew's Gospel. This prophecy was fulfilled in the birth of Christ, yet we know that Micah's prophecy was in existence hundreds of years before that event.

It is important to remember that true prophecy really can be found in the Bible. The Holy Spirit was able to direct writers of Scripture to foretell future events accurately, even when the writers themselves did not fully understand the implications of what they wrote. The Church throughout history has generally accepted an earlier date for other books of prophecy, such as Daniel. It is not that early Christians were uncritical, either. Textual criticism is not modern; there is evidence of robust textual criticism dating from the second century. Modern higher criticism wedded to antisupernatural prejudices is the problem.

This prejudice affects how modernists view even the Gospel account. Yet the Church states, "The Gospels were written under the inspiration of the Holy Spirit, who preserved their authors from every error" (SME). With that said, it will surprise no one that I accept the historicity of the miracles of Jesus as presented in the Gospels, and even the virgin birth of that same Jesus. His Incarnation was possible because of the yes that His mother, Mary, gave to God's plan as presented by the angel Gabriel. Yes, that means I accept the possibility of the supernatural. Along with Christians of every loyal faith tradition, I also believe that Christ will physically return to close the curtain on history. The focus of this book will be on how this last prophecy will occur.

GROUND RULE 2

"NUMBERS ARE SYMBOLS"

Numbers in prophecy denote a symbolic
meaning that trumps any empirical value

In the Old Testament prophetic book of Jeremiah, we encounter our second ground rule. The prophet Jeremiah lived just before the Babylonian captivity. He looked that catastrophe straight in the eye and stated that, although horrible in the suffering it caused, it would have an end. He predicted that the time of captivity for the Jewish nation would be seventy years: "Thus says the Lord: When seventy years are completed for Babylon, I will visit you, and I will fulfill to you my promise and bring you back to this place" (Jer. 29:10).

The prophet Daniel lived through this captivity. When it started, he was a young lad in Jerusalem. He was taken captive to Babylon and rose in the ranks of royal advisors. Later in his life, he came across this prophecy of Jeremiah and realized that the seventy years was close to being completed (Dan. 9). Jeremiah's prophecy was about to be fulfilled — but not with the precision that a modern Western reader might expect.

This prophecy of seventy years is one of the only instances in which we can compare the prophetic time of the Bible with our modern concept of historical time. Both the prediction and the fulfillment are recorded in the Bible. As a result, scholars and historians have struggled to make the historical events of the captivity fit the seventy years that Jeremiah predicted. It simply never works out exactly; rather, the events fit into either sixty-seven years or seventy-one years. Even a staunch literalist such as Walvoord admits this in *Daniel, The Key to Prophetic Revelation*.

If you assume that God is omniscient and omnipotent, the natural question is, "Why would God reveal to Jeremiah a nice round number such as seventy when the actual time period would turn out to be a little less or a smidgen more?" The answer turns out to be quite simple. As Catholic and Protestant scholars alike have long recognized, in Old Testament times, numbers had a symbolic meaning.

Often, this symbolic meaning bears more importance than the literal numerical value. The number *three* was the number of God. The number *four* was the number symbolizing earth. *Seven* (three plus four) and *twelve* (three times four) signified God working in the world. *Ten* was the number of completion. Even multiples of these numbers were important to ancient Jews. In the Jewish calendar, the seventh month was the most sacred, being the month of the Feast of Trumpets, Yom Kippur, and the Feast of Tabernacles. Numbers that relate to dates and times were particularly significant.

The Bible even uses two Greek words for two types of time. Chronological time is *kronos* (the root of the words *chronometer* and *chronology*), whereas symbol-laden, salvific time is *kairos*. This kind of time is described in Ecclesiastes 3:1-8: "For everything there is a season, and a time for every matter under Heaven: a time to be born, and a time to die; a time to plant, and a time to pluck up what is planted. . . ."

So what might be the symbolism of the seventy years in Jeremiah? Seventy is the result of multiplying ten and seven. These numbers signify the completion of God's working in the world. In this case, that work involved the punishment of Israel. The captivity of Daniel and his fellow Jews was not exactly seventy years, but the judgment of God was complete.

This does not match our modern concept of chronological time, but it speaks to something more important — namely, symbol-laden, salvific time. The sixty-seven (or seventy-one) years of the Babylonian captivity was close enough to seventy years for an observer to notice the correspondence, yet the significant number *seventy* was preserved. *Numbers in prophecy denote a symbolic meaning that trumps any empirical value* (GR2).

We must remind ourselves of this ground rule every time we read a number in the Bible. What is its symbolic meaning, if any? For example, the importance of the number *one thousand* is immense. Jewish tradition teaches that this was the length of the Davidic kingdom. But when the Bible states that God owns the cattle on a thousand hills, it is inappropriate to start identifying which hills are being included. One thousand is the product of ten times ten times ten; thus it is a complete and perfect number. The number represents something much more important than 999 plus one. God's wealth is totally complete.

We see the ancient significance of numbers at work even outside of prophecy. In Matthew 1:17, the author organizes Christ's genealogy around the number *fourteen*. There are fourteen generations from Abraham to David, fourteen from David to the Babylonian captivity, and fourteen from the Babylonian captivity to Jesus. This splits the genealogy into "from promise given to promise fulfilled," "from promise fulfilled to promise lost," and finally "from promise lost to promise fulfilled eternally." In addition, some scholars note that the number *fourteen* was the number of King David, which would remind a reader again and again that Jesus was the son of David. All of this is easily lost on the modern reader who does not study the ancient attitude toward numbers and their meaning.

GROUND RULE 3

"HISTORY IS PROPHECY"

An event can be a prophecy of a still-future,
final fulfillment, and when it is, we should
consider the entire historical context of the
events to gain a fuller understanding

In all of Scripture, there is perhaps no prophecy more widely known than Isaiah 7:14: "Therefore the Lord Himself will give you a sign. Behold, a young woman [virgin] shall conceive and bear a son, and shall call his name Immanuel." This prophecy was written hundreds of years before Christ, so it may surprise you to find out that this prophecy was actually fulfilled within the lifetime of Isaiah.

In Isaiah's time, the king of Judah was Ahaz, who was succeeded by his son Hezekiah. Jerusalem was being besieged by Damascus (the Syrians) and Ephraem (the Israelites), or the ten northern tribes. To most of the people of God (Judah) at that time, the situation looked hopeless. Through the prophet Isaiah, God assured the king that their enemies would not be victorious over them. God would send the Assyrians against Damascus and Ephraem. Isaiah promised the king that a young girl would conceive and give birth to a son. This son would eventually be weaned, but before that child was weaned, Judea's enemies would be destroyed.

Isaiah promised Hezekiah that salvation was certain, but there would be a lengthy period before that salvation was fully realized. Isaiah himself writes that this son was born: "The prophetess . . . conceived and bore a son. Then the Lord said to me, 'Call his name Mahershalalhashbaz; for before the child knows how to cry "My father" or "My mother," the wealth of Damascus and . . . Samaria will be carried away' " (Isa. 8:3-4).

Sure enough, when we look back at history, Jerusalem was spared from its enemies during those years. But the story does not stop there. In fewer than seventy years, Ephraem (the ten northern tribes that had rejected the reign of David's heir) was utterly conquered, dispersed, and left without a trace. Jerusalem did indeed experience God's salvation, but not every descendant of Abraham benefited from that salvation. Those Israelites who had rejected the Davidic line of kings were destroyed and forgotten. Even today they are known as the ten lost tribes of Israel.

But an interesting thing occurred to this prophecy after it was initially fulfilled. The leaders of the people of God taught that the events centered on Isaiah 7:14 still had another future fulfillment in mind. We might state it this way: the event itself (the birth of a son via a young woman that signals the coming salvation of God's faithful remnant and the destruction of the faithless majority) was a prophecy pointing to a more important fulfillment in the future. Someday *another* Son would come who would signal the availability of a more universal salvation for a new Israel, the Israel of God. "Israel of God" is the terminology of St. Paul for the Church (Gal. 6:16; Rom. 9:6).

Even before the conception of Christ, many of these Jewish leaders were stating that the young woman of the still-future fulfillment would actually be a virgin. This is evident in the word that Jewish translators used to render this verse into Greek in the Septuagint of Isaiah 7:14. By the time of Christ, this passage from Isaiah was understood to be a Messianic prophecy, and the Gospels reference it as such. When Matthew uses this prophecy of Isaiah in Matthew 1:23, he points to more than just the virgin birth. He includes in his view the entire series of events surrounding Isaiah's time. These events included the salvation of the believing remnant and the destruction of the unbelieving majority that occurred much later than the actual birth of the child.

So we can observe that when a prophecy is fulfilled, that fulfilling event may itself become a prophecy, pointing to another, more final and complete fulfillment. Here is our third ground rule: *An event can be a prophecy of a still-future, final fulfillment, and when it is, we should consider the entire historical context of the events to gain a fuller understanding* (GR3). To put it succinctly, history can become prophecy.

St. Thomas Aquinas enunciated this principle. He wrote that the "allegorical sense" of Scripture is a reading of the Bible that appreciates the fact that events and persons described can point to something beyond themselves, and so build faith in us. For example, Adam is a type of Christ, while Eve is a type of Mary (SUM, 4).

In his thought, even St. Thomas harkened back to an earlier authority, St. Gregory. He wrote, "Scripture transcends all other sciences by the way it uses one and the same discourse to tell history and reveal mystery" (SUM, 4).

We repeatedly see illustrations of Old Testament stories fulfilled in the New Testament. The sacrifices of the Old Covenant foreshadow the one Sacrifice of Christ. The Hebrews' forty years in the desert prefigure the forty days of Jesus' being tempted in the desert. Jonah in the belly of the fish is used by Jesus as a type for His own death and Resurrection. Over and over the Old Testament events give us a picture of what will occur in the New Testament.

This ground rule also leads us to an important caveat. Although ninety-nine percent of all biblical prophecy has been fulfilled already, past events themselves can and do point to the final fulfillment of history when Christ returns. For example, antichrists have come (1 John 2:18) and will continue to come. Each of them foreshadows the one, final antichrist who will embody and perfect all of their evils. The events of the past can be imbued with meaning in the future by the God who is omnipotent and omniscient.

GROUND RULE 4

"ONE EQUALS TWO"

Apocalyptic visions may use one
image to symbolize two realities

If you take great pride in your orderliness, this ground rule might bother you. It is so disconcerting to many Westerners that some ignore it even in the face of a specific teaching of Scripture. But remember, apocalyptic literature was not written for modern Westerners. We must try to be transcultural when we read it.

In The Apocalypse, St. John specifically informs his reader that one object within his vision symbolizes two things. In Chapter 17, we encounter "a scarlet beast . . . and it had seven heads and ten horns. . . . The seven heads are seven hills on which the woman is seated; they are also seven kings" (Apoc. 17:3, 9-10).

The seven heads of this beast have a geographical meaning, "seven hills," and also a personal meaning, "seven kings." When we get to The Apocalypse, we will spend the necessary time to understand St. John's meaning. What is important for us to understand at the outset is our ground rule, which St. John sets forth very clearly: *Apocalyptic visions may use one image to symbolize two realities* (GR4).

GROUND RULE 5
"IT'S ALL POLITICAL"
Apocalyptic literature uses dramatic
imagery of cataclysmic disruptions to describe
changes within the human political sphere

Most Old Testament prophecy has been fulfilled. Scholars generally agree that Isaiah 13:9-13 is one of the fulfilled prophecies: "The day of the Lord comes . . . to make the earth a desolation. . . . For the stars of the heavens and their constellations will not give their light; the sun will be dark at its rising, and the moon will not shed its light. . . . I will make the heavens tremble, and the earth will be shaken out of its place, at the wrath of the Lord of hosts in the day of His fierce anger." Was Isaiah speaking of the end of the world? Hardly.

This prophecy was fulfilled when the Medes destroyed Babylon in 539 B.C. Look at the verses that come next, in Isaiah 13:17-19: "Behold, I am stirring up the Medes against them. . . . And Babylon, the glory of kingdoms, the splendor and pride of the Chaldeans, will be like Sodom and Gomorrah when God overthrew them." Yet although the Bible gives us a record of Babylon's defeat by the Medes, there is no record of any heavenly disturbances such as a darkened sun, moon, or stars. Yet they are undoubtedly fulfilled. The prophet Daniel predicted and then witnessed this event.

Isaiah uses similar language several chapters later. In Isaiah 34:4-10, we read, "All the host of heaven shall rot away, and the skies roll up like a scroll. All their host shall fall, as leaves fall from the vine. . . ." Yet while this prophecy was fulfilled when Edom was destroyed in the sixth century B.C., the physical host of heaven (the stars) still exists today.

The prophet Ezekiel's imagery is equally vivid — so vivid that it is often hard to understand at first reading. In Ezekiel 32, he prophesies the downfall of Egypt and its Pharaoh. Notice his choice of words: "When I blot you out, I will cover the heavens, and make their stars dark; I will cover the sun with a cloud, and the moon shall not give its light. All the bright lights of heaven will I make dark over you, and put darkness upon your land, says the Lord God" (32:7-8). Although this prophecy has been indisputably fulfilled, there is no record that at any time during Pharaoh's downfall there were literal heavenly disruptions such as Ezekiel described.

The only logical reading is to understand the heavenly disturbances described in these prophecies as figurative language signifying the political change God ordained as judgment. So although the prophecies describe massive disturbances in the stars and moon, this is actually apocalyptic imagery that symbolizes the historical overthrow of political powers on earth.

We see the same principle at work in Nahum. He predicted the judgment of God on the mighty city of Nineveh. "The mountains quake before him, the hills melt" (1:5). Some have tried to apply this language to an atomic explosion still to come, but the city of Nineveh was judged by God in fulfillment of Nahum's prophecy long before the canon was closed on the Old Testament.

The Apostles clearly understood this use of vivid apocalyptic language. In his first public sermon, the apostle Peter quoted from Joel and assured his listeners that they were witnessing its fulfillment right there on that first Pentecost Sunday. You can read his entire sermon in Acts 2, but notice the descriptive language: "I will pour out my Spirit upon all flesh, and your sons and your daughters shall prophesy. . . . And I will show wonders in the heaven above and signs on the earth beneath, blood, and fire, and vapor of smoke; the sun shall be turned into darkness and the moon into blood, before the day of the Lord comes, the great and manifest day. And it shall be that whoever calls on the name of the Lord shall be saved" (2:19-21). St. Peter believed this to have been fulfilled on the day of Pentecost. Rather than ask, "Where was the smoke and blood on Pentecost?" we need to accept Peter's appreciation of Joel's apocalyptic imagery.

What is our ground rule? *Apocalyptic literature uses dramatic imagery of cataclysmic disruptions to describe changes within the human political sphere* (GR5).

We should be aware that apocalyptic literature also uses the same hyperbole to describe positive changes. Isaiah 30:26 promises that "the light of the moon will be as the light of the sun, and the light of the sun will be sevenfold, as the light of seven days, in the day when the Lord binds up the hurt of His people, and heals the wounds inflicted by His blow." Notice how the number seven is used symbolically (GR2)? We notice this again in Isaiah 60:19-20: "Your sun shall no more go down, nor your moon withdraw itself."

GROUND RULE 6
"HERE COMES THE JUDGE ON A CLOUD"
*Physical objects can signify spiritual realities; for
example, clouds can signify the glory of God the Judge*

At a critical juncture in their wilderness wanderings, the Hebrews were near mutiny against Moses and Aaron over the lack of meat in their diet. God would eventually send them quail, but just before this, "the people of Israel . . . looked toward the wilderness, and behold, the glory of the Lord appeared in the cloud" (Exod. 16:10).

Later, when God gave the Law to Moses and the Israelites at Mount Sinai, a cloud surrounded the mountaintop. This cloud was a clear physical symbol of the inscrutable power and majesty of God, as God spoke out of it to the Israelites. We are even given the interesting detail that "the Lord descended in the cloud" (Exod. 34:5).

The cloud as a symbol of the power and presence of God later descended on the tabernacle that Moses had commanded to be assembled (Exod. 40:34-38). God specifically stated, "I will appear in the cloud upon the mercy seat" (Lev. 16:2). Of course, mercy is inextricably tied to judgment. Hundreds of years later, when King Solomon built and dedicated the first Jerusalem Temple, "a cloud filled the house of the Lord . . . for the glory of the Lord filled the house of the Lord" (1 Kings 8:10-11).

All of this points us to our next ground rule: *Physical objects can signify spiritual realities; for example, clouds can signify the glory of God the Judge* (GR6).

This common imagery of the Old Testament is reflected in the New Testament when Jesus meets with Moses and Elijah on the Mount of Transfiguration (Matt. 17:1-13). When Peter tries to make a suggestion, "a cloud came and overshadowed them; and they were afraid as they entered the cloud. And a voice came out of the cloud, saying, 'This is my Son, my Chosen; listen to Him!' "

At the Transfiguration, Jesus was still here as the Suffering Servant (see Isa. 53), discussing His coming death in Jerusalem with Moses and Elijah. When Peter, James, and John forget who their humble Master really is, God reminds them with His support of Jesus spoken in glory and power. Once again, the cloud clearly signifies the glory of God, and the fact that the disciples were afraid shows they understood the Old Testament symbolism.

But in some instances, physical clouds are not even present, and the mention of clouds becomes purely symbolic. Psalm 104:1-3 links these symbolic clouds to God in His glory: "Bless the Lord, O my soul! O Lord my God, Thou art very great . . . who makest the clouds Thy chariot." This purely symbolic use of clouds indicates God's coming in judgment.

In Isaiah 19:1, we read, "The Lord is riding on a swift cloud and comes to Egypt; and the idols of Egypt will tremble at His presence." This was fulfilled in Isaiah 20:1-6. Yet no clouds are recorded as having appeared, nor did God make Himself visible in any physical manifestation. God's coming on a cloud was actually fulfilled in the arrival of the Assyrian army! They were the tool of God's judgment. God gloriously came on the clouds, but what was physically seen was the Assyrian army.

A similar use of clouds to signify the glory of God in His judg-ment against Egypt is in Ezekiel: "The day of the Lord is near; it will be a day of clouds" (30:3).

At the Ascension, clouds seem to combine all this symbolism. Jesus "was lifted up, and a cloud took Him out of their sight" (Acts 1:9). His Suffering Servant days were completed. From this point on, the world would see Him as the glorified Son of Almighty God.

The angels hint at this when they tell the disciples that Jesus "will come in the same way as you saw Him go" (Acts 1:11). Some rapturists seem to imply this means that Christ's second advent cannot occur on a clear day, but that is trivializing the meaning of the angels. They meant that next time Christ will return in glory as the Judge of the living and the dead.

The Church has always understood the symbolism of clouds in this way. Victorinus wrote the earliest extant commentary on The Apocalypse in about 270 A.D. He wrote that Christ "shall come with the clouds. . . . For He who at first came hidden . . . shall after a little while come to judgment manifest in majesty and glory" (COA, I). More recently, Pope John Paul II stated in his general audience on April 22, 1998, "In apocalyptic language, clouds sig-nify a theophany: They indicate that the Second Coming of the Son of Man will not take place in the weakness of flesh, but in di-vine power."

GROUND RULE 7
"RESURRECTION EQUALS RENEWAL"
*Physical-resurrection language
can symbolize spiritual renewal*
Ezekiel paints an interesting picture in Chapter 37. He sees a valley strewn with dry bones and is instructed to tell the bones

that God will bring them back to life. Sure enough, as Ezekiel watches, the bones regroup. Then muscle and skin attaches themselves to the bones. Finally the breath of life "come[s] from the four winds" (Ezek. 37:9), and the originally dry, lifeless bones turn into a host of living, breathing people.

Ezekiel is told that this is a picture of what God will do for the people of Israel at the end of their captivity in Babylon. Against all odds, they will once again be brought back to Israel from captivity and become a nation again. We can read of the fulfillment of Ezekiel's prophecy in Old Testament history.

God then describes this renewal of Israel in the most interesting language: "Come from the four winds, O breath, and breathe upon these slain, that they may live. . . . Thus says the Lord God: Behold, I will open your graves, and raise you from your graves, O my people; and I will bring you home into the land of Israel. And you shall know that I am the Lord, when I open your graves, and raise you from your graves, O my people. And I will put my Spirit within you, and you shall live, and I will place you in your own land" (Ezek. 37:9, 12-14).

When we compare these verses carefully with their fulfillment in history, we find no record of a mass resurrection of Jewish people from cemeteries. It is apparent that Ezekiel used physical resurrection as an allegory for the spiritual renewal of God's people.

We can learn from this that in apocalyptic literature, *physical-resurrection language can symbolize spiritual renewal* (GR7). That is the whole point of the dry bones. It is almost as if God were reminding us that sometimes a physical resurrection would be no more difficult than a spiritual renewal. Since a rebirth of faith is every bit as miraculous as a physical rejuvenation, the one can be used to speak of the other.

Jesus used this way of speaking (John 5:25-29). For example, He was criticized by the Pharisees for forgiving the sins of a paralytic man. Jesus said to these critics, "Why do you think evil in your hearts? For which is easier, to say, 'Your sins are forgiven,' or to say, 'Rise and walk'?" (Matt. 9:1-8). We sometimes assume (with Jesus' critics) that the physical restoration is more difficult because it is more readily quantifiable, but that is not God's perspective.

The idea that salvation is a spiritual resurrection is not novel to anyone who pays attention to the teaching of the Church. We hear it every time a child is baptized, in the prayer of the baptizer.

In his General Audience on April 22, 1998, Pope John Paul II reminded the Church faithful that "the resurrection of the dead expected at the end of time already receives its first, decisive realization in spiritual resurrection, the primary objective of the work of salvation. It consists in the new life given by the risen Christ as the fruit of His redemptive work."

GROUND RULE 8
"DON'T CLING TO CHRONOLOGY"
*Chronological order is not always
observed in apocalyptic visions*

When dealing with apocalyptic literature, we must realize that not only does it use vivid, forceful language, but it often portrays its message in short vignettes, or visions. These can follow one right after another in rapid succession. The order in which these visions occur should not be assumed to be chronological. They are more like an envelope of snapshots than a film. The events pictured may overlap, duplicate, or be isolated from one another chronologically. This is true of visionary writings even when they are not a part of apocalyptic literature.

This may not be the way we would have written them, but it is the way apocalyptic writings are. *Chronological order is not always observed in apocalyptic visions* (GR8).

We can see examples of this ground rule all the way back in Genesis. In Genesis 37:5-11, Joseph dreams two dreams. In the first, the eleven sheaves of his brothers bow to Joseph's sheaf, symbolizing that his brothers would one day be his subjects. The second dream overlapped the events of the first, but added new details. In the second dream, not only do eleven stars bow to Joseph's star, but the moon and sun bow as well. This meant that not only his brothers, but even his mother and father would one day be subject to Joseph.

When we compare the later events of Genesis, it seems that the two visions begin with the same events, but that the end of this second vision is later than the first. The brothers visited Egypt and bowed to Joseph at least a year or two before Joseph's entire family came to live in the country where he ruled as Pharaoh's right-hand man.

This duplication of visions crops up again in Genesis. Pharaoh has two disturbing dreams, and he believes the dreams tell two stories. Joseph corrects him, saying, "The dream of Pharaoh is one" (Gen. 41:14-32). The gaunt cows that eat the fat cows in the first dream are parallel to the meager corn that devours the plump corn in the second dream. Both point to a terrible seven-year famine followed by seven years of abundance. (Notice the use of *seven* — GR2).

When we examine visionary literature, we must constantly keep this in mind. The visions might be arranged chronologically. Or they might just as easily not be. They might overlap. Only an examination of the visions themselves will make it clear.

GROUND RULE 9

"THE END IS NOW"

Christ's first advent catapulted
humanity into "the last days"

Ancient Jewish thinkers split history into three ages. First, there was the period before Moses and the Law. Adam, Abraham, Isaac, Jacob, and Joseph lived during this age.

The second age was the time of the Law — the years from Moses until the Messiah's coming. (The Law of Moses loomed large in the Hebrew mind; it is almost impossible to overemphasize its importance.) Most of the Old Testament fits into this second age. It includes Moses, Joshua, Samson, Samuel, Saul, David, and all of the major and minor prophets.

The final epoch expected by the Jews was the Messianic age. The promise of a future Messianic king, or anointed one, can be traced all through the Old Testament, starting in Genesis. The promise even predates Moses and the Law, and that hope is the heart and soul of biblical Judaism.

The advent of the Messiah signaled the start of this third epoch. Since it was the final stage in salvation, it was called the end of the age, or the last days.

To an ancient Israelite, all of history fit into these three ages, and only these three ages. This mindset can be seen repeatedly throughout Scripture, in both the Old and New Testaments. The author of Hebrews states, "God spoke of old to our fathers by the prophets; but in these *last days* He has spoken to us by a Son" (1:1-2). We read a few chapters later that Christ "has appeared once for all *at the end* of the age to put away sin by the sacrifice of Himself" (9:26).

In his sermon on the day of Pentecost, Peter quoted from the Old Testament prophet Joel (ch. 2), and applied it to his day: "In *the last days* it shall be, God declares, that I will pour out my Spirit upon all flesh, and your sons and your daughters shall prophesy" (Acts 2:17). Notice that his assumption is that he and his listeners were in the last days, or the end of the age. Why? Because the Messiah had come! Peter knew that his listeners would accept the idea that the last days were upon them only if they first accepted the fact that Jesus was the promised Messiah.

St. Peter never changed his mind about this. Much later he wrote that Christ "was destined before the foundation of the world but was made manifest *at the end of the times* for your sake" (1 Pet. 1:20).

St. Paul certainly shared this view. He refers to his time as "the *last* days" (2 Tim. 3:1). So did St. John (1 John 2:18).

Twenty-first-century Americans might view this as naive, or even mistaken. After all, look at all the important events that have occurred since the time of Christ's first advent. But we should not dismiss this view with a guffaw. "You must remember, beloved, the predictions of the apostles of our Lord Jesus Christ; they said to you, '*In the last time* there will be scoffers' " (Jude 18).

Every time the phrase "the end" occurs in the Bible, it does not necessarily refer to this last age. It might be the end of a dynasty, the end of a battle, the end of a festival, or just the end of a life. We must never take a phrase out of its context and try to absolutize its meaning.

Nevertheless, we cannot understand the prophecies of Scripture unless we first accept that, for the biblical authors, *Christ's first advent catapulted humanity into "the last days"* (GR9). This means that we have been in the last days for two thousand years. The third age of the Jews started with the first advent of Christ and will extend to His second coming, which occurs at the final eschaton.

It may seem to some that these "last days" are dragging on too long. In that case, we might do well to remember the words of Habakkuk, a pre-exilic prophet who awaited the justice of God on the enemies of Israel. He was in for a long wait, yet he wrote, "For still the vision awaits its time; it hastens to the end — it will not lie. If it seems slow, wait for it; it will surely come, it will not delay. Behold, he whose soul is not upright in him shall fail, but the righteous shall live by his faith" (Hab. 2:3-4). The second Jewish age, the time from Moses to the time of Christ, was probably between 1,300 and 1,500 years. Does it seem so strange, then, that the third age would be two millennia and counting? There is no hurrying God.

Rapture

The Church has always understood the time from the first advent to the second advent as corresponding to the "end of the age" or the "last days" of Scripture. St. Clement was the bishop of Rome from 67-73 A.D., during the intense Neronian persecution. He wrote, "The Books and the Apostles teach that the Church . . . was spiritual, as was also our Jesus, and was made manifest at the *end of the days* in order to save us" (*SEC*, XIV).

The *Catechism* summarizes it well. "Since the Ascension God's plan has entered into its fulfillment. We are already at 'the last hour.' Already the final age of the world is with us, and the renewal of the world is irrevocably under way; it is even now anticipated in a certain real way" (CCC, par. 670).

SUMMARY OF GROUND RULES

If I may make a suggestion: place a bookmark at this page. We will refer back to these ground rules scores of times as we progress, using the notation (GR#).

GR1: Prophecy inspired by God can foretell events in advance of any possible human foresight.

GR2: Numbers in prophecy denote a symbolic meaning that trumps any empirical value.

GR3: An event can be a prophecy of a still-future, final fulfillment, and when it is, we should consider the entire historical context of the events to gain a fuller understanding.

GR4: Apocalyptic visions may use one image to symbolize two realities.

GR5: Apocalyptic literature uses dramatic imagery of cataclysmic disruptions to describe changes within the human political sphere.

GR6: Physical objects can signify spiritual realities; for example, clouds can signify the glory of God the Judge.

GR7: Physical-resurrection language can symbolize spiritual renewal.

GR8: Chronological order is not always observed in apocalyptic visions.

GR9: Christ's first advent catapulted humanity into "the last days."

Part III

The Scriptural Evidence

Chapter Five

Daniel

Now that we have looked at principles for interpreting biblical prophecy, specifically apocalyptic literature, it is time to turn to the relevant passages.

We know that the early Church spent time in the Bible to discover more about the prophecies of Jesus Christ. The Bible they explored was the Old Testament, including the apocraphyl, or deuterocanonical, books. If you expected to jump right into The Apocalypse without gaining an appreciation for the Bible that the writers of the New Testament studied, you are reading the wrong book.

Although some newcomers to the movement try to explain their belief in the rapture by turning to St. Paul's epistles or to The Apocalypse, no one who is thoroughly immersed in this theology would start anywhere but in the Old Testament book of Daniel. That is where Darby allegedly began. The book of Daniel lays the foundation for the entire time framework of rapturist theology.

We will be quite thorough in our treatment of Daniel, and it will pay off when we approach The Apocalypse. Many people are mystified by the symbolism of St. John's vision, but all of biblical prophecy, including The Apocalypse, will come alive if we spend sufficient time in Daniel.

Rapture

THE PRESUMPTUOUS PARENTHESIS

Daniel understood the value of time; it is the overriding concern throughout his visions. Daniel refers to time in one way or another on about a hundred occasions in his twelve chapters! As we will see, Daniel lays out a precise time line for God's plan of salvation. He predicts the rebuilding of the Temple and the coming of the Messiah, and includes some specific details surrounding those two pivotal events.

In their reading of Daniel, rapturists make a preposterously large time miscalculation. Right in the middle of Daniel's time line, they insert a two-thousand-year interruption. They call it a "parenthesis": the parenthetical "Church age." I call it the "presumptuous parenthesis" because it is an egregious distortion of Daniel's timing — yet time is the essence of Daniel's book. This is a presumptuous way to handle God's revelation.

It is important to understand what rapturists are doing here. Daniel asks God for a time line of the events leading up to the Messiah's coming Kingdom, and God reveals it to him. The length of that time line is approximately six hundred years. But to make their system work, rapturists divide that six hundred years into two parts and insert an additional two thousand years in between! In the rapturists' view, God "put one over on Daniel" by claiming to give him a time line, only to have it be off by more than four hundred percent!

Why do rapturists do this? For one simple reason, I believe. They are unwilling to entertain the notion that perhaps Christ founded the Kingdom of God during His first advent. They hold to the firm conviction that the Messianic Kingdom is still in the future, that it will center on ethnic Israel, and — most important — that it is entirely distinct from the Church Christ founded.

Why would rapturists deny the Kingdom of God as a present reality, one awaiting its fullness at the second coming? I believe that on a historical level, Darby — like many other religious innovators in the nineteenth century — was trying to gather a group of followers. Since he was living in a predominantly Christian country, admitting that the Kingdom of God was already present within the world would not jolt people into abandoning their former places of worship to follow him. Admitting the kingdom was already in existence would have scuttled Darby's entire ministry in its infancy.

Furthermore, in the present day, an admission that Christ did set up a kingdom in His first advent is very dangerous to Protestantism. If the Kingdom has been established, the logical response is to look for it. The only Church that can make a credible claim to be the Kingdom of Christ on earth is the Catholic Church. Thus, by denying the present existence of God's Kingdom, the rapturist builds a firewall against Catholicism in his congregation's soul. In this I speak from personal experience.

Why is the rapturists' parenthesis two thousand years? For the same reason we observed earlier in our short history: a sense of immediacy produces converts to their movement.

Based on a misreading of the Olivet Discourse, they would claim that we are in "the generation of the fig tree," meaning that there remains only forty to seventy years before the rapture occurs. Originally the pivotal event that marked the beginning of the generation was identified as the 1948 founding of the modern state of Israel. Now people are proposing that maybe 1967 (the year Jerusalem was reunified) or even 1993 (the year of the Peace Accords) is the real starting point for the final generation. When we pass any critical milestones (just as we did in 1988, which is 1948 plus forty years), we will see rapturists use the rolling end of the world to choose a new date even further in the future. But that new date will still require that the present generation is the final one.

I have no doubt that, in 2200 A.D., they will be inserting a 2,200-year gap into Daniel's visions so that Daniel's last week will

still be imminent. That is the purpose of the presumptuous parenthesis. It pushes the establishment of God's Kingdom into the future — our immediate future.

But this gap is not in the text.

In fact, this gap does great violence to the text, to the funda-
mental message of the vision — all for the purpose of protecting
rapturists from the idea that the Catholic Church might have to
be examined as a possible candidate for the present-day Kingdom
of Heaven.

Throughout this book are charts designed to illuminate both
the rapturist and Catholic time lines. Included as reference points
are accepted historical events as well.

THE VITAL IMPORTANCE OF TIME

In Daniel, we find out the "when" of God's plan for salvation
history. We must never forget that Daniel's questions are fundamentally about *time*. St. Jerome agrees: "None of the prophets has
so clearly spoken concerning Christ as has this prophet Daniel. . . .
He set forth the very time at which He would come . . . stated the
actual number of years involved, and announced beforehand the
clearest signs" (*CID*, prologue).

By the end of our study of Daniel, we will know the overall
timing of God's entire plan of salvation. We will discover which
gentile world empire will be in power when God sets up His Kingdom here on earth. Daniel will even supply details concerning the
reigning Caesar, the rise and fall of Jerusalem and its Temple, the
Passion of the Messiah, and the reaction of good and evil people to
these events.

The rapturist desperately needs Daniel to substantiate his
claim that there is still a seven-year Great Tribulation awaiting
the world. There is nowhere else in the Bible he can turn to support this belief. In Unger's *Bible Handbook* (published by Moody
Press, a bastion of rapturist theology) we read in its comments on

Daniel that this "book is the key to all biblical prophecy. Apart from the great eschatological disclosures of this book, the entire prophetic portions of the Word of God must remain sealed. Jesus' great Olivet Discourse, as well as 2 Thess. 2 and the entire book of the Revelation, can be unlocked *only through an understanding of the prophecies of Daniel*."

The rapturist absolutely must be able to prove that his interpretation of Daniel's time line is the only viable view. If he fails, so does the time line for his entire system, and the whole rapturist house of cards collapses. If there is no future seven-year Great Tribulation, there is no reason for a secret rapture, nor any need for rebuilding the Temple. So we will begin our investigation in Daniel. Timing is everything.

AUTHORSHIP OF DANIEL

Because this is not a thorough commentary on any of the books we are examining, I will not deal comprehensively with the date of authorship, nor with the identity of the human author. I will simply state my relevant conclusions.

A discussion of the authorship and dating of Daniel can make it seem as if there's absolutely no common ground among modernists, rapturists, and Catholics. But there is one important, often-overlooked point on which all scholars agree: the author of Daniel, whoever he was, specifically intended us to read the book as if it were written by the prophet Daniel during the Babylonian exile in the sixth century B.C.

The modernist would claim that the book was written, or more likely assembled from different oral traditions, around the time of the second century B.C. But he would still hold that the author intended us to think otherwise. I do not agree with the modernist's dating, although I can fully appreciate the weight of his arguments. The rapturist would unwaveringly assert that Daniel wrote all of Daniel in the sixth century B.C. The loyal Catholic might question the date of authorship for the three deuterocanonical segments of Daniel, but would otherwise agree in dating the book in the sixth century B.C. Again, all three understand Daniel as a book *intended* to be read as a sixth-century document.

I will refer to the author of this book as Daniel, the sixth-century Jewish prophet in Babylon. That is what the author intended, and I will honor his intention.

OUTLINE OF THE VISIONS

Daniel's theme can be summed up as "The mystery of Messiah's Kingdom revealed: proof that Christ is coming." The book of Daniel was written to encourage God's people when they were being severely persecuted. They had been defeated and dispersed by the Babylonians. Daniel wants God to bless Jerusalem again and witness God's judgment as it falls on Jerusalem's enemies. Even his name means "God is my judge."

Some modernists minimize the suffering of the Jewish people under the Babylonian exile, and so try to claim that the message of Daniel applies better to the persecution of Antiochus Epiphanes. This is simply not true. The Babylonians almost succeeded in obliterating Judaism from the earth, and only the grace of God working through Cyrus the Mede prevented it.

The broad-stroke outline of Daniel is as follows.

Introduction	Historical setting: God's people persecuted	1:1-21
I	Initial vision: The mystery of Messiah's Kingdom revealed	2:1-49
II	Three key personalities in the Kingdom's coming	3:1-6:28
III	Initial vision recapitulated: proof that Christ is coming	7:1-12:13
Epilogue	Thematic summary	13:1-14:42

SECTION I: INITIAL VISION
MYSTERY OF THE KINGDOM REVEALED (2:1-49)

When will the Kingdom of the Messiah come? That is the question that Daniel's initial vision answers. This vision lays the framework for the entire book. All the future visions in Daniel revisit its subject and elaborate on this foundation.

While serving his new king, Nebuchadnezzar, Daniel developed a widespread reputation for his ability to interpret dreams. He firmly established his credentials by interpreting a dream for Nebuchadnezzar even though the king refused to divulge the contents of the dream itself! The other wise men exclaimed that this was a "mystery" that only God could reveal. The word *mystery* is mentioned eight times in this chapter. *Eight* is the number of Christ. Right from the beginning, we can be sure that the "mystery" to be revealed concerns the Messianic Kingdom (GR2).

The king's dream involved a huge statue with four sections. "The head of this image was of fine gold, its breast and arms of silver, its belly and thighs of bronze, its legs of iron, its feet partly of iron and partly of clay" (2:32-33). Daniel told the king that each part of the statue represented a world empire. Looking backward, it is easy to understand that the gold head represents Babylon, the silver represents Medo-Persia, the bronze stands for Greece, and the iron represents Rome. That has been the understanding of most of the Church since before the time of St. Jerome's commentary on Daniel (CID).

The passage tells us that the iron and clay feet symbolize the strength, yet brittleness, of the fourth kingdom. "There shall be a fourth kingdom, strong as iron. . . . It shall break and crush all. . . . And as you saw the feet and toes partly of potter's clay and partly of iron, it shall be a divided kingdom. . . . As you saw the iron mixed with miry clay, so they will mix with one another . . . but they will not hold together" (2:40-43). St. Jerome, who lived and wrote during the time of the Roman Empire, wrote, "Just as there was at the first nothing stronger and hardier than the Roman realm, so also in these last days, there is nothing more feeble, since we require the assistance of barbarian tribes" *(CID)*.

Apart from its accuracy, the startling aspect of this dream is its conclusion. During the fourth empire, "A stone was cut out by no human hand, and it smote the image on its feet . . . so that not a trace of them could be found. But the stone that struck the image became a great mountain and filled the whole earth" (2:34-35). Daniel interprets this to mean that while the fourth kingdom is still in existence, "*the God of Heaven will set up a kingdom* which shall never be destroyed. . . . It shall break in pieces all these kingdoms and bring them to an end, and it shall stand forever" (2:44).

There you have it. During the fourth kingdom, the Messianic Kingdom will be established. The uncut stone symbolizes Christ at His first advent. His reign established through His Passion supersedes all the kingdoms of men. From this point in history, God's Kingdom is predicted to endure forever.

Christians have historically believed that the stone which grows into a mountain is Christ and His Kingdom. (Some modernists view the stone as a symbol of the Maccabees, while the Jews apply it to themselves.) Rapturists agree that the stone is Christ, but there is dissent from the majority of Christians over the advent to which this vision refers. Rapturists believe that this stone does not arrive until Christ's second advent. They cannot agree that the eternal Kingdom of Christ was set up at the first advent without being led to the Church Christ established at that advent. So they deny that *any* kingdom was set up at the first advent of Christ. They believe that the Kingdom of Christ was rejected by the Jewish leaders at the first advent, and so it will have to wait for the second coming to be established.

That is the reason they insert the presumptuous parenthesis. To get the timing of the kingdoms correct, they must split the final (iron) kingdom into two parts (iron legs versus iron-and-clay feet). Then, in between these two parts of the same kingdom, they insert a delay of at least two thousand years and ignore all of that history! They believe that a resurrected Roman Empire is still in our future (many rapturists point to the European Union). They are also forced to conclude that the stone that shall stand forever (Christ) has not arrived on the scene yet!

Rapturists split the Roman Empire into two parts in spite of what the text itself actually teaches. Daniel is clear in his interpretation of the dream that these two parts are one and the same kingdom. "There shall be a *fourth* kingdom. . . . It shall be a divided kingdom" (2:40-41). They reason that, if two kingdoms happen to be in the same geographical area, they can be considered, for prophetic purposes, one and the same — even if they are separated by centuries. This stretches logic to the breaking point.

Further, this twisting of Daniel distorts the entire message of the vision. Remember, time is of paramount importance in Daniel. The events he describes will take about six hundred years to unfold. The rapturists' time gap in effect distorts God's revelation.

In contrast to this rather forced interpretation, the Catholic is free to understand the passage for what it seems intended to convey. The mystery of the Messiah's Kingdom is the focus of this vision. The Messiah and His Kingdom were foretold to be coming during the fourth kingdom of the vision, when Rome ruled over Jerusalem. During that time, Christ would set up His Kingdom, which would grow to encompass the entire world and last forever.

This dovetails with the teaching of Jesus. "The Kingdom of Heaven is like a grain of mustard seed which a man took and sowed in his field; it is the smallest of all seeds, but when it has grown it is the greatest of shrubs and becomes a tree, so that the birds of the air come and make nests in its branches" (Matt. 13:31-32).

We can confidently assert that in the initial statue vision, Daniel has given us the timing for the inauguration of the Kingdom of Heaven. The Catholic has no need to insert two thousand extra years between verses 40 and 41. Christ did set up God's Kingdom on His first advent during the fourth kingdom, the ancient Roman Empire.

SECTION II: THREE KEY PERSONALITIES (3:1-6:28)

Daniel now interrupts the flow of visions to explore important events in the lives of three kings that Daniel served in Babylon: Nebuchadnezzar, Belshazzar, and Darius. We will look at only one of the events, known as "Belshazzar's folly," from which we will be able to learn precisely *how* God "comes in judgment." That will be very important when we start to examine the New Testament.

The events of Belshazzar's folly occurred in Babylon. King Belshazzar precipitated God's judgment by using the holy vessels taken from Jerusalem's Temple for profane uses. This revealed a pride, a penchant for idolatry, and a disregard for Yahweh that resulted in God's judgment. As a result, we get a behind-the-scenes view of the fall of the Babylonian Empire to the Medo-Persians.

When the king used God's holy vessels for an unworthy purpose, "the fingers of a man's hand appeared and wrote on the plaster of the wall of the king's palace. . . . And the king saw the hand as it wrote" (5:5). Daniel interprets the handwriting for Belshazzar. "This is the interpretation. . . . God has numbered the days of your kingdom and brought it to an end" (5:26). Belshazzar was specifically told that God was judging him and his kingdom because he did not honor God (5:23).

But it is important to note that, in this act of judgment, God never actually met with Belshazzar. He never appeared physically in Babylon to judge the king. God was in His Heaven, and any casual observer of the events surrounding the fall of Babylon would have seen Cyrus conquering Babylon with a Persian army. Cyrus the Persian and Darius the Mede were not even believers in Yahweh. Nevertheless they were the appointed instruments of God's judgment on Babylon.

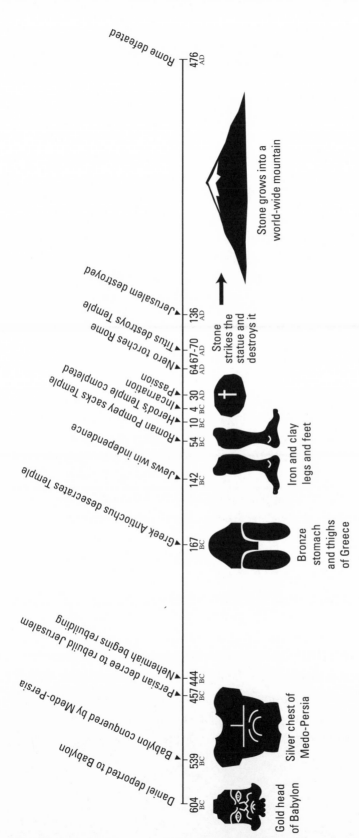

604 BC — Daniel deported to Babylon

539 BC — Babylon conquered by Medo-Persia

457 BC — Persian decree to rebuild Jerusalem

444 BC — Nehemiah begins rebuilding

167 BC — Greek Antiochus desecrates Temple

142 BC — Jews win independence

54 BC — Roman Pompey sacks Temple

10 BC — Herod's Temple completed

4 BC — Incarnation

30 AD — Passion

64 AD — Nero torches Rome

67-70 AD — Titus destroys Temple

136 AD — Jerusalem destroyed

476 AD — Rome defeated

Gold head of Babylon

Silver chest of Medo-Persia

Bronze stomach and thighs of Greece

Iron and clay legs and feet

Stone strikes the statue and destroys it

Stone grows into a world-wide mountain

Daniel:
Mystery of the
Kingdom Revealed

The essential point is that God used a pagan army to execute His "coming in judgment" on a city. Only those who were aware of Daniel's prophecy would have seen God's justice being meted out in the victory of Cyrus's army. Anyone else might just have observed the defeat of a great city by an immense army.

We will see a similar scenario when God's judgment falls on another, newer Babylon in the New Testament. God's prophet, in this case the Messiah Himself, predicted that judgment. Throughout the biblical record, God visits judgment upon political entities *through* other political entities. When predicted by God's prophet, only a fool would doubt that it is indeed God "coming in judgment" (GR6).

SECTION III: VISION RECAPITULATED, WITH PROOF (7:1-12:13)

In Section I, there was only one vision (of a statue). It spoke of the mystery of the Messianic Kingdom revealed. This third section of Daniel contains five visions: the Battle Strategy of the Beast; the Battle Strategy of the Goat and Ram; the Battle Strategy of God's People; the Great Battle; and From Here to Eternity. These do not all directly impinge on our investigation of the rapture, so we will not examine all of them in detail. We will examine the first, third, and fifth, which in our outline we will designate III:A (The Battle Strategy of the Beast), III:C (The Battle Strategy of God's People), and III:E (From Here to Eternity).

Rapturists claim that at least a part of all of these visions are still future, but that is due to an unwillingness to accept the clear teaching of Daniel that the Kingdom was established during the ancient Roman empire. They insert their two-thousand-year parenthesis into the first vision and proceed as though apocalyptic visions always follow a chronological order. We can easily see that this is not the case even here in Daniel if we notice that Chapter 7 of Daniel occurred several years before Chapter 6 (GR8).

VISION III:A: THE BATTLE
STRATEGY OF THE BEAST

This vision will answer the question "What will be the response of the earthly kingdom to the stone that pulverized the statue? Will it fight back?" We will encounter the same four kingdoms as in the vision of the statue. This time, however, these four kingdoms are portrayed as vicious beasts.

That should give us a hint. Will God's Kingdom win an instantaneous victory over the kingdoms of this earth? Probably not, as vicious beasts tend to fight for survival. Will there be any casualties among Christ's faithful subjects? Perhaps, as beasts kill to protect their interests. This might be dubbed the "Empire Strikes Back" vision. The statue in the initial vision is not going to take its own destruction lying down.

The four beasts are portrayed in detail: "The first was like a lion and had eagles' wings. . . . Another beast, a second one, like a bear . . . had three ribs in its mouth. . . . Another, like a leopard with four wings of a bird on its back; and the beast had four heads. . . . And behold, a fourth beast, terrible and dreadful and exceedingly strong; and it had great iron teeth; it devoured and broke in pieces, and stamped the residue with its feet . . . and it had ten horns" (7:4-7).

St. Jerome, the Church's greatest early Scripture scholar, stated that the lion represents Babylon, "on account of its brutality and cruelty." The bear symbolizes Medo-Persia. The three bones stand for the three kingdoms that were subsumed within the Persian: "the Babylonians, the Medes, and the Persians." The leopard with wings is a symbol of Macedonia. Alexander the Great was known for the incredible speed with which he could move his army and conquer territory (CID).

The fourth, terrible beast represents Rome. Its iron teeth remind us of the iron legs and feet of the statue vision. We find ten horns on this beast, which are taken by many commentators as a reference to the ten provinces that made up the Roman Empire. The vast diversity within these ten provinces of the Roman Empire hints at why this last empire might be both strong as iron yet brittle as clay (*TCA*, V, 210, 32).

Just as in the statue vision, the four beasts (earthly kingdoms) are supplanted by "an everlasting dominion which shall not pass away" (7:14). But while the statue implies that these kingdoms will remain passive as the stone destroys them, the beasts are able to fight. This vision supplies the details of the beasts' battle strategy. They will ultimately lose, but have no intention of going into the night softly.

Jewish scholars had a tradition that the transition into the Messianic Kingdom would take about forty years to unfold (*ET*, 356). We will learn that this prediction was amazingly accurate. Christ's Kingdom will not enjoy an instantaneous victory on a worldwide scale. Instead, we read that a new enemy, "another horn, a little one" will arise (7:8).

A modernist mistake

Modernists try to understand this reference to a "little" horn as a symbol of Antiochus, because another little horn, mentioned in a later vision, does refer to Antiochus, who reigned during the third kingdom, about two centuries before Christ. But the details of that vision are different. The little horn we are examining points to Caesar Nero (GR3). We must be careful not to mix these prophecies. They are not arranged chronologically (GR8).

The Jews of Jesus' day made the same mistake that modernists do today. The Jewish scholars assumed that all these visions were speaking of one event, when Antiochus desecrated the Temple just before the rise of Judas Maccabeus. A couple of the visions refer to a coming "abomination." It is a relatively common word in the Law of Moses, but the Jews assumed it referred to the same event every time in Daniel. They actually had some biblical basis for this. The prophet Joel had promised them that God's "people shall never again be put to shame" (2:26-27).

But Jesus specifically disagreed with the prevailing Jewish interpretation of Daniel and Joel. (In doing so, He also argues against modernists.) Jesus said, "So when you see the desolating sacrilege spoken of by the prophet Daniel standing in the holy place . . . flee to the mountains" (Matt. 24:15). Jesus claims the prophecies of Daniel for Himself and the times of His Church. He prophesied to His own generation that they would see yet another abomination of Daniel, that of 70 A.D. We will examine this New Testament text closely when we reach the Olivet Discourse. Actually, the abomination of Antiochus was a historical prophecy of the events of Jesus' generation, culminating in 70 A.D. (GR3).

So we see that, although similar, the various visions of Daniel describe events that occurred in completely different centuries. In Section III, visions B and D point to Antiochus. We are examining visions A, C, and E, which point to the Romans.

The prophecy of Joel apparently applies to those people who chose to be faithful to God's message on the day of Pentecost. It is no accident that the very next two verses after the promise of Joel were applied to the events of Pentecost by the apostle Peter (Joel 2:28-29). God's *new* "people shall never again be put to shame." Of course, all of these passages may very well prefigure events surrounding the final battle between good and evil (GR3).

Who is the little horn?

So if not Antiochus, who was this little horn? Nero ruled Rome from 54 to 68 A.D., and the details of the vision fit him perfectly.

The little horn "had a mouth that spoke great things," and "shall speak words against the Most High" (7:20, 25). Nero blasphemed against God by aggressively enforcing emperor worship.

The little horn is accused of attempting "to change the times and the law" (7:25). This was an attack on the very essence of biblical Judaism: the Law and the Prophets. Nero's disdain for the Law of Moses has been well-documented. And of course, the Law forbade the worship of the emperor.

Even the description of the small horn uprooting three others can be found in the career of Nero. Daniel writes, "There came up among them another horn, a little one, before which three of the first horns were plucked up by the roots" (7:8). Later Daniel learns that the three uprooted horns were of royal lineage. "He shall be different from the former ones and shall put down three kings" (7:24). The Hebrew word used here for *kings* is *melek*. The most common translation is "king," but it also can be translated as "royal" (Gen. 49:20; 1 Kings 10:13; Dan. 6:7).

Nero's life fits this description like a glove. His mother, Agrippina, married the emperor Claudius shortly after Nero was born. At a young age, Nero married his stepsister, Octavia, daughter of Claudius. Agrippina persuaded Claudius to favor this new son-in-law, Nero, as his successor over his own blood son, Britannicus. After becoming emperor, Nero murdered all three of these powerful relatives, whom he saw as rivals. These murders fulfill the vision of the three royal horns that "were plucked up by the roots" (7:8).

Daniel's vision even accurately predicts the death of Nero, who reigned until 68 A.D. During that year, the army, and finally even the Praetorian Guard, rose in rebellion against him. He fled, and when he eventually committed suicide, the dynasty that began with Caesar Augustus died with him. General Vespasian, a man outside of Nero's line, became the next emperor (after a devastating interregnum that witnessed three would-be emperors futilely battling for the throne). Vespasian was not even an aristocrat by birth. Nero and the imperial dynasty from which he came never rose to power in Rome again. "His dominion shall be taken away, to be consumed and destroyed to the end" (7:26).

Daniel's symbolic use of the horns alternates between being a symbol of the ten provinces of the empire and being a symbol of specific people. This type of dualistic imagery in apocalyptic imagery is quite common (GR4).

Daniel's vision continues with more details concerning the battle strategy of the beasts. "This horn made war with the saints, and prevailed over them" (7:21). The leader of the fourth kingdom, Rome, will persecute God's people.

This is the first reference we have to what we will later label the Great Tribulation. This fierce and sustained trial of the Church started when the little horn, Nero, needed a scapegoat for the fire that ravaged the city of Rome. This state-sponsored persecution continued for about three years, until Nero's attention was diverted by the Jewish-Roman War. Nero was the first in a succession of ten Caesars who persecuted the Church with varying intensity (TBR, 37).

For how long does the little horn make war?

Amazingly, we are even told the length of time during which the little horn will wage war against "the law." It will be "for a time, two times, and half a time" (7:25). These times are meant to be added together: one year, plus two years, plus half a year. This is an ancient way of saying three and a half years.

That coincides precisely with events in the first century. Jewish Zealots burned the Roman ruler's palace, slaughtered the garrison of Roman soldiers, killed the high priest Ananias and burned his palace, and put an end to the morning and evening sacrifices for Caesar in the Temple. In response, the Roman general Cestius marched on Jerusalem and burned much of the city. Yet his expedition against Jerusalem was a disaster for Rome, and he lost six thousand soldiers in his retreat.

Caesar Nero was outraged and declared war against Jerusalem in February of 67 A.D. General Vespasian was dispatched at the head of a Roman army. This was the beginning of the Jewish-Roman War. The "little horn" who had been making "war with the saints," even to the point of wearing "out the saints of the Most High," now turned his wrath on "the law" that forbade worship of him (7:21, 25). That war upon "the times and the law" lasted three and a half years.

By April of 70 A.D., the son of Vespasian, General Titus, had tightened the noose of the final siege of Jerusalem. The Roman army had even come from the north, just as Ezekiel 38 and 39 had predicted.

In August of 70 A.D., the Temple of Jerusalem fell before the Roman army of Titus. The Temple was torched and systematically dismantled, piece by piece. This destruction of the Temple was the end of biblical Judaism, as even rabbis of today will attest (*BET*, 154). Their exclusive power to share God with the nations was gone forever with the destruction of the Temple (Isa. 2:2-5, 56).

Just as Daniel had predicted, Nero declared war in February of 67 A.D., and Jerusalem's Temple fell in August of 70 A.D. Count the months. The Jewish-Roman War lasted forty-two months, precisely three and a half years. Jerusalem was to "be given into his hand for a time, two times, and half a time."

We can understand the modernist's desire to date the writing of this vision late and then apply this prophecy to Antiochus! (But remember GR1.) Daniel has been given an amazing amount of detail concerning the "how" of the establishment of God's kingdom here on earth. We knew from the first statue vision that it would occur during the time of the Roman Empire. Now we know that he predicted some of the specific events surrounding the life and reign of Nero Caesar. This includes his murder of his rivals, his egomania, his blasphemy, and his hatred for the law of God. Most amazing, though, Daniel predicted that the Jewish-Roman War would last for three and a half years.

How do rapturists treat this section? They ignore the clear and convincing fulfillment of this vision during the fourth empire of Rome. Instead, they postulate that presumptuous parenthesis, inserting two thousand years between the beast and the beast's horns. They then try to apply all of these prophecies concerning Nero to the future antichrist spoken of elsewhere in the Bible.

Is this Christ's second coming?

Now the vision gets really interesting. Some claim that this part of this vision is a riddle riddled with riddles. Daniel tells us that "with the clouds of Heaven there came one like a son of man, and he came to the Ancient of Days and was presented before Him. And to Him was given dominion and glory and kingdom, that all peoples, nations, and languages should serve Him; his dominion is an everlasting dominion, which shall not pass away, and His Kingdom one that shall not be destroyed" (Dan. 7:13-14).

To solve this riddle, we will approach it like a reporter. We will attempt to answer who, what, where, when, and why.

The *who* question is relatively simple. There are two persons mentioned. Based on details earlier in the vision, it is generally agreed that the "Ancient of Days" is God the Father.

We can be quite certain that the "son of man" is the Messiah, because Jesus referred to Himself as the "Son of man." If you are reading this book, you probably agree that Jesus was the promised Messiah. During His trial before the Sanhedrin, the Jewish religious leaders of Jerusalem, Jesus paraphrased these very verses from Daniel and applied them to Himself (Matt. 26:64).

The high priest understood this to mean that Jesus viewed Himself as the Messiah of Daniel, and so he tore his robe and accused Jesus of blasphemy. In one aspect, the high priest was correct: that is exactly what Jesus was claiming.

Now that we know the two persons involved, *what* is being described? A simple question will help us to clarify our thinking. In Daniel, when the "Son of man" comes, in what direction will He be traveling? In other words, when Daniel describes the Son coming with the clouds of Heaven to be given dominion and glory and kingdom, is He coming toward Jerusalem or the Mount of Olives?

This seems to be the automatic assumption of many commentators, including rapturists, which means this prophecy must refer to either the first or the second advent. But this is an unwarranted assumption that contradicts the text itself. Daniel clearly indicates the direction of the Son's coming. It is not toward His saints, nor even toward earth.

Daniel describes the Son of man as coming "*to* the Ancient of Days." When He comes, He is "presented *before* Him" (7:13). The Son is traveling to the Father in Heaven for the ceremonial bestowal of His Kingdom. This is critical for our interpretation and will be crucial if we are properly to understand Jesus' words in the Olivet Discourse.

This interpretation was the understanding of the early Church. Lactantius has been dubbed the "Christian Cicero" for his defense of Christianity around the beginning of the fourth century. He clearly understood that this passage spoke of a trip *to* the Father by Christ when he connected Daniel's vision to Psalms 110:1. "The Lord says to my lord: 'Sit at my right hand, till I make Your enemies Your footstool' " (*TED*, XLVII). He wrote of it as though it were something, not to be defended, but commonly understood in his day.

So the *what* question is answered in a way few of us probably expected. This prophecy does not describe the coming of the Son of man back to earth at all! Rather, this prophecy concerns the time when Jesus is recognized as the victor over sin because of the Cross. He is publicly given what is rightfully His: God's Kingdom.

Where does this coming occur? The entire scene could very well have occurred in Heaven. In fact, since that is generally where we would expect the throne of the Ancient of Days to be, that is the primary location in view.

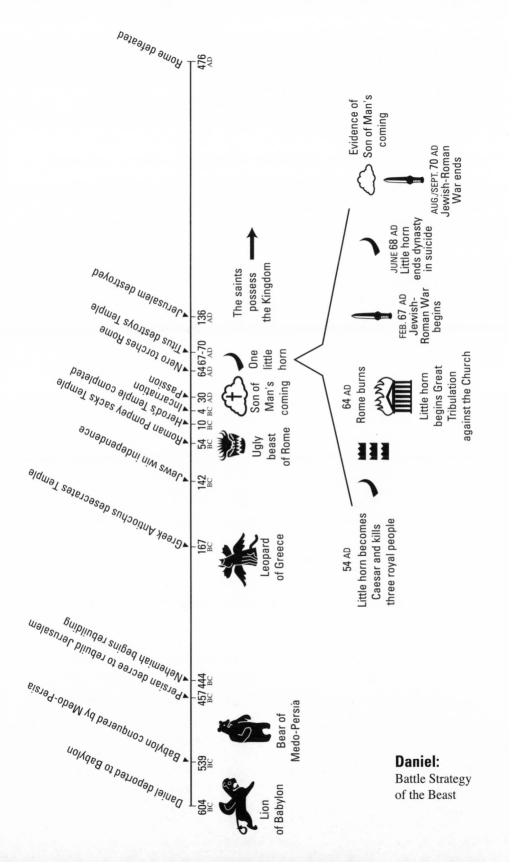

Daniel:
Battle Strategy
of the Beast

However, we have already noted that Jesus applied this prophecy to Himself before the Sanhedrin. In doing so, He gave us a few more tidbits of information about this event. Here is what our Lord said at His trial: "I tell you, hereafter you will see the Son of man seated at the right hand of Power, and coming on the clouds of Heaven" (Matt. 26:64).

Jesus told the men judging Him that they would *see* the coming foretold by Daniel. Since the Sanhedrin's court was not in Heaven, but in Jerusalem, Jesus is expanding the venue of Daniel's vision.

At the very least, we can assume that while the actual coming occurred in Heaven, the Sanhedrin would witness convincing evidence of it in Jerusalem. Some undeniable evidence that Jesus was recognized by God as the victor in Heaven must be seen by the rulers who condemned Jesus to death. This means that this cannot possibly be a future event for us in the twenty-first century, because the men of the Sanhedrin have been dead for thousands of years.

We have already started to answer the *when* part of our investigation. This event, this recognition of the victory of Jesus, must occur within the lifetimes of the men who condemned Jesus for blasphemy. Significantly, Jesus made this prediction after the Jewish leadership had decisively rejected His Kingship.

Since Heaven is outside our earthly sequential time line, the bestowal of God's Kingdom there could easily have preceded the earthly, public evidence. Since we are talking about God's recognition of Christ as King of the Kingdom, most Christians would agree that it occurred in Heaven at the Transfiguration or Ascension. In fact, the Liturgy of the Church connects this prophecy with the Transfiguration.

This understanding certainly does satisfy the details of Daniel. Christ received His Kingdom as a result of the work accomplished in His first advent. Yet Jesus extended Daniel's relatively private event in Heaven to include another earthly event that the Sanhedrin could witness. Since He made His prophecy after the Transfiguration, and since the Sanhedrin were not privy to Christ's Ascension, He must have been referring to another event — quite a public event which Christ could assure the Sanhedrin they would "see." Yet this undeniable evidence of the Son of man's victory must have occurred within the generation of the Sanhedrin.

The riddle of the "coming" in Daniel's vision is coming into focus. The lifetime of the Sanhedrin overlaps with the time frame of this vision in Daniel. Daniel has been describing the little horn, which symbolizes Nero. Was there any public evidence that Jesus was the spiritual victor over the Old Covenant and its leadership during the times of Nero? Hold on to that question, because the answer is an emphatic yes.

I can almost hear you gasp, "Wait just one cotton-pickin' minute! Are you implying that we must believe that the second coming of Christ occurred in 70 A.D.?"

Of course not. In fact, that belief would be soundly and correctly condemned as heresy by all Catholics and most Protestants.

I am making a very limited point about only this passage in Daniel and its partner passage in Matthew. I am proposing that this coming of Daniel's vision could not possibly be a prediction of the second coming at the final eschaton. The Church has always connected it to the first advent in her Liturgy. Our evidence will only become more compelling as we examine Zechariah and the Olivet Discourse.

We are now ready to answer our last question, *why?* Why was Jesus coming? We have already hinted at this answer, but for clarity, we will back up a bit and get a running start.

It is essential to view coming "with the clouds of Heaven" in an Old Testament way. The clouds have nothing to do with the weather on that particular day, but are a sign of coming in glory, in victory, and most of all, *in judgment* (GR6).

Rapture

Perhaps you remember what we learned in Ground Rule 6. We read that "the Lord is riding on a swift cloud and comes to Egypt; and the idols of Egypt will tremble at His presence" (Isa. 19:1-2). In the fulfillment of this passage in Isaiah 20:1-6, God comes to judge the false idols — in the form of the Assyrian army! God promises He is coming to Egypt, and the Egyptians witness a conquering army. The Assyrian army is the physical evidence that God came "on a swift cloud." God's judgment came in the form of the Assyrian army's killing, pillaging, and conquering.

Notice the similarity of the Old Testament language in Isaiah, "The Lord is riding on a swift cloud and comes to Egypt," to Daniel's description, "With the clouds of Heaven there came one like a son of man" (GR3). This is not merely coincidence. God came to Egypt as Judge. Jesus is telling the Sanhedrin, which condemned Him, that they will see the day when He comes to judge them. They fancied themselves the judges, but Jesus tells them that they will live to understand their mistake. When Jesus quoted Daniel at His trial, there was an implied threat. Why is the Son of man coming? To judge. The high priest understood this threat clearly and decided that Jesus had to die.

Although Christ certainly received His Kingdom no later than at His Ascension, the Sanhedrin never saw evidence of that. There was only one event that occurred during the generation of the Sanhedrin that would show them the Christ was their Judge. *The public event that evidenced the coming of Christ in victory was the destruction of Jerusalem's Temple in 70 A.D., as instigated by the little horn, Nero.* It was a public judgment that clearly proved to all mankind that Jesus was the victor in Heaven over His enemies on earth. No other event created the instantaneous, worldwide publicity necessary to illustrate to the Sanhedrin that Christ was seated at the right hand of the Father. Just as God judged Egypt with the Assyrian army, Christ judged Jerusalem with the Roman army.

The fulfillment of Daniel's vision also parallels the Babylonian experience of God's judgment. Remember Belshazzar's folly? The Babylonians witnessed the coming of God in the conquering army of the Medes. Daniel did not include this account just for the fun of telling us the inside story of his political prowess. He was preparing us for the meaning of this vision.

By this understanding, a conquering army around Jerusalem, the city of the Sanhedrin, would fulfill the "Son of man" prophecy of Daniel, as expanded by Jesus in Matthew. The Sanhedrin's defeat was viewed as the earthly evidence of the heavenly acceptance of Christ's victory. This parallel correspondence between events in Heaven and on earth will be seen again when these events are covered in The Apocalypse. We will learn that events in Heaven lead to events on earth and imbue them with significance. The parallel between Jerusalem and Egypt will also be expanded.

As we progress, I will illustrate that the early Church understood the fall of Jerusalem in precisely these terms. But as we have just seen, this understanding certainly fits Daniel's vision, Isaiah's language, and the prophecy of Jesus at His trial.

Summary of the "coming"

Because we firmly believe in the second coming, we automatically assume that any passage that speaks of Christ's coming anywhere is always a reference to that blessed hope. But we must be faithful to the scriptural texts before us.

Jesus said that Daniel's Son of man would come in judgment during the Sanhedrin's generation. This leaves us only three logical choices. Either Jesus was lying to the Sanhedrin (the non-Christian view), or He was mistaken about His timing (the modernist view), or the "coming" in judgment of Daniel 7 and Matthew 26 occurred before the close of the first century A.D. So unless Jesus was untruthful or mistaken, this prophecy has already been fulfilled.

Rapture

Jesus judged Jerusalem with the Roman army in 70 A.D. He predicted that very event: "For the days shall come upon you, when your enemies will cast up a bank about you and surround you . . . and they will not leave one stone upon another in you; *because you did not know the time of your visitation*" (Luke 19:42-44). Now we know that this was evidence to the entire world that Jesus had fulfilled Daniel's "Son of man" prophecy in Heaven.

Daniel tells us that the primary result of Christ's victory is that the saints "shall receive the kingdom." This rings true to the early history of the Church. Even though Christ was already victor in Heaven, as long as the Temple remained, people tended to see Christianity as merely a sect within Judaism. If the sacrifice of Jesus had superseded the Old Covenant ceremonies, people would naturally wonder why animal sacrifices continued in Jerusalem. The letter to the Hebrews stands as a tribute to that confusion in the very early Church. Within the generation of His accusers, Christ with His judgment eliminated the source of confusion. Once the Old Testament system of animal sacrifices had been eliminated, the Church was free to grow unencumbered by the continued existence of biblical Judaism and the confusions it caused.

But a word of caution. This coming of the Son of man in the clouds of glorious victory and judgment must not be confused with the second advent of Christ at the final eschaton. At that time, Christ will come again in the clouds. But then He will be traveling toward earth to judge all of humanity. Daniel's event is a far cry from, and thousands of years before, the second coming of Christ. At the same time, however, the victorious judgment of Christ in Heaven as evidenced in the events of 70 A.D. certainly does point to the final climax of history as a prophetic event (GR3).

Needless to say, rapturists do not agree with this understanding of Daniel. They place the second half of this vision in the future. But when we look at the time line of the rapturists, the problem is even more acute in this vision than in the statue vision. Now the presumptuous parenthesis of two thousand years must appear in the passage between the appearance of the fourth beast and the mere mention of his ten horns. This is proposed even though Daniel specifically informs us that only four kingdoms are involved (7:17). To claim that the fourth kingdom could be reconstituted after two thousand years, and would still be the same kingdom, is grasping at straws.

This brings up another timing problem for the rapturist. Jesus clearly told the Sanhedrin that they would see evidence of the coming of the Son of man as predicted in Daniel 7:13. Yet the rapturist places these events in the future even for our time. He must do this, because he wants to justify a still-future seven-year Great Tribulation. The rapturist is forced to believe that on the eve of His Crucifixion, Jesus made a promise to the Sanhedrin, but that His timing was off by at least two thousand years!

Summary of the beast vision

To summarize this vision's message, thus far we have seen that there will be four empires between Daniel's lifetime and the Messianic Kingdom. During the fourth, the Roman Empire that ruled two millennia ago, God will set up His eternal Kingdom, and the Son of Man will unmistakably begin His reign in glory. Eventually the whole world, even the Sanhedrin, will be forced to recognize the public victory of Jesus when He judges them through Rome. Just as God came to serve justice to the Babylonians through the army of the Medes because of Belshazzar's folly, just as the Assyrians revealed God's coming in His judgment of the Egyptians in Isaiah, just so Jesus publicly judged the Sanhedrin through the Roman army in 70 A.D. The saints will be persecuted by Nero, yet will receive the Kingdom after Jerusalem's defeat in a three-and-a-half-year war. The actions and personality of the little horn, Caesar Nero, are predicted accurately. The details of the vision mesh with the events of the first century with amazing faithfulness.

If you still have residual doubts about Daniel's message, relax. We will examine these ideas again. They are a recurring theme in Scripture (GR6).

VISION III:C: THE BATTLE
STRATEGY OF GOD'S PEOPLE

Time is a recurring element in Daniel, but nowhere is it more important than in this vision. Daniel has foreseen the stone destroy the statue and supplant it. He knows that the little horn will make war for three and a half years and defeat the Law. He anticipates God's saints' receiving the Kingdom that will endure forever. The whole question, to Daniel's mind, is "How long before these events are to be fulfilled, and what must God's people do in the meantime?"

The enormity of Daniel's question may make the complexity of this vision more understandable. As St. Jerome wrote, this is a passage that "has been argued over in various ways by men of greatest learning. . . . Each has expressed his views" (CID).

If you build it, He will come

Perhaps we should first pause in awe over the fact that this prophecy even exists. Daniel has predicted the rebuilding of Jerusalem even before the king let the Jewish people return there. As we know from the reaction of the neighboring peoples in Judea at that time, the decree to rebuild Jerusalem was a bold political move. Jerusalem had been an outpost of rebellion and independence from time out of mind. The concept of an anointed prince of the Jews in a rebuilt Jerusalem would not be popular with the Gentiles.

If we simplify the passage to its very core, and initially ignore all the complex numbers, the message of this vision is quite clear.

Rebuild the Jerusalem Temple to pave the way for the Messiah's coming. In other words, "If you build it, He will come." But the vision does not stop there. Even though the Messiah will bring with Him six tremendous blessings, He will be cut off, and the Temple will be desolated. There is not going to be a "happily ever after" ending to the Messiah's coming.

Seven is a perfect number

One task lies between us and the examination of this vision. We must briefly discuss the significance of the number *seven*. In answer to Daniel's prayers, God sent Gabriel to help Daniel understand the time line of God's plan. Gabriel reveals to Daniel an extremely complex scheme of times and numbers.

"Seven" is obviously the unifying theme of the answer to the question "When will the Jews go back to Jerusalem and rebuild the Temple, paving the way for the Messiah's appearance?" In ancient Jewish literature, the number *seven* signifies God's perfect action in the world. The Babylonian captivity spanned seven decades. Every seventh year in the Hebrew calendar was a sabbatical year, during which the land was to lie fallow, and after every seventh set of seven years (the fiftieth year) was a Jubilee year (Lev. 25). Here the prophecy revolves around seventy sets of seven.

The Hebrew word used here for *seven* is *shabua*. The use of the word *sevens* is analogous to our use of the term *dozens*. When we use the word *dozens*, we might mean dozens of years, or dozens of decades, or dozens of roses, or dozens of eggs. The meaning must be determined from the context. It is the same with *sevens*. The best understanding is that of an unspecified time period; "times" or "time periods" or "seasons" would be a more accurate rendering. Moreover, there is nothing to indicate that they must mean the same thing from one reference to the next (GR2).

Because Daniel bundles these periods into groups of sevens, they are most commonly called "weeks," or "weeks of seasons."

Rapture

Thus, the entire prophecy is referred to as "Daniel's seventy weeks" or "Daniel's seventy weeks of seasons." We will use this common *week* terminology.

The word *years*, which the Revised Standard Version inserts into the text after *seven*, is not in the original language. In this passage, the sevens can be understood as minutes, days, weeks, months, years, decades, or even centuries. To avoid confusion, I have deleted *years* from the text, as do several other translations (e.g., the New American Bible). I have added *seasons* in brackets to clarify the meaning.

For many contemporary readers, the initial response to all these sevens is one of consternation, which rapidly turns to disinterest. We will try to avoid that response because the message of this vision is so important. Although Daniel's style is enigmatic, it is not undecipherable.

Rapturists believe they can prove that there is a seven-year Great Tribulation that is yet unfulfilled in this vision. To come to that conclusion, they insert the presumptuous parenthesis of two thousand years into this vision just as they did in all the others. Here it falls between the sixty-ninth and seventieth weeks. They had better be right. This assertion, about this very passage, lies at the heart and soul of the rapturist system. Both Darby and present rapturists claim that this vision is the basis for their entire time line. Remember that without a future seven-year Great Tribulation, the need for a rebuilt Jewish Temple and a secret rapture of believers disappears, and the entire rapturist system falls like a house of cards.

Let us first read this vision, verse by verse.

> *"Seventy weeks [seventy times seven seasons] are*
> *decreed concerning Your people and Your holy city,*
> > *to finish the transgression,*
> > *to put an end to sin,*

and to atone for iniquity,
to bring in everlasting righteousness,
to seal both vision and prophet,
and to anoint a most holy.

Know therefore and understand that from the going forth of the word to restore and build Jerusalem to the coming of an anointed one, a prince, there shall be seven weeks [seven times seven seasons].

Then for sixty-two weeks [sixty-two times seven seasons] it shall be built again with squares and moat, but in a troubled time.

And after the sixty-two weeks [sixty-two times seven seasons], an anointed one shall be cut off, and shall have nothing; and the people of the prince who is to come shall destroy the city and the sanctuary. Its end shall come with a flood, and to the end there shall be war; desolations are decreed.

And he shall make a strong covenant with many for one week [seven seasons]; and for half of the week [three and a half seasons] he shall cause sacrifice and offering to cease; and upon the wing of abominations shall come one who makes desolate, until the decreed end is poured out on the desolator."

Calculating the sevens

Without a doubt, this is a very unusual passage. The sevens appear four times in the vision. The initial mention of seventy sevens is subdivided into a first set of seven sevens, a second set of sixty-two sevens, and a final, lone set of seven commonly called the final week.

The rapturists' first assumption, however, confounds all their subsequent efforts to understand these numbers. They assume that all of these sevens signify years. As a result, they place the first set of seven weeks (verse 24) and the second set of sixty-two weeks (verse 25) in chronological order. Added together, they approximately equal the 483 years between Daniel and Christ's first advent (GR8).

Although I believe this understanding is flawed, that problem is dwarfed by the presumptuous parenthesis that rapturists insert between the second set of sixty-two weeks and the third, final week. They insert the gap into the middle of verse 26. They teach that up to this point, the vision applies to the first advent. Then, after the cutting-off of the Messiah is mentioned, rapturists try to insert a two-thousand-year hiatus before the Temple and Jerusalem are destroyed in the second half of verse 26. They do this to place the final, lone set of seven as a seven-year Great Tribulation that is still in our future.

Rapturists split every one of Daniel's visions this way. In the first vision, a two-thousand-year gap is introduced into the statue, between the iron legs and the iron-clay feet. In the second vision, this two-millennia interruption is inserted between the fourth beast and that beast's very own horns! And in this third prophecy of time periods, the same presumptuous parenthesis is inserted mid-sentence.

The question remains: where is the textual justification for these massive interruptions in Daniel's time line? The answer is: there is none; not a shred of justification apart from the rapturists' desire to deny that Christ set up a Kingdom during His first advent.

Even the small minority of early Church theologians who believed the seventieth week was still future argued against the introduction of any gap between the sixty-ninth and seventieth weeks. Apollinarius of Laodicea believed in a future seventieth week, but still said, "It is impossible that periods so linked together be wrenched apart, but rather *the time-segments must all be joined together* in conformity with Daniel's prophecy" (cited in *CID*). That is the reason he predicted the end of the world in the sixth century. Of course, that is not a viable alternative for present-day rapturists.

St. Augustine certainly had no patience for any gap inserted between the sixty-ninth and seventieth weeks. He points to Luke's Gospel as proof that this could not be done. "For let us not suppose that the computation of Daniel's weeks was interfered with . . . or that they were not complete, but had to be completed afterward in the end of all things, for Luke most plainly testifies that *the prophecy of Daniel was accomplished at the time when Jerusalem was overthrown*" (*EPA*, 199:31; cited in GCC). St. Augustine was referring to Jesus' Olivet Discourse, which we will examine most closely in Matthew's Gospel. The long and the short of it is this: the rapturist system doesn't work unless you approach the text with preconceived notions that it does not support.

Counting temples

This presumptuous parenthesis totally destroys the unity of this vision. Understood most simply, the vision teaches that there will be one Messiah who will come, and then He will be "cut off." The Messiah's career is preceded by the second Temple (Herod's), which must first be rebuilt for Him and will then be destroyed. There is only one Messiah and one Temple, and their rise and fall are described in relation to each other.

Rapturists see this vision as predicting the first advent after the rebuilding of Herod's Temple. But then they claim that midsentence in verse 26, the vision skips over two thousand years of history. Unbeknownst to Daniel, during this two thousand years, Herod's Temple is destroyed, and the rapturist must now postulate the rebuilding of a third Temple. Without mentioning any of this, the end of verse 26 discusses the destruction of this third Temple (rather than the one already mentioned in verse 25). These mental gymnastics are necessary to substantiate a future seven-year

Great Tribulation. In the meantime, the simple and evident unity of this vision is destroyed.

This leads to perhaps one of the most peculiar beliefs in Christianity. Rapturists believe that Jewish priests will restart the ancient animal sacrifices in a rebuilt Jerusalem Temple about the time that the Great Tribulation begins. This is necessary for the rapturist system to explain the phrase of this vision that states that someone "shall cause sacrifice and offering to cease." The Jewish people cannot stop something they have not been doing.

But ask rapturists why God would ever allow a resumption of animal sacrifices, especially in light of His Son's final Sacrifice, and they have no answer. To make their system coherent, rapturists must believe that the animal sacrifices will be resumed, even in the face of Hebrews 9:24-26: "Christ has entered . . . into Heaven itself, now to appear in the presence of God on our behalf. Nor was it to offer Himself repeatedly, as the high priest enters the Holy Place yearly with blood not his own; for then He would have had to suffer repeatedly since the foundation of the world. But as it is, He has appeared once for all at the end of the age to put away sin by the sacrifice of Himself." Rapturists believe animal sacrifices will resume in a rebuilt Temple, but they are at a loss to explain why.

Blessings bestowed

Daniel states that the purpose of these seventy weeks is to bestow six blessings. As Catholics, we believe that these blessings were bestowed as a result of the first advent. But rapturists must argue that these six blessings have not yet been fulfilled and will not be fulfilled until the end of the future seven-year Great Tribulation.

But look at these six items that they claim have not yet been accomplished. The seventy weeks are decreed "to finish the transgression, to put an end to sin, and to atone for iniquity, to bring in everlasting righteousness, to seal both vision and prophet, and to anoint a most holy." I do not believe it is possible to claim that these six blessings were not bestowed by Christ at His first advent.

Absolutely without exception, the early Church believed they were bestowed then. Tertullian wrote, "The day when Christ was born . . . eternal righteousness was revealed, and the Saint of saints was anointed, namely Christ, and the vision and prophecy were sealed, and those sins were remitted which are allowed. . . . It was because the prophecy was fulfilled by His advent that the vision was confirmed by a seal; and it was called a prophecy because Christ Himself is the seal of all the prophets, fulfilling as He did all that the prophets had previously declared concerning Him" (cited in *CID*). It could not be stated any more clearly.

Julius Africanus (Julius Hilarianus) wrote at the end of the fourth century that there would be no future fulfillment of the seventieth week, but that is not all: "There is no doubt [that this prophecy] constitutes a prediction of Christ's advent, for He appeared to the world *at the end of seventy weeks*. After Him the crimes were consummated, and sin reached its end and iniquity was destroyed. An eternal righteousness also was proclaimed which overcame the mere righteousness of the law; and the vision and the prophecy were fulfilled, inasmuch as the Law and the Prophets endured until the time of John the Baptist, and then the Saint of saints was anointed. And all these things were the objects of hope, prior to Christ's Incarnation, rather than the objects of actual possession" (*CH*, X-XI). Notice his point? If these six blessings have not been accomplished, then New Testament saints are in no better a position than were the Old Testament saints.

St. Augustine strongly argued against any future fulfillment of this vision of Daniel, pointing out instead that the prophetic events fit the first advent very well. "At the end of the age, Christ will *not need to be anointed or put to death*, in order that this prophecy of Daniel may then be expected to be fulfilled" (*EPA*, 199:912; cited in *GCC*).

These six blessings were so clearly bestowed through the Incarnation that it almost sounds as though these six phrases were written by a New Testament writer. And in fact, the New Testament echoes these words. In Hebrews 9:26 and 28, we read, "For [Christ] has appeared once for all at the end of the age *to put away sin* by the sacrifice of Himself. . . . Christ, having been offered once to bear the sins of many, will appear a second time, *not* to deal with sin, but to save those who are eagerly waiting for Him." The phrase "put away sin" is an obvious reflection of Daniel's phrase "to finish the transgression, to put an end to sin, and to atone for iniquity." Hebrews makes clear that this happened in the first advent. He also makes clear that this will not happen at the second advent: "Christ will appear a second time, not to deal with sin."

Further confirmation is seen in Luke's Gospel. At the beginning of His public ministry, Jesus stands in His hometown synagogue of Nazareth and reads the Messianic prophecy of Isaiah 61:1-2: "The Spirit of the Lord is upon me, because He has anointed me. . . ." He then shocks His audience by stating, "Today this Scripture has been fulfilled in your hearing" (4:16-21). Jesus declared Himself to be the Anointed One of the Old Testament, the anointed of Daniel's vision. He came to fulfill the task of the "anointed" described here during His first advent.

The New Testament confirms, then, that all six benefits of the seventy weeks have been bestowed by Christ already. This is not surprising. If not through the Passion, when can we realistically ever hope for these benefits? In this view, we unreservedly agree with the unanimous historical interpretation of the Church.

Yet rapturists must claim that this is not true. If these blessings were bestowed in the first advent, then Daniel's seventieth week is also history. If Daniel's weeks are completed, then rapturists have no basis for a future seven-year Great Tribulation. If there is no tribulation, there is no need for a secret rapture. So, to justify their system, rapturists must contradict both the clear meaning of Scripture and the teaching of the early Church.

This is ironic, for rapturists take great pride in asserting that their theological position most closely resembles that of the early Church. They usually relish the opportunity to inform the Catholic that his Faith is based on later accretions added to the pure, simple Faith of the Apostles. Of course, others may believe them wrong in this assertion, but their stated aim is always to restore the original belief of the early Church — except, it seems, in this case.

They claim that in this instance, concerning the timing of Daniel's seventieth week, the early Church was utterly and completely mistaken. Proponents such as Walvoord try to justify this with vague references to progressive revelation. In reality, however, this rejection of the beliefs of the early Church flies in the face of everything rapturists claim to believe on every other issue of theology.

The end point of the seventy weeks

The fact that the early Church believed that the blessings of the seventy weeks have already been bestowed should make this next issue seem self-evident. Almost all of the early fathers believed that the last week of Daniel *ended* no later than 70 A.D. In this they were in total agreement with the common Jewish interpretation of their time: that Daniel's seventy weeks ended with the destruction of the Temple in 70 A.D. (cited in *CID*).

As we examine the early Church writers on this issue, we will not find unanimity as to the exact end of these weeks. This is largely due to an important handicap of the early Church writers. Some of the early Fathers had a very poor text of Daniel's prophecy from which to work. In addition, they did not have an accurate idea of when Cyrus's reign commenced. This undoubtedly affected some of their opinions when they attempted to work out exact timetables (*ISW*).

Rapture

Yet although various authors chose varying dates as the *"terminus ad quem"* (end) for Daniel's seventy weeks, virtually all the early Fathers agreed that it must be in some way associated with the fall of the Temple. Although the references can be obscure, some writers seem to have proposed 64 A.D., the year Rome burned. Also mentioned is 54 A.D., the year Nero came to the throne. This is justified, because Nero set into motion the destruction of the Temple. But by far the two most common dates are 70 A.D., the year of its burning, and 67 A.D., the year Rome declared war on Jerusalem.

For our purposes, either of these two dates would be satisfactory, which means that we stand with the majority of the early Church. Since 70 A.D. is the date emblazoned in the minds of most people as the year of the Temple's destruction, I will refer to that date. Understand, however, that I use the date with intentional flexibility to mean the events of 67 to 70 A.D.

This date, 70 A.D., seems almost forgotten in modern theology. In spite of their differences, the early Fathers understood the importance of 70 A.D. The early-Church Fathers are so clear; it seems hard to believe that rapturists have even read them. Instead, rapturists insert that presumptuous parenthesis for the express purpose of putting the last week into our future.

Appendix One contains a brief survey of those Fathers I am referencing. I think you will agree, after reading the Fathers, that rapturists have no right to jettison the last week of Daniel into the future, especially when it creates some of the other problems in the vision we have already examined.

The last week first

We are about to explain this vision, one verse at a time, with what I believe is the most consistent Catholic understanding. But first we have to examine the most controversial of the weeks. This is commonly called Daniel's last or seventieth week. This is the week rapturists propel into the future with the presumptuous parenthesis.

We have already seen that the entire Church unanimously believed that the six benefits of these weeks were bestowed by Christ at His first advent. We have also illustrated that the vast majority of the early Church saw all seventy weeks as completed by 67 to 70 A.D. What we have not mentioned concerns the duration of each of the seasons within this final week. How long is a *shabua?*

Rapturists take each of the seasons as one year. That is how they end up with a seven-year Great Tribulation that they call Daniel's last week. But the majority of the early Church understood the last week of Daniel (seven seasons) as encompassing seven *decades*, not seven years. Remember, the word *shabua* is like the word *dozens*; it does not designate the duration of the sevens.

Clement of Alexandria and Origen

Clement of Alexandria is the earliest Church Father to give a clear answer on this issue. St. Jerome informs us that Clement of Alexandria included in his seventy weeks "the reign of Vespasian and the destruction of the Temple." Because Clement also included Christ, this last week must include more than seven years (CID).

Origen was a student of Clement and is the key to Clement's thinking on the seventieth week. Origen makes it explicitly clear that he believes the last week of Daniel does not refer to years, but to decades. He also went to great lengths to demonstrate that the beginning of the Temple's destruction was half a week (thirty-five years) after Pentecost. This was because Origen understood Pentecost as the moment in the last week when the "strong covenant" of Daniel was confirmed (verse 27). He understood Pentecost to be about thirty-seven years before the Temple's destruction. This would mean that the seventieth week of Daniel approximately spans the period from Christ's birth to the assault on the Temple in

67 A.D. Halfway through are the events surrounding the Passion, the Resurrection, and the birth of the Church.

If Origen followed his teacher, which seems likely, we can now understand how Clement would include Christ, Nero, and Vespasian in these seven decades. The fact that Clement never explains this may indicate that this understanding was widely accepted in his day. This also harmonizes with what we have already learned: virtually the entire early Church understood the end of the seventieth week as no later than 70 A.D.

Barnabas

The Epistle of Barnabas already exhibits this view of the last week of Daniel (see Appendix One). "When *the week* is completed, the Temple of God shall be built in glory in the name of the Lord. . . . This is the spiritual Temple built for the Lord" (*EOB*, 16:6). This passage refers to the building of the Church. "The week" is Daniel's final week, which contained the time of covenantal transition between the Old and New Covenants. The Incarnation, the Passion, the Resurrection, the Ascension, Pentecost, and even the judgment of 70 A.D. were all essential to building the Church. These events took seven decades, not seven years to unfold.

Eusebius

Eusebius wrote the first comprehensive Church history. Rapturists fail to notice his assertion that most of the early Church accepted the final week of Daniel as seven decades rather than seven years. "*Most authorities* extend the one [last] week of years to the sum of *seventy years*, reckoning each year as a ten-year period. They also claim that thirty-five years intervened between the Passion of the Lord and the reign of Nero, and that it was at this latter date when the weapons of Rome were first lifted up against the Jews" (cited in *CID*).

The authorities Eusebius refers to were obviously from before his time. They probably included Barnabas, Clement of Alexandria, and Origen, along with undoubtedly many others whose writings are no longer extant. Eusebius minces no words. "Most authorities" in the early Church held a position that was straightforward and easy to understand: the last week of Daniel encompassed seven decades, not seven years.

Yet this seems to be forgotten today. Even many well-educated Catholics assume that the final tribulation of the Church must last seven years. This is simply never taught in Scripture nor by the Church.

We are now ready to examine the vision verse by verse. This insight into the final week will enable us to understand the other sets of weeks of Daniel as well. As we will see, Daniel's first set of sevens (seven weeks) is also best understood as forty-nine decades, not forty-nine years. The middle set of sevens (sixty-two weeks) is best understood as 434 years.

Verse 24: Blessings bestowed when Messiah comes

The vision starts with a summary of how many seasons will be under consideration: seventy weeks, or seventy times seven. The first mention of the seventy weeks does not point to years or decades. They are only a signal of how many "seasons" must transpire to bestow the six blessings. They carry the symbolic importance of the numbers *seven* and *ten* (GR2).

As we have noted, these blessings were all gained for God's people at Christ's first advent. The sixth blessing speaks of anointing a most holy. The Hebrew does not make it clear whether this is a person, place, or thing. The most straightforward understanding is to take every mention of "anointed" in this vision as a reference to the Messiah. That is what the word *Messiah* means, "anointed one." The coming of the Messiah during the seventy weeks is one of the blessings.

Rapture

The second half of verse 24 gives the reader a specific length of time before the "anointed one, a prince" arrives on the public scene. That length of time is "seven weeks" (forty-nine seasons). Again, the simplest method of understanding this vision is to take both the last set and this first set of seven weeks as decades. This would mean that the duration before the Messiah's arrival would be seven times seven (forty-nine) decades. This would, of course, span 490 years. But when does the clock start ticking?

The vision declares that the time line starts with a decree "to restore and build Jerusalem." In 538 B.C., Cyrus decreed the rebuilding of the Temple (Isa. 44:26-28, 45:1-4; Ezra 1:2-4). Darius issued a second decree in 520 B.C. (Ezra 6:3-12), and in that year the people started to rebuild the Temple in earnest under Zerubbabel.

But both decrees have the same problem. They do not mention the rebuilding of *Jerusalem*, but only the reconstruction of the Temple. A decree allowing the building of the Temple (for spiritual worship) is one thing. Allowing the building of a city with walls (for political protection) is another issue entirely. The building of the Temple might be included in the building of the city, but not vice versa.

Finally, King Artaxerxes of Persia issued a decree to rebuild the city of Jerusalem in about 457 B.C. (Ezra 7:11-26). This is the decree for which we have been waiting. The beginning point for Daniel's seventy weeks of seasons is therefore 457 B.C., since it is the initial "word to restore and build Jerusalem."

If we take the beginning of this seven weeks to be years, they end in the middle of nothing, around 408 B.C. But if we understand these sevens to be decades, as a complement to the Church's clear understanding of Daniel's last week, then this first segment makes perfect sense. The first set of seven weeks denote the forty-nine decades from 457 B.C. to 32 A.D. This spans the time from the decree to rebuild Jerusalem to the public arrival of the Messiah, the

Anointed One. The prophecy certainly matches history well! Scholars now estimate that the public ministry of Jesus occurred sometime between 25 and 33 A.D.

Verse 25: The Temple must be rebuilt first

We now encounter the second set of weeks, sixty-two times seven seasons. Rapturists insist that these weeks must follow chronologically after the first set of seven weeks. But this is not necessary (GR8). In fact, the text itself argues against that understanding. The vision states that the actual building of Jerusalem will span this second set of weeks. This means that the beginning point of the second set of weeks is not the end of the first set, but whenever the building project actually began.

Did the building start immediately in 457 B.C.? No, history is clear that it did not. While the decree to rebuild Jerusalem was first issued in 457 B.C., Nehemiah received word from Jerusalem several years later. "The wall of Jerusalem is broken down, and its gates are destroyed by fire" (Neh. 1:3). Nehemiah asked Artaxerxes to write another decree between 446 and 444 B.C. (Neh. 2:3-13). The actual rebuilding of Jerusalem began around 444 B.C., which makes this the beginning of the sixty-two weeks.

If we count this middle segment as years, we find that this segment ends in 10 B.C. That certainly meets one of the criteria for this second segment mentioned in the next verse (26): it must end before the Messiah is cut off.

This understanding also fits history exceedingly well. The 434 years from 444 to 10 B.C. saw plenty of "troubled times" for Jerusalem. During Nehemiah's rebuilding project, the threat was so imminent that the construction workers labored with weapons at their sides. By 400 B.C., the controlling political force in Jerusalem was the priests, but they found themselves beholden to a series of conquerors. First the Persians, then Alexander the Great, then the Ptolemies of Egypt, and then the Seleucids of Syria conquered

Jerusalem. Around 168 B.C., the priestly dominance was challenged by the Syrian king, Antiochus Epiphanes. In his effort to minimize Roman influence, he profaned the Temple with the sacrifice of swine to the Greek god Zeus Olympios (1 Macc. 1:44-59). The Jews rose in rebellion. By 165 B.C., the priestly family of the Hasmonians had prevailed in the war, and the Temple was reconsecrated by Judas Maccabee. The Jewish nation won complete independence by 142 B.C.

But any sense of tranquility was short-lived. The two competing Jewish groups we read about in the Gospels, the Pharisees and Sadducees, fought over religion and power. Their infighting enabled Pompey to conquer Jerusalem with a Roman army in 63 B.C. In 54 B.C, he sacked the Temple. At this point, the Temple had not been destroyed, but it was certainly not in functional shape. In fact, there was hardly a moment in these four centuries when Daniel's description "troubled times" did not fit Jerusalem's situation.

But this ruin of a Temple that Zerubbabel had built was not the one Jesus entered during His first advent. In 37 B.C., the Romans installed Herod the Great as king of the Jews. He initiated a massive reconstruction project on the Temple in 20 B.C. Everyone agreed this was still the second Temple, the Temple of Zerubbabel, being finally completed for glory (AJ, XV, 11).

Herod really outdid himself. This construction project enlarged the Temple greatly. While annexes and adjoining buildings were still under construction until about 63 A.D., Herod's Temple, the culmination of Zerubbabel's efforts, the Temple of Jesus' day, was in fact finally completed in a peaceful, protected, and rebuilt Jerusalem by about 10 B.C. (The Jews who spoke of a forty-six-year project in John 2:20 were including the annexes and adjoining buildings.) You couldn't ask for a more accurate, historical fulfillment of Daniel's middle sixty-two weeks of seasons. They began in 444 B.C. and ended in 10 B.C., 434 years (sixty-two weeks) later.

Now it becomes clear why the Jews of Jesus day were so overwrought with Messianic anticipation. They knew that Daniel's time line pointed to their generation. The Temple had been completed in 10 B.C. The forty-nine decades of the first set of weeks ended around 32 A.D. So where was the Messiah?

Verse 26: The Temple and the Messiah will meet ruin

Perhaps because we already know the ending of the Greatest Story Ever Told, the "cutting off" of the Messiah does not startle us in the same way it would have startled Daniel. Daniel tells us that after the Temple is rebuilt and the Messiah has come, He "shall be cut off, and shall have nothing." After His coming had been awaited for centuries, the Messiah will somehow be "cut off"! We can clearly understand this proposition as a reference to the Passion, but it must have been a mystery to Daniel.

As if that were not bad enough, Daniel learns that Jerusalem will also be destroyed. This statement in Daniel seems to be related to the Messiah's death. At some point after the Messiah's being cut off, an evil people will destroy both Jerusalem and its Temple. This sets up a very nice parallel in the vision. The Messiah will come; the Temple will be rebuilt. The Messiah will be cut off; the Temple will be destroyed.

We know something at which Daniel only hinted. The destruction of Jerusalem was a direct result of the cutting off of the Messiah. Jesus warned the leaders of Jerusalem that the destruction of their city and its Temple was a direct result of His being cut off, which they helped engineer. He prophesied, "Would that even today you knew the things that make for peace! But now they are hid from your eyes. For the days shall come upon you, when your enemies will cast up a bank about you and surround you, and hem you in on every side, and dash you to the ground, you and your children within you, and they will not leave one stone upon another in you; *because you did not know the time of your visitation*" (Luke 19:41-44). The city is destroyed because the Messiah is cut off.

But if this is true, who is the prince mentioned here in Daniel? "The people of the prince who is to come shall destroy the city and the sanctuary." The Messiah is the focus of this vision, and the Prince described here is none other than he. Christ is the Prince. The parallel is clear: the Messiah comes and is then cut off; Jerusalem is rebuilt and then destroyed. The prince does not destroy the city; his "people" do. The people of the Prince who destroyed Jerusalem through their own folly were Jesus' own kinsmen. The Jewish people destroyed their own city.

The historian Josephus claims just this point, that the Jews destroyed themselves through the abominations they performed. Josephus was a Jewish priest and general of the first century, who led the army that met General Vespasian when the Romans invaded Israel in 67 A.D. The Jewish army was utterly defeated, and only Josephus and one companion survived to surrender. Josephus became a Roman historian for Vespasian, and while in time he became sympathetic to Rome, in no way was he ever a Christian sympathizer. He wrote an extensive eyewitness account of the Jewish-Roman War titled *Wars of the Jews*. Unfortunately, few rapturists have read it.

Josephus tells of three warring factions within the walls of Jerusalem that created unimaginable devastation before the Romans ever entered the city in 70 A.D. Jewish tradition claims that there was initially enough food in Jerusalem to withstand a siege for twenty-one years. But the three factions burned one another's stores of grain, initiating a severe famine (*WJ*, V, 1:4). The Jews of Jerusalem "never suffered anything that was worse from the Romans than *they made each other suffer*" (*WJ*, V, 6:1).

According to Josephus, no other "age ever [did] breed a generation more fruitful in wickedness than this was. . . . *They overthrew the city themselves*" (WJ, V, 10:1). He continues, "The writings of the ancient prophets . . . foretold that this city should be taken when somebody shall begin *the slaughter of his own countrymen. . . .* It is God, therefore, it is God Himself who is bringing on this fire, to purge that city and Temple by means of the Romans" (WJ, VI, 2:1). Traditional Jewish thought even today teaches that Herod's Temple was destroyed because of *sinat hinam,* which is hatred without cause. They believe that at this time the Jewish people turned on one another for no reason, and that was the cause of the Temple's destruction. The Messiah's own people destroyed Jerusalem and its Temple.

When we look at the time line of Daniel's vision, this means the destruction of Jerusalem and its Temple occurred at the very end of the seventy sevens. Daniel links the war over Jerusalem to the time of "the end." "The end" is the third and final epoch in Jewish thought. The end is that period after which the Messiah has come and set up the promised Kingdom (GR8).

Verse 27: The strong covenant, sacrifice, and judgment

Here the vision seems to rewind to give us more details. Up to now, the Messiah was introduced and then cut off. In parallel, the Temple was rebuilt and then destroyed. That destruction brings us to the "end" of the seventy weeks. But Daniel needs to give us more information about how the Messiah's activities secure the six blessings. Daniel's vision does not end in despair (GR8).

We have now come to the last week of Daniel. It begins with the Incarnation, around 4 B.C., and spans the seven decades to 67 to 70 A.D. These seven decades are the time of covenantal transition of which the early Fathers spoke (Appendix One). The Prince, Christ, will make a *"strong covenant"* that will bring a halt to the Temple sacrifices during this one week. In fact, Daniel correctly envisions all of the Messiah's activities as contained in this final week.

Rapture

I believe that the covenant of the Messiah is the unifying theme of the four major prophets. The "strong covenant" of Daniel is that New Covenant which Christ made with His own Precious Blood. Isaiah called this covenant everlasting: "I will make with you an *everlasting covenant*, my steadfast, sure love for David" (55:3). Ezekiel said it was a covenant of peace: "I will make a *covenant of peace* with them; it shall be an everlasting covenant with them; and I will bless them and multiply them, and will set my sanctuary in the midst of them forevermore" (37:26). Jeremiah was told by God, "I will make a *new covenant* with the house of Israel and the house of Judah. . . . I will put my law within them, and I will write it upon their hearts; and I will be their God, and they shall be my people" (31:31, 33). The Liturgy of the Church links this Jeremiah passage to the Gospel passage in which Jesus foretells His death. It is undeniable. The new everlasting covenant of peace, the strong covenant, is inextricably linked to the death, the cutting off, of the Messiah.

Daniel predicts just that. This could explain why the early Church moved Daniel from the canonical section of historical writings into the prophetic section. Like the modernist, the pre-Christian Jew understood Daniel only as history. But Jesus emphatically declared that Daniel was prophetic. Daniel writes that halfway through the last week of seven decades, the Messiah caused the animal sacrifices of the Old Covenant to cease by sacrificing Himself to usher in a new, strong covenant.

This is certainly how the early Church interpreted these verses. Eusebius, the early-fourth-century bishop of Caesarea, wrote that "after our Lord's Passion, the sacrifice and offering ceased in the *middle of the week*. For whatever took place in the Temple after that date was not a valid sacrifice to God" (CHR).

A Christian can scarcely read the vision's phrase "shall cause sacrifice and offering to cease," without thinking of Hebrews 10:11-12: "Every priest stands daily at his service, offering repeatedly the same sacrifices, which can never take away sins. But when *Christ had offered for all time a single sacrifice for sins,* He sat down at the right hand of God."

Placing the end of the seventieth week at 67 to 70 A.D. would mean that when Daniel refers to events about halfway through this seventieth week, he is referring to something that would happen around 32 A.D. In prophetic reckoning, 32 A.D. is certainly close enough to the date of the Passion of Christ and Pentecost to be a bona fide fulfillment of Daniel's prophecy (GR2).

Scholars now date the Passion between 28 and 33 A.D., with the birth of Jesus around 4 or 5 B.C. I will refer to the Passion as occurring in 30 A.D. *(TDY)*. If the symbolism of numbers had not been important to Daniel and his readers, he might have described this cutting off of the Messiah as occurring forty-seven percent of the way through the final seven decades. But even to a modern reader, this sounds a bit odd. To an ancient reader, the time of the cutting off would have lost much of its symbolic importance (GR2).

But the vision is not quite done yet. The last phrase of verse 27 completes Daniel's vision of the battle strategy of God's people. So far, they have been told that it is their responsibility to build God's Temple; that when it is complete, the Messiah will come; and that He will set up a New Covenant even though He and the Temple will somehow be "cut off" and "desolated." Now Daniel learns that at the end of these seven decades, the desolator will come.

The Jewish people believed even this last part of the prophecy was fulfilled in 70 A.D. The Jewish historian Josephus recorded that Daniel "wrote about the empire of the Romans and that [Jerusalem] . . . would be desolated . . . by them." (AJ, X, 11, 7). Chapter 21 of Luke's Gospel certainly agrees.

These events do not predict a future abomination in a new, rebuilt Temple, as rapturists would have us believe. The Romans certainly came on "the wing of abominations"; the very fact that a foreign army was on Judean soil was considered an abomination to the land. The symbol of Roman might was the ensign with the eagle held high at the front of that army. Being a scavenger, the eagle itself was a winged abomination to the Jews. The Romans ended up dismantling the Temple down to the very last stone. Without question, when the Romans came, they did make the city desolate.

The vision promises that the desolator will not escape God's justice. The one who sent the "wing of abominations" in 67 A.D. met his "decreed end" when judgment was "poured out on the desolator." Nero met his Maker after committing suicide. All three Caesars involved, Nero, Vespasian, and Titus, lost their dynasties in the "decreed end."

Even the "people of the prince," the Jewish Zealots, were destroyed along with Jerusalem. They desolated the Temple, and they were, in their turn, desolated themselves. Eventually everyone involved ended up the loser, save Christ and His Church. He had successfully set up His "strong covenant" and saved His fledgling Church from Jerusalem's devastation.

A Catholic summary of the seventy weeks

Let us pause here to reflect. On close examination of Daniel's seventy-week vision, we can be certain that no two-thousand-year gaps must be introduced to make the prophecy's timing work out. God did not try to slip one by Daniel. We can take the vision's timing at face value and agree with the early Church in her overwhelming consensus that these events were entirely fulfilled by the year 70 A.D. Daniel's seventy weeks clearly point to Christ's first advent and its blessings, the most important event in all of history.

Daniel's last week denotes seven decades, from about 4 B.C. to 67 to 70 A.D. This is the period during which the Messiah will be active: the time of covenantal transition. After the Anointed One

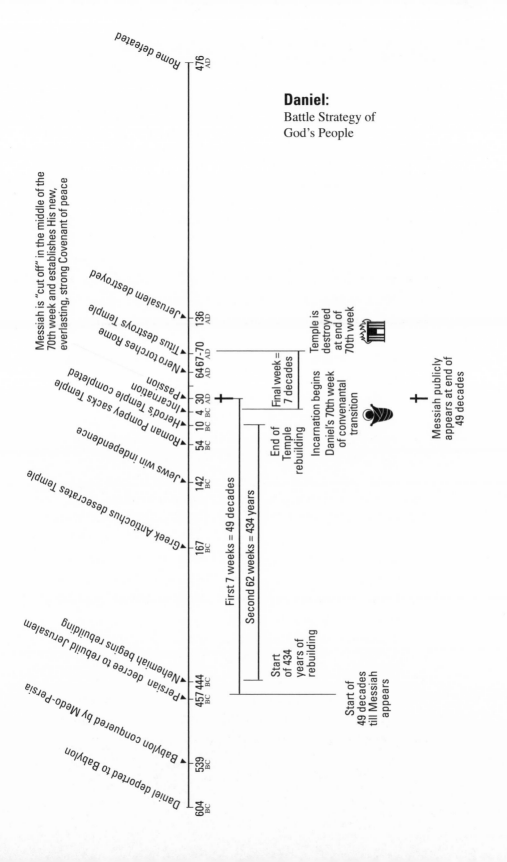

brings sacrifices to a halt, which we have determined would be around 32 A.D., someone will come to desolate Jerusalem and its sanctuary. Once the weeks began with the decree to rebuild in 457 B.C., they progressed without interruption until the end, in 70 A.D.

Is this view consonant with present Church teaching? Yes! "The ancient view . . . maintains that the prophecy of the seventy weeks refers directly to the appearance of Christ in the flesh, His death, His establishment of the New Covenant, and the destruction of Jerusalem by the Romans" (CE). We worked hard to get here, but now that we have arrived, we find we are in agreement with the early Church, the "ancient view."

Our work here has been important. The problems in the rapturist system are so immense that I can honestly say that the person who throws up his hands in consternation at all of these sevens is in better shape than the rapturist who inserts that presumptuous parenthesis.

Turn back a few pages, and reread this vision carefully. These few verses form the entire biblical foundation for the rapturists' claim that a future seven-year Great Tribulation is about to break upon the world and that the antichrist must appear and make a peace treaty with ethnic Israel. This is a good portion of their proof that the Old Covenant Temple must be rebuilt in Jerusalem.

The simplest understanding of Daniel's seventy weeks will ultimately undercut premillennialism itself, leaving us to choose the only viable option left, Catholic amillennialism. But we are not at that point just yet. We will get there, but not just yet.

We have learned much that will help us as we progress. Many passages written after Daniel will view the first advent through the lens of Daniel's seventieth week — the seven decades of covenantal transition from the Annunciation to the destruction of Jerusalem's Temple. Rapturists tend to view salvation as a three-day accomplishment. Catholics tend to view the first advent as a three-decade event. Yet the events put into motion by Mary's yes were not fully played out until seventy years later. As we continue, remember that Daniel predicted exactly this. In Zechariah, this seven decades of covenantal transition will be called "the day of the Lord." In The Apocalypse, these seven decades will dominate the central, pivotal chapter (ch. 12).

VISION III:E: FROM HERE TO ETERNITY

The heavy lifting in Daniel is over. Our work here will help us immensely in the New Testament. But it would be a mistake to overlook completely the last vision of Daniel before we leave this book.

Tribulation and resurrection

Just before this vision begins, there is a description of a resurrection that occurs immediately after a severe tribulation. "Many of those who sleep in the dust of the earth shall awake, some to everlasting life, and some to shame and everlasting contempt. And those who are wise shall shine like the brightness of the firmament; and those who turn many to righteousness, like the stars forever and ever" (12:2-3). Rapturists claim that the resurrection language requires this passage to be placed at the end of the Great Tribulation, when they claim that one of the final resurrections occurs. (Yes, they believe in more than one!)

However, as elsewhere in Daniel, their system seems to be built without a clear understanding of how Scripture uses language. Elsewhere the Bible uses resurrection language to refer to a spiritual rebirth. Remember Ezekiel's vision of dry bones that come back to life (GR7)?

This mention of a spiritual resurrection is still referring to the time of Antiochus's persecution. This phrase describes the revival of biblical Judaism under the Maccabees after the great battle of Vision III:D. After the defeat of Antiochus, the Temple was restored, the people of God were renewed, and biblical Judaism was resurrected. Indeed, there was a spiritual rebirth in Jerusalem.

Seal the mystery

The final vision begins with Daniel 12:5. Daniel is told that he cannot understand more than he already knows. What is he trying to understand? Why, it is the mystery of the Messianic Kingdom! We encountered it in the initial vision, and its details and timing have been on Daniel's agenda ever since. The mysteries of the Kingdom "are shut up and sealed until the time of the end." This should give us a clue about the time frame of this last vision. The events under discussion are specifically about "the time of the end." The time of the end begins with the arrival of the Messiah and His Kingdom (GR9).

Increase in knowledge

This helps us to make sense of the last phrase in 12:4, which leads into this vision. Daniel is told to "seal up the book, until the time of the end . . . and knowledge shall increase." One of the more fantastic claims of rapturists is that this is a reference to the explosion in scientific knowledge in the twentieth century. But look at the context of these verses: Daniel is being told about a very specific knowledge, which will shed light on the meaning of his visions. This knowledge concerns the mystery of the Messiah's Kingdom. That is the knowledge that will increase at the end, when the Messiah appears. Cars and computers are wonderful developments, but I doubt that Daniel had them in mind in this vision.

The wicked and the wise

Daniel is told that none of the wicked will ever understand the mystery of the Messiah's Kingdom. "None of the wicked shall understand; but those who are wise shall understand" (12:10). This was certainly true of the Jewish leaders during the public ministry of Christ, continuing right through the Passion and the Resurrection. Even after the Church was founded, the Jerusalem leaders never understood the true significance of what had happened in their own lifetime. They never comprehended the mystery of Christ's Kingdom or what it meant for Judaism.

This continued to be true in 70 A.D. Even after the Roman army had breached two of the three walls protecting Jerusalem, the people stood on the wall and jeered at the Roman army. They shouted that "*this Temple would be preserved* by him that inhabited therein, whom they still had for their assistant in this war, and did therefore laugh at all his [Titus's] threatenings, which would come to nothing, because the conclusion of the whole depended upon God only" (*WJ*, V, 11:2).

They did not understand that their conquest was an inevitable result of the earlier rejection of the Messiah and His spiritual Kingdom. Jesus Himself had prophesied these events. When He entered Jerusalem for the Passover, He "wept over it, saying . . . 'The days shall come upon you, when your enemies will cast up a bank about you and surround you, and hem you in on every side, and dash you to the ground, you and your children within you, and they will not leave one stone upon another in you; because you did not know the time of your visitation' " (Luke 19:41-44). Throughout the entire covenantal transition of Daniel's seventieth week, the wicked remained oblivious.

But there is a second group of people in this vision — namely, the "wise." The mere mention of them must have given Daniel some hope. "Those who are wise shall understand" (12:10). They would understand what Daniel could not: the mystery of the Kingdom. Therefore, they would act on the advice of the King. Indeed, the Church historian Eusebius informs us that the wise of those seven decades *did* understand when the time came. They fled to Pella in response to Christ's warning, recorded for us in the Olivet Discourse (*EH*, III, 5:4).

The abomination

The wise will understand that, at a certain point in history, "the continual burnt offering" will cease, and "the abomination that makes desolate . . . [will be] set up" (12:11). These events are related to the "shattering of the power of the holy people" (12:7). When these events occur, the wise will understand the mystery of the Kingdom that Daniel's visions have so illuminated. These two events would be the trigger that would enable the wise to understand what Daniel could not. (This interpretation of Daniel 12:10-11 ignores the Masoretic *silluk* inserted by the Jewish scholars into this passage. See Appendix Two.) Did these events occur in history at a juncture that would seem to fulfill this prophecy? If so, when?

In the summer of 66 A.D., Jerusalem halted the daily sacrifices for Caesar Nero. This action was largely responsible for starting the forty-two month war between the Jews and the Romans. This could be the meaning of the phrase "the continual burnt offering."

This phrase might also refer to the regular, daily sacrifices that the priests of the Temple had always performed, even before the influence of Rome. These were halted "for want of men to offer it" just days before the overthrow of the city by the Romans. (*WJ*, VI, 2:1). Either (or both) of these fulfills the first half of this phrase, the cessation of the offering in the Temple.

What about the "abomination"? Unfortunately for the Jews of Jerusalem, any number of abominations occurred in Jerusalem and its Temple during the years surrounding the war. Most of them were perpetrated on the Temple by the outlaw Jewish Zealots who had taken over the Temple and proceeded to treat it like a secular fortress. Shortly after the Zealots gained power, they installed a high priest who made a mockery of the Law. Battles were continually waged, and blood was shed on holy ground. Ceremonially unclean men lived in the Temple. Temple supplies were used for unholy purposes. Any one of these outrages could qualify as the abomination that Daniel predicts.

Josephus records Ananus the high priest as saying, "Certainly it had been good for me to die before I had seen the house of God full of so many abominations, or these sacred places that ought not to be trodden on at random, filled with the feet of these blood-shedding villains." Not long after uttering these words, this high priest was also systematically hunted down and murdered by the Zealots. Josephus tells us, "The death of Ananus was the beginning of the destruction of the city" (WJ, IV, 5:2).

But if we must choose a single event, the "abomination that makes desolate" most likely refers to the invasion of Judea by the Roman army. We will note later in the New Testament that this is also the understanding of Luke. Famine, disease, and death were the inevitable desolation left behind in the wake of any army of this magnitude. The Roman army came in 66 A.D. and then returned en masse between 67 and 70 A.D.

The Roman army marched behind the ensign of an unclean bird, the eagle. They were Gentiles who practiced idolatry. When the Temple fell to the Romans, they promptly worshiped the eagle, which led their troops in battle within the ruins of the Temple. They "brought their ensigns to the Temple, and set them over against its eastern gate; and there did they offer sacrifices to them" (WJ, VI, 6:1). Even modern Christians can appreciate the abomination that this must have been to the Jews.

Their actions certainly fulfilled the vision of Daniel. Bishop Eusebius wrote, "The abomination of desolation, proclaimed by the prophets, stood in the very Temple of God, so celebrated of old, the Temple which was now awaiting its total and final destruction by fire" (EH, III:5).

Within five years, a pagan Roman temple was erected on the Temple site in Jerusalem. Daniel was more right than even the Jews of 70 A.D. knew. "The shattering of the power of the holy people" that Daniel predicted had been accomplished. Biblical Judaism had been obliterated. It has never been resurrected.

Rapture

By this understanding of Daniel, the signs of the Olivet Discourse are actually an enlargement upon this vision of Daniel. As we will see when we get to the New Testament, Jesus urged His disciples to flee Jerusalem at the emergence of certain signs. If these signs were heeded, they would be the salvation of His infant Church.

When that infant Church in exile then observed what happened to Jerusalem, at that point "those who are wise" understood completely. What did they understand? They understood the mystery of the Kingdom. Christ's dominion would be worldwide, not merely Jewish. The Kingdom of Christ was no longer inextricably tied to the fate of Jerusalem's Temple, because it was spiritual and ecclesiastical rather than physical and political. This interpretation dovetails precisely with the understanding of the earliest Christians. They believed that these prophecies of Daniel spoke primarily about the decades surrounding the first advent, and ending in 70 A.D. And they put feet to their belief by fleeing when the time was right.

The three times?

Before we leave our last vision in Daniel, we must note that there are two new time periods introduced in it. In the first half of the vision is the original three and a half years, or 1,260 days. Then the vision introduces 1,290 days. As if that were not enough, the passage finally mentions 1,335 days. What are we to make of this extra thirty days, and then forty-five?

Rapturists find this passage a bit awkward. There are three periods mentioned. Because rapturists have already placed their presumptuous parenthesis of two thousand years before the vision begins, they contend that the three and a half years, or 1,260 days, refer to the last half of a still future seven-year Great Tribulation. (Strictly speaking, some rapturists would refer to only the last three and a half years of the tribulation as the Great Tribulation.)

The 1,290 days in this passage they understand to include an extra thirty days after the Great Tribulation ends. These thirty days will give Christ a month to judge the Gentiles who have survived the Great Tribulation. Rapturists claim that this thirty-day period starts with Christ's second coming and ends when the judging is complete.

But the passage also mentions 1,335 days. Rapturists believe that these extra forty-five days begin when the judging of the Gentiles is completed. During this additional month and a half, the new thousand-year Messianic kingdom will be set up. Rapturists assert that Christ will need those forty-five days to establish and staff the various bureaucracies that will oversee His reign on a worldwide basis.

I am not making this up.

Remember, rapturists view Christ as an earthly potentate ruling from a throne in the Middle East during the thousand-year period following on the heels of the seven-year Great Tribulation and the second coming.

Of course, this is based entirely on conjecture. The best that can be said of their argument at this point is that at least these gaps (of thirty and forty-five days), which they place between the Great Tribulation and the Millennium, are mentioned in the Bible, whereas the major gap (the parenthesis of over two thousand years) between the sixty-ninth and seventieth week of Daniel 9 is not. But there is a better way to understand this passage.

The extra thirty days

The extra thirty days mentioned in this vision of the end refers to the additional time it took for the total conquest of the entire city, both lower and upper, after the Temple proper was torched. The Temple was defeated within the 1,260 days that Daniel predicted. But as with any real war, it takes some time to mop up the opposition. Josephus wrote that the Temple burned on the tenth day of the month *Av*, probably August 10, 70 A.D. (WJ, VI, 4:5) and wrote that complete control of the city did not occur until the eighth of *Elul*, about thirty days after the ninth or tenth of *Av* (WJ, VI, 10:1).

This extra thirty days was still a time of tremendous bloodshed. Josephus wrote, "Around the altar a pile of corpses was accumulating; down the steps of the sanctuary flowed a stream of blood, and the bodies of the victims killed above went sliding to the bottom." The Romans "set fire to the houses . . . but they ran *everyone* through whom they met . . . and made the whole city run down with blood, to such a degree indeed that the fire of many of the houses was quenched with these men's blood" (WJ, VI, 8:5).

Finally on the eighth of *Elul* (September 9, 70 A.D.), Titus ordered the Roman army to halt the wholesale slaughter of Jews, "since his soldiers were already quite tired with killing men" (WJ, VI, 9:2). While some killing occurred after that point, the worst was over.

This is the best understanding of the additional thirty days. It took 1,260 days for the conquest and fall of the Temple, but there was still urban warfare in the rest of Jerusalem for another thirty days. "There shall be a thousand two hundred and ninety days" of killing and abominations when the city is overthrown (12:11).

The extra forty-five days

The vision has just one more detail. The vision encourages readers to "wait and come to the thousand three hundred and thirty-five days" (12:12). In other words, forty-five days after all of Jerusalem fell, safety would finally be attainable. To what could this extra time refer?

The inhabitants of Jerusalem who had escaped death during the urban warfare of the last thirty days still had somehow to survive this next forty-five-day period. After Titus had ordered a halt to the wholesale killing at the 1,290th day, the Roman soldiers herded the inhabitants of Jerusalem into the women's court of the Temple, which was walled. One of Titus's friends by the name of Fronto was "to determine everyone's fate, according to his merits. So this Fronto slew all those that . . . were impeached one by another; but of the young men he chose out the tallest and most beautiful, and reserved them for the triumph; and as for the rest . . . he put them into bonds, and sent them to the Egyptian mines. Titus also sent a great number into the provinces, as a present to them, that they might be destroyed upon their theaters, by the sword and by the wild beasts; but those that were under seventeen years of age were sold for slaves. Now, during the days wherein Fronto was distinguishing these men, there perished, for want of food, eleven thousand; some of whom did not taste any food" (WJ, VI, 9:2).

It was a gruesome forty-five days. One had to hope for food, all the while watching others die of starvation, or be executed as potentially seditious, or be sorted into one of the many slave pools.

The events that occurred in Judea from 66 to 70 A.D. were seen by more than just the Church as the fulfillment of Daniel's visions. No doubt the prophecy of Daniel gnawed on the minds of these Jews during these forty-five days as well. Upon his capture three years earlier, Josephus had informed the Romans that "he was not unacquainted with the prophecies contained in the sacred books." (WJ, III, 8:3). But for the wicked, they did not understand the meaning of these events until it was much too late. It is doubtful that any of them ever understood the mystery of the Kingdom.

During these forty-five days, the Roman army captured virtually all the outlaw Zealots, who had retreated to the many subterranean caves around Jerusalem in the hope of waiting out the Romans and re-emerging when they had left (WJ, VI, 8:5). The Jewish Zealots very well may have thought that if they could just wait out the forty-five days, they might experience the promise of Daniel: "Blessed is he who waits and comes to the thousand three hundred and thirty-five days" (12:11).

But they didn't make it that far. Virtually to a man, the rebels were caught. The Romans worked particularly diligently to capture the two major leaders of the Jerusalem revolt, John and Simon. John was sentenced to life imprisonment, and Simon got the death sentence. It seems that none of the Zealots survived the extra forty-five days to the relative peace that Daniel foresaw.

Josephus tells us that after Titus thought that he had Judea completely subdued, the Roman army regrouped and rewarded its heroes of the war. A month and a half after the city had been completely taken, much of the anger of the Roman soldiers had dissipated, and much of the army had been rewarded and had disbanded. The remaining army concerned itself with the task of dismantling the Temple stone by stone.

But "the wise" did "understand," and those who were patient and faithful in their waiting were "blessed." This mention of the blessed brings to mind the Church that fled into the wilderness before Jerusalem's defeat, following Christ's warning in the Olivet Discourse. They patiently waited in relative safety, and their faithfulness to Christ's warning had secured their survival. The blessed were still safe when the 1,335 days were fulfilled. To them was entrusted the mystery of Christ's Kingdom. That Kingdom now was free to blossom in the ancient Roman Empire without the confusion that Temple worship engendered.

So we see that this vision actually has two endings. The wicked are caught in the consequences of their own choices, blind to the truth until it is too late. For God's people, it ends with the "blessed," who have survived the desolation and destruction of Jerusalem and its Temple, and are ready to enjoy the Kingdom's benefits.

The general judgment

Even though Daniel will not live long enough to understand completely his visions and their mysteries, he is given personal

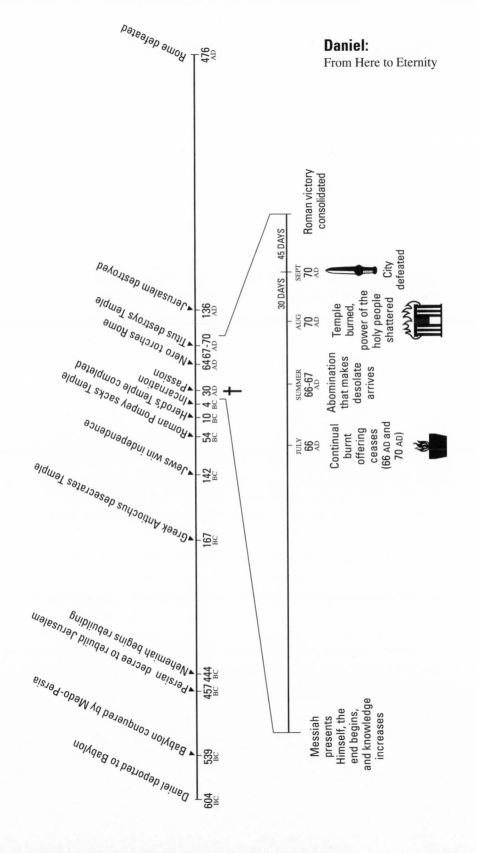

hope at the end of this vision. Daniel is informed that he will die, but still "shall stand in your allotted place at the end of the days" (12:13). For the first time in Daniel, the scope extends all the way to the final eschaton. When the final judgment occurs, Daniel will be rewarded appropriately. This is one of the earliest promises in the Bible regarding the immortality of the human soul. For Daniel it is good news, but in fact, all humans will be judged at the end of time. This is the general judgment, the "Great White Throne" judgment of The Apocalypse.

This is as close as Daniel gets to envisioning the second coming. But this vision of Daniel has taken us from here to eternity, right up to the final eschaton. No more details of the final judgment are given, but it is quite clear in the vision that the timing of Daniel's judgment is not to be confused with the time of the "shattering."

In this vision, the mention of the final events is almost an afterthought, a personal consolation given to Daniel. This structure will be borrowed in The Apocalypse, when St. John's last vision also extends its scope to the final eschaton.

SUMMARY: DANIEL'S LESSONS

Let us sum up the evidence we have gleaned from Daniel. Rapturists claim that Daniel gives the entire timetable of their system: the seven years of Great Tribulation that follow on the heels of the rapture, the refocusing of God's redemptive work exclusively through ethnic Israel during those seven years, the rebuilding of the Temple at the very beginning or even before those seven years, the coming of an antichrist who sets up his covenant with Israel at the beginning of the seven years, the breaking of the antichrist's covenant halfway through the seven years, and the resurrection immediately after the seven years are completed.

On closer examination, this is clearly not the best way to understand these texts; in most instances, it is not even a reasonable way. In every case, rapturists have had to insert a massive gap into the time line that Daniel delineates. This is their colossal mistake. They do not take the visions for what they are plainly trying to teach — the timing and meaning of the first advent — and thus they completely twist the meaning of Daniel's predictions concerning the time of salvation that was to come. The presumptuous parenthesis is necessary because of the rapturists' refusal to accept Daniel's overall message: God's spiritual Kingdom came when the Messiah appeared during the ancient Roman Empire. The seventy weeks ended in 67 to 70 A.D., by which time the blessings bestowed on Christ's Church were evident to the world.

This view, the Church's historical understanding, emerges as both reasonable and superior. Christ's birth, death, Resurrection, and founding of the Church, and the judgment upon those who rejected His new Kingdom are the fulfillment of these prophecies. From Daniel's perspective, the drama of the Incarnation spanned seven decades of covenantal transition. Other than the final judgment of the man Daniel, there is nothing in these visions still awaiting fulfillment, except in the sense that all these events point to a still future death and resurrection of our world itself, and the founding of a new Heaven and a new earth at the final eschaton (GR3).

Four hundred years ago, a famous mathematician, Blaise Pascal, summed up Daniel very well: "One must be bold to predict the same thing in so many ways. It was necessary that the four idolatrous or pagan monarchies, the end of the kingdom of Judah, and the seventy weeks, should happen at the same time, and all this before the second Temple was destroyed. . . . The time foretold by the state of the Jewish people, by the state of the heathen, by the state of the Temple, by the number of years. . . . Christ will then be killed . . . in the last week. . . . In the seventieth week of Daniel . . . the heathen should be . . . brought to the knowledge of the God worshiped by the Jews; that those who loved Him should be delivered from their enemies, and filled with His fear and love. . . . *And it happened*" (PEN, XI, 708-722).

Pascal summarized these visions well. Daniel predicted the Roman Empire would be in power when Messiah came. And it happened. He predicted the rebuilding of Jerusalem and its Temple as a precondition for the first advent. And it happened. He predicted the Great Tribulation of Christ's fledgling Church. And it happened. He predicted the Passion of our Lord along with its benefits. And it happened. He predicted the establishment of the new strong covenant. And it happened. He predicted the destruction of Jerusalem, the Temple, and biblical Judaism. And it happened. Daniel even predicted his own final judgment. What he did *not* predict is the second coming of Christ. That would have to wait for another Prophet.

We have now completed Daniel, which contains the most difficult passages in the entire Old Testament, and we are ready to proceed to the New Testament. You might first want to read Appendix Three, however, for a brief discussion of the Old Testament book of Zechariah. Rapturists claim that there are events in Zechariah that require that Jerusalem's Temple be rebuilt and the animal sacrifices of the Old Covenant be reinstituted. They claim that this plan for ethnic Israel will be independent of the Church. Yet we have already seen that Daniel allows no time for that.

What we will find is that rapturists are working under a minor misunderstanding. Zechariah makes it crystal clear that God will never return to His Old Covenant with ethnic Israel — that God broke that relationship forever during Daniel's seventieth week.

LOOKING AHEAD

After Daniel, the rapturist argument boils down to one simple assertion: the events portrayed in the apocalyptic passages of the Bible have not yet been fulfilled. Central to this assertion is the refusal to accept that Christ did indeed set up the Kingdom of God during His first advent. As we saw in Daniel, this leads to the pre-sumptuous parenthesis, the rapturists' colossal mistake.

We must give credit where it is due. Rapturists believe that the prophecies of the Bible must be fulfilled. I do not disagree in the least. I do disagree with the claim that there remains much unful-filled prophecy.

Because this is the sum and substance of their argument, we will approach the New Testament passages differently from the way we approached Daniel. In the New Testament, we will at-tempt to determine whether the key prophetic proof texts in the rapturists' system could already have been fulfilled.

Of course, at least some New Testament passages have not yet been fulfilled, because the second advent is still in the future. We will examine these passages to determine whether they teach a two-stage coming: a secret rapture first with the second advent seven years later. If all the passages have either been fulfilled or are easily understood without resorting to a secret rapture, then the heart will have been ripped out of the rapturist position. Without any biblical support, why believe it?

Chapter Six

The Olivet Discourse

Perhaps no other part of the Gospels has caused the casual reader as much confusion as has the Olivet Discourse. It undoubtedly contains important information, because all three of the synoptic Gospel authors (Matthew, Mark, and Luke) deemed it important enough to include.

Because of its complexity, we will focus on Matthew's account. It is a long passage, encompassing all of Matthew 24 and 25. There are slight variations from Matthew in both Mark and Luke, but once Matthew is understood, the other two are not difficult to understand. We will borrow an insight from Mark or Luke when it sheds further light on Jesus' meaning, but I will leave it to you to investigate the other two passages further.

AN UNFAIR INSULT

C. S. Lewis was a former agnostic who became one of the most eloquent apologists of the twentieth century. His books on Christianity have helped thousands; I am one of them. I first read Lewis in college, and over the years his books have helped me answer many questions.

Lewis defended Christ and God's Word when most intellectuals scoffed. But when it came to the Olivet Discourse, Lewis was embarrassed by some of Jesus' predictions. Of Matthew 24:34 he wrote, "It is certainly the most embarrassing verse in the Bible." ("World's Last Night," 1960 essay in *TEL*, 385).

What in the Olivet Discourse could embarrass a faithful Christian apologist such as Lewis?

The Olivet Discourse contains Jesus' answers to two very short questions asked by the disciples: "Tell us, when will this be, and what will be the sign of Your coming and of the close of the age?" (24:3).

In response, Jesus predicts many signs and events. About halfway through this long passage, Jesus promises the coming of the Son of man within a generation by stating, "They will see the Son of man coming on the clouds of Heaven with power and great glory. . . . Truly, I say to you, this generation will not pass away till all these things take place" (24:30, 34).

This was the source of Lewis's embarrassment. He believed that Jesus had not kept His word to return within a generation. As far as Lewis could tell, the signs and the coming that Jesus had predicted did not occur within His generation either. Lewis believed that Jesus was God, but that in this case He was showing the "man side" of His personality. Lewis could not understand how Jesus could be anything but wrong in this case.

WAS JESUS A FALSE PROPHET?

With all due respect to Lewis, I believe that his view of the Olivet Discourse insults Christ. But Lewis was not the only person who found the promises of Jesus to be ingenuine. In his book *Why I Am Not a Christian*, Bertrand Russell cited the Olivet Discourse as one of the reasons Jesus could not have been God. Russell pointed to what he considered the obvious fact that the "coming" that Jesus foretold had not happened within a generation. To make matters worse, Jesus did not stop at predicting certain signs and events within a generation. To add emphasis, Jesus continued, "Heaven and earth will pass away, but *my words will not pass away*"

(24:35). Jesus seemed certain these events would transpire before His disciples all passed away.

Perhaps without knowing it, Russell was actually using the Old Testament criterion recorded in Deuteronomy for determining the trustworthiness of a prophet. "When a prophet speaks in the name of the Lord, if the word does not come to pass or come true, that is a word that the Lord has *not* spoken. The prophet has spoken it presumptuously; you need not be afraid of him" (18:22). Russell was right to hold Jesus to the same standard. In fact, he was being more consistent than was the Christian apologist Lewis.

But that leaves the issue unsettled. Was Russell correct in his conclusion? Was Jesus a false prophet? Or is this an unfair insult? You probably know what my answer will be, but we need to work our way through the evidence.

A DEFICIENT SOLUTION

We will look at two ways of handling Lewis's embarrassment and Russell's skepticism. The first is the rapturists' method. Rapturists agree with Russell that the events Jesus foretold in the Olivet Discourse did not come to pass within the generation of the Apostles. This is in spite of Jesus own words: "This generation will not pass away till all these things take place" (24:34).

They squirm out of the situation by claiming that Jesus did not mean *exactly* what the Gospels record Him as saying. They usually take one of two mutually exclusive tacks. Rapturists propose both of them in the hope that you might find one or the other plausible.

Both tacks can be found in the *New Scofield Reference Bible*, in a footnote under Matthew 24:34. "The word 'generation' (Gk. *genea*), though commonly used in Scripture of those living at one time, could not mean those alive at the time of Christ, *as none of 'these things' — i.e., the worldwide preaching of the Kingdom, the tribulation, the return of the Lord in visible glory, and the regathering of the elect — occurred then*. The expression 'this generation' here 1) may mean that the future generation which will endure the tribu-lation and see the signs, will also see the consummation, the re-turn of the Lord; or 2) it may be used in the sense of race or family, meaning that the nation or family of Israel will be preserved 'till all these things be fulfilled,' a promise wonderfully fulfilled to this day" (emphasis mine).

SOME FUTURE GENERATION?

First, rapturists claim that the "generation" of which Jesus was speaking is not the one that heard Him say these words. Jesus gave various signs to warn His followers of a tribulation about to break over them. Rapturists say that the generation Jesus refers to is the one that first sees the signs Jesus has described.

Most rapturists today believe that this generation began when Israel was formed as a modern state in 1948, although some main-tain 1967 is a more likely date. They call the people who saw this event the "final generation" or the "generation of the fig tree." This expression comes from this same passage: "From the fig tree learn its lesson: as soon as its branch becomes tender and puts forth its leaves, you know that summer is near" (Matt. 24:32). Rapturists unequivocally claim that we, the people of the early twenty-first century, are the final generation.

This solution has its problems. The reinterpretation of the word *generation* is just plain dishonest and inconsistent with the Greek word's meaning. Jesus uses the phrase "this generation" many times, as does the rest of the New Testament. The word *generation* is used thirty-four times in the New Testament, and the phrase "this generation" is used twenty times. Without exception, it always refers to the people who were alive, listening to the speaker. In fact, Jesus uses this same word just a few verses before the Olivet Discourse to refer to His own generation. No one tries to reinterpret the meaning of this word on that occasion (Matt. 23:36).

Further, the word *generation* is not used in a vacuum. Jesus continually speaks during the discourse in the second person, *you* (Matt. 24:9, 15, 20, 25, 32, 33, 34). He obviously meant the generation of those hearing Him. One of these references within the Olivet Discourse is particularly interesting: "You will be beaten in synagogues" (Mark 13:9). It would be hard to imagine this prophecy being fulfilled anywhere in the twenty-first century. When was the last time you heard of a Christian taken away to the local synagogue for a good, old-fashioned whipping? Jesus must have been referring to the generation of those listening, the "you." That is the meaning of the word and the implication of the context.

GENERATION EQUALS RACE?

The second rapturist attempt to explain this word is to say that Jesus did not mean *generation* at all, but *race*. In other words, the Jewish people would exist as a distinct race within humanity until these signs were fulfilled. They hold to this position even though the Gospel writers had other words they could have used to express *race* more clearly. If they understood Jesus to mean something other than the people living at the same time as His disciples, they could have used the Greek words *ethnos* ("nation"), *genos* ("kindred"), or *suggenes* ("kinsmen").

This second solution seems to imply that Jesus was pulling the wool over the disciples' eyes with virtually meaningless statements. His prediction could wait almost forever, as long as there remained a distinct Jewish race.

Yet Jesus was specifically answering a *when* question from His disciples. Just as in Daniel, we must be very careful about interpreting any passage in such a way that it makes it seem as though a straightforward question regarding time is answered by God in a deceitful way. The listener at that time would have thought Jesus was claiming that these events would occur in forty to sixty years, yet rapturists push them back two thousand years or more. That presumptuous parenthesis rears its ugly head again.

The most obvious conclusion from all of this is that Jesus really did mean the generation that included His disciples. To explain that away clumsily is no less insulting than is Russell's claim that Jesus was simply wrong. Indeed, Christians deserve to be the objects of scorn when they propose the type of word-parsing that rapturists perform on this statement of Jesus. It comes across as dishonest, because it is. It is insulting to the original speaker's intent.

Both of the attempted solutions are demolished by a parallel passage in Luke. In Luke's version of the Olivet Discourse, specifically Luke 21:20-24, there are details that were entirely fulfilled in 70 A.D. Even the *New Scofield Reference Bible* admits this. But the rapturist tries to claim that Matthew and Mark, because they omit some of the identical details of Luke, are actually talking about a different event! In notes on Matt. 24:16 and Luke 21:20 Scofield writes, "The passage in Luke refers in express terms to a destruction of Jerusalem which was fulfilled by Titus in A.D. 70. . . . Two sieges of Jerusalem are in view in the Olivet Discourse, the one fulfilled in A.D. 70, and the other yet to be fulfilled at the end of the age."

We would not interpret other parallel passages in Scripture in this way. For example, there are multiple descriptions of Jesus' Resurrection, each containing different details. Do rapturists believe in more than one Resurrection as well? Of course not, but that heresy would be entirely consistent with the hermeneutic they employ in the Olivet Discourse. Isn't it much more likely that Luke merely chose to add a few details of the Olivet Discourse that Matthew omitted?

Besides relying on a faulty hermeneutic, both rapturist solutions are based on circular reasoning. They claim Jesus could not have meant His generation, because the events didn't pan out (from their perspective) as He had prophesied. They are forced to twist the obvious meaning of Jesus' statement because the prediction did not come to pass.

When Jesus predicted the events of the Olivet Discourse, He fully expected those in the first century to understand that *they* would see the events transpire. He didn't expect them to have to reinterpret the meaning of simple, common words. Jesus never intended us to question our understanding of what "is" is.

The only convincing response the rapturist can muster is Scofield's note referenced previously — namely, that "none of 'these things,' i.e., the worldwide preaching of the Kingdom, the tribulation, the return of the Lord in visible glory, and the regathering of the elect," has yet occurred anytime in history (*SRB*).

But what if there *has* been a fulfillment of the Olivet Discourse? That would destroy the rapturist argument at its root. Russell would be proven wrong, and Lewis would be relieved that His Savior was not a false prophet.

A BETTER SOLUTION: ANSWERING TWO CONFUSING QUESTIONS

A different and potentially more satisfying solution to the problem is to understand correctly the two questions asked by the disciples in Matthew 24:3.

Two questions combined into one sentence can cause confusion if we are not careful listeners. For example, suppose your teenage daughter asks for permission to go to the prom, because she and her date would like to go afterward with a group of friends to a summer cottage for a sleepover. Contained in that sentence are two very distinct questions: First, can I go to the prom? Second, can I go to a sleepover with my date? I do not know about your home, but for our children, the answers to those two questions would be very different indeed!

The key to understanding the Olivet Discourse is to understand that it contains two *distinct* questions. Jesus gives distinct answers to each, but some people insist on confusing them. They really have no excuse. Matthew, Mark, and Luke all record this discourse with essentially the same responses. Luke, however, places the two questions, with their two answers, in entirely different chapters. In other words, if someone is confused about which question is being answered at any given point, he need only turn to Luke, where the separation is crystal clear.

The early Church knew there were two questions with different answers. The fourth-century archbishop of Constantinople, St. John Chrysostom, split this text into two sections. "When the Lord had finished all that related to Jerusalem, He came in the rest to His own coming" (cited in GCC in Matt. 24:23).

St. Augustine agreed: "In answer to the disciples, the Lord tells them of things which were from that time forth to have their course; whether He meant the destruction of Jerusalem, which occasioned their question . . . or the end itself, in which He will appear to judge the quick and the dead" (*EPA*, CXCIX:9).

The division between these two questions is still recognized by many scholars. It should be. It is really quite obvious. Keeping their distinctly different answers separated in our minds will overcome Russell's objections in this passage. We need to determine what events Jesus claimed would be fulfilled within a generation, and whether they actually were. If they were fulfilled within the generation of those listening to Jesus, then Russell is dead wrong in using this prophecy to question the divinity of Jesus. Furthermore, if the fulfillment is apparent, the rapturists' parsing of words will be unnecessary.

The first question of the disciples was "When will this be?" Jesus had just condemned the Temple to destruction. The disciples were anxious to know when this would occur.

The second question was "What will be the sign of Your coming and the close of the age?" This is a very different question, pertaining to events separated from the first question by thousands of years, and requiring an entirely different answer. The simplest and most straightforward method of understanding this passage is to accept that Jesus answered these questions one at a time, in the order in which they were posed.

I propose that Matthew 24:4-35 (along with Mark 13:1-31 and Luke 21:5-33) answers the question of when the Temple would be destroyed. Matthew 24:36-44 (along with Mark 13:32-37 and Luke 17:22-37) answers the second question, which is essentially "What signs can You give us that history is coming to its eschatological climax with the second advent?"

We will take the two questions in order, one at a time. If the early Church was right, and Russell was wrong, then all the details of the first question should be fulfilled in one generation, as Jesus predicted, and the details of the second question are awaiting the future coming of our Lord and Savior, Jesus Christ.

We will proceed verse by verse through the two answers of Jesus. Then we will look at four stories immediately following the Olivet Discourse that will help explain how we should live given the events that Jesus foretold. We will briefly glean some lessons from those also.

THE FIRST QUESTION:
WHEN WILL THE TEMPLE BE DESTROYED?

As we would expect, Jesus answers the disciples' the first question first. The opening verses of the Olivet Discourse set the scene for the first question: "Jesus left the Temple. . . . When His disciples came to point out to Him the buildings . . . He answered them . . . 'Truly, I say to you, there will not be left here one stone upon another that will not be thrown down' " (24:1-2). No one disputes the historical fulfillment of this prophecy within that first generation of the Church. Some modernists try to avoid any real prophecy by claiming that the early Church was merely inserting history into Jesus' mouth, after the fact. (Remember GR1!)

Rapture

But rapturists and loyal Catholics can agree that prophecy is real and that Jesus was absolutely trustworthy in this prediction. He was speaking to His disciples just before the Passion. This places the event at the halfway point of Daniel's final week. Jesus is predicting the events that will transpire at the end of those seven decades of covenantal transition.

Between 70 and 73 A.D., the Temple complex was destroyed by the Roman army. In their rage in 70 A.D., the Roman legions disobeyed General Titus's orders and set fire to the Temple. As a result, the gold in the Temple melted down between its huge stones. To their chagrin, these same Roman soldiers were then ordered to dismantle everything stone by stone over a period of three years. By the time they had finished recovering the gold, nothing was left but a field. The Romans then plowed the field under.

The Jewish Talmud understood the defeat at the hand of Titus to be the final fulfillment of Micah 3:12. It states that the Romans "ploughed up Sion as a field, and made Jerusalem become as heaps, and the mountain of the house as the high places of a forest" (cited on Matthew 24 in XGM). Micah 3:12 and Jeremiah 26:18 predicted the destruction of the Babylonian conquest. The Babylonian destruction, in turn, stood as a prophetic event pointing to the Roman destruction (GR3).

The fourth-century Church historian Eusebius would have agreed with the Talmud on this issue, with the caveat that he believed that Jesus elaborated on the message of Micah and Jeremiah. Eusebius believed that we can take the prophecies of the Olivet Discourse at their straightforward best. Jesus made certain predictions and claimed that His disciples' generation would live to see His words fulfilled. "All this occurred in this manner, in the second year of the reign of Vespasian [70 A.D.], according to the predictions of our Lord and Savior, Jesus Christ" (*EH*, III:7). Yet he also still firmly believed in the future second advent. These are not mutually exclusive beliefs.

Much of the Olivet Discourse involves a discussion of the signs leading up to the destruction Jesus has just predicted. This is the extended answer to the first question. This makes sense when we realize that the defeat of Jerusalem could very well have also meant the destruction of the early Church in Judea. So the eight signs that Jesus said would lead to the Temple's destruction were important for the Apostles to recognize. They are important for us, too.

Sign 1: False messiahs

"Take heed that no one leads you astray. For many will come in my name, saying, 'I am the Christ,' and they will lead many astray" (Matt. 24:4-5). During the period leading up to the Jewish-Roman War that culminated in the destruction of the Temple in 70 A.D., there were several supposed messiahs in Judea who collected an army to fight the Romans. Every one of these messiahs was hunted down and killed by the Roman legions. Their followers were killed or sold into slavery.

Josephus mentions these false messiahs: "Imposters and deceivers persuaded the multitude to follow them into the wilderness, and pretended that they would exhibit manifest wonders and signs that should be performed by the providence of God. And many that were prevailed on by them suffered the punishments of their folly" (AJ, XX, 8:6).

In his fourth-century commentary on the Olivet Discourse, St. Jerome also discusses these deceivers: "At the time of the Jewish captivity, there were many leaders who declared themselves to be Christs, so that while the Romans were actually besieging them, there were three factions within" (cited in GCC). This is a reference to the armies of Simon and John, who fought each other and the Sanhedrin's followers inside Jerusalem while the Roman siege was underway outside the walls.

In the eighth century, St. Bede also recognized this prediction as fulfilled in the crisis of 70 A.D.: "For many came forward, when destruction was hanging over Jerusalem, saying that they were Christs" (on Mark 13:6, cited in GCC).

Jesus gave fair warning to Jewish Christians of that first century that they should avoid following these deceivers. False messiahs were sign 1. The Temple destruction that Jesus had just predicted was on its way, although not imminent.

Sign 2: Wars

"You will hear of wars and rumors of wars" (Matt. 24:6). The decade before 70 A.D. began with rebellion in Britain and ended with rebellion in Judea. The *Pax Romana*, the Roman-imposed peace that reigned throughout the ancient world, was deteriorating. As if that were not bad enough, there was civil war within the city of Rome itself, among generals fighting for the throne. This fighting was one reason Vespasian suspended his efforts in the war with the Jews in 68 A.D. He "foresaw already the civil wars which were coming upon them, nay, that the very government was in danger" (*WJ*, IV, 8:1). He was also maneuvering into position for the throne himself. His troops declared him emperor on July 1, 69 A.D., when word reached his army headquarters that civil war was raging within the city of Rome itself.

This was sign 2. Amazingly, Jesus said Christians should not be disturbed by these wars. "See that you are not alarmed; for this must take place, but the end is not yet" (24:6). Imagine that! The civilized world is disintegrating into civil war, and Jesus tells His followers not to let it bother them. The fighting was only a necessary preliminary stage before "the end," meaning the end of the wait for the Temple's demolition (GR9).

Signs 3 and 4: Famines and earthquakes

Signs 3 and 4 each merit only a word each in the text. "There will be famines and earthquakes in various places" (24:7). Many Christians today are aware of the famine that plagued the Jews in

Jerusalem. St. Paul wrote about it in his letter to the Corinthian Church. He seems to have been regularly collecting donations from the gentile Christians to ameliorate the suffering of the Church in Judea (2 Cor. 8).

Eusebius also documents the famine: "Under [Claudius] the world was visited with a famine, which writers that are entire strangers to our religion have recorded in their histories" (*EH*, II:8).

Modern Christians seem to be less aware that earthquakes frequently erupted during the decades leading to the destruction of Jerusalem. The city of Colossae was totally destroyed in an earthquake in the 50s. That was the end of the Church there, the same Church that St. Paul addressed in the letter to the Colossians.

Perhaps the most famous earthquake of ancient times was the one in 63 A.D. in Pompeii. The ruins have been excavated by archeologists in our own day. (This earthquake is now famous because Pompeii was utterly destroyed by volcano in 79 A.D.) The earthquake of 63 A.D., along with others, would have been a warning to the Christians about three or four years before the Jewish-Rome War began.

These were signs 3 and 4, but Jesus was careful to let His disciples know that this was not yet the time for action: "All this is but the beginning of the sufferings" (Matt. 24:8). As we will see, the time would come when immediate obedience would mean the difference between life and death, but not just yet. These signs are preliminary, and the situation could get much worse before it got any better.

Sign 5: Persecution

In the very next sentence, Jesus tells His disciples that it *does* get much worse. Up until now, the signs have been rather general and impersonal, but now the tone changes: "They will deliver you up to tribulation, and put you to death; and you will be hated by all nations for my name's sake" (Matt. 24:9).

Sign 5 is a prediction of religious persecution. Christians would be called upon to endure tribulation and even death. This must have been a chilling prospect for the disciples. In Matthew 10:17-21, Jesus had predicted that even family members would turn their Christian relatives over to the authorities for punishment.

Actually, persecution came early, very early, in the Church's life. The Sanhedrin persecuted Christians in Jerusalem and used the synagogues as a base for persecution elsewhere in the empire. But the persecution of sign 5 would come not only from the Jewish leaders in the synagogues. Jesus tells His followers, "You will be hated by all nations for my name's sake." The Gentiles enthusiastically joined in persecuting the young Christian Church.

Nor would this persecution be an anomaly within certain parts of the empire, escaping the attention of the emperors. Mark 13:9 and Luke 21:12 add that the Christians would be hauled before the highest authorities: the gentile governors and kings. The persecution Jesus predicts would be sanctioned by the government itself.

This was a new development. Ever since the day of Pentecost, the Christians had been persecuted by the Jewish religious leaders. But Rome had viewed this as a squabble between two groups of Jews and had not taken sides. As far as Rome was concerned, both groups were a bit of a problem because of their resistance to emperor worship.

In July of 64 A.D., that all changed when two-thirds of Rome burned to the ground. Nero, in his desire to deflect the anger of Rome's citizenry, singled out the Christians as the scapegoat. Rome officially sided with the Sanhedrin: the Christians were declared seditious. In this new persecution, the entire weight of the Roman political bureaucracy was brought to bear against the tiny Christian community.

The ancient Roman historian Tacitus has documented Nero's persecution. Christians became hunted creatures in the empire.

Many met their death in the Coliseum in Rome as the audiences cheered and jeered. Some were strapped to stakes in Nero's gardens and burned alive as human torches (*AIR*, XV, 44). St. Peter and St. Paul seem to have been martyred in Rome during this time. In Jerusalem, Bishop James, the cousin of Jesus and the author of the New Testament book that bears his name, was martyred.

Although intense, Nero's persecution did not last even three years. When Jerusalem revolted in 66 A.D., Nero's attention was diverted to the Jewish-Roman War. Finally in 68 A.D., the Roman army, along with the Praetorian guard, rose in rebellion against Nero. He fled from Rome, committing suicide in June of that year.

Eusebius, along with the early Church writer Tertullian, points to Nero as the first Roman emperor to persecute the Christians as part of state strategy (*EH*, 11, 25). Nero would be followed by others even more ruthless than he, but Clement of Rome wrote that *"the Neronian persecution had been a wholesale onslaught of reckless fury"* (*TBR*, 28).

This sign was sure to get the attention of the early Church. The end — the destruction of the Temple, to which all eight signs pointed — was approaching when the gentile state turned on the Christian Church.

Sign 6: Apostasy

Jesus predicts the reaction of His followers to this new and concentrated form of persecution. "Many will fall away, and betray one another. . . . Many false prophets will arise and lead many astray. . . . Most men's love will grow cold" (24:10-12). Jesus emphasizes again the coming of false prophets. He was obviously concerned about His young Church holding fast to the Truth. But the main focus in this sign is the reaction of His followers. Many Christians would desert the Christian community; some would turn upon their fellow Christians; some would fall into heresy; and "most" would find their love abating. We can call this sign 6.

We find evidence of this apostasy in the letters to the seven churches that St. John includes in The Apocalypse. The letter to the Hebrews was written in the decade preceding 70 A.D. and gives further evidence that all of this occurred as Jesus predicted.

Times would be extremely difficult during the Great Tribulation of 64 to 67 A.D. But Jesus predicts that even the Roman Empire will not be able to snuff out His Church. The Christians that endure the trials all the way to the end are assured of salvation by the Savior Himself: "He who endures to the end will be saved" (Matt. 24:13). We will encounter this promise in The Apocalypse as well.

Sign 7: The gospel worldwide

All this is well and good, say rapturists. Perhaps much of this did occur in the first-century Church. But rapturists claim that the seventh sign proves that this passage is still speaking of a future fulfillment. Jesus predicts, "This gospel of the Kingdom will be preached throughout the whole world, as a testimony to all nations; and then the end will come" (Matt. 24:14). The rapturist rests confident in the belief that even today the gospel has not been preached throughout the whole world, and so the end spoken of by Jesus cannot have come yet.

Is that a truly scriptural perspective? No. St. Paul states that in his lifetime, the Faith of the Church in Rome "is proclaimed in all the world" (Rom. 1:8). In Colossians 1:5-6, he writes, "You have heard . . . the gospel . . . as indeed in the whole world it is bearing fruit and growing." There was certainly no doubt in St. Paul's mind, while writing under inspiration, that the gospel had gone out into the whole world.

Although some Christians seem confused on this point today, the early Church certainly understood that the gospel had been preached to the entire world before 70 A.D. Clement of Rome was bishop when the signs of the Olivet Discourse were being fulfilled

(67-73 A.D.). He wrote that Peter and Paul had been martyred, but not before they "taught righteousness to the *whole world*, and [they came] to the extreme limit of the west" *(FEC)*. Since both Peter and Paul were martyred before the fall of Jerusalem, Clement must have believed the seventh sign was fulfilled before the fall of Jerusalem.

Justin Martyr, born around the turn of the first century, wrote that "from Jerusalem there went out into the world, men, twelve in number, and these illiterate, of no ability in speaking: but by the power of God *they proclaimed to every race of men* that they were sent by Christ to teach *to all* the word of God" (FA, XXXIX).

Eusebius even connected the seventh sign to Jerusalem's desolation: "The teaching of the new covenant was borne to *all nations*, and at once the Romans besieged Jerusalem and destroyed it and the Temple" (POG, I:VI). Eusebius reiterated the relationship Jesus enunciated. He said that the gospel would be preached, "and then the end will come" (Matt. 24:14).

St. Bede adds that the Apostles determined to spend their lives fulfilling sign 7: "All the Apostles, long before the destruction of the province of Judea, were dispersed to preach the gospel over the whole world" (cited in GCC). They did this *specifically to remove any obstacle* to the fulfillment of Christ's prophecy.

So, given this evidence from both Scripture and the early Church, how can rapturists be so confused about this point? In part, it is because they do not take stock of the two Greek words for *world*. The Olivet Discourse uses the word *oikoumene* at this point, which specifically means the civilized world, delineated at the time by the boundaries of the Roman Empire. In other words, the gospel would be preached throughout the entire empire. There is another word for *world* that designates the entire earth, *kosmos*. Rapturists act as though this word is used, but it is not.

Kosmos appears later in this same chapter: "from the beginning of the world until now" (Matt. 24:21). Since both words are used in the same passage, it seems quite certain that the Apostles were fully cognizant of these two concepts. Therefore, we can be confident that Jesus taught His disciples that the "end" of the Temple would follow the preaching of the gospel throughout the civilized world, the Roman Empire.

Sign 7 is the first sign that seems to be linked rather closely in time to the end of the Temple. It was also the only sign over which the followers of Jesus had any control. They proceeded diligently to do their part.

Sign 8: Daniel's desolating sacrilege

All the signs up to this point have been preliminary warnings to the Christians that the time of the destruction of the Temple was coming. Sign 8 is the last sign. It is so closely associated with the end of the Temple that Jesus exhorts His followers to immediate action when it appears. Jesus urges Christians, "When you see the desolating sacrilege spoken of by the prophet Daniel, standing in the holy place (let the reader understand), then let those who are in Judea flee to the mountains" (Matt. 24:15-19). The previous signs have been a warning. Now danger is imminent for anyone near Jerusalem's Temple.

We can easily miss the direct affront posed by this teaching to the Jewish leaders of Jesus' day. The Jewish scholars at the time taught that Daniel's desolation had been fulfilled in 167 B.C. by Antiochus Epiphanes, and there would never be another abomination in the Temple. But as St. Jerome pointed out, the desolation in the second century B.C. lasted only for three years, not the three and a half years that Daniel specifically predicted (CID). Jesus specifically teaches here that there was yet another "desolating sacrilege" of Daniel that was still in the future.

The "sacrilege" Jesus spoke of in the discourse would be the result of the Jewish leaders' rejection of the Messiah Himself. It would result in a change of covenantal relationship for ethnic

Jews forever. Antiochus's actions were a true abomination on the Temple, but at the same time they were merely a foretelling of worse things to come (GR3). The Seleucid Syrians of Daniel 8 and 11 were only a prophetic foretaste of the final desolation foretold in Daniel 9 and 12, when God allowed the Romans to destroy biblical Judaism forever.

Both Matthew and Mark add a phrase to Jesus' prophecy that was obviously not spoken by Him: "Let the reader understand." They evidently believed that this "desolating sacrilege" would be so obvious that the average Jewish Christian *of the first century* would automatically recognize it for what it was.

Luke gives us more specific direction as to what to look for in this "desolating sacrilege." He writes, "When you see Jerusalem surrounded by armies, then know that its desolation has come near" (Luke 21:20). St. John Chrysostom illustrates that the early Church linked the Matthew and Luke passages. "The abomination of desolation means the army by which the holy city of Jerusalem was made desolate" (*ANF* on Matt. 24:15).

Even casual students of history are familiar with the desolation that foreign armies leave in their wake. But to a devout Jew, the mere presence of any gentile army in Judea would be considered a sacrilege. Add to this the fact that the Romans marched under the banner of an unclean bird, the eagle. For the Roman legions, "the entire religion of the Roman camp consisted in worshiping the ensigns, in swearing by the ensigns, and in preferring the ensigns before all the gods" (*APO*, XVI, 162). The Jews knew that the Roman legions would worship their ensign and their emperor upon victory.

FULFILLMENT OF THE DESOLATION

So what does history tell us about these eight signs? In the summer of 66 A.D., the Roman general Cestius Gallus attacked Jerusalem in response to the cessation of the sacrifices for Nero in the

Temple. He actually led his soldiers up to the gates of the Temple, and many Jews thought the Romans had won the battle. The Temple was about to fall. For some unknown reason, however, Cestius unexpectedly retreated.

At this sign of weakness, the Jews pursued the retreating army and killed hundreds of Roman soldiers while acquiring a great amount of war materiel. The Roman garrison, now an island in a sea of hostile territory, was promised safe conduct, but the Roman soldiers were slaughtered once they laid their weapons aside. This repulsion of the Roman army left Jerusalem with the impression that God would continue to protect His Temple, and that they could defeat Rome when it came to battle (WJ, II, 17-19).

Nero was livid when he was informed of this fiasco. He immediately declared war and dispatched Rome's best general to Israel in February of 67 A.D. General Vespasian set about subduing Galilee and the Judean countryside. He was not about to make the mistake Cestius had. Vespasian fought a campaign in the summer of 67 A.D., and then again the following summer. Upon the completion of these campaigns, he planned to bring his entire army to the siege of Jerusalem.

Suddenly everything changed. Nero committed suicide in June of 68 A.D. Vespasian immediately withdrew from the battlefield. He had something more important on his mind: the emperor's throne in Rome. Although ultimately successful in that quest, he had to leave Jerusalem unconquered in the meantime. Vespasian fought a third, very brief campaign in the summer of 69 A.D. By then his first rival, Galba, had been murdered (January 69 A.D.), and his second rival, Ortho, had been defeated and had committed suicide (April 69 A.D.). His third rival, Vitellius, arrived in Rome in July. The legions of the east declared Vespasian the emperor, and Vitellius was killed in the fall of 69 A.D. by his own troops. Vespasian's son, Titus, finally returned to Jerusalem in 70 A.D. to complete the job his father had left undone.

What does this have to do with the escape of the Christians? During the initial withdrawal of troops at the news of Nero's suicide, it seems that the Romans had left Jerusalem entirely free from siege. This error was quickly remedied, but there was a short period during which no Roman army was surrounding Jerusalem.

Vespasian's exit did not stop the outlaw Zealots from waging war against each other. One group of them had holed up in Jerusalem for the relative safety it offered. Those within Jerusalem would not allow anyone to leave for fear they would help those outside the city. The outlaw Zealots outside the city would not allow any to leave for fear they were spies.

When Vespasian had secured Rome and its throne for himself, Titus could turn his full attention on Jerusalem. Titus was not about to leave undone the job his father had been enticed to abandon by the death of Nero. By this juncture, the rest of Judea had either sued for peace or been conquered, and Titus was now free to turn his full attention to this rebellious city of Jerusalem (WJ, IV, 10:5).

He paused to let the factions of Jews within the city further decimate each other. The Temple itself was controlled now by one of the groups of outlaw Zealots, battling the priestly class and city residents. The Idumeans, who were the descendants of Esau, had gained entry and were rampaging through the city. And a band of lawless Zealots, who had been encamped outside the walls, eventually got into the city and joined the fray (WJ, IV, 6:2).

The Romans built ramparts to breach the walls, just as Jesus had predicted. "Your enemies will cast up a bank about you and surround you, and hem you in on every side, and dash you to the ground. . . . They will not leave one stone upon another in you" (Luke 19:43-44).

Many Jews tried to escape the city once this final siege by Titus was underway, but the opportunity to flee had long gone. It seems that the only opportunity had been either during the brief retreat and pursuit of Cestius, or during the moment when Vespasian decided to seek the throne after Nero's suicide. Vespasian momentarily pulled his entire army from Jerusalem at that point. Then he thought better of it and sent a portion back.

Jesus knew the margin for error would be razor-thin. "Let him who is on the housetop not go down to take what is in his house; and let him who is in the field not turn back to take his mantle. And alas for those who give suck in those days! Pray that your flight may not be in winter or on a Sabbath" (Matt. 24:17-20). The Christians had to escape without hesitation when the opportunity presented itself.

Cestius came in 66 A.D. Vespasian came in 67, 68, and 69 A.D. Then Titus conquered in 70 A.D. In each of these instances, the Jewish people did what they had always done when invaded by foreign armies. They fled *into* Jerusalem and thanked God for its relative safety. It was a well-fortified city and had withstood attack throughout history more often than not.

So, Jesus' admonition to His disciples in the Olivet Discourse was diametrically opposed to the instincts of every Israelite. He commanded His followers to "flee to the mountains" immediately when they observed the desolating abomination of Daniel, which Luke identifies as armies surrounding Jerusalem. The Christians were to flee *away from* Jerusalem! This advice would test the faith of even the most devout and trusting Christian of Jerusalem. Did the Christians follow their own best judgment and hide within the city walls; or did they obey their Master by leaving Jerusalem when they had the chance?

Eusebius recorded that the Christians fled en masse because of the prophecy of Jesus, probably in 68 A.D. "The whole body, however, of the church at Jerusalem, having been commanded by a divine revelation, entrusted to men of approved piety there before the war, removed from the city, and dwelt at a certain town beyond the Jordan, called Pella. . . . And when those that believed in Christ had come thither from Jerusalem . . . the judgment of God at length overtook . . . and totally destroyed that generation of impious men" (*EH*, III, 5:86).

This area across the Jordan was primarily a gentile land, under the protection of King Agrippa. Most Christians escaped to Pella in Transjordan, but some traveled down to Alexandria in Egypt, and a few escaped to Asia Minor.

Josephus tells us that many Jews fled Jerusalem immediately after the defeat of General Cestius in 66 A.D. Were they Christian Jews? Eusebius places the flight in June of 68 A.D., when Vespasian temporarily pulled his troops away from the siege of Jerusalem.

It is really not important exactly which opportunity was seized. In either instance, there would have been a very short period in which to escape. Of course, both were at the precise moment when any clear-thinking Christian would have been least convinced he needed to flee.

But the Christians did not look at events without the benefit of a supernatural perspective. They remembered Christ's words. St. Athanasius informs us that the revelation that Eusebius mentions was the very words of Christ that we have been examining. After quoting the warning of Jesus, Athanasius describes the actions of the Judean Church: "Knowing these things, the Saints regulated their conduct accordingly" *(DHF)*. Without thought of possessions, they fled for their lives.

Virtually no one escaped the Roman army alive once the siege was staged in earnest. Those trying to escape Jerusalem were caught, whipped, and then crucified by the Romans: five hundred people or more each day. Titus "hoped the Jews might perhaps yield at that sight, out of fear. . . . Their multitude was so great, that room was wanting for the crosses, and crosses wanting for the bodies." (*WJ*, V, 11:1).

Eusebius records that not a single Christian was caught within Jerusalem when Titus successfully surrounded the city (*EH*, III,

V)! The early Church had seen the signs of the fulfillment of Jesus' prophecy. Their faith in Christ's words had saved the fledgling Judean Church from extinction.

NO FLEEING ON THE SABBATH?

Some commentators have pointed to Jesus' statement concerning the Sabbath as evidence of His loyalty to legalistic Judaism: "Pray that your flight may not be in winter or on a Sabbath" (Matt. 24:20). But this shows the typical modernist disregard for context. It is not that the Christians would be observing the Sabbath themselves. Rather, Jesus is concerned that nothing delay His followers in their flight from danger. The gates of Jerusalem would be locked for the Sabbath, and the prohibition on traveling would be enforced by the Temple authorities. This would slow the flight of the Christian community.

Jesus knew that when the eighth sign appeared, there would not be enough time to go back into the home for cherished belongings or even to retrieve a coat. Jesus felt particular pity for pregnant mothers or those slowed by a nursing child. Winter would slow their flight, as would the Sabbath restrictions on travel. All these statements signify the necessity for speed.

SUMMARY OF THE EIGHT SIGNS

Thus far in the discourse, Jesus has predicted the total demolition of the Temple. More important, He has given eight signs to indicate when to flee to the mountains, to prevent the decimation of His infant Church when Jerusalem's Temple was destroyed.

The first seven signs — the appearance of false messiahs; wars and rumors of wars; famines; earthquakes; state-sponsored religious persecution; the falling away of some Christians; and the worldwide preaching of the gospel — are not linked too closely in time with the Temple's destruction. The disciples only knew they would happen while the Temple was still standing, as they were the warning of its demise. Here are the seven preliminary signs.

In contrast, the eighth sign — the desolating sacrilege of Daniel (gentile armies surrounding Jerusalem) — is accompanied by an urgent warning to flee immediately when it appears. Jesus stresses, "Let nothing delay you when you see this last sign."

As we have seen, all of these signs appeared within a generation of Jesus' prediction (30 A.D. to 67 A.D.). In fact, there were some "Rabbins alive at the time when Christ spoke these things, that lived till the city was destroyed, viz. Rabban Simeon, who perished with the city, Rabban Jochanan Ben Zaccai, who outlived it, Rabban Ishmael, and others" (CNT, II:320).

Could it be that Lewis and Russell are mistaken in their embarrassment and skepticism? Could it be that rapturists are just plain wrong in looking for some future fulfillment of these signs?

St. Bede would have thought so. Speaking of the Olivet Discourse in Mark, he wrote, "It is on record that this was literally fulfilled, when on the approach of the war with Rome and the extermination of the Jewish people, all the Christians who were in that province, warned by the prophecy, fled far away, as Church history relates, and retiring beyond Jordan, remained for a time in the city of Pella under the protection of Agrippa (cited in GCC).

FIVE AMPLIFICATIONS ON THE SIGNS

Jesus has warned His Church with eight signs. He now elaborates on His descriptions of the events that will accompany the Temple's destruction. We will refer to them as five amplifications on the eight simple signs He has already enumerated.

Amplification 1: Great Tribulation

The first amplification elaborates on the nature and the intensity of the tribulation of sign 5. Rapturists assert that this first amplification proves that the Olivet Discourse is still unfulfilled.

Jesus states, "There will be *great tribulation*, such as has not been from the beginning of the world until now, no and never will be. And if those days had not been shortened, no human being would be saved; but for the sake of the elect those days will be shortened" (Matt. 24:21-22). Rapturists believe that this Great Tribulation will occur during the seven years immediately after the secret rapture. But is that what the text teaches?

Jesus is borrowing the language of Daniel 12:1. This vision of Daniel (III:D) speaks of a severe tribulation during the reign of Antiochus. Daniel is told that the trouble during Antiochus's time would be the worst ever experienced up to that point. But Jesus states that there is another tribulation that will be even worse than that of Antiochus. It would be the greatest tribulation "from the beginning of the world until now, no and *never will be [surpassed]*" (Matt. 24:21).

Although rapturists automatically assume this Great Tribulation must refer to Daniel's final week — a future seven-year trial of ethnic Jews — they lost that part of their time line in Daniel. (Remember that the early Church viewed that week as seven decades of covenantal transition.)

Moreover, the text here in Matthew argues against that understanding. Jesus is speaking here to Christians. He is elaborating on the eight signs He has just given the disciples to protect His infant Church. Those signs were fulfilled before 70 A.D. He has already referred to tribulation in the fifth sign (Matt. 24:9). These all make it apparent that Jesus is referring here to the Great Tribulation of His Church under Nero from 64 to 67 A.D. Jesus is warning His new Church that they are on the eve of an intense battle for survival; the one mention in sign 5 wasn't enough.

But even granting the severity of the trial under Nero, can we validly claim that this was the worst trial the Church would ever suffer? Was it really a "great tribulation, such as has not been from the beginning of the world until now, no and never will be"? I

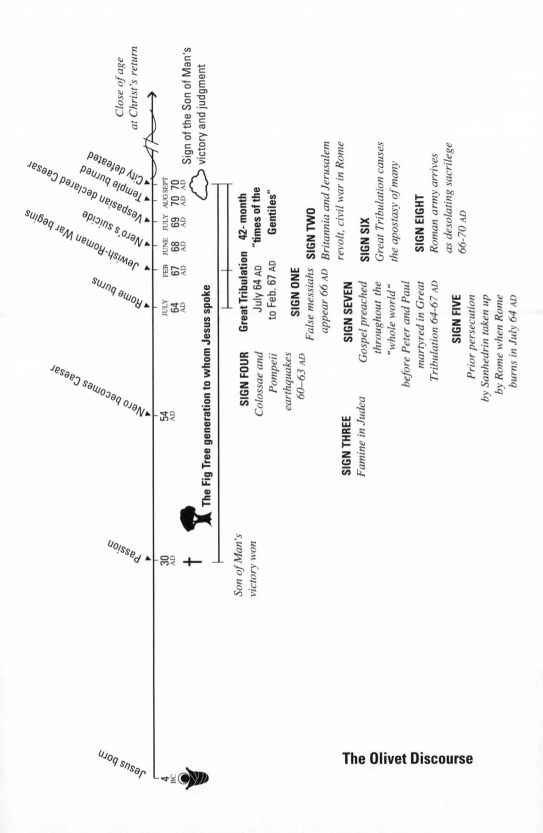

The Olivet Discourse

Jesus born
4 BC

Passion
30 AD

Son of Man's
victory won

The Fig Tree generation to whom Jesus spoke

Nero becomes Caesar
54 AD

SIGN THREE
Famine in Judea

SIGN FOUR
*Colossae and
Pompeii
earthquakes
60–63 AD*

Rome burns
JULY 64 AD

Great Tribulation
July 64 AD
to Feb. 67 AD

SIGN FIVE
*Prior persecution
by Sanhedrin taken up
by Rome when Rome
burns in July 64 AD*

SIGN SEVEN
*Gospel preached
throughout the
"whole world"
before Peter and Paul
martyred in Great
Tribulation 64-67 AD*

Jewish-Roman War begins
FEB 67 AD

SIGN ONE
*False messiahs
appear 66 AD*

SIGN EIGHT
*Roman army arrives
as desolating sacrilege
66-70 AD*

Nero's suicide
JUNE 68 AD

Vespasian declared Caesar
JULY 69 AD

SIGN TWO
*Britannia and Jerusalem
revolt, civil war in Rome*

SIGN SIX
*Great Tribulation causes
the apostasy of many*

Temple burned
AUG/SEPT 70 AD

City defeated
70 AD

**42- month
"times of the
Gentiles"**

Sign of the Son of Man's
victory and judgment

*Close of age
at Christ's return*

believe the answer is an unqualified yes. There has never been, nor will there ever be (until the final eschaton), anything rivaling it (GR3). The Church could have easily been smothered in its cradle if Nero had continued any longer or if the Jerusalem Christians had not escaped to Pella.

Look at the situation. The Christian Church was young and small. For the first time, under Nero, the full might of the Roman Empire was turned against this tiny group of believers. The Church at this time was primarily still Jewish in orientation, yet the Jewish leaders were using their power against the Church as well.

From a human standpoint, it was rather touch-and-go for the Church during this time. Of course, now we know that the Church would survive. But most contemporary observers would probably have given this new sect within Judaism less than even odds of survival. The forces lined against it were too formidable. One commentator has written that the only reason the Church survived at all is that Rome ran out of hungry lions.

Jesus gives us a different reason for the Church's survival during the Great Tribulation of the first century; there is a supernatural explanation. He predicted that "for the sake of the elect those days will be shortened" (Matt. 24:22). In fact, that is exactly what happened. The Neronian persecution of the Church had begun after the burning of Rome in July of 64 A.D. For two years it progressed in full force, and might have succeeded in stamping out that minor Jewish heresy called Christianity. But in 66 A.D., Jerusalem revolted against Rome. When Rome subsequently declared war on Jerusalem in February of 67 A.D., the focus of Rome's wrath shifted from the Christian community to its former ally, Jerusalem. With Rome concentrating on a rebellion on its eastern edge, it had decidedly less appetite for picking a fight with the Christians scattered throughout its empire.

Jesus imbues the timing of these secular events with supernatural meaning. The Church survived the persecution of the Jewish and Roman authorities because of God's merciful intervention. Humanly speaking, the Church probably could not have endured the unabated wrath of Rome and Jerusalem much longer. It is too easy from our perspective in the twenty-first century to assume that the Church would have survived. The disciples did not have that perspective . . . yet.

This was the Church's greatest tribulation, because never again would it be in such a vulnerable position. Thank God He "shortened" those days. By the time Rome again focused its hatred on the Church, it had grown stronger, able to survive future persecutions.

This means the Great Tribulation is history! While it can stand as a prophetic event of the final test of the Church (GR3), Jesus' words cannot be used as a prediction of something still in the future. The Great Tribulation that Jesus prophesied has been fulfilled (GR3).

Amplification 2: Heresy

Jesus now turns the attention of His disciples to a danger more sinister than the Great Tribulation: heresy. "Then if anyone says to you, 'Lo, here is the Christ!' . . . do not believe it. For false Christs and false prophets will arise . . . so as to lead astray, if possible, even the elect. Lo, I have told you beforehand" (Matt. 24:23-25).

The concern of Jesus for the survival of His Church extends well beyond it physical safety. He has given them eight signs that will warn them of the time to flee from Jerusalem. He has promised that the time of the Great Tribulation will be shortened. But what eternal benefit is gained in saving the physical lives of the Christian community, only to have them lose their faith through false teaching? As He said elsewhere, "What does it profit a man if he gains the whole world and loses or forfeits himself?" (Luke 9:25).

Tribulation can damage the Church from without, but heresy destroys from within. Jesus has already warned His disciples of the false messiahs in signs 1 and 6: "Take heed that no one leads you astray. For many will come in my name" (Matt. 24:4-5). He is elaborating on His two major concerns for the early Church: tribulation and heresy.

At this point, Jesus seems to have detected an aura of consternation among His disciples. It is not difficult to discern what their problem was. Jesus promised to return at the final eschaton; how would they know that these false messiahs are not really the Lord come again? It is a good question that deserves a thorough answer, and Jesus gives them one: a litmus test for His second coming.

In the next two verses, Jesus contrasts His second coming with the arrival of the false messiahs. The heart of the message is this: "As the lightning comes from the east and shines as far as the west, so will be the coming of the Son of man" (Matt. 24:27). We will examine these two verses in more depth when we answer the second question, but the sum and substance of the contrast is this: when Christ's second advent occurs, no one will need to be told about it; there will be no need for a public-relations campaign. False messiahs will have to build a base of support; Christ coming in glory as Judge will not. It will be obvious to all, both good and bad, that the final event of history will have descended upon them.

These two verses are a brief tangent. They contrast the true Christ in His return with the false messiahs who would come first. Jesus needed to assure His disciples that they need not worry about missing His second advent. We will examine these two verses later because they supply details concerning the second question of the disciples. (Remember that Luke's account makes this division between questions very clear.) In a moment, Jesus will return to the topic of His eschatological return, but He is not done yet with the events of 70 A.D.

Amplification 3: Political upheaval
At this point in His discourse, Jesus further amplifies our understanding of the events accompanying the destruction of the

Temple. He uses accepted Jewish apocalyptic language to describe what will happen to those who will persecute His people during the Great Tribulation: "Immediately after the tribulation of those days the sun will be darkened, and the moon will not give its light, and the stars will fall from heaven, and the powers of the heavens will be shaken" (Matt. 24:29).

Rapturists look at these verses and claim that they must be fulfilled literally. They want to see the sun stop shining. They demand the spectacle of shooting stars. But this ignores how the Bible itself uses such language. Apocalyptic prophecy repeatedly uses heavenly disruptions to describe political upheavals (GR5).

Even the Jewish literature that described the fall of Jerusalem after the fact used this type of language to describe the events surrounding 70 A.D. The *Sibylline Oracles*, written sometime after 70 A.D., says, "He seized the divinely built Temple. . . . For on his appearance the whole creation was shaken and kings perished" (*SO*, 5:150-154; *OTP*, 1:396).

There is nothing here in Matthew that is at all unlike the language of Isaiah. "The stars of the heavens and their constellations will not give their light; the sun will be dark at its rising and the moon will not shed its light. . . . I will make the heavens tremble, and the earth will be shaken out of its place" (Isa. 13:10-13). Isaiah is predicting the defeat of Babylon. Remember Belshazzar's folly?

Jesus is foretelling the overthrow of those political dynasties that persecuted His Church. He draws a parallel between the "shaking" of Babylon (the conqueror of God's Old Covenant people) and the "shaking" of Jerusalem (the persecutor of God's New Covenant people). One disciple, John, will remember this parallel and use it as a backdrop for Vision III:D in The Apocalypse.

Actually, Jesus was not the first to draw this parallel. The prophet Haggai told Jerusalem that one day it would be "shaken" just as Babylon had been: "Thus says the Lord of hosts: Once again, in a little while, I will shake the heavens and the earth and the sea and the dry land; and I will shake all nations, so that the treasures of all nations shall come in, and I will fill this house with splendor, says the Lord of hosts" (Hag. 2:6-7).

What was this "splendor"? In explaining this Haggai passage, St. Augustine wrote that the "splendor" that filled this house was Christ, while the "house" was the New Covenant Temple, the Church. Haggai was predicting the shaking, or overthrow, of Jerusalem so that "the treasures of all nations," the Church, could be revealed (COG, XVIII:48). The shaking of Jerusalem in 70 A.D. cleared the way for the unimpeded growth of the Church.

The New Testament book of Hebrews makes it clear that Christianity remained in a precarious position as long as the Temple sacrifices continued. Many Jewish Christians were turning back to the Temple worship as Jesus had predicted in sign 6. Hebrews reiterates a favorite passage (Hab. 2:3-4) calling for patience in the promises of God. "Do not throw away your confidence. . . . You have need of endurance. . . . 'For yet a little while, and the coming one shall come and shall not tarry; but my righteous one shall live by faith . . . ' We are not of those who shrink back and are destroyed, but of those who have faith and keep their souls" (Heb. 10:36-39).

Jesus' amplification on the political upheaval accompanying the end of Daniel's final week in 70 A.D. is a message of hope designed to build up "confidence," "endurance," and "faith." Any Jewish reader with an elementary grasp of his own history would have understood this at once. The nations that hate and persecute God's people will be judged, but only in God's good time (GR3).

In point of fact, both of the political dynasties that instigated the Great Tribulation of Christians were destroyed. Nero was the last in his dynasty. The next Roman emperor, Vespasian, was not of his lineage. Yet in just one more generation, Vespasian's dynasty was also obliterated.

But this prophecy probably speaks even more directly to the end of the Sanhedrin of Jerusalem. This Jewish political machine had hounded the Christians since Pentecost. The Romans joined in the persecution only after three decades of pestering by the Sanhedrin. After the Temple's destruction in 70 A.D., no high priest could lay legitimate claim to Aaron's mantle. The Sanhedrin was uprooted forever, never to be validly re-established again.

Amplification 4: Sign of the Son of man

We now come to the heart of the Olivet Discourse. It is here that Lewis, Russell, and rapturist all agree. Surely, they say, we cannot claim that this prophecy of Jesus has been fulfilled already! Yet because we did our homework in Daniel, that is exactly what we will discover.

Here is how the Revised Standard Version of the Bible translates this verse: at the judgment of Jerusalem, there "Then will appear the sign of the Son of man in heaven, and then all the tribes of the earth will mourn, and they will see the Son of man coming on the clouds of heaven with power and great glory; and He will send out His angels with a loud trumpet call, and they will gather His elect from the four winds, from one end of heaven to the other" (Matt. 24:30-31).

When the context of Daniel is understood, a strong case can be made for its fulfillment in 70 A.D. Jesus uses the term "Son of man" to describe Himself. This ought to prompt us at least to investigate the possibility that this might be referring to the same event as in Daniel's prophecy.

The sign

Neither the Jewish historian Josephus nor the Roman historian Tacitus ever claimed to be a Christian, nor was either particularly sympathetic to the Christian cause. Yet without ulterior motive, both recorded the appearance of strange heavenly signs at the time of the fall of Jerusalem (*WJ*, VI, 5:3; *THI*, 1:5-7, 1:2-3). These could have been "the sign of the Son of man in the Heaven."

Lest we think that both historians were just gullible ancients, Josephus assures his readers that these events were hard to believe and credible only because of the eyewitnesses involved: "I suppose [this] account . . . would seem to be a fable, were it not related by those who saw it, and were not the events that followed it of so considerable a nature as to deserve such signals.

"There was *a star resembling a sword*, which stood over the city, and a comet, that continued a whole year. . . . Before the Jews' rebellion . . . so great a light shone round the altar and the holy house, that it appeared to be bright daytime; which lasted for half an hour. . . . Moreover, the eastern gate of the inner court of the Temple . . . was seen to be opened of its own accord about the sixth hour of the night. . . . The men of learning understood it, that *the security of their holy house was dissolved* of its own accord. . . . So these publicly declared that *the signal foreshowed the desolation* that was coming upon them. . . . A few days after . . . before sunsetting, chariots and troops of soldiers in their armor were seen running about among the clouds. . . . Moreover, at that feast which we call Pentecost, as the priests were going by night into the inner court of the Temple, as their custom was, to perform their sacred ministrations, they said that, in the first place, they felt a quaking, and heard a great noise, and after that they heard a sound as of a great multitude, saying, 'Let us remove hence.' "

This cross-like star could easily have been the "sign of the Son of man." Three centuries later, something very similar to this sign appeared to Constantine just before he fought the battle that made him emperor of Rome. Add the heavenly chariots and the angels that were witnessed in the sky in 70 A.D., and it seems even more likely that the "sign of the Son of man" really did appear above Jerusalem to warn them of their coming judgment by "the Son of man coming on the clouds of Heaven with power."

The clouds

We must be careful not to assume that the coming of the Son of man on clouds means that the Son must be coming to earth. Jesus lifted the "Son of man" language directly out of Daniel 7:13-14, so we must respect that context (GR3). We already determined that in Daniel it is perfectly clear that the Son of man is coming toward the Ancient of Days, not to earth!

We have already seen that Daniel's "Son of man" was publicly recognized as the victor at the judgment of the Sanhedrin in 70 A.D. This is the point at which Christ was vindicated as Judge of His accusers, and the Kingdom was publicly given to the saints, as Daniel's vision foretold. "The greatness of the kingdoms under the whole Heaven shall be given to the people of the saints of the Most High; their kingdom shall be an everlasting kingdom" (Dan. 7:27). What happened here on earth was just the by-product of the heavenly reality.

Of course, the "clouds of Heaven" symbolize the majesty and glory of the Son of man when He judges His enemies. It does not mean that this event of coming could not have occurred on a cloudless day (GR6).

Here comes the Judge

Never lose sight of the fact that Daniel's Son of man is a *judge*. In this case, there will be a judgment of the Sanhedrin of Jesus' generation for what they had done to the Messiah. This is exactly what Jesus predicted when He stood before those very men: "You will see the Son of man . . . coming on the clouds of Heaven" (Matt. 26:64).

Luke 19:41-44 draws this connection clearly. "When [Jesus] . . . saw the city, He wept over it, saying . . . 'The days shall come upon you, when your enemies will cast up a bank about you and surround you, and hem you in on every side . . . and they will not leave one stone upon another in you; *because you did not know the*

Rapture

time of your visitation.' " The Sanhedrin's rejection of their Messiah had consequences.

When we start to understand the significance of 70 A.D., the words of Jesus at the Transfiguration take on new meaning. Jesus said to those present, "For the Son of man is to come with His angels in the glory of His Father, and then He will repay every man for what he has done. Truly, I say to you, there are some standing here who will not taste death before they see the Son of man coming in His Kingdom" (Matt. 16:27-28). If Jesus publicly came into His Kingdom in 70 A.D., then He was absolutely correct in telling His disciples at the Transfiguration that some of them would live to see that event. Notice that Jesus links His "coming in His Kingdom" to the fact that "He will repay every man for what he has done." This need not be primarily a reference to the final judgment, but to the judgment of the Sanhedrin.

The view we are developing understands the prophecies in Daniel, in the Transfiguration, in the Olivet Discourse, and in the trial of Jesus before the Sanhedrin as all relating to the same event. They all occurred within the generation that Jesus had promised. At the same time, the judgment of 70 A.D. is also a prophecy of the final eschaton (GR3).

By this view, Jesus and His Kingdom were progressively revealed to more and more people through a series of revelatory events. First, there were the miracles of His birth and childhood, to which only a very small group were privy. Then His glory was revealed to a few disciples in the Transfiguration. His glorious power was made evident to many more in the Resurrection, but still primarily to those who believed. Then even His enemies saw the glorious power of Christ when He judged Jerusalem in 70 A.D. The same Christ whom they had rejected was publicly exalted by God the Father. Finally, at the second advent, this same Christ will return in glory for all to see. All will be rewarded for their loyalty, or punished for lack of it.

The modernist does not like this view. He enjoys claiming to the uninformed Christian in the pew that the Apostles expected the second coming very quickly. He points to these very passages as proof that even Jesus thought the final eschaton would occur within a generation. I hate to rain on the modernists' parade (I take that back; I enjoy raining on their parade), but their exegesis of these passages lacks an in-depth understanding of Daniel's "Son of man" prophecy.

The mourning
We now come to the response of people who would witness this coming of the Son of man in judgment. As Appendix Three notes, this response reflects the language of Zechariah: "Then all the tribes of the earth will mourn" (Matt. 24:30).

What does Jesus mean by "all the tribes of the earth"? This certainly need not imply that the entire planet is mourning over the events in Jerusalem. The Greek word for *earth* here is *ge*. It is often better translated as "land." In Jewish literature, it was common to use *land* as a reference for Israel and *sea* to refer to the gentile nations.

In other words, if these signs that Josephus and Tacitus recorded really occurred (and we have no good reason to doubt that they did, aside from our twenty-first-century rationalistic prejudices), then the mourning would be done by the tribes of the land of Israel. It is not at all hard to believe that the Jewish tribes would mourn the impending destruction of the Temple. In fact, they still commemorate that destruction on the ninth of *Av* every year, in a solemn day called *Tisha B'Av*.

The four winds
Finally, Jesus completes the details of what will happen when the Son of man judges the Sanhedrin for their faithlessness: "He will send out His angels with a loud trumpet call, and they will

gather His elect from the four winds, from one end of Heaven to the other" (Matt. 24:31). Rapturists are quite sure this has not occurred yet because they view this as some sort of physical resurrection. But if we understand the Old Testament use of this phrase, we will see that it clearly did occur in 70 A.D.

The "four winds of Heaven" is a common image in the Old Testament. When God providentially scattered a people, the Old Testament described it as being scattered to the "four winds" of Heaven. In other words, God was thorough. In Jeremiah, we read of God's scattering Elam to the four quarters of Heaven with the four winds: "There shall be no nation to which those driven out of Elam shall not come" (Jer. 49:36). This can happen even to political dynasties, as Daniel describes the split of the kingdom of Alexander the Great as being "divided toward the four winds of Heaven" (Dan. 11:4).

Conversely, when God regathers His scattered people after tribulation, He is said to be gathering them from the four winds of Heaven. In Zechariah 2:6 and Isaiah 11:12, God regathers His chosen people after spreading them to the four winds (or "corners").

In the Olivet Discourse, Jesus is reflecting the regathering language of Ezekiel. "Come from the four winds . . . and the breath came into them, and they lived" (Ezek. 37:9-10). In this passage, God resurrects a valley of dry bones (GR7). Ezekiel uses this resurrection language to predict the spiritual rejuvenation and regathering of the Jewish nation after the Babylonian exile. They will be renewed even though they were coming "from the four winds."

The message of Ezekiel was one of hope to the scattered people of God. At this point, so is the Olivet Discourse. After warning the disciples about tribulation, heresy, flight, and destruction, Jesus predicts the revitalization and reunification of the young Christian Church. By 70 A.D., Christians had been disheartened by Jewish and Roman persecutions. They had been dispersed throughout the known world. First, they had fled the Sanhedrin in response to persecution, and then they fled from the surrounding Roman armies.

It is reassuring to note that Jesus' message starts but does not end with the destruction of Jerusalem and its Temple. Much had to be said about the tribulations and destruction that were to come. The very survival of early Christianity depended on this warning. But Jesus would not end on this hopeless note. He returned to a familiar Old Testament theme: after tribulation there is always a renewed outpouring of God's grace and love. Jesus would not have His followers doubt that the end of His story would be filled with grace as well.

Summary of the coming of the Son of man

Once we understand its first-century context, we can say with confidence that Jesus kept His word in the Olivet Discourse. The coming of the Son of man in judgment can certainly be viewed as validly fulfilled in 70 A.D.

Much of my analysis here reflects the research done by David Palm for his master's thesis at Trinity Evangelical Divinity School (awarded "Thesis of the Year" by the faculty). After working with the Greek words and phrases of Matthew 24:30, Palm retranslated the verse as follows: "Then the tribes of the land will see in the destruction of Jerusalem an unmistakable sign that the rejected Son of man is in Heaven, enthroned. They will mourn. The Son will come in glory to the throne of God."

Palm does an excellent job of making aspects of this prophecy very clear, while remaining absolutely loyal to the Greek text. As we have already seen, God came on "the clouds" in judgment to the Egyptians via the Assyrian army (GR6). Later, King Belshazzar witnessed God's coming in the Persian army as it meted out His judgment on Babylon. Any educated Jew would have understood the Roman destruction as exactly that: the Messiah's vindication. Since those who heard Jesus make this prophecy were well-versed in Old Testament usage, the advance of the Roman army and its victory over Jerusalem would have been universally understood as the fulfillment of this prophecy. Jesus promised He would come in judgment on His accusers within their lifetime.

There is good evidence that even the ancient pagan world understood the destruction of Jerusalem by the Romans as God's punishment for their treatment of Jesus. Mara Bar Serapion was a pagan Syrian Gentile who wrote a letter to his son sometime after 73 A.D., trying to encourage him in their struggle against injustice: "What advantage did the Athenian gain from putting Socrates to death? Famine and plague came upon them as a judgment for their crime. What advantage did the men of Samos gain from burning Pythagoras? In a moment their land was covered with sand. *What advantage did the Jews gain from executing their wise King?* It was just after that that their kingdom was abolished. God justly avenged these three wise men" (cited in *NTD*, X). The events surrounding 70 A.D. were a pronouncement of the Kingdom of Christ that even the pagans of that day could understand. Jesus was recognized by all as the victor when the Temple was judged.

Our understanding of this prophecy dovetails with that of the early Church, which held that biblical Judaism was destroyed because of its rejection of the Messiah. Before 70 A.D., Christianity was assumed by most in the ancient world to be a small sect within Judaism. The Temple's destruction cleared the way for the unimpeded growth of Christ's Church.

The third-century bishop Clement of Alexandria wrote, "[Jesus] confidently set forth, plainly as I said before, sufferings, places, appointed times, manners, limits . . . and [that] this generation shall not pass until the destruction begins. . . . He spoke in plain words the things that were straightway to happen, which we can now see with our eyes, in order that the accomplishment might be among those to whom the word was spoken" (*CLH*, 3:15, cited in *ANF*, 8:241).

Origen challenged all doubters: "I challenge anyone to prove my statement untrue if I say that the entire Jewish nation was destroyed less than one whole generation later. . . . For forty and two years, I think, after the date of the Crucifixion of Jesus, did the destruction of Jerusalem take place" (*CCE*, IV:XXII).

Origen draws the right conclusion: only God could make the type of prediction that Jesus made and have it come true. "Consider how, while Jerusalem was still standing, and the whole Jewish worship celebrated in it, Jesus foretold what would befall it from the hand of the Romans. . . . At that time there were no armies around Jerusalem, encompassing and enclosing and besieging it; for the siege began in the reign of Nero [three decades after His death]" (*CCE*, II:XXIII).

Amplification 5: The fig tree

Jesus finishes His answer to the first question with the famous fig-tree analogy. This final amplification elaborates on the certainty of the signs pointing to the Temple's judgment. "From the fig tree learn its lesson: as soon as its branch becomes tender and puts forth its leaves, you know that summer is near. So also, when you see all these things, you know that He is near, at the very gates. Truly, I say to you, this generation will not pass away till all these things take place" (Matt. 24:32-34).

Fig trees are plentiful in Judea, so Jesus uses this familiar image as an object lesson. When the fig tree puts out its leaves, summer is upon Israel. In like fashion, when the eight signs occur, the coming of the Son of man in judgment will be near as well. In fact, He will be at "the very gates." What gates would those be? Jesus means the gates of the rebellious city of Jerusalem, of course.

Rapturists claim that the generation of the fig tree did not start with the people listening to Jesus that day. They believe that it did not start until the signs started, which they usually assume to have been in 1948 or 1967. But they do not accept, or have not learned, that all eight signs appeared, and were fulfilled, in the first century.

From our perspective, the entire discourse up to this point is history. This is a biblical perspective. St. John Chrysostom tells us that the reason St. John did not include the Olivet Discourse in his Gospel was that the events surrounding 70 A.D. had already been fulfilled by that time. "John wrote none of these things . . . (for indeed he lived a long time after the taking of the city), but they, who died before the taking, and had seen none of these things, they write it, in order that in every way the power of the prediction should clearly shine forth" (HOM, LXXVI on Matt. 24:16). There was no point in giving the eight signs to a reader who had already witnessed their fulfillment. The generation of the fig tree had already passed by the time St. John wrote his Gospel.

Ours is not the generation of the fig tree. That generation is long dead.

Perhaps the best indication of the belief of the early Church as regards the Olivet Discourse is not found in a book. We need only examine the actions of the Jerusalem Church in the years surrounding the Jewish-Roman War. It is unambiguous: the early Christians voted with their feet at the time of the Temple's destruction: they fled. Discounting all the history of their nation, they fled. The early Judean Church believed this warning of Jesus; they fled. And they survived. There can be no clearer evidence of how the early Church originally understood this passage.

We have completed the answer of Jesus to the first question of His followers. "Tell us, when will this [the Temple's destruction] be?" (Matt. 24:3). Jesus gave His disciples everything they needed to recognize the signs of the coming destruction of Jerusalem. He predicted the Great Tribulation. He predicted He would come as a judge upon their persecutors, the Sanhedrin, and He did. It all happened in the generation listening to Him that day.

As the father of Church history wrote, "If anyone compares the words of our Savior with the other accounts of the historian concerning the whole war, how can one fail to wonder, and to admit that the foreknowledge and the prophecy of our Savior were truly divine?" (*EH*, III, 7:7). We can trust the word of Jesus, even beyond the point when "Heaven and earth will pass away" (Matt. 24:35).

THE SECOND QUESTION:
WHAT WILL BE THE SIGN OF YOUR
COMING AND OF THE CLOSE OF THE AGE?

Here in the Olivet Discourse there is a marked change of tone. Until now, Jesus has spoken of the signs pointing to the destruction of the Temple. He has been very specific with eight signs and then expanded our understanding in five amplifications. He has presented a great deal of knowledge and detail. Now He speaks of the timing of an event of which no one, not even the Son, has any knowledge: "But of that day and hour no one knows, not even the angels of Heaven, nor the Son, but the Father only" (Matt. 24:36).

This is clearly a different event; the verses that follow will answer the disciples' second question: "What will be the sign of Your coming and of the close of the age?" (Matt. 24:3).

No signs left for you

The answer to the second question reminds me of the song that laments, "No time left for you." In this case, the eight signs refer to the first question, and there are no signs left for the second question.

While the disciples were promised that the events surrounding the Temple's destruction would occur within their own generation, the events surrounding the eschatological second advent of

Christ will occur at a time that even the Son could not pinpoint. I find this to be one of the most amazing statements in the Bible.

Notice how many times Jesus returns to this refrain in the next nine verses. "No one knows. . . . They did not know. . . . You do not know. . . . You do not expect" (Matt. 24:36, 39, 42, 44). Perhaps Christ was anticipating the voracious appetite of many Christians for any hint as to the timing of His second advent. Yet His advice is that we should not bother to try to determine the time. "No one knows. . . . You do not know."

It certainly is startling enough to give the disciples warning that they were passing from the first question to the second. For readers who have difficulty sensing this change in tone, however, it is an easy matter to turn to the parallel passages in Luke. In Luke's account, the two questions and answers are separated by more than three chapters. The first question is answered in Luke 21:5-36, and the second is briefly answered in Luke 17:22-37.

A sudden coming

As the answer to this second question unfolds, the contrast between the first and second answers becomes even more evident. "As were the days of Noah, so will be the coming of the Son of man . . . until the day when Noah entered the ark, and they did not know until the flood came" (Matt. 24:37-39). People will be living normal, happy lives, oblivious to the judgment about to befall the world. They will be "eating and drinking, marrying and giving in marriage," just as they did just before the flood in Noah's time.

The contrast between the events surrounding 70 A.D. and the events leading up to Christ's second coming are striking. The second advent is unexpected, whereas eight dramatic signs presage the judgment upon Jerusalem.

Jesus earlier contrasted His second coming to the appearance of many false messiahs. These were parenthetical verses inserted into the answer to the first question. Let us now return to them.

The analogy then was one of lightning: "For as the lightning comes from the east and shines as far as the west, so will be the coming of the Son of man. Wherever the body is, there the eagles will be gathered together" (Matt. 24:27-28). These parenthetical verses tell us three aspects of the second advent of the real Christ.

• *First, Christ's second advent will be sudden.* There will be no immediate warning preceding it. There will be no eight signs with five amplifications. As with lightning, we may be aware that storm clouds are gathering, but there is no way to predict precisely when or where the lightning will strike.

• *Second, the return of Christ will be very public and unmistakable.* There is nothing private or secretive about lightning; no one need tell anyone else about its advent. It is immediately experienced by all.

• *Third, at the second coming, Christ will draw to Himself those who are His.* I believe this is the best interpretation of the enigmatic statement, "Wherever the body is, there the eagles will be gathered together."

Luke records this statement as an answer to the disciples' question, "Where will those taken at the second coming go?" (17:37). The false messiahs must drum up support for their leadership through recruiting drives out in the desert. In contrast, Jesus' followers will be inexorably, irresistibly, and immediately drawn to Him when He returns. In other words, don't worry about finding Christ at the second advent: the connection will be automatic.

To summarize, the second coming of Christ will be unmistakable because it will be so public. Everyone will experience it firsthand. It will come with no immediate warning. Christ's presence at that moment will draw His faithful people to Him automatically and immediately. This does not resemble a secret rapture in the least.

You must be ready

The entire thrust of Jesus' message in this second question is readiness: there will be no signs, so we must live each day as though His coming could occur that day. "You also must be ready; for the Son of man is coming at an hour you do not expect" (Matt. 24:44).

Matthew includes an interesting play on words. Jesus is recorded as saying, "You do not know on what day your Lord is coming" (24:42). Then He starts the very next sentence with the command "Know this" (24:43). We may not know the time, but we must know our duty: to "be ready." It is our duty to wait watchfully, lest we be unprepared for the second coming. This second answer is written for you and me. We do not know, so we must always live as though we were ready for eternity.

Will some be "left behind"?

The coming of Christ will be so sudden that two men will be outside doing chores together, and "one is taken, and one is left" (Matt. 24:40). Two women will be preparing food together and "one is taken, and one is left" (Matt. 24:41).

Now, we must give credit where credit is due. Rapturists have done a magnificent job in convincing Christians that this is a prediction of the rapture, when Jesus will return secretly for His Christians, take them to Heaven, and leave the unbelievers to suffer here on earth. They insert the word *behind* into the passage. They understand it as "one is taken, and one is left behind."

But this is not what the verses say, nor does the Greek language support this interpretation. Jesus does not mean one of these people will be left behind. Jesus is speaking here of the second coming that will usher in eternity. It will be impossible to be left behind, because the world will come to an end. No, Jesus is saying they will be left *out*, left out of His eternal Kingdom when He returns.

The Gospel account uses the Greek verb *aphiemi*, which most commonly has the meaning of being left, left alone, forsaken, or even sent away. There is another Greek word that would have made it clear that Jesus meant "left behind." This word is *apoleipo*, or *hupoleipo*. The idea that the first person will be taken to Heaven and the second left behind is not justified by the Greek text.

But the context of Jesus' discourse argues even more strongly against the rapturist understanding of being left behind. How do we know this? Jesus proceeds to tell three parables. When we get to the second parable, we will see that the only reasonable understanding of Jesus' meaning is not "left behind," but "left out" — left out of the eternal marriage feast of the Lamb.

The "left behind" controversy should not obscure an important assertion of Jesus: the daily lives of loyal Kingdom subjects will remain entirely comingled with those of the disloyal. People are not sorted into or out of Christ's Kingdom by physical or national boundaries. Christ's subjects will be neighbors and friends with unbelievers until the very end, at His second coming. They will be working, living, and socializing together. Some will enter the Kingdom of Heaven in the end, and some will be left out of it. This is the part of these verses that would have shocked any first-century citizen of Rome. This is unlike the four earthly kingdoms that the Kingdom of Heaven replaces in Daniel's vision. Christ's Kingdom will not have physical boundaries, because it is spiritual.

Three parables to clarify the answer

Jesus was a master at using parables to clarify His meaning. This case is no exception. The next three stories illustrate how we must live in the light of Jesus' teaching concerning the suddenness of His second coming.

Parable of two servants

The first story is about two servants. One of them is faithful and wise; when his Master returns, he is rewarded. The other servant is wicked, and he is punished for his wickedness when his

Master unexpectedly returns to find him abusing his freedom. Notice that at the return of the Master, the judgment is the final one, and the return has no warning: "The master of that servant will come on a day when he does not expect him . . . and will punish him, and put him with the hypocrites; there men will weep and gnash their teeth" (Matt. 24:50-51).

Jesus is clearly alluding to His second coming, which will usher in the final judgment of all humankind. The only thing after the judgment is eternity. Unfortunately for the rapturist, Jesus does not mention any hint of a seven-year tribulation or a Millennium after this coming. All that remains is either eternal bliss or eternal damnation.

Our lesson in this? Never do anything of which you would be ashamed if your Master caught you in the act of it at His second coming. He will come suddenly and unexpectedly. We will be judged. Eternity will immediately follow.

Parable of ten maidens

The second story is about ten maidens waiting for the bridegroom, an obvious picture of the Church waiting for the second coming. Five of the maidens were wise and took extra oil for their lamps, so that when the bridegroom was slow in coming, they were still ready. Oil in the New Testament is usually a symbol of the Holy Spirit. These five maidens had prepared themselves for a marathon rather than a quick dash to the final eschaton. The other five maidens were foolish. They ran out of oil before the bridegroom appeared and left to buy more. "While they went to buy, the bridegroom came, and those who were ready went in with him to the marriage feast; and the door was shut" (Matt. 25:10). When the bridegroom took the five wise maidens into the marriage feast, the five foolish maidens were left out.

The mention of the marriage feast is a hint that once again we are in eternity. The joy at a wedding reception is analogous to the joy of Heaven. We will encounter the marriage supper again in The Apocalypse.

The main message of this parable? Be ready. You may have associated with Christians your entire life. You may know all the right answers. But you must still remain prepared. Don't be like the foolish maidens.

Notice how the parable expands our understanding of the earlier phrase "one is taken, and one is left" (Matt. 24:40-41). This parable substantiates our claim that Jesus meant "left *out* of the eternal Kingdom." He never meant "left *behind* at the secret rapture," as rapturists claim. Jesus is talking about the taking of Christians into eternal bliss. Two men will be working together. One will be taken, and the other left out of the marriage feast (Matt. 24:40). Two women will be together. One will be taken into the marriage feast of the Lamb, and the other left out (Matt. 24:41).

Parable of talents

The third parable concerns three servants, each entrusted with a sum of money: one received five talents, another received two, and the third received one. The master left and did not return for "a long time" (Matt. 25:19). When the master returned, he rewarded the servants based on how they had managed the talents he had given them. The obvious message is that our talents — our material goods as well as our abilities — are God-given, and He expects us to use them for Him.

In addition, this third story states explicitly something at which the second story merely hinted. In the second story, the bridegroom came much later than the five foolish maidens expected. In this story, Jesus specifically tells us that the Master did not return for "a long time."

Jesus was absolutely right; we have been waiting for His coming for a long time. It has been two millennia since the Master left

His Church on earth to work for His Kingdom. We might easily wait for two or three more.

This parable is another blow to modernists who assert that Jesus led His Apostles into an unrealistic view of how soon the second coming would occur. In fact, neither Jesus nor His Apostles are guilty of this mistaken belief. Jesus taught that it would be a "long time," and His followers believed Him.

The final judgment

These three parables are completed by Matthew 25:30. Jesus ends His discourse by giving His disciples a few more details concerning the second question.

First, we learn that at the second coming, the Son of Man will complete the work He set out to accomplish here on earth. How do we know this? Jesus tells us, "When the Son of man comes in His glory, and all the angels with Him, then He will sit on His glorious throne" (25:31). Sitting signifies the consummation of the Son of man's work. All the battles are won at that point. All enemies have been subdued. All that remains is the final judgment. Need I say it again? There is no mention of a seven-year tribulation or a thousand-year kingdom *after* this coming.

"Before Him will be gathered all the nations, and He will separate them one from another as a shepherd separates the sheep from the goats" (Matt. 25:32). Because Jesus mentions the gathering of "all the nations," some rapturists have tried to read into this passage a judgment different from the final judgment each of us will individually experience at the close of history. Some rapturists foresee two or even three judgments.

But look carefully at the judgment being described. Although we are gathered as nations, we are sorted into the "sheep" side or the "goat" side on the basis of our individual actions: "He will place the sheep at His right hand, but the goats at the left" (Matt. 25:33).

Those who have exhibited the greatest gift, charity, are rewarded for all eternity: "Then the King will say . . . 'Come, O blessed of my Father, inherit the kingdom prepared for you . . . for I was hungry and you gave me food; I was thirsty and you gave me drink; I was a stranger and you welcomed me; I was naked and you clothed me; I was sick and you visited me; I was in prison and you came to me" (Matt. 25:34-36). These are the actions of individuals, not of nations, that are being rewarded. Our response to the needs of others will be credited to our eternal account, as though we had helped Jesus Himself: "Truly, I say to you, as you did it to one of the least of these my brethren, you did it to me" (Matt. 25:40).

Those who have not shown charity to the needy will experience the results of their rejection of God's commandments: "Depart from me, you cursed, into the eternal fire prepared for the Devil and his angels; for I was hungry and you gave me no food, I was thirsty and you gave me no drink" (Matt. 25:41-42). Suddenly, the use of our talents for the Master in the earlier parable becomes apparently important. We must use our talents for the sake of the least of His — and our — brethren. Our eternal destiny depends on it.

SUMMARY OF THE TWO CONFUSING QUESTIONS

Surely, by the end of the Olivet Discourse Jesus has given His disciples much more information than they had expected when they asked two short questions! They were wondering about when the Temple would be destroyed, and perhaps they assumed that the final judgment would occur at the same time. But as we have determined, by the time the Olivet Discourse was recorded for us in all of the synoptic Gospels, the distinction between the two events was well understood.

Summary of the first question

Jesus told the Apostles that within their generation, eight signs would point to the destruction of the Temple. He then detailed five amplifications. These all occurred. The signs warned of His judgment upon the Sanhedrin — the "Son of man" coming in judgment that Daniel foresaw six centuries earlier. The judgment occurred within a generation, as Jesus had predicted.

Summary of the second question

The reliability of Jesus' first answer gives us confidence in His second answer, which is still unfulfilled. Of course, the events surrounding 70 A.D. can act as a prophecy pointing to the second advent, but the two events should not be confused (GR3).

Christ's second coming will be sudden. It will be public and unmistakable. Christians will be irresistibly attracted to their Lord immediately. We cannot determine its precise timing, so we should live each day in anticipation, yet prepare for the long haul. Christians will be living and working alongside non-Christians when it occurs. Every person will receive his just reward in the end based on the charity he has shown. History itself will end because Jesus will sit on His throne, judge humanity individually, and take His faithful into eternal bliss with Him. Some will be taken into the Kingdom, and some will be left out.

This is nothing less than the Church's traditional belief in the second advent of Christ. Nothing we have uncovered even remotely suggests the private rapture that rapturists try to deduce from these verses. Nowhere is anyone "left behind." There is no secret rapture preceding a seven-year Great Tribulation; indeed, the Great Tribulation Jesus predicts here has already come to pass. There is no mention of a separate millennial reign of Jesus as Messiah after the judgment. And nowhere is there any hint of two or three future judgments. The beliefs integral to the rapturist system are conspicuously absent from the teachings of Jesus.

Chapter Seven

The Epistles

At this point, the rapturists' case is looking tenuous, to say the least. In Daniel, we learned that there really was no prediction of a seven-year tribulation, but rather a seven-decade period of covenantal transition that ended in 70 A.D. In the Olivet Discourse, we learned that Jesus keeps His promises. The signs He predicted were fulfilled in the first century, the Great Tribulation occurred as predicted, and Christ came in judgment to His accusers in the Sanhedrin. When Christ returns, it will not be a secret, and no one will be left behind. Rather, we will all be judged and admitted into — or left out of — God's eternal Kingdom.

Yet rapturists still use certain passages from New Testament epistles to try to salvage their case. Even very knowledgeable Catholics can get confused about how to answer these rapturist claims. Examining these verses, we will see that the confusion stems from the rapturist tendency toward "deceptive double vision."

In the movie *It's a Wonderful Life*, George Bailey's Uncle Billy looks for his hat after drinking too much at a party. When George holds it out to him, he looks at it and asks, "Which one is mine?" The audience laughs because everyone knows that there is only one hat.

We will encounter a similar scenario with the rapturist treatment of the epistles. One, and only one second advent is taught in the New Testament. Yet in each passage, the rapturist will ask which "hat" is being discussed: the secret rapture or the second coming.

After examining the "double vision" passages, we will look at two epistles that will give us valuable insight into the mindset of the Apostles. These passages will "sober us up" after the "double vision" passages. After we glean what we can from the wisdom of these epistles, we will be ready for The Apocalypse.

DECEPTIVE DOUBLE VISION
The time line is assumed: 1 Corinthians 15:20-26

This passage lays out a general time line of the events of the end. This is certainly not Paul's primary purpose — which is to convince his readers of the resurrection of the body — but this makes the order of events even more compelling:

> Christ has been raised from the dead, the first fruits of those who have fallen asleep. . . . As in Adam all die, so also in Christ shall all be made alive. But each in his own order: Christ the first fruits, then at His coming those who belong to Christ. Then comes the end, when He delivers the Kingdom to God the Father after destroying every rule and every authority and power. For He must reign until He has put all His enemies under His feet. The last enemy to be destroyed is death.

The order is clear. First, Christ was raised bodily from the dead. This event stands as a prophecy concerning our own personal future. Christ was "the first fruits of those who have fallen asleep" (GR3). Second, Christians will be raised from the dead. Third, "the end" comes.

That is the order. If St. Paul had believed in the rapturist system, this would have presented a perfect passage in which to include it. But Paul does not allude to the rapturist time line of the end; moreover, he lays out a time line that excludes its possibility. There is no mention of a two-stage coming split into a secret rapture and a later, public second advent. In fact, there is not even a hint of a secret rapture. There is *one* resurrection mentioned (not two) and only *one* coming "event" (not two, or in two stages). *Immediately* after this coming (not seven or a thousand or 1,007 years later), "the end" arrives, at which time Christ "delivers the Kingdom to God."

This is a major problem for the rapturist system. Even leading rapturists admit that the idea that Christ's second advent will be split into two stages is not taught in a single passage of Scripture. The only way to justify their system is to assign certain passages to the first stage and other passages to the second stage, even though the passages themselves do not encourage this. This is what I call "deceptive double vision."

The end is really the end: 1 Corinthians 15:51-54

This tendency on the part of the rapturist to assign certain passages to one stage or the other in an arbitrary way is nowhere more apparent than just a little further on in 1 Corinthians:

Lo! I tell you a mystery. We shall not all sleep [die], but we shall all be changed, in a moment, in the twinkling of an eye, at the last trumpet. For the trumpet will sound, and the dead will be raised imperishable, and we shall be changed. . . . Then shall come to pass the saying that is written: "Death is swallowed up in victory."

(Church nursery workers like to claim that this passage describes their experiences with babies: "We shall not all sleep, but we shall all be changed.")

Rapturists would say that this passage describes the secret rapture. But why? There is certainly nothing in this text that cannot be understood perfectly well as happening at the traditional second coming. In fact, that is a better way to understand the text. St. Paul tells us that not all Christians will die, but that "in a moment, in the twinkling of an eye . . . we shall all be changed." The Church has always understood this to be an event that will occur at the second coming of our Lord and Savior.

We read that this will occur "at the last trumpet." Trumpets always proclaim public events in the Old Testament (Exod. 19:10-20; Lev. 25:8; Num. 10:1-10; Jos. 6; Ps. 81:3-5; Isa. 27:13, 58:1; Jer. 4:19-21; Ezek. 33:3-6; Joel 2:1, 15; Amos 3:6; Zeph. 1:14-16; Zech. 9:14). The image of trumpets' boldly announcing Christ's coming certainly does not resemble a secret rapture.

Further, this is not just any trumpet. This is the "last" trumpet. "The dead will be raised imperishable, and we shall be changed" at the end of time. The rapturist tries to place this last trumpet 1,007 years before the second coming! But the "last" trumpet will not occur seven or 1,007 years before the end. It seems too evident to require pointing out, but the "last" trumpet will sound *last*.

A few verses later, we see further evidence that these are the final events being described. "When the perishable puts on the imperishable, and the mortal puts on immortality, then shall come to pass the saying that is written: 'Death is swallowed up in victory.' " At the time of this trumpet and resurrection, death will be destroyed. Yet St. Paul has already mentioned that "the last enemy to be destroyed is death" (1 Cor. 15:26). That would place these events at the final eschaton. Yet rapturists still foresee the battle of Armageddon and the battle with Gog and Magog as transpiring after this passage. That would mean death had really not yet been "swallowed up in victory."

Rapturists claim that these verses speak of the secret rapture before the Great Tribulation and the Millennium. But they believe that during this time, people will continue to be born, to live, and to die. That, quite simply, does not fit this passage. When death is destroyed and we are all raised, all tombs will be forever empty, just as that one tomb outside Jerusalem was empty two thousand years ago. The bodies will be gone.

The scriptural evidence points much more convincingly to the Church's historical teaching. Christ will come back one more time. At that time, all mankind will be resurrected, will be judged, and will enter into eternity. It is a simpler system; it is what the early Church believed; it is what the Bible teaches.

Our glorious bodies: Philippians 3:20-21

Our commonwealth is in Heaven, and from it we await a Savior, the Lord Jesus Christ, who will change our lowly body to be like His glorious body.

These verses promise that our bodies will be changed "to be like His glorious body."

When Jesus' body was resurrected, the old body was subsumed into that resurrected body. There was no longer any body on earth to decompose. When we have a resurrected body, our old bodies will not be in graves any longer. This will happen at the final eschaton, and the caskets will all be empty.

There is nothing to indicate that this is not at the second advent of Christ — the historical understanding of the Church. Only a case of deceptive double vision would necessitate the insertion of a secret rapture. There is no textual reason to insert an intermediary event before the second coming.

Appearing with Christ: Colossians 3:4

When Christ who is our life appears, then you also will appear with Him in glory.

The most straightforward understanding of this verse avoids any double vision. Christ will gloriously return to earth to close the curtain on history. When He does come, it will be in glory and power.

Rapture

This glorious coming does not match the secret rapture that is sometimes read into this verse. There is certainly nothing in the context of this verse that suggests a secret rapture before Christ's glorious return.

Parousia in the clouds: 1 Thessalonians 4:13-5:3

This is a favorite passage of the rapturists. They seem quite certain that this passage clearly teaches their version of the future. But does it?

> But we would not have you ignorant, brethren, concerning those who are asleep, that you may not grieve as others do who have no hope. For since we believe that Jesus died and rose again, even so, through Jesus, God will bring with Him those who have fallen asleep. For this we declare to you by the word of the Lord, that we who are alive, who are left until the coming of the Lord, shall not precede those who have fallen asleep. For the Lord Himself will descend from Heaven with a cry of command, with the archangel's call, and with the sound of the trumpet of God. And the dead in Christ will rise first; then we who are alive, who are left, shall be caught up together with them in the clouds to meet the Lord in the air; and so we shall always be with the Lord. . . . The day of the Lord will come like a thief in the night. . . . Sudden destruction will come upon them as travail comes upon a woman with child, and there will be no escape.

St. Paul wrote to the Thessalonian Christians because they were worried about those who died before Christ's return. Many in the ancient world believed that a person simply ceased to exist upon death, as do many modern unbelievers. There seems to have been a rumor in Thessalonica that the dead Christians had lost out on any chance of a physical resurrection. St. Paul assures them that it was not so. In fact, "the dead in Christ will rise first" to meet

Christ, and those still alive at the second coming will immediately follow them. But all will meet Christ at that time.

Rapturists make a point of the fact that we will "meet the Lord in the air" — the Lord who has come "in the clouds." They infer from this that Christ will not actually touch down on *terra firma* and that we will go back to Heaven with Christ for the duration of a seven-year Great Tribulation. If so many people did not accept this explanation, I would dismiss it immediately as silly.

The word St. Paul uses for meeting the Lord "in the air" is *aer*, the Greek word for *atmosphere*. This same word is used to describe Satan as "the prince of the power of the air" (Eph. 2:2). Yet no one would claim that, because of this word, Satan has no influence over people who keep their feet firmly planted on earth. A consistent rapturist reading of this word here would mean that only astronauts, balloonists, pilots, and airplane passengers are influenced by Satan's power.

No, when Christ returns to the earth's atmosphere, He has returned to *earth*. Read the verses again! We will meet Christ, but it will be at His second coming to earth. Any other use of the language stretches credibility.

Rapturists bolster their argument by pointing to the description of Jesus' coming "in the clouds." But this does not mean that Christ cannot return on a clear, cloudless day. Elsewhere, even rapturists do not claim that Jesus must be seated upon a stallion when He returns (Apoc. 19:11). Certain symbols appear in Scripture repeatedly. Clouds indicate that Christ will be coming again in glory as Judge. His Suffering Servant (cf. Isa. 53) days are over, and He is now victorious over His enemies (GR6).

Rapturists, however, do not want to lose this passage for their cause. They sometimes point out that the word Paul uses for *coming* in verse 15 is the Greek word *parousia*. During my childhood, rapturists were taught that this word always refers to the rapture. Even today rapturists still talk of the *parousia* when referring to the rapture. We were taught that two other Greek words in the Bible, *epiphaneia* ("appearing") and *apokalupsis* ("revelation") refer exclusively to the second advent of Christ. If this were true, it would be a clear indication of which passages refer to the secret rapture and which refer to the second coming.

Unfortunately for rapturists, however, their own Bible scholars have disproved this assertion. These three Greek words are used interchangeably. This leaves each reader to pick and choose which passages refer to the rapture and which refer to the second coming, based on his own subjective reading. This should be a clue to all of us that perhaps the entire system is a fabrication with no basis in the Bible whatsoever.

There is just no good reason to insert a secret rapture into this passage — unless you come to the text with pre-existing double vision. Look at the passage itself. The coming of Christ is anything but secret and silent. Christ will come with "a *cry of command*, with the archangel's *call*, and with the sound of the *trumpet* of God." These are descriptions of loud, public events.

Jesus is not trying to be discreet or secretive in His coming. This passage reflects the Olivet Discourse, when Jesus predicted His coming would be "as the lightning comes from the east and shines as far as the west" (Matt. 24:27). Jesus Himself prophesied that everyone would immediately be aware of His coming. He was specifically contrasting His coming with the false Messiahs who would appear on the scene discreetly. Christ will not be discreet. Yet the rapturist claims that at this point, the rest of the world will not know what happened. The "cry of command," "the archangel's call," and "the trumpet of God" make this impossible.

The phrase "the Lord will come like a thief in the night," must be understood in this context of commands, calls, and trumpets (5:2). In addition, the next verse makes it clear that St. Paul is not speaking of the stealth of the thief, but the unanticipated suddenness with which thieves strike. He calls it "sudden destruction"

(5:3). Notice the destruction comes suddenly on the *unbelievers*. This is the last judgment.

A further problem for rapturists appears when we examine the assumed time line of the passage. St. Paul clearly states that immediately after this event, eternity begins. He writes, "and so we shall always be with the Lord." That is precisely the time line taught by the Church throughout her history. Yet rapturists teach that this coming (the rapture) will be followed by the seven-year Great Tribulation and then a thousand-year earthly Kingdom. Why does St. Paul not at least allude to these events?

But, rapturists respond, the details in this passage are different from those we encounter elsewhere in the New Testament, suggesting two entirely different events. But this is just a symptom of the preconceived conclusions, the deceptive double vision, that they bring to the passage.

Rapturists usually understand that this is a very bad method for handling Scripture. For example, the Bible talks about the Passion of the Lord on several occasions, each time giving us different details about one historical event. But they'd never interpret this to mean that there was more than one Passion. In like manner, various passages provide different details about the second advent. But this doesn't mean they should be sorted into two piles — those about a rapture and those about the second coming. All the passages speak of *one and only one* more advent of Christ.

In this passage, St. Paul related a few new details about the second coming to encourage the Thessalonian church. Since he had founded the church in that city, he had already taught them the basics of the Faith, including the blessed hope of Christ's coming. In this epistle, he clarifies something of which they already had some knowledge.

If there were two stages to the second advent, we would be able to find one passage that speaks of them both together, teaching us in one place of the differences. That we are not able to do so is a

Rapture

terrible handicap to rapturists. It is evidence of their deceptive double vision. Of course, we have not been able to find a passage that unequivocally teaches about a secret rapture at all, much less a passage that speaks of it side-by-side with the second coming.

Since none of these passages contains details inconsistent with the second advent, why not simply accept the simplest, most consistent understanding? There is only one remaining coming of the Lord, and the Bible uses three Greek words interchangeably to describe that coming. It will occur at the end of history, just before the final judgment and eternity.

Antichrist in the Temple: 2 Thessalonians 2:1-10

Here St. Paul is again writing to the Thessalonians, probably shortly before the Jewish-Roman War began in 67 A.D. For this reason, some have tried to understand this passage as being fulfilled in the coming in judgment that we described surrounding the events of 70 A.D. But the passage mentions the "assembling" of Christians to meet Christ. This will occur at the second advent, so the only adequate understanding of this passage is that it speaks of the second advent. In addition, the Church has universally understood this passage as still future even after the destruction of the Temple (CCC, pars. 673-677).

> Concerning the coming of our Lord Jesus Christ and our assembling to meet Him, we beg you, brethren, not to be quickly shaken in mind . . . by letter purporting to be from us, to the effect that the day of the Lord has come. . . . That day will not come, unless the rebellion comes first, and the man of lawlessness is revealed, the son of perdition, who opposes and exalts himself against every so-called god or object of worship, so that he takes his seat in the Temple of God, proclaiming himself to be God. . . . For the mystery of lawlessness is already at work; only he who now restrains it

will do so until he is out of the way. And then the lawless one will be revealed, and the Lord Jesus will slay him with the breath of His mouth and destroy him by His appearing and His coming. The coming of the lawless one by the activity of Satan will be with all power and with pretended signs and wonders, and with all wicked deception for those who are to perish, because they refused to love the truth and so be saved.

This paragraph says a lot in a few sentences. We will examine it one piece at a time.

The MIA rapture

Rapturists agree that this passage focuses on the events leading up to Christ's second advent. They believe the antichrist will appear after the rapture. When Christ comes, He "will slay [the antichrist] with the breath of His mouth." Early Christians associated this statement with the sword that comes out of Christ's mouth in The Apocalypse (COA). The "breath" and the "sword" both signify the truth of the gospel. The power of Christ is in the truth that the Word proclaims. Truth will always win the victory, particularly at the final eschaton.

We do disagree over who is on earth when these events take place. Rapturists claim that Christians have been secretly raptured at the very start of the passage — three and a half years before the Temple worship is corrupted, and a full seven years before Christ returns to "destroy [the man of sin] by His appearing."

Notice deceptive double vision at work. Rapturists place the one event (the rapture) at the very start and apply all the rest of the passage to the second advent. Yet if that is true, why does not St. Paul make it clear that his readers would not be present to see this antichrist "proclaiming himself to be God"? He is writing to encourage a group of Christians who are afraid they had been "left behind"! Why does he not explicitly speak of the "blessed hope of the rapture" to comfort the worried Thessalonians? Nowhere in this passage is there even a mention of the rapture. This would certainly have been more reassuring than a description of events that would transpire after they were gone! In this passage, the rapture is missing in action.

The reason St. Paul does not mention the rapture as occurring before the appearance of the antichrist and before the second coming is simple: it never entered into his mind that anyone would believe Christ would rapture His Church before the final eschaton. The passage assumes that the Church will be around to witness the man of lawlessness revealed. That will be during the final confrontation between good and evil. In The Apocalypse, that is referred to as the battle with Gog and Magog. Christians will *participate* in that confrontation because there will be no secret rapture before it. Our comfort rests in Him who will emerge from that confrontation as the Victor. *That* is the reassurance St. Paul offers, not the promise of escape from the Great Tribulation.

Restraint of the antichrist

The passage also describes a "restraining" force that prevents the antichrist's power from taking full effect right now. Various alternative interpretations have been proposed. Rapturists claim the restraining force is the Holy Spirit within the Church. Tertullian, Cyril of Jerusalem, Jerome and Augustine all understood the restrainer as the rule of law as enforced by the state (*APO*, 32; *CAT*, XVII:12; *EPJ*; *COG*, XX:19).

Most important, we need to notice that this restraining force is active at the same time that Satan is "bound" in The Apocalypse. We are getting a little ahead of ourselves, but the restraint is taken out of the way at the same time that Satan is "loosed" just before the final battle with Gog and Magog (Apoc. 20:1-7). This does not happen twice, as rapturists assert, but once.

The antichrist in the Temple

"Wait a minute," rapturists might interject. "You are ignoring that St. Paul teaches here that the final antichrist will set himself up in the Temple: 'The son of perdition . . . takes his seat in the Temple of God, proclaiming himself to be God.' "

Because this passage predicts an attack on the Temple, in which the antichrist forcibly subverts its worship of the true God, rapturists believe that the Jerusalem Temple must be rebuilt before the antichrist can be revealed. How can the man of sin, the antichrist, proclaim something from a Temple that has not been rebuilt?

But unfortunately for rapturists, this is a poor proof text for their beliefs. The Greek word for *temple* in this verse is *naos*. Although *naos* is sometimes used to designate the physical Temple of the Jews in Jerusalem, it is used in the New Testament to designate other temples. But even more to the point, St. Paul, the author of 2 Thessalonians, *never once* uses this Greek word to designate the Jerusalem Temple of the Jews — always preferring to use the more common New Testament word for Temple, *hieron* (1 Cor. 9:13). Whenever St. Paul uses the word *naos*, he is referring to New Covenant temples. These include either the Church or the individual Christian, both of which are New Covenant temples indwelt by the Holy Spirit (1 Cor. 3:16-17, 6:19; 2 Cor. 6:16; Eph. 2:21).

St. Paul understood the word *temple* to have different senses (Appendix Five discusses some of them), but he always uses the word *naos* in a New Covenant context (GR3).

St. Paul was not alone in this understanding of the New Testament Church as the new Temple. The Fathers of the Church adopted his perspective. We encounter this in the Epistle of Barnabas (Appendix One). Clement of Alexandria also refers to the Church as the Temple of God (*STO*, VI, 14:114).

This makes eminent sense. St. Paul, along with all first-century Christians, believed that Christ had predicted the destruction of the Jerusalem Temple within their generation. But they never believed that this destruction would leave the world without any Temple. The new Temple was God's spiritual Temple, the Church, for which Paul always used *naos*.

So if not in the rebuilt Jerusalem Temple, where will the man of lawlessness set himself up "to be God"? Although it may be difficult to ascertain in advance, as is true of most biblical prophecy, it will likely be very evident at the time. The crucial element is that he will claim to be God. This goes even further than what Antiochus Epiphanes did when he defiled God's Old Covenant Temple with sacrifices to Zeus (Dan. 8:24; 11:36-38). It goes beyond what Pompey did when he defiled the inner Temple with his visit. It goes beyond what the Romans did in 70 A.D. when they introduced pagan worship in the Temple. It is reminiscent of Caligula's intention of being worshiped within the old Temple in 40 A.D., although he died before he could implement his plan. Each of these events points to the final antichrist (GR3).

A clue to our understanding of the final antichrist is his title, the "son of perdition." In His prayer for the infant Church, Jesus gives this very title to Judas Iscariot (John 17:12). Does this mean that St. Paul believed the antichrist would be someone who had been privileged to know the entire truth about Christ and had purposefully rejected it? Or perhaps, like Judas, the man of perdition would attempt to bring in the fullness of God's Kingdom through his own machinations. Perhaps the antichrist will thrust upon the world a hope for a secular Millennium, as was attempted in the century just past. We do not know for sure, but it can make for interesting discussion (CCC, pars. 675-677).

My belief is that the man of sin will somehow try to insert himself or his symbols into the worship of the Church, the new Temple. Perhaps it will even involve the Mass in some way. The word *naos* can be translated as "sanctuary," which is a place within every Catholic Church in the world. Will the final antichrist somehow use these sanctuaries to proclaim "himself to be God"? Perhaps. This would fit in with his being called a "son of perdition," a "Judas-priest" perhaps.

We can be certain, however, that even though the antichrist might be a priest, he cannot possibly be the Pope. In Matthew's Gospel, Peter and his successors are promised that "the gates of Hades" will not prevail against Christ's Church (16:18). This includes an assurance that, although the Pope may not be the best leader possible, he will never *teach error*. Since proclaiming "himself to be God" would certainly qualify as error, we can be sure the Pope cannot be the antichrist.

Some of what this passage means will never be known for certain until it happens. But of one thing we can be certain even now: this passage does not teach a two-stage coming, nor the necessity of a rebuilt Jerusalem Temple. It does teach that Christians will still be here on earth when the battle with the final antichrist rages.

Our blessed hope: Titus 2:11-13

Many rapturists nonetheless refer to the rapture as their "blessed hope." They find this language in St. Paul's epistle to Titus:

> For the grace of God has appeared for the salvation of all men, training us to renounce irreligion and worldly passions, and to live sober, upright, and godly lives in this world, awaiting our *blessed hope*, the appearing of the glory of our great God and Savior Jesus Christ.

Rapturists believe that the "blessed hope" refers to the secret, imminent rapture. (The Greek word here is not *parousia*, but *epiphaneia* ["appearing."]) But the passage speaks of glory, and what is glorious about secretly stealing away your followers and shuffling them off to safety while your enemy runs rampant for seven more years?

No, when Christ comes in glory, it will be in the glory of "our great God." The entire world will see Him, as we recognize lightning that blazes across the sky. The entire world will immediately know Him as the one the antichrist has led them to reject. The entire world will promptly be judged by Him. We already know these facts from other passages. The idea of a secret rapture does not fit this passage at all. Unless we see with double vision, this passage pictures a *victorious* return of the King as Judge at the final eschaton.

Catholics are well aware that we have the real presence of Christ even now, in the Eucharist. But His Real Presence with us now is veiled, requiring the eyes of faith to see Him. The "blessed hope" points our hearts to the moment when we will see Christ unveiled, as He is in all His glory and power (CCC, par. 1404).

A CORRECTIVE PRESCRIPTION
FOR DOUBLE VISION

In Daniel, the rapturists lost their future seven-year Great Tribulation. In the Olivet Discourse, they lost their signs for the generation of the fig tree, as well as their "left behind" language. In the epistles, the lack of biblical support for their system continued.

We will soon enter The Apocalypse, in which there is such tremendous interest today and about which there is so much sensationalistic speculation. But before we do, there are two epistles that will help us to "sober up" from any double-vision hangover we may still have from the rapturist view of the last few epistles.

Galatians

St. Paul wrote his epistle to the Galatians to explain the relationship of the Christian Church to the Old Covenant Law. On the one side stands the Church with her freedom in Christ and the gift of the Holy Spirit. On the other is the Law as practiced by the Jewish leaders in Jerusalem.

Galatians was written midway between the Passion and the destruction of Jerusalem. At this point, the Roman Empire viewed the Christian community as a small sect within official Judaism. From the perspective of the civil Roman government, the Jewish religious authorities in Jerusalem had a perfect right to influence beliefs within the Church.

Certain Jews had parlayed this Roman attitude into undue influence within the Galatian church. They claimed that Christians had to continue fulfilling the requirements of the Jewish ceremonial law.

St. Paul writes powerfully and persuasively to convince the Christians that this is not only untrue, but also dangerous to their faith. He reviews the first Church council in Jerusalem and his interactions with the Apostles to prove that the Apostles and bishops had determined that Gentiles did not have to keep the Jewish law to become members of Christ's Church. He develops the theme that the gospel of Jesus Christ is superior to the Law because it is based on the faith of Abraham, which preceded the Law given to Moses.

He then takes the argument a step further by telling a story:

Abraham had two sons, one by a slave and one by a free woman. . . . Now, this is an allegory: these women are two covenants. One is from Mount Sinai . . . Hagar. . . . She corresponds to the present Jerusalem, for she is in slavery with her children. But the Jerusalem above is free, and she is our mother. . . . We, like Isaac, are children of promise. But as at that time he who was born according to the flesh persecuted him who was born according to the Spirit, so it is now. But what does the scripture say? "Cast out the slave and her son; for the son of the slave shall not inherit with the son of the free woman." So, brethren, we are not children of the slave, but of the free woman (4:22-31).

St. Paul reminds the Galatians that Abraham had two sons. The younger son, of Sarah, was the child of faith. The older son, of Hagar, was the child of slavery. Being older, this first son persecuted the second. This situation went on for years until Sarah finally convinced Abraham that it was no longer tolerable. The household of Abraham was not suitable for either son when both were there. St. Paul reminds the Galatians of the solution to this family discord by quoting the passage in Genesis 21: "Cast out the slave and her son; for the son of the slave shall not inherit with the son of the free woman."

Now, here is the truly riveting aspect of this story. St. Paul tells the Galatians that this entire story "is an allegory" of their own situation (GR3). The Church is the child of faith, like the younger son. The Sanhedrin is the child of bondage, like the older son. The Sanhedrin (the earthly Jerusalem) is persecuting the Church (the heavenly Jerusalem). This situation would only worsen until it culminated in the Great Tribulation of Nero.

Like these two sons of Abraham, earthly and heavenly Jerusalem coexisted for quite some time, about forty years. But the situation could not go on forever.

The only solution was to cast out the son of bondage. This is precisely what Jesus had predicted in the Olivet Discourse. He had warned the Jewish leaders that their rejection of the Truth would be the cause of their destruction. But He had also implied that the two children of God, Old Covenant and New Covenant, would coexist for some time, a "generation" (Matt. 24:34). Before the end of that generation, about forty years, the earthly Jerusalem would be destroyed.

After the older son was "cast out," the younger son of faith would be free to grow. Only then could the younger brother of faith, the Church, develop unimpeded by persecution and confusion. St. Irenaeus understood this well: "The law originated with Moses, [and] it terminated with John as a necessary consequence.

Christ had come to fulfill it. . . . Therefore Jerusalem . . . must have an end of legislation when the new covenant was revealed" (AG, IV:4).

Confusion over loyalties could be a serious problem in the early Church. This was the point of St. Bede in his comments on Mark 13:2: "It was ordered by divine power that after that the grace of the faith of the Gospel was made known through the world, the Temple itself with its ceremonies should be taken away; lest perchance someone weak in the faith, if he saw that these things which had been instituted by God still remained, might by degrees drop from the sincerity of the faith, which is in Christ Jesus" (cited in GCC).

If we keep this allegory from the life of Abraham in mind when we examine the conflict between the Old and New Covenants in the first century, we will understand the entire New Testament more clearly. For example, The Apocalypse is primarily a prophecy that describes the complex process of casting out the Old Covenant system. Because it illustrates how God keeps His promises to His children, we can trust its promise of the second advent. But much of The Apocalypse does not predict the future to us in the twenty-first century, but tells of the past. We must remember, of course, that even these past events may themselves be a foretaste of the future, just as Sarah and Hagar were a foretaste of the events surrounding 70 A.D. (GR3).

This theme runs throughout the Bible. We find another example in the reign of King David, who was a type of Christ. He was anointed by Samuel, just as Jesus was baptized by John the Baptizer. David was rejected by the leadership of Israel, just as Jesus was. Eventually, the faithful remnant of Abraham's seed, Judah, acclaimed David as their king after the death of King Saul. So, too, the believing remnant of Old Israel accepted Christ as their Redeemer King after the King's death on the Cross. There was a period of warfare between those who accepted King David's authority and those who did not. Eventually, King David's followers were victorious over those who rejected him, and David sat upon the throne. Just so, Old Covenant Israel made war upon the New Covenant followers of King Jesus. Eventually, however, the followers of King Jesus were victorious, and the King was publicly recognized as seated on the throne of David in the New (spiritual) Jerusalem.

Please keep in mind that these parallels are not simply my idea. Nor is it just the idea of some other theologian. St. Paul wrote under divine inspiration when he outlined this conflict between biblical Judaism and Christianity in Galatians. Jesus predicted the "casting out" in the Olivet Discourse. The first nineteen chapters of The Apocalypse relate the details of the conflict between these two children of God, the Old versus the New. We will see the persecution, and we will see the casting out of the older brother in vivid detail.

Hebrews

In the epistle to the Hebrews, the author develops some of the same themes we found in Galatians and will find foundational to The Apocalypse, especially this: Christ and His New Covenant are better than physical Jerusalem and its Old Covenant.

Hebrews was probably written toward the beginning of the Great Tribulation, before the Roman Empire turned its fury on Jerusalem. Hebrews gives evidence, as does The Apocalypse, that the religious leaders of Jerusalem instigated and participated in the Christian persecutions.

As an aside, rapturists sometimes claim that Hebrews criticizes Catholic belief in the sacrifice of the Mass. Out of the other side of their mouths, they try to claim that belief in the Mass as an unbloody sacrifice did not appear in the Church until as late as the Middle Ages. Of course, they cannot have it both ways! How could the author of Hebrews be criticizing the sacrifice of the Mass if it was not believed to be a sacrifice yet? But more to the point,

Hebrews has the Mosaic sacrifices, not the Mass, in view when it refers to sacrifices. The Jerusalem Temple was still operational, performing the endless series of daily animal sacrifices.

It is interesting that in Hebrews 8:13, written just before the destruction of Jerusalem's Temple, we find this statement: "In speaking of a new covenant, He [the Lord] treats the first [covenant] as obsolete. And what is becoming obsolete and growing old is ready to vanish away." Although this verse is not usually treated as a prophecy, that is exactly what it is! The author of Hebrews is looking for the destruction of the Old Covenant system as Jesus had foretold it in the Olivet Discourse. When we get to The Apocalypse, we must keep in mind that its message is not unique. We saw it predicted in Daniel. We saw it predicted by Jesus. We saw it in Galatians. It keeps popping up throughout the Scriptures. It was even a common topic when St. Peter and St. Paul preached in Rome. Yet we have somehow forgotten this pivotal event in modern theology. Keeping it in mind will help us recognize the double vision of the rapturist.

Hebrews also makes it clear that there is a heavenly Jerusalem, of which the earthly Jerusalem is only a type or precursor: "Without the shedding of blood there is no forgiveness of sins. Thus it was necessary for the copies of the heavenly things to be purified with these rites [animal sacrifices], but the heavenly things themselves with better sacrifices than these [Christ's Sacrifice]. For Christ has entered, not into a sanctuary made with hands, a copy of the true one, but into Heaven itself, now to appear in the presence of God on our behalf" (Heb. 9:22-24). We will be introduced to the New Jerusalem in The Apocalypse. The tension between the New Jerusalem in Heaven and the Old Jerusalem on earth will be developed in depth there. But this theme is essential to our understanding.

Hebrews 12:22-24 could actually be viewed as a rather good summary of the climax of The Apocalypse. In contrasting the New

Rapture

with the Old Jerusalem, the passage states, "But you have come to Mount Zion and to the city of the living God, the heavenly Jerusalem, and to innumerable angels in festal gathering, and to the assembly of the first-born who are enrolled in Heaven, and to a judge who is God of all, and to the spirits of just men made perfect, and to Jesus, the mediator of a new covenant." Every time we celebrate the Mass, we join our voices to the realm of this heavenly Jerusalem. We get a foretaste of what God has in store for us in eternity. When we examine The Apocalypse, we should remember that this message is not unique to the last book of the Bible.

Chapter Eight

The Apocalypse

The Apocalypse, also known as the Revelation of St. John, or simply Revelation, is perhaps the most misunderstood — and misused — book in the Bible. Certain groups within the early Church so misconstrued its message that the early Eastern churches even questioned the book's canonicity. Wiser heads eventually prevailed, and its canonicity became universally accepted.

From the outset, St. John informs us of his purpose. He hopes to encourage an appropriate Christian response, "patient endurance" to the "tribulation," which they are undergoing (1:9). It will become apparent that an integral part of "patient endurance" is the celebration of the Eucharist. Finally, John will investigate the mysterious nature of the Kingdom that Christ established by His blood during His first advent (1:6, 9).

The rapturist position has already been proven inadequate in every passage we have so far examined, so we could probably skip the entire Apocalypse. But then I am afraid rapturists would cry, "Foul!" They have an elaborate scheme of how this book will one day be fulfilled, a scheme that deserves to be rebutted. It is not within our purpose to attempt an exhaustive commentary of this beautifully crafted book. Instead, we will read it with an eye always focused on its meaning, and whether the rapturist scheme can be reasonably derived from the text.

THE WINKLE WARP

It was an ordinary September day, and the man who commanded the world's most powerful army looked over the great city in silence. Just a few weeks earlier, thousands had died in an attack on it. The burning at the city's heart could be seen from miles away.

The attack on this major center of world trade was the result of the religious fanaticism of a group of zealots in the Middle East, who, according to other adherents of their religion, had hijacked the meaning of their faith. The whole world witnessed the massive destruction visited upon the city that day.

The man who quietly looked over the destruction was the scion of a powerful political family. At this point in history, he was in charge of the only superpower remaining in the West. The man was the oldest son of the one person who might have, maybe even should have, ended the conflict with these extremists years earlier. Instead, the resentment continued to brew for years, and more than a few cheered and celebrated at the destruction.

Who was this man in charge?

Caesar Titus of Rome. And Caesar Vespasian was his father. The city that was overrun was Jerusalem, and the building that burned was Herod's Temple. In The Apocalypse, we will investigate a day that changed the world forever: August 10, 70 A.D.

If you thought we were describing September 11, 2001, do not feel bad. You were caught in the "Winkle Warp." As the story goes, Rip van Winkle fell asleep for twenty years in the Catskill Mountains. When he awoke, an entire generation had died off. He looked for his young daughter, only to find her holding a child of her own. He saw himself leaning against a tree, only to realize it was actually his grown son. Rip van Winkle had experienced a time warp, a "Winkle Warp."

Rapturists experience a Winkle Warp when they read The Apocalypse. They look at the descriptions of events and misplace them by two thousand years. They are still waiting for Daniel's seventieth week, when in fact it encompassed the seven decades of covenantal transition during the first century. The Apocalypse is a series of visions describing this transition, including the Great Tribulation of the Olivet Discourse and the casting out of Hagar explained in Galatians. The bulk of the visions are not primarily about our future, and only a Winkle Warp can make it seem as if they are. True, we must not make the mistake of assuming that the lessons of The Apocalypse do not apply to our daily lives. When we meditate on the evil in our modern world, we need to keep the lesson of The Apocalypse before us. Yet the book must be interpreted within its frame of reference: 68 to 70 A.D. (GR3).

I believe one reason for the rapturists' Winkle Warp is their doctrine of *sola Scriptura*. In Church-history class, they doze off at the end of the Acts of the Apostles and do not wake up until the Great Awakening (the first major Protestant revival in America, in the 1730s). Some pay slight attention to St. Augustine, but otherwise miss all of the Church's development from 65 to 1700 A.D. Their Winkle Warp spans more than one and a half millennia!

In the process of our examination, we will try definitively to answer the question, "Will you be left behind when Jesus returns?" We have already come to a solid conclusion, but there are those who still will withhold their decision until we examine the last book of the Bible. That suits our purposes just fine, as this is the only book of the Bible that promises a special blessing to anyone who reads it: "Blessed is he who reads aloud the words of the prophecy, and blessed are those who hear, and who keep what is written therein; for the time is near" (1:3).

PRELIMINARIES
Authorship, date, and frame of reference

I will interpret The Apocalypse on the premise that the apostle John was its author. This has the weight of long tradition in its favor.

Rapture

As far as the frame of reference, there is substantial agreement among scholars, except rapturists, that St. John intended much of the book to be read as though it were written during the reigns of Nero and Vespasian. The switch between the two dynasties took place in 68 A.D., when Nero committed suicide. This scholarly conclusion is very well accepted for at least a major part of these visions and is the crucial conclusion for our purposes.

I go a step further than most modern scholars in that I believe the 68 A.D. frame of reference was also the actual date of authorship. Therefore I will refer to the author as St. John and to the frame of reference and the date of authorship as 68 A.D.

Although my conclusions on the author and frame of reference of The Apocalypse are very broadly accepted, that is not true as regards the date of authorship. I have discussed thoroughly my reasons for rejecting the more commonly accepted 96 A.D. date in Appendix Four. Whether you read it or not, remember the important point: there is wide scholarly support for the position that 68 A.D. is the frame of reference intended by St. John, regardless of the actual date of authorship.

Milieu of Daniel's final week

Although we have discussed this period, let us review the events that scholars widely agree form the intended backdrop to The Apocalypse. Until 63 A.D., Rome considered Christianity to be a sect within Judaism, a recognized religion within the empire. The Romans had a policy of tolerating indigenous religions. Thus, Christians were free to practice their Faith without state interference.

In July of 64 A.D., that all changed. Nero finally agreed with the Sanhedrin that Christianity was not a part of Judaism. For the first time, Rome started to persecute Christians. Many Christians died, and even more deserted the young Church. The epistle to the Hebrews is evidence of the Church's concern about this trend toward apostasy.

This state-sponsored persecution lasted from July 64 until February 67 A.D. At that point, the empire changed its mind about where the real danger to the empire lay. Jerusalem had revolted in 66 A.D. The Jewish Temple in Jerusalem stopped daily sacrifices for the emperor. This enraged Nero (who may have actually believed his own claims to divinity), and Rome soon mobilized a massive army to defeat the Jews. In turning upon Jerusalem, Rome's attention was diverted from the intense persecution of the Church. The Roman war upon the Jews lasted precisely forty-two months, from February 67 until August 70 A.D.

St. John clearly wanted the reader to understand that his visions were a commentary on events of his time. He says that the visions describe "what *is* and what is to take place hereafter" (1:19).

John also references the prophecy of the Olivet Discourse to reaffirm that his visions are the fulfillment of Jesus' predictions concerning the end of Daniel's final week of covenantal transition. "Behold, He is coming with the clouds, and every eye will see Him, everyone who pierced Him; and all tribes of the earth [better translated as "land"] will wail on account of Him. Even so. Amen" (1:7). St. John obviously believed that Jesus' predictions were occurring within the generation He mentioned. His book supplies us with the details.

One important note concerning translations should be made. The Revised Standard Version uses *earth* for the Greek word *ge*. St. John uses this word profusely throughout his visions. But this Greek word is translated as "land" about two-thirds of the time in the New Testament. That is a better translation much of the time in The Apocalypse as well. The land of *Israel* was the one suffering under these seals, because the Sanhedrin had first rejected their Messiah and then the message of His followers. This word will rear its head again and again in The Apocalypse. Rather than call attention to it each time, as in the quotation above, I will simply translate *ge* as "land" when appropriate.

Rapture

When we read the book as a divine commentary on the events of Daniel's seventieth week, it comes alive. This was an exciting time of covenantal transition. The first nineteen chapters are short, intense glimpses of the events affecting the Church during this period. It is apocalyptic literature to be sure, and so its imagery is vivid (GR 5, 6, 7); but the events that God says "must soon take place" (1:1) did just that! God kept His promise, just as the Messiah did in the predictions of the Olivet Discourse.

Outline and theme

The theme of The Apocalypse is identical to that of Daniel: "The mystery of Christ's Kingdom: proof that Christ is coming again." The only difference is generated by the six hundred years of events that transpire between the two books. While Daniel envisions the time from the re-establishment of the *earthly Jerusalem* Temple to the *first* advent, St. John envisions the time from the establishment of the *New Jerusalem* Temple to the *second* advent.

Here is an outline of the structure of The Apocalypse:

Introduction	Historical setting, God's people persecuted	1:1-3:22
I	Initial vision: mystery of the Messiah's Kingdom revealed	4:1-11:19
II	Three key personalities in the Kingdom's coming	12:1-12:17
III	Initial vision recapitulated: proof that Christ is coming	13:1-21:5
Epilogue	Thematic summary and concluding remarks	21:5-22:21

The roots of this general outline are in the Church's earliest understanding of The Apocalypse. Until the thirteenth century, virtually everyone in the Church believed that the initial vision of the seals (chs. 6-7) and trumpets (chs. 8-9) are recapitulated in the ensuing visions. The visions are linked like the visions of Daniel: they tell the same story from different angles and perspectives, while the time periods of the individual visions overlap. This is perfectly normal in apocalyptic literature and would have been understood by St. John's initial readers — especially since they were familiar with Daniel's outline (GR8).

St. Augustine certainly taught that the visions were not chronologically related, but that they repeatedly reviewed the time span from the first advent to the Last Judgment (GR8). In fact, this view concerning recapitulation of the visions can be traced at least as far back as Victorinus of Pettau (Victorinau), a martyr under Emperor Diocletian in 303 A.D. His is the earliest extant commentary on The Apocalypse. Some have questioned its authorship and integrity, but modern scholarship has put those issues to rest (NCE, XIV, 651).

Victorinus understood the visions as recapitulating the same events from different perspectives to provide emphasis and new information. Referring to the seals, trumpets, and bowls, he writes, "Although the same thing recurs in the phials [bowls], still it is not said as if it occurred twice, but because what is decreed by the Lord to happen shall be once for all; for this cause it is said twice. What, therefore, He said too little in the trumpets, is here found in the phials. We *must not regard the order* of what is said, because frequently the Holy Spirit, when He has traversed even to the end of the last times, returns again to the same times, and fills up what He had before failed to say. *Nor must we look for order in The Apocalypse;* but we must follow the meaning of those things which are prophesied" (COA, VII). In other words, the visions are not chronologically organized (GR8).

The *New Catholic Encyclopedia* states that this original understanding is still the best. "Section 12:1-21:8 covers the same period (as the initial vision), but centering on the role of the Church. . . .

Rapture

Even the description of the heavenly Jerusalem [recapitulates this period] (21:1-22:5), although it offers a transcendent image of the Church" (*NCE*, I).

Recently, however, this original view has been drowned out by the cacophony of rapturist voices trying to understand these visions chronologically. This system of interpretation did not really gain credence until the thirteenth century, winning more notoriety when the Reformers insisted on using this novel interpretation to justify their identification of the Pope with the antichrist. It is difficult at times to believe that, even today, interpretive choices are uncolored by the common rapturist desire to use The Apocalypse to condemn the Catholic Church as the Whore of Babylon.

If you have a good memory, you may have noticed that the theme and outline of St. John's Apocalypse are identical to Daniel's! This is very important. Here is a combined outline of Daniel and The Apocalypse.

Introduction	Historical setting, God's people persecuted	Daniel 1 Apocalypse 1-3
I	Initial vision: mystery of the Messiah's Kingdom revealed	Daniel 2 Apocalypse 4-11
II	Three key personalities in the Kingdom's coming	Daniel 3-6 Apocalypse 12
III	Initial vision recapitulated: proof that Christ is coming	Daniel 7-12 Apocalypse 13-21:5
Epilogue	Thematic summary and concluding remarks	Daniel 13-14 Apocalypse 21-22

St. John consciously borrowed the outline of Daniel as he wrote The Apocalypse. Both books start with God's people standing up for Him, but finding it dangerous to do so. Both then relate the central, initial vision, revealing the mystery of the Messiah's Kingdom. After that, both authors insert events from the lives of important historical people to help the reader understand the initial vision more fully. Both books proceed to recapitulate the initial vision, while providing proof concerning the coming of the Messiah. Finally there is a thematic summary of each book. (In Daniel, this thematic summary is part of the deuterocanonical portion of the book.)

This reliance on Daniel is evident in more than just the outline of The Apocalypse. St. John alludes to or quotes from the Old Testament 518 times in the 404 verses of this book. Almost seventeen percent, or eighty-eight, of these allusions and quotations are from Daniel alone. Since there are twenty-two chapters in The Apocalypse, on average there are four references to Daniel in every chapter.

The similarities go beyond language. Daniel was a man of God suffering under a government that commanded him to disobey his God by eating the food of idols and worshiping the king; the Christians of The Apocalypse were suffering under a government that commanded them to disobey Christ by worshiping the emperor. Daniel's response was worship and prayer, which St. John recommended to the early Church. When both Daniel and the Christians continued to worship and pray to their God, the state used deceit and power to throw them to the lions. In both cases, the faithful response was always prayer.

With all of these similarities, it should not surprise us that the visions of The Apocalypse reflect the visions of Daniel. We will be seeing many of the same events being described. The Apocalypse concentrates on the time during which the Old Covenant passes away and is publicly replaced by the New Covenant. Daniel focuses on the last of his seventy weeks — as will St. John in The Apocalypse. This week encompasses the seven decades of covenantal transition. As in Daniel, The Apocalypse deals with the final eschaton only briefly, at the end of the visions. This is as we would expect.

Rapture

No one should ever try to understand St. John's Revelation without first becoming thoroughly immersed in Daniel. If you ignore Daniel's outline when examining The Apocalypse, you can easily fall into the mistake of placing the visions of The Apocalypse in chronological order. As anyone can attest who has carefully studied under a rapturist, this makes the book absolutely indecipherable! Rather, the visions of The Apocalypse reveal the same events from different perspectives, with different details over slightly different periods — in precisely the same manner as Daniel's visions did.

This outline does not, as far as I can determine, negate the idea that St. John also wrote The Apocalypse to parallel the Liturgy of the Mass. The Eucharist is essential to understanding St. John's visions. When the Church on earth celebrates the Eucharist, it is united to the triumphant New Jerusalem in Heaven. These ideas could certainly be investigated more fully, but that is not the purpose of this book.

Timetable of The Apocalypse

But before delving into St. John's masterpiece, we need a timetable to determine which prophecies are past, which are present, and which are future. For those reading the book in 68 A.D., almost all of The Apocalypse would have been future, but not for us. The same was true of Daniel's prophecy. When he wrote it, it was almost all future, but later readers must take into account the fulfillment of some of his prophecies. We will make this timetable reflect our perspective in the twenty-first century, not that of the first century.

Past events

Introduction	Historical setting	1:1-3:22
I	Initial vision describing the events surrounding 70 A.D.	4:1-11:19

| II | Three key personalities | 12:1-12:17 |
| Early III | Initial vision recapitulated, the strategies and events of 70 A.D. | 13:1-20:2 |

Present events

| Middle III | Millennium | 20:2-20:6 |
| Epilogue | Thematic summary | 21:5-22:21 |

Future events

| Late III | The final eschaton | 20:7-21:4 |

Notice that the timetable overlaps the book outline. Events present to us in the twenty-first century take up only five verses, until St. John returns to the present state of affairs in the thematic summary at the book's end; future events encompass only about one chapter. The vast majority of The Apocalypse is history now. We will refer back to this timetable, but will use the outline for headings.

Rather than proceed exhaustively and meticulously verse by verse, which would entail writing a complete commentary on The Apocalypse, we will look at the overall flow of the book, paying particular attention to how the symbols relate to the events of the Great Tribulation and the Jewish-Roman War. We will examine all the symbols that have become well-known in the rapturist system, but we cannot hope to discuss every single symbol here.

We will keep in mind two questions: Were these prophecies fulfilled adequately in 70 A.D.? Is there anything that necessitates our acceptance of the belief in a future secret rapture, future seven-year Great Tribulation, or future Millennium?

Much of our work will be to illustrate that the events surrounding 70 A.D. really do fulfill the visions of St. John. Then there will be no reason to look to the future, except as these events themselves may foreshadow the future eschaton (GR3).

INTRODUCTION
The historical setting

The first three chapters of The Apocalypse give the historical setting. Immediately, St. John begins using numbers in a symbolic way. *Seven* is the number that symbolizes God's perfect workings in the world (GR2). The speaker in the vision, Christ, is envisioned standing in the midst of "seven golden lampstands . . . and . . . in His right hand He held seven stars. . . . The seven stars are the angels of the seven churches, and the seven lampstands are the seven churches" (1:12-20).

Letters to the seven churches

The next two chapters contain letters to the seven churches in Asia Minor, struggling to stand for God in the midst of evil. For the visions in The Apocalypse describe a battle, with Christ and His truth on one side and Satan and his deceitful use of power on the other. False teachings and carnal practices are always Satan's approach to the Church, whether in the first century or in the twenty-first.

Despite the faithfulness of many Christians, there was apostasy in these churches, which has led some to believe that The Apocalypse was written later than 68 A.D. But that view is wrong. Apostasy came early and often in the Church. In fact, Jesus warned in the Olivet Discourse that false teachers would appear before the judgment of 70 A.D. These letters prove that the heresy promised in the Olivet Discourse did in fact appear before the judgment of the Sanhedrin. The rest of The Apocalypse proves that the Great Tribulation and the Temple's destruction that Jesus predicted appeared as well.

Church One: Ephesus

We learn that the Ephesian Church opposes the Nicolaitans (2:6). We can possibly trace the Nicolaitans to one of the first seven deacons ordained by the Apostles (Acts 6:5). According to Victorinus, they were morally permissive, promising "that whoever [had] committed fornication might receive peace on the eighth day" (COA, II).

Jesus promises to "grant to eat of the tree of life" to the Christian who "conquers" (2:7). We will encounter this tree again at the end of the book. St. John repeatedly uses the literary technique of briefly alluding to a subject and then promptly dropping it. Later, when that subject returns as the central theme of another vision, the reader is familiar with it. This gives unity to visions that otherwise might seem disjointed. We will call this technique anticipation.

Church Two: Smyrna

The Church in Smyrna is under persecution from "those who say that they are Jews and are not, but are a synagogue of Satan" (2:9). This should give us clear notice that the tension between the Jewish leaders and the Christians was in full bloom in Smyrna. Christ warns them that they will have a short but complete time of trial ahead, "ten days" (GR2). This reflects the ten days of trial that Daniel underwent at the beginning of his captivity. After his trial, the king granted him a role in ruling.

Christ ends with a promise of reward after successful endurance: "He who conquers shall not be hurt by the second death" (2:11). It is significant that here, in the middle of trials, this Church is not promised deliverance from trouble. There is no hint of a secret rapture that will spare them the Great Tribulation ahead.

The second death will reappear later in The Apocalypse. We will discuss it then, but even in this brief instance of anticipation, it is clearly a reference to eternal damnation (COA, II).

Church Three: Pergamum

Pergamum's church had succumbed to the evil of the Nicolaitans: eating "food sacrificed to idols and [practicing] immorality"

(2:14). A careful reading of these churches' problems illustrates that in the early Church there were serious heresies that sprang up almost immediately.

The parallel to Daniel's test is interesting. The government ordered Daniel to eat royal food sacrificed to idols. He refused, and God rewarded Daniel and his three friends for their faithfulness to His Law. Christ promises the same if Pergamum repents. If not, Christ states that He "will come to [them] soon and war against them with the sword of my mouth" (2:16). This anticipates the sword that later represents the Truth of the gospel.

Church Four: Thyatira

The Church of Thyatira had in their midst a woman whom Christ calls "Jezebel." She was "teaching and beguiling my servants to practice immorality" (2:20). This may have been linked to one of the Gnostic cults, because they had secret teachings, "what some call the deep things of Satan" (2:24). The Gnostics can be linked to Simon Magus, whom we read of in Acts. He said, "I am the Word of God, I am the Comforter, I am Almighty, I am all there is of God" (GHF).

Christ assures Jezebel of the coming of His judgment if she does not repent. The result of this judgment "anticipates" one of the major themes of The Apocalypse: "And all the churches shall *know that I am* He who searches mind and heart" (2:23). The judgment of Christ vindicates His claims to godly power. It also serves as an assurance that He will judge everyone in the final eschaton, as He has predicted. Of course, those who die before the final eschaton will witness the coming of Christ upon their death for their own particular judgment.

Church Five: Sardis

The Church of Sardis is bluntly urged to awaken. Anyone who responds, Christ "will not blot his name out of the book of life"

(3:5). Many rapturists also are strong proponents of eternal security. They do not believe that anyone can be blotted out, even if they stay asleep throughout Christ's warnings. The letter to Sardis ought to give them pause.

St. John also anticipates a common future use of *coming*. As we saw in Daniel and the Olivet Discourse, God comes in judgment at times other than just the second advent. Christ threatens to "*come* like a thief, and you will not know at what hour I will *come* upon you" (3:3). Since this is spoken only to those who refuse to awaken, it is obviously not a reference to the final eschaton. Christ possesses the ability to judge people because He is the Lion who has conquered like a Lamb.

Church Six: Philadelphia

Christ praises the Philadelphian Christians for their faithfulness. He refers again to "the synagogue of Satan." Christ promises to make these persecutors of His Church "learn that I have loved you" (3:9). This phrase could have easily been spoken by Abraham to Sarah when they discussed Hagar! This anticipates one of the major themes of The Apocalypse. Christ wants it to be clear to all the world that from this point forward, He loves His Church as His chosen people. As we noted in Galatians and Hebrews, one major reason the Temple had to be destroyed was to clear up latent confusion over where one met God, in the Jerusalem Temple or in the Church.

To those who "conquer" by remaining faithful to Christ, He promises to "write on him the name of my God, and the name of the city of my God, the new Jerusalem which comes down from my God out of Heaven, and my own new name" (3:12).

He has already anticipated the Jewish persecution of the Church with two references to "the synagogue of Satan." That persecution will take center stage very soon in the book. He also has anticipated eternal damnation in the "second death" and eternal life in the "book of life." Now he anticipates the "New Jerusalem," which we will not see in its full manifestation until the very end of the visions. St. John is preparing us by mentioning it here. Finally, he alludes to the writing of "the name of my God" on the conqueror. This is preparing us for the mark of God that will take center stage soon, in juxtaposition to the famous mark of the Beast.

Church Seven: Laodicea

Christ accuses the last Church, Laodicea, of complacency stemming from their material wealth. He warns them that "those whom I love, I reprove and chasten" (3:19). This is a sobering thought, especially since the rest of the book will discuss tribulation. Notice there is not a hint of a secret rapture to save them from hardship. God shows us His love through chastening.

Christ continues, "Behold, I stand at the door and knock; if anyone hears my voice and opens the door, I will come in to him and eat with him, and he with me" (3:20). Protestants often use this verse to invite a prospect to be "born again." But notice the context. Christ is inviting *Christians*, not unbelievers, to eat with Him. This is an invitation to share in the Eucharist. At the Eucharist, Christians are invited to open their lives to Christ's Kingdom and "eat with Him." Christ always keeps His promise: "I will come in to him" (cf. John 6). As we will see, even this mention of the Mass is an anticipation of a major theme of this book.

Summary of the seven letters

Yes, these churches were struggling against complacency, materialism, immorality, heresy, and persecution — just like any age. We encounter the struggle against apostasy and error in almost all of the epistles. These were real churches, with real people struggling against real hardships to be the kind of Christians Christ was calling them to be. The solution to these problems is the sacraments, particularly the Eucharist. It will become crystal clear in later visions that this is where Christ strengthens us through His supernatural presence. That is why St. John ended his letters with an invitation to commune with his Lord.

SECTION I: THE INITIAL VISION

In Chapters 4 through 11, we encounter St. John's vision of the scroll. All other visions recapitulate this first one. It comes in two parts: the seven seals of a scroll and the seven trumpets contained in the last seal. The seals view the judgments from the perspective of the King (Christ), and the trumpets recapitulate these judgments from the perspective of the judged. (This uses the same plan of visions as Daniel did. The statue vision looked at the four kingdoms to come through the monarch's eyes, and the beast vision saw these empires through the eyes of the conquered peoples.)

Perhaps we should mention that rapturists make a rather large issue out of the fact that there is no mention of the Church in Chapters 4 through 18. They take this as a signal that the Church is not present on earth because all the born-again Christians have been secretly raptured away from the Great Tribulation.

This holds no water. The saints — those who make up the Church — are mentioned eleven times in these chapters, on average almost once every chapter. These saints are *on earth*. If they had been "raptured" away, it would have been a very secret rapture indeed — so secret that St. John never even mentions it!

We must not lose sight of the major message, however. Yes, the vision is punctuated with the seven seals and seven trumpets. But the central element is the scroll. What does the scroll contain? No one knows until it is opened, and at first it seems as if no one will be able to reveal it.

The throne room

The visions begin with St. John on earth, and a door to Heaven opens. A voice invites him to enter Heaven and says, "I

will show you what must take place after this" (4:1). This estab-
lishes the book's historical setting. The letters to the churches
have been read. The events to be examined immediately follow
the time of these churches: the first century.

Once in Heaven, St. John encounters "a throne [that] stood in
Heaven, with one seated on the throne" (4:2). Twenty-four elders
and four beasts worship God there. The twenty-four elders hearken back to the twenty-four sets of twenty-four priests that we find
in 1 Chronicles 24. The Temple of the Old Covenant had twenty-
four priests on duty at any given time, and they would take their
turns every twenty-four days. These twenty-four elders in The
Apocalypse probably represent the entire priesthood of the New
Covenant (GR3). They might also represent the twelve Apostles
and twelve patriarchs (GR4).

Victorinus took the "jasper and carnelian" appearance of God
to symbolize judgment by flood (clear jasper) and judgment by fire
(reddish carnelian). The rainbow symbolizes the eternal promise
of God never to judge by water again (Gen. 9:11). The "sea of
glass" reminds us that we can approach this fearsome, judging God
only through the grace bestowed at Baptism (COA, IV).

The four living creatures are probably cherubim, as were the
four living creatures in Ezekiel's vision. "They never cease to sing,
'Holy, holy, holy is the Lord God Almighty, who was and is and is
to come!' " (4:8).

This is the "holy, holy, holy" to which we join our voices during every Mass. As other authors have noted, the Liturgy of the
Church is never far from St. John's mind as he records his visions.
The Apocalypse will circle back again to the praise that Heaven is
continually pouring upon God: He is worthy because of who He is
and what He has done. The twenty-four elders join in the praise of
God: "Worthy art Thou, our Lord and God, to receive glory and
honor and power, for Thou didst create all things, and by Thy will
they existed and were created" (4:11).

The mysterious scroll

The scroll that "no one in Heaven or on earth or under the earth was able to open" (5:3) is the central, unifying element of the entire first vision, which, encompassing seven chapters, is the longest single segment of The Apocalypse. Yet rapturists usually ignore the scroll and its significance. They spend time on other details, such as the locust, the scorpions, the wormwood, and the falling stars, but not on the scroll. This is a mistake. The rest of this vision entails the opening of the seven seals that hide the contents of this scroll. The seven seals encompass also the seven trumpets, the three woes, and the seven thunders.

Origen wrote that the scroll was the Old Testament. In this he was following Victorinus's commentary on The Apocalypse. I agree with Origen. But we must always keep in mind that the entire Old Testament points to Christ and His Kingdom, whose true nature remains shrouded in mystery until the seals are broken. What was hidden in the Old Testament was revealed in the Messiah.

Even though the scene is in God's throne room, the only one able to break the seals on the scroll is "the Lion of the tribe of Judah, the Root of David" (5:5). Why? Because He "has conquered." When He opens the scroll, Heaven "sang a new song, saying, 'Worthy art Thou to take the scroll and to open its seals, for Thou wast slain and by Thy blood didst ransom men for God from every tribe and tongue and people and nation, and hast made them a kingdom and priests to our God, and they shall reign on earth" (5:9-10).

We must take a moment to understand this song, because it reveals the scroll's message. Christ is able to open and reveal the contents of the hidden message in the scroll because of His Passion. That sacrifice established a Kingdom with priests, an ecclesiastical Kingdom containing people — both Jew and Gentile — of every nation. These people will unite and reign on earth in a spiritual, ecclesiastical Kingdom, rather than a physical, political one.

Rapture

The hidden message of the scroll reveals the true nature of the Messiah's Kingdom.

To us in the twenty-first century, this may not seem like exciting news. To those in the first century, it was earth-shaking. No longer was Jew-versus-Gentile the important distinction. Now it is ransomed-versus-unbelieving. The Kingdom was established, but not in the manner the Sanhedrin had expected. This was a priestly Kingdom, the Church.

That is the message of the scroll. It is the hidden message of the Old Testament. The message is revealed to the entire world *when the seals of this scroll are opened*. Although the chosen of God understood this before 70 A.D., the world did not. The seals relate the details of the destruction of the Temple. That event signaled to the world that Christ had delivered on His promise of judgment in the Olivet Discourse. Until that event, many might have thought of Jesus as just an interesting Jewish boy. No longer!

The scroll's message was hidden in the Old Testament. It was conceived on Calvary. It was publicly proclaimed at Pentecost. It was finally affirmed and vindicated when the seals were opened and the Temple was judged. There is now a new people of God, made up of Jew *and* Gentile. God's *ekklesia* (Church) is not limited to one ethnic group or one geographical location. All peoples will come to the one table of this Kingdom and eat together. Further, the leader of this New Covenant is not just an inspiring human, but someone who can reach from beyond the grave to judge His enemies, because He has conquered death.

That is the central message of this vision. Do not lose sight of it as the seals, the trumpets, the woes, and the thunders unfold. Christ and His Church are being vindicated in the judgment on the Sanhedrin. His Church is being publicly proclaimed as God's New Covenant People.

St. John will return to this mystery at the very end of this vision. He will make explicit what we have just drawn out of

Heaven's song. We will discuss the mystery of the Kingdom further at that point, but it helps to know ahead of time that this is the message of the scroll and its seal. Christ is being publicly vindicated for the victory already won when He "wast slain."

The Lion and the Lamb

St. John looks for the Lion that has conquered, but he actually sees "a Lamb standing, as though it had been slain, with seven horns and with seven eyes" (5:6). Again the symbolism of numbers in The Apocalypse becomes apparent (GR2). No one I know of has in his home an image of Christ as a seven-eyed, seven-horned lamb.

The glory of the Lion is that He gave Himself as a Lamb for the redemption of the world. He "has conquered so that He can open the scroll and its seven seals" (5:5). This self-sacrificing path to victory is to be an example to His followers. We will see that the victory of the saints will come through spiritual strength, by keeping their faith in the Truth while enduring suffering — not by reliance upon physical strength, deception, or political power.

The Lion's exclusive ability to open the seals should remind us that He is still in control. Even when events on earth look as though they are careening out of the Almighty's control, they are not. The Lamb is still the only One who opens the seals of history.

The conquering Lion, the slain Lamb, has already established a Kingdom. This reign of Christ on earth will be examined in detail when we reach Chapter 20. But notice that even here in the very first vision, the coming of this Kingdom is already spoken of in the past tense. The Kingdom is in existence even before the events of The Apocalypse take place, even before we get to the description of the Millennium.

This is impossible for rapturists to explain. They do not believe God's Kingdom was established when the Lamb "didst ransom

men for God from every tribe and tongue and people and nation."
In fact, they do not believe the Kingdom will even be established
until seven years after this scene in Chapter 5 of The Apocalypse.
St. John's obvious reference to the Passion assures us that the
Church is correct: "As Eve was formed from the sleeping Adam's
side, so the Church [the Messianic Kingdom] was born from the
pierced heart of Christ hanging dead upon the Cross" (CCC, par.
766).

The singing

Christ's sacrifice established His Kingdom and motivates thanksgiving to and worship of the Lamb. They "sang a new song" in
honor of the Lamb (5:9). We will closely examine this act of singing, later, in the second recapitulating vision.

For now, let us just say that it is the same event as the "marriage
supper of the Lamb" (19:9). This marriage supper is commonly
recognized by Catholic commentators as the Mass. The Mass can
be described not only as a sacrifice, but also as a meal, and here as a
song.

It may be easy for us to miss the significance of this for those
in the first century. In taking Communion, a Catholic eats with
everyone else present. But when the Church began, Jews obeyed
the Old Covenant dietary laws. Gentiles ate unclean foods in unclean circumstances. These two groups just did not intermingle!
Before the Church, no one could even imagine these two groups
eating together.

But Christ could. He established a new Kingdom whose sacramental meal was the Eucharist, and at that meal were people
"from every tribe and tongue and people and nation" (5:9). The
Mass is intimately tied to the mystery of the Kingdom. Until this
Kingdom, no one would have dreamed that Jew and Gentile could
commune together in peace. This mystery is contained on the
scroll about to be opened by the breaking of the seals.

The seven seals

We now approach the details of the judgment that reveals to the whole world the true nature of the Messianic Kingdom: the mystery of the scroll. The symbolic importance of the number *seven* continues to be evident in the seals and trumpets: seven of each of them. They signify the perfect judgment of God upon the leadership of an unbelieving Jerusalem. In Leviticus, Moses had warned Israel that they would be punished seven times if they forsook God: "If you will not hearken to me . . . I will chastise you again sevenfold for your sins" (26:14, 18). St. John emphasizes that history is firmly within the grasp of the Lamb with the seven horns and seven eyes.

Rather than seeing the seals and the trumpets as chronologically related, the passages should be viewed as portraits of this period from different angles. The seals look at these events from the perspective of the Lion/Lamb who opens them. His Church had been ruthlessly persecuted during the Great Tribulation of 64 to 67 A.D., and justice is finally being meted out upon those persecutors from 67 to 70 A.D.

First seal: Rider on a white horse

The opening of the first seal reveals a message of hope, given by the King for the encouragement of the persecuted Christian community: "I saw . . . a white horse, and its Rider had a bow; and a crown was given to Him, and He went out conquering and to conquer" (6:2). This Rider symbolizes Christ, armed with the conquering Truth He proclaims. The picture of Christ the Word on a white horse is reminiscent of an Old Testament passage in Wisdom: "Thy all-powerful word leaped from Heaven, from the royal throne, into the midst of the land that was doomed, a stern warrior carrying the sharp sword of Thy authentic command" (18:15-16).

Christ appears on a white horse riding in victory over His enemies again at the end of The Apocalypse (19:11). This first seal is an anticipation of that event. The visions of The Apocalypse begin and end with the white-horse Rider. The first seal reminds the Christian community that even though there is much suffering to undergo first, the final outcome is assured: Christ will be victorious. From Heaven's perspective, He already is.

Second, third, and fourth
seals: war, famine, and death

The next three seals are also horses with riders. The red horse signifies war: "Its rider was permitted to take peace from the land" (6:4).The black horse signifies famine, with outrageous prices for foodstuffs. The pale horse symbolizes death: "I saw . . . a pale horse, and its rider's name was Death, and Hades followed him" (6:8). As history attests, famine follows war, and death follows them both. The events of Ezekiel's time (Ezek. 6:11-7:15) foreshadowed St. John's time (GR3).

It is noteworthy that the seals are opened in the same order that Jesus used in warning His disciples about the fall of the Temple (signs 2 and 3 in the Olivet Discourse). St. John is describing the fulfillment of his Lord's predictions spoken about four decades earlier.

The fifth seal: martyrs under the altar

The fifth seal reveals the martyrs of the Church, killed during the intense persecution of the Sanhedrin and Nero (sign 5 in the Olivet Discourse). Their souls are obviously awaiting the final resurrection, but why are they under the altar in Heaven? This is a reflection of the Old Covenant Temple. In the Temple, the blood of the sacrifices flowed under the altar. The Old Testament taught that the life of a creature was in its blood (Lev. 17:11). These martyrs were New Covenant sacrifices. They had joined their suffering to those of Christ's Passion. St. Paul alludes to his own desire for this union of suffering. In Colossians, he writes, "I rejoice in my sufferings for your sake, and in my flesh I complete what is lacking in Christ's afflictions for the sake of His body" (1:24).

From an earthly perspective, these martyrs had wasted their lives as a burning lamp in one of Nero's garden parties, or as lion bait for entertainment at the Coliseum. But from a heavenly perspective, their earthly loss of life was a Christian sacrifice. In reality, their lives were not lost, but preserved under the altar in Heaven. Their sacrifice had eternal significance in God's Kingdom in Heaven.

These martyrs cry out to God for justice against their persecutors. (Even from the perspective of a Christian in Heaven, evil should be punished.) They are told to be patient; it will be only "a little longer" (6:11). Indeed, history records that it was less than three years before the fall of Jerusalem. More martyrdom must be accomplished before God will be ready to exact justice. We are reminded that the purpose of our earthly existence is not human happiness, but human divination. This idea may sound strange to us, but was a common theme of the early Church Fathers.

The sixth seal: heavenly disruptions

The sixth seal is actually the final one, since the seventh seal recapitulates these events in trumpets, thunders, and woes. This seal uses the apocalyptic language to which we have now become accustomed, especially in our examination of this event in the Olivet Discourse (Matt. 24:29). This is the climax to the disruptions of 70 A.D.: political dynasties will be dislodged (GR5).

The events leading up to 70 A.D. saw not only the fall of the most prominent religious dynasty of the Roman Empire (the institutional Jewish priesthood, which could trace itself back to Aaron and Moses), but also, with the suicide of Nero, the blotting out of the line of Augustus. The next true emperor of Rome was Vespasian, who was not of the lineage of Augustus. Even his dynasty would not extend past his two sons.

Josephus tells us that in the upheaval surrounding the Temple's fall, many Jews actually hid in the caves around Jerusalem, just as the sixth seal predicts (6:15).

• *The Great Tribulation.* Before St. John starts the seventh seal's recapitulation, he pauses in Chapter 7 to expand on this climactic sixth seal. By now it should be clear to any careful reader that St. John's vision is following the blueprint of the Olivet Discourse. Jesus assured His disciples that they were on the winning side in the battle with evil, but there would still be a time when their prospects looked bleak. They would suffer from the effects of famine, persecution, and war in the "Great Tribulation." But then "the Son of man" would come to the "Ancient of Days" and "be presented before Him" to be recognized by all in His kingdom as victorious ruler (Matt. 24:30; Dan. 7:13).

The phrase "Great Tribulation" is used only three times in the New Testament. Jesus used it in the Olivet Discourse, referring to the time when the Roman Empire would sponsor a persecution of Christians just before the Temple's destruction (sign 5). The other two uses are in The Apocalypse. St. John uses the term in 7:14 just as Jesus did: to refer to the Neronian persecution. Only a severe case of Winkle Warp could place this verse into the future after a secret rapture.

• *Four winds and the mark.* The sixth seal contains an interesting scene of "four angels standing at the four corners of the land holding back the four winds" (7:1). This is very likely a reference to the four winds of Daniel 7:2 that stir up the gentile nations. These gentile nations, when stirred up, would "harm the land" of Israel. Before these angels are allowed to release the winds of wrath, however, God demands more time to complete the identification of Christ's followers. No evil will be allowed "till we have sealed the servants of our God upon their foreheads" (7:3). This is the "mark" that was mentioned in the letter to the Church in

Philadelphia, in anticipation of the mark of God that would later stand in contrast to the mark of the beast. The fact that God's servants are sealed with this mark "upon their foreheads" shows that their minds are right. They think as Christians should because their loyalty is to God and His Kingdom.

Just as more time was needed to allow for more martyrs in the fifth seal, in the sixth seal a delay is granted to garner more followers for Christ. These delays are one and the same, not consecutive. The purpose: to gather more Jewish Christians into the Church before the destruction of Jerusalem.

These new Christians would be protected in much the same way that the ancient Hebrews were protected in Egypt when the angel of death decimated the Egyptians. In Egypt, the mark was the physical blood of a lamb that the Hebrews put on their doorposts in obedience to God's command. Then they fled in haste the next morning. In the Jerusalem Church, the mark most likely refers to the spiritual mark received at Mass. Those in the Jerusalem Church also fled in haste at a moment's notice. The mark of God's sacrifice saved them both.

It is an interesting aside that this picture of the four winds and their devastation was a very understandable image to the residents of Jerusalem in the decade before 70 A.D. Four years before the war began with Rome, before even the start of the Great Tribulation, an unnamed Jewish prophet appeared in Jerusalem to warn its residents of their coming destruction. He roamed the streets shouting, " 'A voice from the east, a voice from the west, a voice from the four winds, a voice against Jerusalem and the brides, and a voice against this whole people!' This was his cry, as he went about by day and by night, in all the lanes of the city." He did this until he was killed in the war after more than seven years of prophesying (WJ, VI, 5:3). Was he a Christian? We really have no way of knowing. Was he a faithful prophet of God? Absolutely. He stood solidly in the tradition of Jeremiah.

Rapture

• *The 144,000.* The introduction of the number *144,000* shows again the significance of symbolism to St. John (144,000 is twelve squared times ten cubed.) He writes that this would be the number of Jewish Christians brought into the Church before the fall of the Temple. Notice that it specifically excludes the non-Jewish Christians who have continued to come to Christ since St. Peter opened the door to the Gentiles: "A great multitude which no man could number, from every nation, from all tribes and peoples and tongues" (7:9) were seen entering the Church, praising and worshiping God.

This number need not be exact. Symbolically, it is a very complete number (GR2). Here it represents the complete number of Judean Christians to enter the Church before Jerusalem is destroyed by the unleashing of the four winds; before the gentile nations would come to destroy the Temple.

The vision continues by reminding us that the victory of Christ's forces is assured. The remainder of Chapter 7 gives us a quick glimpse of the celebration that has continually been occurring in Heaven since the victory of Christ on the Cross. "Salvation belongs to our God who sits upon the throne, and to the Lamb! . . . Amen! Blessing and glory and wisdom and thanksgiving and honor and power and might be to our God forever and ever! Amen" (7:10-12). There will be more descriptions of this celebration later in The Apocalypse. It reflects Heaven's eternal joy.

At this point in the vision, we have reached the end of the main story of The Apocalypse, the period leading up to the judgment of Jerusalem in 70 A.D. In typical apocalyptic fashion, St. John proceeds to look at the same events from a different perspective. The reader must resist the modern temptation to organize these seals and trumpets chronologically. Remember Daniel's vision of the statue? The statue events were revisited in the vision of the four beasts, the seventy sevens, and the vision of the end. In this way, Daniel was able to give more detail (GR8).

The seventh seal: trumpets, thunders, and woes

After bringing the vision to a climax in the sixth seal, St. John links the seals with the trumpets by having the seventh seal contain all seven trumpets. (The last three trumpets are also the three woes.) The trumpets themselves are reminiscent of those that Jesus told us about in the Olivet Discourse. They were to announce His public coming into His kingdom (Matt. 24:31).

That is what this scroll vision is all about. The scroll's opening reveals the mystery of the Messianic Kingdom. The trumpets describe the same events as the seals do, but from a different perspective. Whereas the six seals view the coming judgment from the perspective of Christ, the trumpets view these events through the eyes of the Sanhedrin. Evidence of this non-Christian perspective is found in the climax of the last trumpet and its woe, announcing the coronation of Christ: "The kingdom of the world has become the Kingdom of our Lord and of His Christ, and He shall reign forever and ever" (11:15). This could be viewed as a "woe" only by an unrepentant unbeliever being judged by the victorious Christ. The masterful use of recapitulation is breathtaking!

An interesting aside revolves around the "prayers of the saints" (8:4-5), shown as having a direct influence on earthly events. These are the same saint/martyrs of the fifth seal. Their prayers are mingled with "much incense." In the epistle of James we read, "The prayer of a righteous man has great power in its effects" (5:16). This holds true *even after* the righteous man dies and enters Heaven. This principle anticipates a message of the Millennium that we will encounter in Chapter 20.

• *The first trumpet: hail and fire.* The first trumpet uses vivid apocalyptic language to describe the effects of the Jewish-Roman War on the land of Israel. All seven trumpets closely parallel the signs that Jesus gave in the Olivet Discourse, particularly in Luke 21.

The first trumpet is followed by "hail and fire, mixed with blood" (8:7). This is a picture of destruction and death beyond the ability of any human to stop; a devastated ecosphere, with "a third of the trees" destroyed (8:7). The Roman army actually used so many trees for their siege engines and their crosses that the area around Jerusalem was completely deforested for miles (WJ, XI).

• *The second trumpet: mountain into the sea.* At the second trumpet "something like a great mountain, burning with fire, was thrown into the sea" (8:8). This symbolizes the destruction of a monarchy, as does similar language in Amos 1 and 2. The Sanhedrin were the remnant of the Hasmonean dynasty. The priests traced their lineage all the way to Aaron's day. Nero was of the royal dynasty of Augustus. All were overthrown during this period, Daniel's last week.

• *The third trumpet: poisonous wormwood.* Wormwood is not only the third trumpet, but also the name of an extremely bitter plant. "A third of the waters became wormwood, and many men died of the water, because it was made bitter" (8:11). Rapturists try to interpret this bitter water to be the result of a future biochemical or nuclear war. Even the accident at Chernobyl has been read into this trumpet. But a Winkle Warp is not the way to understand this prophecy.

This view fails to appreciate the Old Testament background of this word. The message of the third trumpet reflects the language of Jeremiah 23:15. As is so often the case in the New Testament, a mere word or phrase is meant to evoke an entire scene from the Old Testament (GR3).

Jeremiah lived in a time when Jerusalem was under attack by the Babylonians. He predicted the defeat of Jerusalem. In the middle of a beautiful description of God's promised Messiah, one who will be a "righteous Branch" that "shall reign as king," Jeremiah stops to lament the false prophets of Judah (23:5). They were falsely predicting peace and safety when Jeremiah knew Jerusalem would surely fall. The leaders of Jerusalem persecuted Jeremiah as a naysayer. God makes a promise to Jeremiah, telling him that He "will feed them with wormwood, and give them poisoned water to drink" (23:15). A modern equivalent to this idiom might be to say that God would make the false prophets "eat their words."

The connection to the third trumpet of The Apocalypse is apparent. When the Messiah, the righteous Branch, finally appeared, the Jewish Sanhedrin turned the people of Jerusalem against Him. The Sanhedrin's leader, the high priest, is the star that "fell from Heaven," and poisoned the waters (8:10). He led the assault on the Messiah and encouraged the false prophets.

All throughout the Roman siege, the leadership of Jerusalem was predicting the salvation of God for Jerusalem. Josephus tells us that there were many "false prophets suborned by the tyrants to impose on the people . . . that they should wait for deliverance from God; and this was in order to keep them from deserting, and that they might be buoyed up above fear and care by such hopes" (WJ, VI, 5:2). They believed to the very end that God would defeat the Roman army for them.

The third trumpet bears evidence again that God keeps His promises against false prophets. They will be fed "with wormwood." The prophets who predicted victory for Jerusalem would have to "eat their words."

Unfortunately, their false hopes resulted in the unnecessary and brutal deaths of many Jerusalem residents. These residents are split into thirds, and the mention of "a third" here is another example of anticipation (8:11). We will examine its background and fulfillment shortly.

• *The fourth trumpet: sun, moon, and stars darkened.* The fourth trumpet once again employs vivid apocalyptic imagery to warn of political upheaval (GR5): "A third of the sun was struck, and a third of the moon, and a third of the stars" (8:12). The significance of "a third" is rooted in the Old Testament prophecy of Ezekiel, and we will examine it in more depth in a later passage. Suffice it to say here that this symbolizes the utter defeat of the leadership of Jerusalem. In 70 A.D., biblical Judaism was utterly destroyed and was eventually replaced by the Rabbinic Judaism of today. Rabbinic Judaism finds its home in the synagogue rather than in the Temple, its meaning in the moral law rather than in the sacrificial law, and its leadership in the teacher rather than in the priest.

• *The fifth trumpet, first woe: the fallen star and the locusts.* The fifth trumpet serves also as the first of three woes, introduced by an eagle (8:13). The eagle was an unclean bird and would have immediately brought the Roman Empire's army to the mind of any attentive Jewish reader.

With the blowing of the fifth trumpet, St. John "saw a star fallen from Heaven to earth, and he was given the key of the shaft of the bottomless pit" (9:1). Some commentators believe that the star that falls from Heaven is probably Satan. Jesus told the seventy-two disciples on their successful return to Him that He "saw Satan fall like lightning from Heaven" (Luke 10:18; Isa. 14:12-17).

But in apocalyptic writings, stars usually denote earthly, political leaders. The best interpretation is that this fallen star symbolizes either Nero or the Jewish high priest. It could symbolize both (GR4). Nero was responsible for the initial decision to declare war upon Jerusalem. Alternately, the high priest has already been described as a fallen star in the third trumpet. By his misguided leadership, he incited Nero to declare war.

This fallen star unleashes a swarm of locusts with "the power of scorpions" upon Israel (9:3). The word *locust* literally means "burners of the land."

Amos 2:1-20 describes the fear and destruction locusts could bring. Locusts were an instrument of God's judgment on any people who rejected His entreaties. Pharaoh discovered this in Exodus 10:1-20. Here in The Apocalypse we see the plagues that had been unleashed upon the Egyptians being brought upon Jerusalem. God had promised as much to the Israelites if ever they rejected His ways (Deut. 28:38).

The advancing Babylonian army is likened to a swarm of locusts in Joel 2:1-11. That is probably the primary picture drawn here as well. In this instance, it was the Roman army that would devour the land like an invasion of locusts, just as the Babylonians had done centuries earlier (GR6).

We will hear much of this army's "power" (9:3). They were the warriors (the red horse of the seals) that brought famine (the black horse) and death (the pale horse) to Israel. The fifth trumpet recaps the second, third, and fourth seals.

The detailed description of this locust army is quite obviously that of the Roman cavalry in battle armor under the bright Judean sun: "The locusts were like horses arrayed for battle; on their heads were what looked like crowns of gold; their faces were like human faces, their hair like women's hair . . . teeth like lions' teeth; they had scales like iron breastplates, and the noise of their wings was like the noise of many chariots with horses rushing into battle" (9:7-9).

The only description that does not sound like a human army on horseback is the description of "teeth." Of course, the fourth beast of Daniel (Rome) had iron teeth. More specifically, the reference to "teeth like lions' teeth" recalls Joel 1:4-6. Joel prophesied the judgment of God upon Israel, and St. John subtly reminds us that this is exactly what is occurring in this trumpet (Joel 2:2).

What makes this locust army particularly frightful is its purpose. They would not "harm the grass," as most locusts would. This invading locust army would prey upon "those of mankind who have not the seal of God upon their foreheads" (9:4). This is the mark of God already mentioned in the sixth seal.

During this trumpet, we encounter the first of several specific time references. This scorpion army would torment the Jews for five months, which was the length of the season in Israel for these insects (May to September). Those are precisely the months during which Titus completed his final assault upon and siege of Jerusalem in 70 A.D.

This locust army brings with them the "torture of a scorpion" — not merely death, but "torture." Read St. John's description carefully: "Their torture was like the torture of a scorpion, when it stings a man. And in those days, men will seek death and will not find it; they will long to die, and death will fly from them" (9:5-6). This was written by a man who had witnessed the Crucifixion of his Savior up close (John 19:25-27). The locust army stung like scorpions in the hand and foot by using the nails of crucifixion. Imagine the hills around Jerusalem completely filled with Jews being crucified; that was the scene during the final five months of the siege. During these five months, well over one million Jews died, many of them from crucifixion. This passage describes the horrific judgment that fell upon Jerusalem for its rejection of the Messianic Kingdom. It is not a future event.

Abaddon the King

These locusts have a king, who is "the angel of the bottomless pit" (9:11). As we will see with other symbols in The Apocalypse, this beast serves as a symbol for more than one person. In its broadest sense, the beast symbolizes the Roman Empire's government. This should not surprise us at all if we remember Daniel. He predicted four beasts. The fourth one symbolized Rome. Yet in a specific sense, some of what this beast does points directly to the individual Caesar ruling at that particular time. There were three during this period: Nero, Vespasian, and Titus (GR4).

When we compare the descriptions of the king of the locust army (9:11), the beast that kills the two witnesses (11:7), and the beast with seven heads that "was, and is not, and is to come" (17:8), we can determine that this king "of the bottomless pit" is General Titus. We will return to this later when we examine Chapter 17.

The name of the army's king, *Abaddon*, literally means "destruction." This Hebrew word leads the careful student to Obadiah 12. In the Old Testament, the elder son of Isaac, Esau by name, was denied the promises of God's blessing. The younger son, Jacob, was blessed instead. Esau and his descendants (Edomites, or Idumeans) deeply resented this, and so would later revel in the persecution of Jacob and his descendants (Israelites). But the prophet Obadiah promised a day of reckoning, of *abaddon*, to the Edomites. Obadiah spoke judgment against the Edomites, because they gloated over the destruction of the Israelites.

Obadiah chastises the Edomites: "You should not have gloated over . . . your brother in the day of his misfortune; you should not have rejoiced . . . in the day of their ruin; you should not have boasted in the day of distress" (Obad. 12). In fact, the Edomites cooperated with the Arabians and Philistines when they plundered the home of Israel's king. The conquering army carried off all of the royal sons except one (2 Chron. 21). Obadiah prophesied to the Edomites that "as you have done, it shall be done to you; your deeds shall return on your own head" (Obad. 15).

These events stand as prophecy pointing to 70 A.D. (GR3). The Sanhedrin had reveled in the persecution of this young sect called Christianity. They were the elder brother (Esau and Edom) in the family of faith, while the Christians were the younger brother (Jacob and Israel). But by their persecution of their younger brothers, they had turned their advantage into a curse. The Messiah's coming in judgment through the Roman army would constitute their "day of the Lord" (GR6). "Abaddon" had arrived.

Rapture

- *The sixth trumpet, second woe: invasion by a great army* . When the sixth trumpet blows, we find four angels have been waiting — reflecting the four angels in the sixth seal. They "had been held ready for the hour, the day, the month, and the year, to kill a third of mankind" (9:15). Might the holding back of the four angels be a reference to the prediction of Jesus that His followers would be given a small window of opportunity to flee Jerusalem? It is a historical fact that the Christian community heeded the warning of their Lord and that no Christians remained in Jerusalem during its final siege and destruction. The destruction had to wait; it "had been held ready for the hour, the day, the month, and the year." Remember that at the beginning of the seals and the trumpets, only the Lamb was able to break the seal of the scroll. Even now He controls the flow of events. One moment too soon would not do. Jesus had a promise to keep, down to the exact hour of the exact day.

This trumpet unleashes the gentile horde. Even the ancient protective boundary of the Euphrates will not impede the advance of the locusts, the Roman army (9:13-14). The details of the invasion extend all the way through 11:14.

The size of the army is almost universally understood as a symbolic number. The "cavalry" alone is "twice ten thousand times ten thousand" (9:16). If taken literally, that would be two hundred million! Since the cavalry is a small percentage of an army, imagine the size of the army itself! Clearly, no army that size could have existed in the ancient world. Some have calculated that it would encompass every eligible male alive even today. It makes better sense as a symbolic number.

Significantly, this cavalry is exactly double the size of "ten thousand times ten thousand," the number who attend to the Lamb as they "encircled the throne" (5:11, NIV). That is the crucial issue for St. John. The number of God is *three*, and man's number is twice that, *six*. The army of man is twice the size of God's loyal following, even in Heaven.

256

On an earthly level, the locust army outnumbers the Lamb's loyal following. It is a complete army of ten thousand, multiplied by another of the same size, and then doubled for good measure. It is an overwhelming force. Any thought of victory against this force is ludicrous. Indeed, when the Jews saw the size of the army that Vespasian and Titus had actually mustered, much of the Jewish army deserted in despair (WJ, III, 6:3).

The *loipos*

But even with all this, there is still a group "who were not killed by these plagues [and] did not repent of the works of their hands nor give up worshiping demons" (9:20). This is the remnant, *loipos*, that will appear later in the book. St. John mentions them here in anticipation. In Daniel's previous vision, they were called the "wicked." Josephus calls them the "scum." Historically, we know them as the "outlaw Zealots." We will eventually learn what happens to these men who refused to "repent of their murders or their sorceries or their immorality or their thefts" (9:21). It is not a pretty picture.

Seven thunders

Like the climactic sixth seal, the sixth trumpet has many details. A powerful angel now unleashes seven thunders, but St. John is not permitted to write these details for us. How ironic: Jesus' nickname for John and his brother was *boanerges*, or "sons of thunder" (Mark 3:17), yet John is forbidden to tell more about these seven thunders.

At this point, an angel announces that when the seventh trumpet is sounded, "the mystery of God, as He announced to His servants the prophets, should be fulfilled" (10:7). We have not arrived at the seventh trumpet; this is another example of anticipation. We will wait until we arrive at the seventh trumpet to discuss this "mystery of God." It is the message of the scroll, the mystery of

Christ's Kingdom, that will be revealed for the entire world to see when the seals are all opened.

The little scroll

St. John is instructed to eat a second scroll, a little scroll, from the hand of a powerful angel, and he says, "It was sweet as honey in my mouth, but when I had eaten it, my stomach was made bitter" (10:10). This is a clear reference to the scroll of Ezekiel that contained "words of lamentation and mourning and woe" (Ezek. 2:8-3:14). At first blush, the deliverance of the Church from the Great Tribulation was a sweet prospect. But the result of that deliverance was the destruction of St. John's kinsmen and hometown.

The forty-two-month trampling

We now encounter the second specific time reference in The Apocalypse. This one will be repeated. We read that Jerusalem, "the holy city," will be trampled for forty-two months (11:2). This is the biblical period of judgment, as is evidenced as far back as the prophet Elijah, who withheld rain from Israel for three and a half years.

These forty-two months are still within the sixth trumpet. The trampling is made possible because the protective river Euphrates has dried up. The trampling will be accomplished by the locust army of "two hundred million" cavalry.

This specific period is identical to the "one thousand two hundred and sixty days" during which the "two witnesses" of prophesy (11:3). We see this period when the woman flees from Satan (12:6, 14). It appears again when the beast is given "authority" over Israel for "forty-two months" (13:5). Remember Daniel? This same three and a half years appeared in Visions III:A and III:E.

While most of the numbers in apocalyptic literature are round, significant numbers, such as *three, seven,* or *ten* (or multiples of these numbers), the four references to this period are not, so they possess the aura of actual historical time (GR2). And when we examine history, we find a precise fulfillment of these forty-two months in the three-and-a-half-year Jewish-Roman War.

The repetition of the time reference in four visionary contexts gives further evidence to the position that the visions of Daniel are not to be viewed chronologically. They look at the same events and periods from different perspectives (GR8).

It is no wonder this sixth trumpet was considered the "second woe" by the Jewish leadership. "The nations . . . will trample over the holy city for forty-two months" (11:2). The picture of Jerusalem being overrun by pagan Gentiles is lifted from the teaching of Jesus in the Olivet Discourse. Jesus prophesied that "Jerusalem will be trodden down by the Gentiles, until the times of the Gentiles are fulfilled" (Luke 21:24).

This picture can be found in the Old Testament as well. Jesus was expanding on Daniel's visions. Daniel had seen a gentile nation trample the holy places of the Jews. He witnessed the Babylonians as they conquered Jerusalem and carried off all the holy vessels within the Temple. This defeat was a fulfillment of Isaiah 63:18.

But that was not the last time the Temple would be desecrated. During the time of the Maccabean Wars, Antiochus Epiphanes defiled the Temple by entering its walls and even sacrificing a pig on its altar. This was foretold by Daniel (8:13-14; 11:31). That overrunning of the Temple's holy places lasted for 1,150 days (2,300 evenings and mornings). It ended with the victories of Judas Maccabee, and that victory is still celebrated today as the Jewish holiday of Hanukkah.

During the time of Jesus, Jewish commentators claimed that Antiochus would be the last to desecrate the Temple as foretold by Daniel, but Jesus specifically taught otherwise. In the Olivet Discourse, Jesus referred to "the desolating sacrilege spoken of by the prophet Daniel" as a future event (Matt. 24:15). Although the

Antiochan insult would last 1,150 days, and was in the past by the time Jesus spoke in the Olivet Discourse, the sacrilege that Jesus foretold best fits the details of Daniel 9:27 and 12:11. As we saw in Daniel, this period of judgment spans three and a half years.

So we have come full circle in the entire scope of our examination of the Old and New Testaments. The three and a half years that appear in Daniel, and are described in the Olivet Discourse, are now mentioned in the sixth trumpet. By using this time reference four times in Chapters 11 and 12 of The Apocalypse, St. John effectively emphasizes that these events all occur within the three and a half years that Daniel and Jesus predicted.

Jesus had prophesied that this judgment would occur within the lifetime of His hearers: "This generation will not pass away till all these things take place" (Matt. 24:34). By referencing the Luke passage, we can determine that these forty-two months are "the times of the Gentiles" (Luke 21:24). St. John writes that, during these forty-two months, the Gentiles "will trample over the holy city" (11:2).

According to Josephus, the daily sacrifice dedicated to Nero in the Temple in Jerusalem was halted in July of 66 A.D. (WJ, II, 17:2). This Jewish provocation led to the declaration of war by Rome in February of 67 A.D. (WJ, III, 1:2). The war ended precisely forty-two months later when the Temple was burned by Titus's troops in August of 70 A.D. Daniel predicted these things more than six centuries earlier, Jesus predicted them four decades earlier, and St. John expands on their prophecies. The Jewish-Roman War might have already started by the time St. John wrote, but was not anywhere near a resolution.

Make no mistake. The "times of the Gentiles" cannot be a present or a future time. Indeed, there can no longer be a "times of the Gentiles" because the categories of Jew and Gentile are no longer relevant in the Kingdom of Christ. "For there is no distinction between Jew and Greek; the same Lord is Lord of all" (Rom. 10:12).

The distinction is meaningless because there is now a new Lord, who is ruler of His eternal Kingdom here and now. That Kingdom supersedes any national or ethnic identity. "Every nation, from all tribes and peoples and tongues" is invited to eat at the Table of the Lord (7:9).

The two witnesses

There are more important events during this sixth trumpet. During the trampling by the Gentiles, there will be two witnesses who prophesy for God. They are described as the "two olive trees and the two lampstands which stand before the Lord of the earth" (11:4). This description should tell us that they may not be just normal human beings.

The identity of the two witnesses in 11:3-14 has been much debated: the Law and the Prophets, Moses and Elijah, Peter and Paul, the Prophets and the Apostles, and Zerubbabel and Joshua have all been proposed.

The symbolism is definitely taken from Zechariah 4, where Joshua the priest and Zerubbabel the ruler are described in similar fashion. But the Old Testament events are meant to foreshadow the New Testament (GR3). These witnesses might also represent the ministries of Sts. Peter and Paul. They were both killed by the beast, when they were martyred in Rome during the Great Tribulation. Anyone who has done his homework in Daniel would expect the beast to be nothing other than Rome. But Peter and Paul were martyred before these 1,260 days began.

The best interpretation of the witnesses seems to be as symbols for the Law and the Prophets. If we remember the vision of the battle strategy of the beast in Daniel 7 (III:A), this will not surprise us. Daniel informed us that the little horn, Nero, would make war on *the times and the law* for three and a half years. This was the first time we encountered the forty-two months. The times and law that Daniel mentions are the parallel of the two witnesses.

Rapture

As we have seen with the beast, and will see again, St. John also had the personification of the Law and the Prophets in mind. Moses and Elijah serve as the personification of all that the Law and the Prophets represented. St. John uses this literary technique enough that we can be sure of this (GR4).

Moses and Elijah were the two most important men in each of their respective roles. Moses gave Israel the Law, and Elijah was the epitome of God's prophet. Elijah prophesied during a similar three-and-a-half-year period of judgment in the Old Testament. The powers attributed to these two witnesses in The Apocalypse recall the high points of the careers of Moses and Elijah. "They have power to shut the sky, that no rain may fall during the days of their prophesying, and they have power over the waters to turn them into blood, and to smite the land with every plague," and even the power to breathe life back into the dead (11:6).

It was Moses and Elijah who came to bear witness to Christ in the Transfiguration (Matt. 17:1-13; Mark 9:2-13; Luke 9:28-36). We see the symbolic importance of Elijah as Jesus uses him as a type for John the Baptizer. This was an allegorical fulfillment of the Old Testament prophecy concerning Elijah's return.

At this point in his vision, St. John does something noteworthy. While his book is apocalyptic literature, and much of that literature is vividly symbolic, St. John specifically points out the allegorical nature of his language in this vision (11:8). Nowhere else in The Apocalypse does he remind us that he is writing allegorically. So in this vision especially we must not expect too literal a fulfillment. In fact, we will find that this section of The Apocalypse has the least "literal" fulfillment.

So how were the events surrounding these two witnesses fulfilled? As long as the Temple stood, the Mosaic system gave voice to the Law and the Prophets. They witnessed against the paganism of both the Romans and the unfaithful Jews. This witness annoyed many Romans.

The Law and the Prophets were killed by the beast when biblical Judaism was destroyed forever by the Roman army in 70 A.D. The world would have thought that, at the burning of the Temple, they could forget about this Law that prohibited the worship of the Roman emperor. When the Temple was destroyed, the world would have thought that the prophets who condemned their selfish lifestyles and immoral practices had been silenced forever. After all, the earthly center of Judaism was destroyed. Surely Judaism, and even this small sect within Judaism (the common view of Christianity at the time) would dissipate when Jerusalem was eliminated. Pagan Rome was so overjoyed that people made "merry and exchange[d] presents" (11:10). But the world was wrong to think that God's Truth could be silenced by war.

The Law and the Prophets came back to life. Even now they continue to proclaim their message of moral uprightness and godly worship within the heavenly city of the New Jerusalem, which is the Church. God's New Covenant was beyond the reach of armies. They "went up to Heaven in a cloud" (11:12). The heavenly city of God is a theme that St. John develops in some detail later. Heaven is the location of the New Jerusalem at this point in The Apocalypse. The use of a cloud speaks of their more glorious associations in the New Covenant. We participate in that glory in the Mass.

From this point forward, the message of the Law and the Prophets is beyond the power of earthly kingdoms to silence. That is the significance of their being protected in Heaven. They continue to bear witness against the evil of emperor worship and immoral lifestyles from their home in the New Jerusalem, the Church. This is the significance of St. John Chrysostom's comment: "The Romans conquered countless thousands of Jews, but could not overcome twelve unarmed, unprotected men" (HOM, LXXXVI).

The early Church assiduously used the Jewish Law and Prophets of the Old Testament (the Scriptures) to point people to Christ (Acts 1:16, 8:35, 17:2, 17:11, 18:28; Rom. 1:2-3; 1 Cor. 15:3-4).

The situation became so distressful to the Jewish rabbis that they revised the list of the canon a few decades after the fall of Jerusalem, and some very Messianic books of the Old Testament were demoted to deuterocanonical status. The irony of the situation is that this revision by the Jewish scholars in about 90 A.D. gave the Protestants an excuse to delete some of the books of the Bible that they found distressing almost fifteen centuries later.

Yet the Church continued to use the Law and the Prophets as an apologetical tool. It was very effective, for the simple reason that Christ really was to be found in the Old Testament (GR1). Through the efforts of the early Church, the Law and the Prophets really did rise again to bear witness to God's undefeated Truth.

The theme of the two witnesses will later be counterbalanced with the two evil beasts in Chapter 13 of The Apocalypse. This theme will then be complemented by the two women: a good woman in Chapter 12 and an evil one in Chapter 17. We will see the same dual symbolism that St. John used with the two witnesses. The characters symbolize an entity or group of people, but also point to a particular individual as representative (GR4).

The witnesses were dead for three and a half days, or half a week, while the Roman world celebrated. It is only slightly longer than the three days that Jesus was in the grave. The time of Israel's trial was three and a half years, or half of a week of years (GR2). In a fraction of the time it had taken to silence the Old Covenant, the Law and the Prophets were promoted to a City the world could not defeat with armies. It did not take long at all for the empire to realize that it had not permanently silenced the Truth. This is a major theme that rings throughout The Apocalypse: God's Truth will reign eternally triumphant from this point forward.

The great earthquake
This all occurs within the sixth trumpet, which we know extends for three and a half years. Now St. John gives us a major

event by which to date this vision within history. If you are unsure of our analysis, here is a reality check. When did the voice of the Old Testament witnesses transfer to the Church? "At that hour there was a great earthquake, and a tenth of the city fell; seven thousand people were killed in the earthquake" (11:13; GR5).

The Temple occupied about a tenth of the land within Jerusalem. We know when this tenth of the city fell: in August of 70 A.D. On the day the Temple was torched, a large number of Jews also died. *Seven thousand* — ten cubed, multiplied by seven — is a symbolically large number. Yet when the outlaw Zealots were defeated in the Temple, they shifted their defensive stand to the royal palace, slaughtering in cold blood 8,400 Jews who had taken refuge there (WJ, VI, 7:1). Yes, they slaughtered their own kinsmen, a shaking of all that was considered important within the holy bloodline of Judaism. Even today, this killing of Jew by Jew is referred to as the *sinat hinam* that precipitated the defeat of the Temple.

By this point, it should be obvious why Victorinus and St. Augustine believed these visions recapitulated one another. This earthquake illustrates again that these visions are not chronological. There was an earthquake in the sixth seal that exactly mirrors this earthquake in the sixth trumpet (6:12 and 11:13; GR8).

The great city

The specific location in which these two witnesses are killed is now identified. All of these events transpire in "the great city which is allegorically called Sodom and Egypt, where their Lord was crucified" (11:8). This city is obviously Jerusalem. First, it is the location of Christ's Crucifixion, and second, the term "great city" is used elsewhere in reference to Jerusalem. Josephus uses the term as well (WJ, VII, 8:7).

St. John uses the allegorical names Sodom and Egypt for Jerusalem. Perhaps it is to protect himself and his readers in case his manuscript were to fall into the hands of the authorities. Perhaps it is merely because his book is apocalyptic. But it should not surprise us, because it is not an innovation. Jerusalem is allegorically called both Sodom and its sister city, Gomorrah, in the Old Testament (Isa. 1:10; Jer. 23:14; Ezek. 16:48).

St. John does not just spring this on the reader, however. As he does so often throughout his work, he has anticipated this theme. In two of the letters to the churches, Christ refers to the "synagogue of Satan," while warning the Church to prepare for a period of suffering. St. John has let us know that the Jewish leaders were persecuting the Christians. Of course, this was not news to the original readers, since they were living under that very persecution. But the alert reader of the first three chapters would expect the Jewish leaders in Jerusalem to be among the Church's persecutors during the Great Tribulation.

As we progress in the book, we must keep our minds alert to other allegorical names for Jerusalem that equate it with evils of which other ancient peoples were guilty. Sodom's primary sin was its blatant disregard for God's moral law. Egypt's leaders sinned by trying to keep God's people in bondage, denying them the freedom to worship. This parallels the actions of the Sanhedrin in 68 A.D.

The beast
During this vignette, we are subtly introduced to a new character in The Apocalypse. He is "the beast that ascends from the bottomless pit" (11:7). We will see more of evil beasts shortly. This is another example of St. John's use of anticipation.

• *The seventh trumpet, third woe: the Kingdom comes.* The seventh and last trumpet is also the third and last woe. The seventh angel with his trumpet declares, "The kingdom of the world has become the Kingdom of our Lord and of His Christ, and He shall reign forever and ever" (11:15). This phrase and its meaning are so well

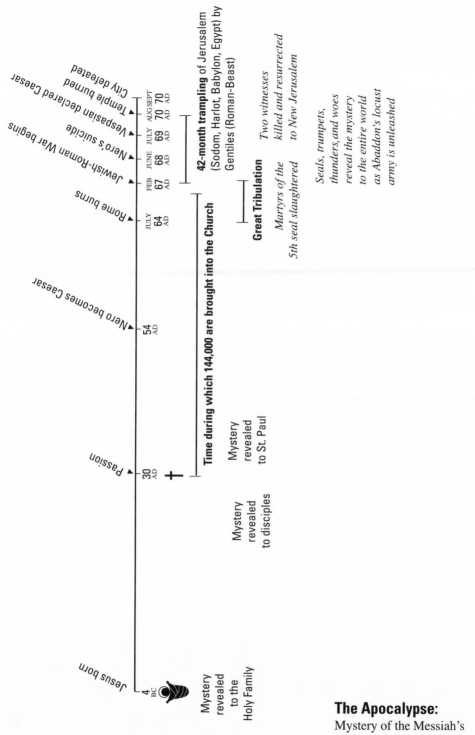

The Apocalypse:
Mystery of the Messiah's
Kingdom Revealed

Jesus born

Mystery
revealed
to the
Holy Family

4 BC

Passion

30 AD

Mystery
revealed
to disciples

Time during which 144,000 are brought into the Church

Mystery
revealed
to St. Paul

Nero becomes Caesar

54 AD

Rome burns

JULY 64 AD

Jewish-Roman War begins

FEB 67 AD

Nero's suicide

JUNE 68 AD

Vespasian declared Caesar

JULY 69 AD

Temple burned
City defeated

AUG SEPT 70 70 AD AD

42-month trampling of Jerusalem
(Sodom, Harlot, Babylon, Egypt) by
Gentiles (Roman-Beast)

*Two witnesses
killed and resurrected
to New Jerusalem*

Great Tribulation

*Martyrs of the
5th seal slaughtered*

*Seals, trumpets,
thunders, and woes
reveal the mystery
to the entire world
as Abaddon's locust
army is unleashed*

known to us that it is easy to forget that during the sixth trumpet, this was identified as the mystery of God: "In the days of the trumpet call to be sounded by the seventh angel, the mystery of God, as He announced to His servants the prophets, should be fulfilled" (10:7).

The mystery of God

What is this mystery of God being fulfilled in The Apocalypse? In all of the Gospels, Jesus refers to a "mystery" (or "secret") only once. In all three synoptic Gospels this mystery is put into the same context (Matt. 13:11; Mark 4:11; Luke 8:10). It is the mystery of what the Kingdom of the Messiah would really be like. It would not be the physical, political, conquering power for which the Jewish leadership had hoped. No, the Messianic Kingdom would be an *interior* kingdom — the rule of an omnipotent Christ within the lives and hearts of men and women all over the world. For this reason, it would never be defeated or uprooted, as Daniel had foretold in his visions of the statue and the beasts. Because it was a spiritual rule, no unbeliever would be able to enter it, as Zechariah had stated at the end of his oracles (Appendix Three).

The spiritual aspect of the Kingdom of the Messiah was a theme throughout much of the Old Testament prophets. Jesus even reminds His disciples that "many prophets and righteous men longed to see what you see, and did not see it" (Matt. 13:17). Even at the moment of death, Christ emphasized to an unbelieving Pilate that His was a spiritual Kingdom: "My kingship is not of this world; if my kingship were of this world, my servants would fight, that I might not be handed over to the Jews; but my kingship is not from the world. . . . For this I have come into the world, to bear witness to the truth" (John 18:36-37).

If you look for Jesus' teaching on what the Messiah's Kingdom would be like, you will see the obvious silhouette of the Church. The parable of the sower and the soils teaches that entrance to the

Kingdom is open to all, but dependent on a personal response to the "word" (Matt. 13:3-23). The public encounter with His family reveals that, in the Kingdom, what matters is no longer a holy bloodline, but doing "the will of my Father in Heaven" (Matt. 12:50). In the parable of the weeds and the wheat, Jesus explains that His Kingdom will have loyal, obedient subjects mingled with the evil and traitorous. Even though His servants recognize this, they are to leave the final judgment to Christ (Matt. 13:24-30, 36-43). This lesson is so important that it is reiterated in the parable of the fishes (Matt. 13:47-51).

In another parable, the mustard seed is a picture of how the Kingdom will be small and hidden in the beginning, yet contain within itself all things necessary to grow into a huge and fruitful tree (Matt. 13:31-32). This is the fulfillment of Daniel's stone growing into a mountain. This reflects precisely the development of the Church. The *Catechism* clearly teaches that "The Church was catholic [i.e., having correct and complete confession of faith, full sacramental life, and ordained ministry in apostolic succession] on the day of Pentecost and will always be so until the day of the Parousia" (CCC, par. 830).

This growth that starts with a small beginning is re-emphasized in the parable of the leaven: it starts out small and invisible, but slowly and surely it changes the very nature of the dough. Just so, the Church does not rule the world as a political entity, but through the unseen process of changing men's hearts (Matt. 13:33-35). Finally, Jesus gives His disciples two parables to hammer home the idea that His Kingdom, although it would not be visible on the worldly scene at first, would be worth the nurture, effort, and sacrifice. These are the parables of the hidden treasure and the pearl of great value (Matt. 13:44-46).

So the Kingdom of God that Christ offered was radically different from what the Jewish Sanhedrin desired, even though it was in perfect harmony with the Old Testament prophecies. The Jewish leaders were yearning for the good old days; they wanted a return to the thousand-year dynasty of David, with its political power and military muscle. As a result, they missed the unifying theme of the four major prophets: Isaiah, Jeremiah, Ezekiel, and Daniel.

Because Christ's kingdom would be internal, it would supersede ethnic and national distinctions. Jew and Gentile would be accepted on an equal footing. This teaching is integral to the message of the later prophets of the Old Testament. Isaiah prophesied that God would gather His believers from all the nations of the world, and "some of them also I will take for priests and for Levites, says the Lord" (66:21). Isaiah was teaching that these newcomer Gentiles would be accepted on a par with the most worthy of the Jews. I am sure that turned some heads in Isaiah's day! The Jewish leaders of Jesus' day seem to have forgotten this promise. The make-up of Christ's Church, with Jew and Gentile at peace as equals, was a mystery in the Old Covenant.

The Church's Liturgy connects this prophecy of Isaiah with the teaching of Jesus in Luke. Jesus proclaimed publicly to His Jewish listeners, "You will weep and gnash your teeth, when you see Abraham . . . in the Kingdom of God and you yourselves thrust out. And men will come from east and west, and from north and south, and sit at table in the Kingdom of God. And behold, some are last who will be first, and some are first who will be last" (13:28-30). The Sanhedrin rejected this vision of the Kingdom, so they were left out.

St. Paul did not reject this mystery, but embraced it enthusiastically. In Colossians he writes, "This mystery . . . is Christ in you, the hope of glory" (1:27). In whom was Christ? He dwelt in the gentile Christians of Colossae. St. Paul devotes an entire section of his letter to the Roman church (chs. 9-11) to this mystery. In Romans 10:12-13, he drives the point home. "The scripture says, 'No one who believes in Him will be put to shame.' For there is no distinction between Jew and Greek; the same Lord is Lord of all and bestows His riches upon all who call upon Him. For, 'everyone who calls upon the name of the Lord will be saved' " (note also Rom. 11:25).

The apostles became the "stewards of the mysteries of God" (1 Cor. 4:1). To put it succinctly, the sum of "the mysteries of God" throughout the ages was that the Kingdom of the Jewish Messiah would be the Church! To think that the Kingdom of the Son of David would not be political, but ecclesiastical; not physical, but spiritual; not ethnic, but personal. To think that, because of the very nature of the Kingdom, a Gentile could be accepted alongside the descendants of Abraham. To think that a master would be no more privileged in this Kingdom than his slave. To think that women and men would be equals in dignity in the Kingdom. But more than anything else, to think that Jews and Gentiles would *eat together at one Table*. The celebration of the Eucharist by the New Testament Church did more to proclaim the gospel than anything else ever could!

All of these conclusions flowed logically and inexorably from the major premise that Jesus taught His disciples: His Kingdom would not be "of this world" (cf. John 18:36). His would be a spiritual Kingdom within the hearts of human beings, working outward from there. His would be an ecclesiastical Kingdom.

This was the message the world was to glean from the destruction of the Temple. "In the days of . . . the seventh angel, the mystery of God, as He announced to His servants the prophets, should be fulfilled" (10:7). This was the hidden message of the scroll whose seven seals are opened in this initial vision. The Kingdom of Christ is not physically a part of political Judaism. It does not depend on Jerusalem or its Temple. Rather, it extends an invitation to all men and women who desire communion with the one true God.

Was this really such a mystery? Absolutely! Although every Catholic communicant probably understands this well, the Jewish leaders never quite caught on to what the Kingdom was to be like. In fact, even today, there is a group of Christians who do not seem to understand the mystery: that the Messiah came to set up a spiritual Kingdom, and that He was not and never will be interested in ruling the world as an earthly potentate enthroned in Jerusalem. Such Christians are called rapturists.

This was the thrust of Dr. Walvoord's quotation early in this book. He is the leading, living proponent of rapturist theology, yet he admits that the pretribulationalism (the rapture theology we have been examining) is not taught anywhere in Scripture. Today's rapturists insist on the same physical Messianic Kingdom that the leaders of Jerusalem did because their view of the Church demands a return of ethnic Israel into the center of God's plan.

Once again we see that eschatology is closely tied to ecclesiology. Our theology of the end times is inextricably bound to our theology of the Church. So how do average rapturists view the Church? They believe that it is *not* the zenith of God's plan throughout the ages or even anticipated in the Old Testament. They call it rather a "parenthesis" in God's eternal plan — a temporary stand-in for Old Covenant Israel. They believe that the Jews' rejection of the Messiah in His first advent forced God to initiate "Plan B." So God is left with two plans, the one foretold in the Old Testament for the Jews, and the last-minute substitute that became the Church. "Most premillenarians . . . would agree that *a* new covenant has been provided for the church, but not *the* new covenant for Israel" (*TMK*, 214). Because the original plan with its Messianic Kingdom could not be established without the Jews' approval, God set up the Church for a couple of thousand years, waiting for the right time to offer His Kingdom to the Jews again.

That is the purpose of the future seven-year Great Tribulation: to prod the Jewish people into accepting their Messiah. It will do nothing for the Church, which will already have been raptured to the safety of Heaven — put forever onto the back burner of God's eternal plan. Those Jews who "accept Christ" during the Great Tribulation and the Millennium will never become a part of the Church. Rather, they will remain an eternally separate, chosen Israel.

One major reason rapturists insist that a tribulation and millennium are necessary is God's supposed failure to make good on His physical promises to Abraham. Abraham was promised that his kingdom would extend "from the river of Egypt to the great river, the river Euphrates" (Gen. 15:18). Rapturists claim that this has never been fulfilled, but the Bible tells us another story. At the pinnacle of the Davidic kingdom, King Solomon dedicated the Temple he built to God, and he claimed that this promise had already been fulfilled in his lifetime! In fact, he blessed the people of Israel by saying, "Blessed be the Lord . . . not one word has failed of all His good promise" (1 Kings 8:56).

According to rapturists, the Millennium will be the Messianic Kingdom that God had promised to David but never delivered. Ignoring the scriptures that indicate that the physical promises have already been fulfilled, they believe that Jesus must physically rule from an earthly throne in the Middle East.

As hard as this is to imagine, rapturists believe that during this reign of Jesus in Jerusalem, the Temple will be in operation again. Hal Lindsey opines, "Obstacle or no obstacle, it is certain that the Temple will be rebuilt. Prophecy demands it" (LGP, 56). This means that even its sacrificial system of animal sacrifices must be reinstituted.

But this does not conform with the New Testament writers' view of the Church: as the fulfillment of all the Old Testament prophecies about the heavenly Jerusalem and the new Temple. As the Old Testament progressed, the prophets revealed more and more that the promises of God pointed to an everlasting, spiritual reign, rather than a merely physical kingdom. The spiritual graces we enjoy in the Church are the sum of all that God has been working toward in this world since the sin of Adam. In fact, St. Justin and Tertullian are not unique in teaching that the Church is the whole reason the world, along with Adam and Eve and everyone since, was ever created in the first place (*TSV*, II:4; *ACR*, II:7; *APO*, XXXI:3, XXXII:1)!

Have we lost sight of where we were in The Apocalypse? The angel informed us in the sixth trumpet that there would be "no more delay." This mystery of God must soon be revealed for all to see. The powerful angel predicts that when the seventh trumpet is sounded, the "mystery of God, as He announced to His servants the prophets, should be fulfilled" (10:7).

It has now been sounded, and the voices in Heaven proclaim, "The kingdom of the world has become the Kingdom of our Lord and of His Christ, and He shall reign forever and ever" (11:15). At the seventh trumpet, the New Covenant has publicly and unmistakably superseded the Old Covenant. This is one of the major messages of The Apocalypse: that the Old Jerusalem, with its sacrifices and rules, must make way, permanently and visibly, for the public establishment of the New Jerusalem. It is the picture of what St. Paul promised in Galatians.

And so it was in 70 A.D., if we follow the chronology given by Christ in the Olivet Discourse. When the Temple fell, it became obvious even to pagan Rome that Christianity was not a sect within Judaism. The Church was free to grow unencumbered by the baggage of the Old Covenant sacrifices being performed daily in the Temple in Jerusalem. The mystery of the Church was free to be fulfilled in the sight of all.

The Apostles understood the pre-eminence of Christ's Church on the day of Pentecost. In Heaven it was understood from before the foundation of the world and completely accomplished with the Passion. We saw Heaven celebrating the Kingdom's establishment back in the initial vision, before the very first seal. But the public establishment of the mystery of Christ's Church became evident to non-Christians with the events of 70 A.D. The stone of Daniel's vision had arrived and destroyed the statue of earthly kingdoms, and now everyone could see it.

This seventh angel, who announces the Kingdom to the world, is a parallel to the angels in the Olivet Discourse: "He will send out His angels with a loud trumpet call, and they will gather His elect from the four winds" (Matt. 24:31). At this point, the gospel message has been proclaimed throughout the civilized world. The mystery of Christ's Kingdom is evident for all who care to notice. Now, after its dispersal and persecution, it is time for the spiritual revival of the young Church. After the public demise of the Old Covenantal system, the New Covenant could flourish unimpeded by confusion or mixed loyalties. Daniel's time of covenantal transition has run its course and fulfilled its purpose.

Summary of the initial vision

We have now completed the initial vision: all seven seals, all seven trumpets, all seven thunders, and all three woes.

St. John used the seals and trumpets to give us a double look at the fall of the Temple in Jerusalem — first from the perspective of Christ, and then from that of the Sanhedrin. In so doing, he has mimicked Daniel. Daniel's initial vision is about the statue: the ancient empires viewed from the king's perspective. The first recapitulating vision of Daniel (the four warlike beasts) views the same empires from the perspective of the conquered. St. John has used both of these perspectives in his initial vision.

Now that we have finished the initial vision, ask yourself, "Is there really anything in this vision that was not already fulfilled in the events surrounding 70 A.D.?" Admittedly, St. John's descriptions are vivid, but undoubtedly there has already been an adequate fulfillment in the events of the Temple's destruction. And that is not the only problem for rapturists. Remember that before we examined The Apocalypse, we determined that there is no biblical evidence for a future seven-year Great Tribulation at all! Without it, there is no need for a secret rapture, so it is not surprising that we could find no biblical evidence for that event either. Even rapturists do not claim to be able to find any mention of their secret rapture in these first eleven chapters of The Apocalypse.

SECTION II: THREE KEY PERSONALITIES IN CHAPTER 12

Take a deep breath and congratulate yourself. St. John's first vision is completed. If you understand The Apocalypse through Chapter 11, you are over the hump. The mystery of the Kingdom has been revealed to the world. The remaining visions will recapitulate this initial vision, and some will extend all the way to the final eschaton.

Following Daniel's outline, however, St. John will first insert a section that will focus more closely on the three key personalities behind the drama of Daniel's final week of covenantal transition. This personality section provides the background for the rest of The Apocalypse.

The activities of these three personalities span the entire last week of Daniel, which encompasses seven decades. It should not surprise us that Daniel covered the events of three key personalities as well: the Kings Nebuchadnezzar, Belshazzar, and Darius. St. John will tell us the history of the Child, the Woman, and the dragon.

The Child

The first key personality of Daniel's seventieth week is "a male Child, one who is to rule all the nations with a rod of iron" (12:5). The idea of ruling with a rod of iron comes from Psalms 2:9, which is generally accepted as a Messianic psalm pointing to Jesus. This Child who will rule with a "rod of iron" is identified in a later vision as "the Word of God" and "King of kings, and Lord of lords" (19:13, 16). The birth of the Child initiates the beginning of Daniel's seventieth week.

There can be no doubt that the Child is Jesus Christ. That is the overwhelming view of all scholars. Further evidence that the Child symbolizes Jesus is that the "Child was caught up to God and to His throne." This language is reminiscent of how the Scriptures have described the Ascension of Christ in Mark 16:19, Luke 24:51, and Acts 1:9.

The Woman

The second key personality of these seven decades is a Woman. In the heavenly Temple, the ark appears as "a Woman clothed with the sun, and the moon under her feet, and on her head a crown of twelve stars" (12:1). Like the two witnesses (11:3), the Woman symbolizes both a group and one specific person who ideally represents that group (GR4).

• *Mary.* Everything said about the Woman is true of one person, and some of what St. John writes about the Woman is true of no one in all of history *but* that one person: Mary, the Blessed Mother of our Lord and Savior, Jesus Christ.

Of course, this makes perfect sense, since, in the vision, the Woman's identity is inextricably tied to her motherhood. If the Child of the Woman is Jesus, the Woman must be Jesus' Mother.

Perhaps we read the end of the seventh trumpet so quickly that we missed something. St. John saw "the ark of His covenant . . . within His Temple" in Heaven (11:19). The Old Covenant ark resided in the Temple's holy of holies (Exod. 26:33). There, between its two cherubim, God took up His abode with His people. In St. John's vision, however, there are two temples: the one on earth about to be destroyed, and the one in Heaven, which will endure forever.

The Temple St. John sees is in Heaven, and then he immediately notices a "Woman clothed with the sun." This is the Woman who bore the Child. Her womb nurtured the God-man before His birth. This makes her the perfect "ark of His covenant." Mary is the ark of the New Jerusalem Temple.

So both Scripture and Church history point to one and only one woman at this point: Mary, the Mother of Jesus. She is the Ark of the New Covenant. No one, absolutely no one, other than Mary fits this description.

Some rapturists, along with other Protestants, are very uncomfortable with Mary, especially the idea of her being enthroned in some role of authority in Heaven. They seem to think it is a doctrine the Church "invented" relatively recently. But this is not true. This teaching concerning Mary goes back to the earliest of the Church Fathers.

In fact, it can be traced back even further than that. Like virtually all the psalms, Psalm 45 is replete with Messianic overtones. Verse 9 speaks of the queen standing at the "right hand" of her King, her Son. The context of Psalm 45 makes it rather clear this is the King's mother, not His daughter or wife. This can be taken as a small glimpse into the Messiah's throne room in Heaven (cf. 1 Kings 2:19). Mary sits in Heaven in a place of honor because her Son is the King (cf. Songs 6:9-10).

• *The Church.* At the same time, the symbolism of the woman goes deeper than just Mary, the individual. Just as Moses and Elijah were particular representatives of the Law and Prophets, Mary has been accepted since the early Church as a symbol and type of the Church. This Woman "clothed with the sun" also symbolizes the Church, just as the witnesses pointed to the Law and the Prophets (GR4).

We rapidly find assurance that our identification of the Woman is correct. "Her offspring" are identified as "those who keep the commandments of God and bear testimony to Jesus" (12:17). These offspring are clearly the children of Mother Church. From one of the seven letters, we know that even the responsibility to rule the nations will be delegated to the faithful of the Church (2:26-27).

The dragon

The story of the woman does not progress very far before a third key personality is introduced. This new character is "a great red dragon, with seven heads and ten horns, and seven diadems upon his heads" (12:3). This dragon is none other than "that ancient serpent, who is called the Devil and Satan, the deceiver of the whole world" (12:9). In typical apocalyptic language denoting political upheaval (GR5), "his tail swept down a third of the stars of heaven" (12:4).

Those who would deny the existence of a personal Satan cannot adequately explain this passage. He is certainly described as more than just a force or influence for evil. In fact, the Church has always described him as more than just an evil influence. The Church speaks of Satan as an evil *person* or spirit who tempted man in his first sin (CCC, pars. 397-398).

Daniel's last week

In the interactions of these three key personalities, St. John summarizes Daniel's entire seventieth week. This is the only time in The Apocalypse that all seven decades of Daniel's seventieth week are in focus, making this the pivotal chapter of the book. John has just finished describing the victory of Christ over His foes in the first half of the book and will examine the parallel victory of the Church over her foes in the second half. But here St. John pauses to put into focus the entire seven decades of covenantal transition from the birth of the Messiah until the destruction of Jerusalem's Temple. Everything else in The Apocalypse flows from the historical events described here. In fact, everything in salvation history flows from these events.

One of the first things we notice again is apocalyptic literature's disregard for our twenty-first-century obsession with chronology (GR8). There are three vignettes that overlap chronologically, just as Daniel's visions did. In 12:6, we see the Woman (the Church of Jerusalem) fleeing into the wilderness for "1,260 days." Then the story on earth is interrupted with some events in Heaven that explain the earthly events. The story returns in 12:14 to the same three-and-a-half-year period, expressed as "time, and times, and half a time," during which the Church was in flight from Jerusalem. In the initial vision, we already encountered this as the time of the "trampling" of Jerusalem and as the time during which the two witnesses were slain and resurrected.

This period comprises the same forty-two months we have noticed since Daniel: the time during which the Roman Empire was at war with Jerusalem and its Temple (February of 67 to August of 70 A.D.) Because the Church had heeded the warning of Jesus in the Olivet Discourse, her members fled from Jerusalem at its outbreak and were protected at Pella in Transjordan and elsewhere while the siege progressed around Jerusalem. As we noted in Daniel, this three and a half years are the final five percent of Daniel's seventieth week.

Events on earth

Now that we have met the Child (Jesus), the Woman (Mary and the Church), and the dragon (Satan), we can examine the pivotal events of Daniel's seventieth week.

So how do the seven decades of covenantal transition begin? The Woman, Mary, gives birth to the Child, Jesus (12:2). Immediately, the dragon tries to destroy the Child. "The dragon stood before the Woman who was about to bear a Child, that he might devour her Child when she brought it forth" (12:4). This is widely understood to be a reference to Satan's use of Herod when he tried to kill Jesus as an infant. This, too, would have been at the very beginning of the seventieth week of Daniel.

Mary's Child is born and destined to rule the nations. But something unexpected happens. Mary's "Child was caught up to God and to His throne." This is a clear reference to Christ's Ascension and coronation in Heaven. That would place us at the halfway point of Daniel's last week, around 30 A.D.

Until this point, the primary focus of the Woman is as a symbol of the Blessed Mother, Mary. Now the symbolism of the Woman expands to include the Bride of Christ, the Church. The Woman is forced by the dragon to flee into the desert, where she is protected by God. This is a good picture of what the Jewish Christians did when they saw the Roman army surrounding Jerusalem: they fled from Jerusalem into the desert area of Pella. This event is at the very end of Daniel's seventieth week, either in 66 or 68 A.D.

Parallel events in Heaven

At this point, the vision changes focus for a second vignette. St. John gives us the heavenly perspective on the quick overview of Daniel's final week just completed, and he focuses our attention on the events surrounding the Passion of our Lord. In Daniel, the entire seventieth week pivots and centers on the Passion. It is halfway through the seven decades and is the basis of the "strong covenant" of Daniel. It holds center stage in this vision as well, as it does in the entire Apocalypse and in all of history.

The Passion was an earthly, historical event, but more important, it was also a heavenly, spiritual event. St. John describes it here as a war in Heaven between Satan's angels and God's angels. Through the power of the risen Christ, God's forces, led by the archangel Michael, are victorious. An announcement is made: "Now the salvation and the power and the Kingdom of our God and the authority of His Christ have come, for the accuser of our brethren has been thrown down, who accuses them day and night before our God. And they have conquered him by the blood of the Lamb" (12:10). Satan is cast out of Heaven and grows bitter because of his defeat.

St. Augustine summed up this section of The Apocalypse well in one of his sermons: "The victory of our Lord Jesus Christ came when He rose and ascended into Heaven. . . . The Devil jumped for joy when Christ died; and by the very death of Christ, the Devil was overcome: he took, as it were, the bait in the mousetrap. He rejoiced at the death, thinking himself death's commander. But that which caused his joy dangled the bait before him. *The Lord's Cross was the Devil's mousetrap:* the bait which caught him was the death of the Lord" (SSA, 222).

Events on earth resumed

Now that he has described the heavenly battle that imbues the corresponding earthly events with meaning, St. John can return to the Woman's flight into the wilderness. He had to interject the events in Heaven so we would know what truly made the flight necessary. It was the hatred of the dragon for anyone associated with this Child. The third vignette resumes the interrupted story on earth to fill in the details.

After the Ascension, the Woman primarily symbolizes the Church. The salvation of God's people is assured by the aid of Yahweh, "the two wings of the great eagle" (12:14 and Deut. 32:10-12). God protects them for the same three and a half years in this flight, as in the flight before the heavenly scene, because they are one and the same flight (12:6; 12:14). The flight illustrated the obedience of the Church to the warning of Christ in the Olivet Discourse: "Then let those who are in Judea flee to the mountains, and let those who are inside the city depart" (Luke 21:21).

But Satan is not about to give up his designs on this Woman, the Church, so easily. The serpent attempts to "sweep her away with the flood" (12:15). This flood reference reflects Daniel 9:24-27. In that vision of Daniel (III:C), the war that destroys Jerusalem and its Temple is described as a flood. We have already determined that this refers to the Jewish-Roman War at the end of Daniel's final week. So St. John gives us a tidbit of information that we did not learn in Daniel. It was Satan's plan to use the Roman army to destroy the Church of Jerusalem during the war in Judea.

But Satan's plan was foiled. The Christians obeyed the command of Jesus in the Olivet Discourse, and they fled at the beginning of this three-and-a-half-year period. The flood, which was the Roman army, was "swallowed" by the land (12:16). This is an accurate picture of what Josephus describes in the Jewish-Roman War. Conquering Jerusalem was no easy task. It exhausted all of Rome's energy and patience. By the time of their victory, the Roman Empire had no stomach for tracking down and destroying the Church as Satan had planned.

Of course, Satan had surely planned to trap the Christians in Jerusalem along with everyone else. If the Church had stayed in Jerusalem, she would have been destroyed along with the Temple. But the Church heeded the warnings of the Olivet Discourse and so was not in Jerusalem when the flood came.

The next sentence must have sent chills down the spine of any early Christian reading The Apocalypse aloud in Church: "Then the dragon . . . went off to make war on the rest of her offspring" (12:17). The dragon does not give up when the Roman army fails to destroy the Woman and her offspring, the Church. Satan redoubles his efforts to destroy "those who keep the commandments of God" (12:17).

As history attests, Satan has continued to hate the Woman's offspring even after the events of 70 A.D. were completed. Emperor after emperor persecuted the early Church. Diocletian, in the late third century, is perhaps the most infamous persecutor of the Church. He vowed to wipe even the word *Christian* from his empire (CE, IV).

This hatred has continued down through the ages into modern times. Muslims have been ruthless in their treatment of Christians who refuse to convert. Hitler's hatred for the Church is well documented. The communists of the Soviet Union and China have shown no remorse for their persecution of Christians. Although the names change through time, the motive behind it all remains the same: the hatred of the dragon for the Woman, stemming from the dragon's defeat by the Child.

Another Winkle Warp

Rapturists make such a convoluted mess of this passage that it hardly warrants a point-by-point refutation. Let me just mention one problem with their time line, caused by yet another instance of Winkle Warp.

Some rapturists understand these two forty-two-month periods (12:6 and 12:14) as consecutive, giving them their future seven-year Great Tribulation. But these are clearly *identical* times, both involving the flight of the Woman "into the wilderness." Indeed, if we must start to place all these periods end to end, we could end up with fourteen or more years in the rapturist Great Tribulation.

There is a more serious problem with rapturists' time line, though. They believe it will occur at the very end of history, during a seven-year tribulation that immediately precedes Christ's second coming. Yet the dragon "went off to make war on the rest of her offspring" when his initial assault failed. When would he find the time to do this if the second advent occurs immediately? There is no room for any more war in the rapturist time line.

It is much better to understand this as St. John clearly intended. These events are history from Daniel's final week. The events of Chapter 12 are the pivotal events in all of history. This was when Christ established the "strong covenant" with His New People.

SECTION III: INITIAL VISION RECAPITULATED

St. John has completed his descriptions of the three key personalities around which the covenantal transition revolves. The rest of The Apocalypse is a series of visions that add details to the initial vision of seals and trumpets from Chapters 4 through 11 (plus the epilogue). While the initial vision ended when Daniel's final week ended in 70 A.D., the last of these recapitulating visions will extend right up to the final eschaton and eternity. This is exactly what Daniel did when he recapitulated his initial vision. His final vision (III:E) extended all the way to the final judgment, his own.

There are differing opinions about how to divide the remaining visions. How many are there? The rapturist tends to see the remainder of The Apocalypse as one long chronological account of the future. That position was unheard of in the *first thirteen centuries* of the Church, when the dominant position was that they are a recapitulation of the initial vision, as in Daniel's outline. As St. Augustine taught, the visions of The Apocalypse repeatedly review the same events and period. Most scholars would probably separate the rest of the book into four or five visions. Either way, it would not alter our interpretation one whit, although I find five to be more helpful and understandable. The first three visions relate to the three key personalities we examined in the last section.

III:A   The battle strategy of the dragon
Parallels Daniel's vision of the battle strategy of the beast

III:B   The battle strategy of the Lamb
Parallels Daniel's vision of the battle strategy of the goat and ram

III:C   The battle strategy of God's People
Parallels Daniel's vision of the battle strategy of God's People

III:D   The Great Battle
Parallels Daniel's vision of the Great Battle

III:E   The vision of From Here to Eternity
Parallels Daniel's vision of From Here to Eternity

We skipped treatment of two of Daniel's visions (III:B and III:D) because they do not impinge directly on our topic. In The Apocalypse, we will examine all five of them in order.

Section III:A: The Battle
Strategy of the Dragon

After the Child of the Woman escapes the dragon in Chapter 12, St. John relates that the dragon targets the Woman's off-spring: the Church. In Vision III:A, we learn the strategy of the dragon in his pursuit of revenge on the Child for his defeat in Heaven. This emphasis on battle strategy in the first recapitulating vision should not surprise us. Daniel did the same thing. He had five recapitulating visions, and much of the content of those (including the ones we did not examine) involved the battle strategy of the combatants.

What is the dragon's battle strategy? Basically, it is to use power and deceit to coerce people into accepting his distorted view of reality. He denies the possibility of judgment after death. His deceit is popular even today: "What you see is all you get." If deceit fails, he intimidates and even annihilates his opponents.

Two beasts rise up

In Chapter 13, St. John introduces us to the two beasts that the dragon uses to implement his strategy. The Church (the Woman and her offspring) encountered them and their full power in the Great Tribulation. We will dub them the sea-beast and the land-beast. "And I saw a beast rising out of the sea. . . . Then I saw another beast which rose out of the land" (13:1, 11). The sea traditionally symbolized the gentile nations, and the land traditionally stood for the Jewish people. This means that the sea-beast symbolizes gentile Rome, and the land-beast symbolizes the Jewish leadership of St. John's day. Both are the dragon's servants. Satan cannot have a child, like the Woman, but he does have slaves.

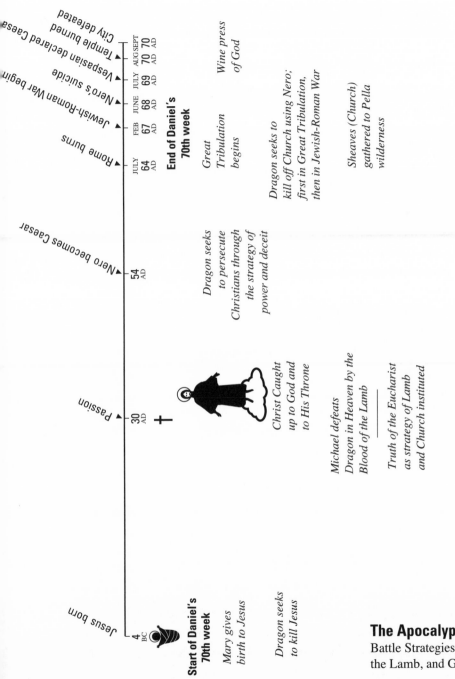

The Apocalypse:
Battle Strategies of the Dragon,
the Lamb, and God's People

Jesus born

**Start of Daniel's
70th week**

*Mary gives
birth to Jesus*

*Dragon seeks
to kill Jesus*

4
BC

Passion

30
AD

*Michael defeats
Dragon in Heaven by the
Blood of the Lamb*

*Truth of the Eucharist
as strategy of Lamb
and Church instituted*

*Christ Caught
up to God and
to His Throne*

Nero becomes Caesar

54
AD

*Dragon seeks
to persecute
Christians through
the strategy of
power and deceit*

Rome burns

JULY
64
AD

**End of Daniel's
70th week**

*Great
Tribulation
begins*

*Dragon seeks to
kill off Church using Nero;
first in Great Tribulation,
then in Jewish-Roman War*

*Sheaves (Church)
gathered to Pella
wilderness*

Jewish-Roman War begins

FEB
67
AD

JUNE
68
AD

Nero's suicide

JULY
69
AD

Vespasian declared Caesar

Temple burned

City defeated

AUG SEPT
70 70
AD AD

*Wine press
of God*

Rapture

The gentile sea-beast

Rapturists assume that the sea-beast of Chapter 13 is the antichrist. Some Catholics follow their lead. But nowhere in the entire book is there any indication that this is the final antichrist foretold to appear at the final confrontation between good and evil. In fact, by the time we get to the final battle, St. John foresees that both beasts will have been in the lake of fire for centuries! No, this sea-beast lived in the first century, although he might certainly stand as a type for the final antichrist (GR3).

When reading the description of the sea-beast, we cannot avoid being reminded of the four beasts in Daniel's vision. The beast has attributes of "a leopard . . . a bear . . . and . . . a lion." From this we can be absolutely certain that St. John saw the Roman war machine as the fourth beast of Daniel 7. The beast even has the same ten horns. Modernists who try to interpret Daniel without including Rome must answer to St. John.

The sea-beast is the dragon's protégé, so it has seven heads and ten horns just like the dragon (13:1). The ten horns represent the ten provinces of ancient Rome, as a later vision will make clear (17:9-13).

That later vision also reveals that the seven heads have a double meaning (GR4). The vast majority of scholars would agree that these seven heads are the seven emperors who ruled Rome, and that is the meaning that concerns us here.

There is controversy over when to start counting emperors. Who was the first emperor? Modernist scholars begin with Augustus, the heir of Julius Caesar. But St. John was not a modernist scholar. He was a Jewish native of Judea, like the ancient historian Josephus. And because Josephus was a contemporary of St. John, he is illustrative of how St. John's original Jewish readers would have numbered the emperors. Josephus started counting the imperial rulers of Rome with Julius Caesar. Even though Julius technically ruled during the Republic, he was considered by St. John's

contemporaries to be the first of the emperors. After all, he established the Julio-Claudio dynasty that ruled Rome for generations.

This dynasty began with Julius Caesar and continued through
Augustus, Tiberius, Caligula, Claudius I, and Nero. This makes
six, with the seventh head being Emperor Vespasian, under whose
rule Jerusalem was sacked and the Temple destroyed by General
Titus, his son and future heir to the throne. The interregnum of
three short-lived rulers is ignored by Josephus, just as it is by most
present-day scholars when numbering the emperors.

St. John mentions seven heads, including Vespasian, because
that was the number of emperors before Jerusalem was judged and
the Church vindicated. In early 68 A.D., Nero was Caesar, and so
stands as representative of the empire. By July 1, 69, Vespasian was
declared emperor by his troops. He was confirmed by the Senate in
Rome on December 21, 69. Of course, the number *seven* was also
very important symbolically (GR2).

Yet in this vision of the sea-beast, Nero is the primary focus.
Why? The reason should be obvious. He was the emperor during the Great Tribulation implemented by the two beasts. In this
vision of the dragon's battle strategy, the destruction of the Temple takes a back seat to the greater conflict between Satan and
Christ's Church from 64 to 67 A.D. — a conflict that extends
even to today.

Remember, that spiritual conflict is what imbues the destruction
of the Temple with significance. Christ pointed to the judgment of
the Temple and the Sanhedrin as the public vindication of His
message and ministry. The destruction of the Temple revealed to
the world the message of the scroll: the mystery of the Church. We
encountered this scroll in God's throne room in the initial vision.

Overall, the symbolism of the beasts is similar to that of the
Woman and of the two witnesses. Nero, Vespasian, and Titus each
stand at different times as a specific focal point for the entire Roman Empire in its vindictive destruction of Jerusalem. Later in the

book (17:11), the beast is identified as General Titus, who became the eighth emperor of the Roman Empire. At other times, it is evident that what is said of the beast is meant to refer to the entire Roman Empire and its government. St. John uses his symbols to signify dual realities (GR4).

The mortal wound

The beast suffers a wound on one of its heads. "One of [the beast's] heads seemed to have a mortal wound, but its mortal wound was healed, and the whole earth followed the beast with wonder" (13:3). Nero is the personification of the empire in much the same way as Moses was the personification of the Law. At this point, the beast signifies Rome, and the wounded head symbolizes Nero.

Rome certainly endured what "seemed to [be] a mortal wound" during the tumultuous reign of Nero. Nero's reign was disastrous in many respects: Rome was plagued by uprisings and civil wars; the Senate hated him; and the provinces, the army, and even the praetorian guard finally revolted against him. In the end, he committed suicide. On an individual level, that not only seemed to be a mortal wound; it was.

On a political level, the suicide of Nero caused a wound that seemed mortal as well. Nero's sudden suicide, preceded as it was by his incompetence, led to a total disarray in the Roman Empire. Many Romans, including General Vespasian, were afraid the empire might disintegrate after Nero's suicide (WJ, IV, 8:1).

During the interregnum between Nero and Vespasian, three men reigned for a very short time each. There were three rulers from the suicide in June 68 A.D., to the Senate's confirmation of Vespasian in December 69 A.D. These nineteen months of turmoil saw civil war within the city of Rome itself. Rome was perhaps in more danger during this interregnum than at any other point in its history (WJ, IV, 8-10). Some historians are amazed that the empire avoided implosion. Rome's failure to suppress the revolt of the Jews spawned insurrections throughout the empire, up until Titus's victory in 70 A.D. Then "the mortal wound was healed," as Vespasian ruled over a peaceful Roman Empire for nine years. Indeed, the empire had been wounded through Nero's actions, but the empire would be healed.

Worshiping the beast

A careful reading of the text reveals that, although the "head" suffers the mortal wound, it is the beast that is followed. After the mortal head wound, that particular head is not mentioned again. This is, of course, because Nero is dead, but the Roman Empire has survived. "The whole world followed the beast with wonder."

By Nero's reign, the ancient Roman world had given itself unreservedly to the worship of the emperor as divinity. St. John equates this with worship of Satan himself: "Men worshiped the dragon . . . and they worshiped the beast, saying . . . 'Who can fight against it?' " (13:4). Rome truly was invincible in the eyes of much of the ancient world. St. John understands the power of Rome as a gift from the dragon.

This worship of the sea-beast led to blasphemy, as Daniel had predicted (7:25). The beast (Rome as personified in its Caesars) "was given a mouth uttering haughty and blasphemous words . . . for forty-two months" (13:5). This is the same three and a half years that we have seen repeatedly throughout The Apocalypse. Historically it refers to the time when Rome and Jerusalem were at war, from February of 67 to August of 70 A.D. During this time, three men were Caesar: Nero, Vespasian, and Titus (Titus was declared Caesar by his father before Jerusalem fell; SH, XXX:403). In demanding worship, the Caesars had crossed the line between political loyalty and idolatrous blasphemy.

Nero's arrogance and blasphemy are well known, but the next two emperors were no better. Jewish tradition states that after the

Romans overran the Temple, Titus took a prostitute into the innermost chamber of the Temple, the holy of holies, spread out a scroll of the Torah (the Old Testament Scriptures), and proceeded to engage in an act of fornication on the scroll. Such was the arrogant blasphemy of the Caesars who conquered Jerusalem and persecuted the Christians. They were beasts.

How to fight the invincible beast

In the face of this invincible beast that demands and accepts worship, what is a Christian to do? St. John makes clear one thing they are *not* to do. Lest the early Church take up arms to protect itself in a futile and suicidal revolt, The Apocalypse warns that "if anyone slays with the sword, with the sword must he be slain" (13:10). This warning parallels that of Jesus in the Olivet Discourse: do not join the army of false Messiahs if you value your life. "Here is a call for the endurance and faith of the saints" (13:10). Endurance and faith are the only paths to victory in what amounts to a spiritual battle with a political foe.

This can also be taken as a promise. The pleas for justice by the Christian martyrs under the altar in the fifth seal have not been forgotten. In the midst of the description of these two evil beasts, the reader is reminded that justice will be served in the end. But the role of the Christian is to plead his case before God's throne. It is a lesson that applies to many ages beyond just the first century.

The Jewish land-beast

The second beast, the land-beast, now enters the scene. As is so often the case in The Apocalypse, earth in 13:11 would better be translated as "land." This land-beast "had two horns like a lamb, and it spoke like a dragon" (13:11). So the land-beast will speak just as deceitfully as Satan, but will appear harmless and holy. This beast must be a symbol of the Sanhedrin.

This interpretation dovetails with how many scholars view the essence of these two beasts. "Satan calls up two lieutenants: the 'beast from the sea,' the political [adversary of the Church, which is] . . . the Roman Empire with its emperor worship . . . ; and the 'beast of the earth,' the philosophical and theological [adversary]" (NCE). The Jewish land-beast provides theological "cover" for the political machinations of the Roman sea-beast.

Josephus mentions two men whom Nero sent to administer his will in Jerusalem (AJ, XX, 11:1): Albinus and Gessius Florus. They are probably the most logical interpretation of the two lamb-like horns on the beast.

In a few chapters, this same land-beast is referred to as "the false prophet." "False prophet" is actually a description of what the land-beast does: "It works great signs, even making fire come down from Heaven to earth in the sight of men. . . . It deceives those who dwell" in the land (13:14). This false prophet is able to imitate even that sign of the greatest of the Old Testament prophets, when Elijah brought fire down from the sky. But his main stratagem is deceit.

This passage parallels the prophecy of Jesus. In the Olivet Discourse, Jesus predicted that, at the time of the destruction of the Temple, "false christs and false prophets will arise and show great signs and wonders." The land-beast uses signs and wonders to deceive people. St. John is careful to show that Jesus has kept His promise. The signs He pointed out in the Olivet Discourse came to pass within that generation.

This land-beast stands in a long line of false prophets who have assured God's people that they were safe, when they were anything but safe. The Sanhedrin in 70 A.D. certainly fit the description. Not only had they led Jerusalem in revolt against her Messiah almost a generation earlier, but during the war, "there was a great number of false prophets suborned by the tyrants to impose on the people [in Jerusalem] . . . that they should wait for deliverance from God" (*WJ*, VI, 5:2). As we learned in the initial vision, they were forced to drink wormwood (8:11).

This land-beast is given authority by Rome and "makes the land and its inhabitants worship the first beast, whose mortal wound was healed" (13:12). The Roman system of government required great autonomy on the part of the provincial governments. The empire was simply too large to be administered by a centralized bureaucracy in Rome. So Nero used the provincial governments within his empire to enforce emperor worship. Judea was no exception. This cooperation with Roman idolatry was one reason the outlaw Zealot hated the Sanhedrin and the priesthood in Jerusalem. They thought the leaders of Jerusalem were blaspheming the Law of Moses in their cooperation with Roman religion.

Although some of the earlier Caesars accepted worship, it seems doubtful they genuinely believed it themselves. But many historians think that Nero did believe in his own divinity, and so he rigorously enforced his edict of worship on all his subjects. One ancient writer called the enforcement of Nero's edict "maniacally rigorous." In fact, "the Neronian persecution [was] the most cruel that ever occurred" (*HCC*, I, 386). During Nero's reign, even simple trade became impossible without submitting to the worship of Nero in the town square: "No one can buy or sell unless he has the mark, that is, the name of the beast" (13:17).

The Jewish leadership had compromised to survive, by performing daily sacrifices in the Temple for Nero, but the Christian Church refused to participate in anything that even bordered on idol worship. In the letters to the churches of Pergamum and Thyatira, St. John encouraged them to hold to the Faith in this regard. No idol worship! For obeying Christ, Christians were viewed as traitors. As traitors, they were hunted down and killed by Rome.

Rome did not act in isolation from its provincial governments. The land-beast caused "those who would not worship the image of the beast to be slain" (13:15). Jerusalem encouraged and cooperated with Rome because the Sanhedrin had their own motive for hating the Christians. Christianity taught that the Temple worship was obsolete, and that the divisions between Jews and Gentiles had been superseded by Christ's atonement. That was the initial vision's mystery of the scroll that was unsealed for the entire world to see.

Although it seems shocking to the modern Christian, Jerusalem not only cooperated fully with the Roman persecution of the early Church, but it even instigated that persecution. Although it is not true of modern Israel, the description of the land-beast in this passage actually matches the Jewish leadership of first-century Jerusalem perfectly. Not until 66 A.D. did they rebel against Rome, and at that point the Roman Empire turned its wrath on them. St. John describes the rift between Rome and Jerusalem in a later vision.

St. John's description of the image of the beast has an uncanny resemblance to the image that Nebuchadnezzar built after his dream of the statue in Daniel. Three Hebrews were thrown into the fiery furnace because they would not worship the king's gods. It is likely that St. John used this reference to remind his Christian readers about how that story ends. The three faithful Hebrews were spared death by the intervention of God, but they had clearly demonstrated their willingness to die rather than engage in idolatry.

The human number, 666

The land-beast also makes life difficult for those who will not submit to "the mark" of the sea-beast. Just what this mark of the beast is has been the subject of almost unlimited speculation. But before we examine the mark, we should realize that St. John understands that the reader may be a bit confused.

He pauses to clarify the identity of this sea-beast with the mark. He instructs his readers to "reckon the number of the beast, for it is a human number, its number is six hundred and sixty-six" (13:18). This may have clarified the situation for the Christians of the first century, but these numbers have caused havoc ever since. Everyone agrees that it must refer to a human man. Beyond that, the number 666 has been taken to identify everyone from the Pope to Luther, from Hitler to Mussolini, from Stalin to Mikhail Gorbachev, from FDR to Ronald Reagan. But remember, the writer was trying to make his message clear to his *original* readers, without subjecting them to charges of treason or blasphemy. The number 666 is one of *sixteen* clues to the identity of the sea-beast that St. John gives in The Apocalypse.

Today's scholars agree: to reveal the identity of the beast to Jewish Christians, while hiding it from outsiders, St. John used the rabbinic numbering system for names, called *Gematria*. When the Gematrian numbers of Nero's official name in Hebrew are added together (fifty plus two hundred plus six plus fifty plus one hundred plus sixty plus two hundred), they total 666. The original Hebrew Christian readers of this vision would have understood this immediately. Without endangering the Church, St. John succeeds in fingering the present Roman emperor, Nero, as the sea-beast (GR4, 8).

The early Church universally understood these numbers to refer to Nero. Even the futurist Irenaeus mentions that Nero is the Gematrian solution to the puzzle of the 666. In some manuscripts of The Apocalypse, the number had been copied as 616. Irenaeus points out that even this number would work as the solution to Nero's abbreviated name. This is further evidence that the early Church understood the 666 as a reference to Nero, the personification of the sea-beast.

The significance of the number *six* in triplicate would not have escaped the original readers either. *Six* stood symbolically as the number of man. Nero might be powerful, but he was only a man. Even the trinity of Nero, Vespasian, and Titus would never add up to more than just finite man. Nero could never be 777 (perfection), much less 888 (Christ conquered death on the eighth day).

The mark of the beast

Now we understand that the sea-beast clearly symbolizes Rome during Nero's time. But we still need to examine "the mark" of this beast. Could it really be a microchip that will be imbedded in the forehead or hand at some point in the future, as some believe?

No. That is simply Winkle Warp again. Although everything that happened in 70 A.D. in the destruction of the Temple might give us a picture prophecy of what may happen in the still-future final battle, we cannot assume willy-nilly that details of this sort will be repeated (GR3).

The "mark" was a common symbol in the Old Testament, signifying loyalty. Cain was given a mark for disloyalty after he killed his brother (Gen. 4:15). The mark of lamb's blood on the doorposts in Egypt just before the exodus of the Hebrews was a public announcement of loyalty. In Ezekiel 9:4-6, a mark was put on each loyal man's forehead before God destroyed those in Jerusalem who were doing evil. This mark was the Hebrew letter *tau*, or *T*, and those without it were killed in judgment. The early Church saw it as a prophecy pointing to the sign of the Cross.

As the prophets preached to Israel over the centuries, this mark of loyalty evolved into a primarily interior reality that paralleled the evolving vision of a spiritual Kingdom. Jeremiah prophesied, "I will put my law within them, and I will write it *upon their hearts; and I will be their God, and they shall be my people*" (Jer. 31:33). No serious scholar of Jeremiah assumes that God meant that He would write the words of the law on their hearts with a ballpoint pen. Nor could the "law within them" be something an X-ray machine could detect. The loyalty of the New Covenant, which is the focus of this beautiful passage in Jeremiah, is an inward commitment of the will that manifests itself in the way we live.

Rapture

Rapturists are not the first to take the spiritual meaning of a Bible passage and interpret it in an overly physical way. The Pharisees did the same thing. In Deuteronomy, Moses instructed the Israelites in the "Great Commandment": "Hear, O Israel: The Lord our God is one Lord; and you shall love the Lord your God with all your heart, and with all your soul, and with all your might" (6:4-5). He explains that this commandment should be kept always in mind and continually taught to the next generation. He goes on to say, "And you shall bind them as a sign upon your hand, and they shall be as frontlets [or phylacteries] between your eyes" (6:8).

How did the Pharisees interpret this instruction of Moses? Many of them seemed to miss entirely the spiritual meaning of Moses' message: that this "Great Commandment" had to affect the way they thought, the way they saw the world, and the way they lived their lives. Instead, they literally tied phylacteries onto their foreheads and right arms. Phylacteries were small leather boxes with leather straps, and inside the boxes was printed the "Great Commandment." Yet as Jesus makes clear, their adherence to the literal, physical interpretation of this passage lulled them into a false security. They failed to keep the spiritual command of Moses: to be ever mindful of the presence of their awesome God in everything they thought or did (Matt. 23:1-7).

Like the Kingdom that is being revealed, the marks of The Apocalypse are *internal*. There are two marks: the mark of the beast and the mark of the Lamb. Popular sentiment concentrates on the mark of the beast, but God's mark — the mark of the Lamb — is actually much more important in The Apocalypse. It is first alluded to in the sixth letter to the churches, the letter to Philadelphia. God's mark is mentioned specifically in the sixth seal of the initial vision (7:3). The four angels are held back from judgment until God's children can be marked with His name. In the later vision of the Child's strategy, the redeemed 144,000 all have been marked by God (14:1). This mark of God is evident even in eternity. In Heaven God's faithful "servants shall worship Him; they shall see His face, and His name shall be on their foreheads" (22:4).

The mark of the beast and the mark of the Lamb are inward and discernible only through the actions of those marked. Having it on the hand signifies the change in what we Christians *do* as a result of our loyalty, while the forehead mark signifies how our loyalties change the way we *think*. The loyalty to God's Law within the Christian community would be obvious to everyone when emperor worship was demanded in the marketplace. Christians refused to "go along to get along," and they ended up as a people marked by Rome for death. At the same time, God marked these martyrs for eternal life.

In a later vision, we see evidence that St. John intended us to understand the mark of the beast in this spiritual fashion. In the vision of the winepress, "anyone [who] worships the beast and its image" is equated with "receiv[ing] a mark on his forehead or on his hand" (14:9). This spiritual understanding of the marks dovetails best with the mark of God's presence even in eternity.

God's mark is actually much more important to the message of The Apocalypse. Yet for some reason, few try to understand it in the physical, literalistic way in which the mark of the beast is portrayed in contemporary prophecy novels.

Summary of Vision III:A

Rapturists try desperately to place all of this in the future. But the fulfillment would have been clear to the first-century Christian, so why bother?

At the time of St. John's writing, Nero personifies the Roman Empire. He is the human whose symbol is 666, and he demands worship in violation of God's Law. This is the only time in history that the Church was persecuted by both the Roman beast and the Jerusalem beast. Even the eighth emperor of the later vision has already lived and died. We know him as Titus, the son of Vespasian. Unless we have slept through the history of the first century and are suffering from Winkle Warp, there is no reason to look for any future fulfillment.

That said, the lesson of the two marks is timeless. Throughout history, the strategy of the dragon has been to make it socially advantageous to compromise with evil. Derision and death have always accompanied those who have refused his deceptions (GR3).

In the first century, the mark of the beast was the willingness to worship Rome's power. God's mark was revealed in the refusal to worship Satan's great deception. *It still is today.* Deception of any kind is straight from Hell, and it usually still stinks like smoke.

SECTION III:B: THE BATTLE STRATEGY OF THE LAMB

Now in beautiful fashion, St. John uses these opposing marks to make the transition from the battle strategy of the dragon and his beasts to the battle strategy of the Child and His followers who have "His Father's name written on their foreheads" (14:1). As you may remember, the Child is none other than the Lion and the Lamb of the initial vision.

What can be the battle strategy of Christ in response to this powerful, deceitful strategy of Satan? That is the question of this vision. We will learn not only how the Lamb opposes the dragon, but also the benefits that the Lamb's followers can expect. Remember, the Lamb's followers are the same people as the offspring of the Woman.

The famous 144,000

This vision begins with a scene on Mount Zion in Heaven. The author of Hebrews mentions Mount Zion as being associated with the heavenly Jerusalem. "You have come to Mount Zion and to the city of the living God, the heavenly Jerusalem, and to innumerable angels in festal gathering, and to the assembly of the first-born who are enrolled in Heaven, and to a judge who is God of all, and to the spirits of just men made perfect" (Heb. 12:22-23).

On Mount Zion stands "the Lamb, and with him a hundred and forty-four thousand who had His name and His Father's name written on their foreheads" (14:1). These martyrs have God's mark of loyalty upon them. They should remind us of the "saints" in the heavenly scene of the initial vision (5:9).

The number 144,000 was used in Chapter 7 to symbolize the entire number of those who came into the Church from biblical Judaism. But we noted that it also had all the earmarks of a symbolically large number. There is no good reason to change our mind here.

In this instance, the 144,000 are all "chaste." But the Greek word, *parthenos*, is more accurately translated "virgins" (14:4). Without a doubt, this is a difficult passage for the average rapturist. As a group, rapturists vehemently disagree with the Church's historical teaching concerning the need for sexual continence within the leadership of the Church. Lest there be any doubt, St. John emphasizes his point by describing them as those "who have not defiled themselves with women." "Defiled" is probably too strong a translation for the relatively rare Greek word *moleno* in this passage. It carries with it the idea of becoming ceremonially unfit for service. (The only other occurrences in the Bible are 1 Corinthians 8:7 and Apocalypse 3:4.) Although rapturists and modernists hate to admit it, here is evidence that the early Church's demand for episcopal celibacy was just that — very early. Although the marriage bed is certainly holy, the sexually continent are held up to the reader as exemplary. They are to be esteemed precisely because of their virginity.

Once again the Catholic is free to take the text for what it actually says. Being "eunuchs" for the Kingdom is a sacrifice that does not go unnoticed in Heaven (Matt. 19:12). Although some

Rapture

modernist Catholics try to argue the point, the Church's historical teaching is that this is a higher calling (CEC).

Singing a new song

The 144,000 "sing a new song before the throne and before the four living creatures and before the elders" (14:3). St. John acts as though we should know who these creatures and elders are, and so we should. They appeared at the very beginning of the initial vision in the throne room. This indicates that these two visions have the same starting point, the throne room of God. In fact, the events are almost identical. Because of this, we will use the symbolism mentioned in both places to clarify the battle strategy of the Lamb.

The entire passage revolves around the actions of these 144,000 who are "redeemed from the land." The 144,000 "sing a new song" along with the twenty-four elders (5:9; 14:3). This song is the battle strategy of the Child.

"Wait a second," you think. "What kind of battle strategy is this?"

It does seem ludicrous! After all, the dragon has two beasts of power that deceive, imprison, and kill their opponents. How could it be that the entire battle strategy of the Child involves nothing more than a choir of virgins singing a song so unsingable that "no one [else] could learn" it (14:3)? This is not what we expected. We were promised a "rod of iron" from this Child. Where is it? It is nice that the chaste in this choir are "spotless," and it is wonderful that they do not "lie," but this is a *battle with a dragon* (14:5)!

The strategy of God has always been a mystery to those who think like the dragon. In a passage with Messianic overtones, Zechariah is told, "This is the word of the Lord. . . . Not by might, nor by power, but by my Spirit, says the Lord of hosts" (Zech. 4:6). The dragon's mindset has so permeated our modern culture that our minds reel under the full implication of these words.

That greatest of the prophets, Elijah, was in a battle with the powerful and evil queen Jezebel. He went into the wilderness to hide in a cave near Mount Horeb. There God promised to come to Elijah: "Behold, the Lord passed by, and a great and strong wind rent the mountains . . . but the Lord was not in the wind; and after the wind an earthquake, but the Lord was not in the earthquake; and after the earthquake a fire, but the Lord was not in the fire; and after the fire a still, small voice" (1 Kings 19:11-12). No matter what the age, God is not found in power, but in the still, small voice speaking Truth.

The eucharistic song

But the song these virgins sing is special. The song that the celibate 144,000 sing is the Eucharist. We touched briefly on this in the throne room of the initial vision; let us now consider it more closely.

The elders "sang a new song" (5:9), and the chaste "sing a new song" (14:3). This is the eucharistic song of Heaven. It was not a part of the Old Covenant, but is integral to the New. When we sing "holy, holy, holy," we join all the choirs of saints and of angels in Heaven (4:8).

The connection to the Eucharist becomes apparent when we investigate the Greek words used by St. John. The verb form *sang* is a translation of the Greek word *ado,* and the noun form *song* is from the word *ode.* These Greek words are the source of our English word *ode.*

Webster's Dictionary defines *ode* as "a poem suitable for singing that is addressed to some person and characterized by lofty feeling and dignified style." Think about that. That is a pretty good description of the Mass.

Other than the three times we see them in The Apocalypse, *ado* and *ode* are used only twice elsewhere in the New Testament: in Ephesians 5:19 and Colossians 3:16, where they are linked to *eucharisteo*. This is the root of our word *Eucharist*, meaning "thanksgiving."

Where does this lead us? "Singing an ode" is a specialized phrase in the New Testament that is linked by context to the thanksgiving we give to God in the Mass, the Eucharist. Our thanksgiving is due to the salvation Christ won for us when He "wast slain" (5:9).

We will encounter one more case of people singing an ode in the next vision, and they will also refer to the thanksgiving we give to God in the worship of the Mass.

The reason the initial vision identifies the Lion with a slain Lamb becomes apparent: it is an obvious reference to the sacrifice of the Passion. Every Catholic should know that the Church celebrates and joins itself to that ultimate sacrifice in the unbloody Sacrifice of the Mass.

Now it makes sense why the first throne-room scene makes a point of the presence of "priests" (5:10). This Kingdom of God on earth requires priests. Without priests, there is no sacrifice of the Mass. The priest is an essential element in bringing the sacrament of the Eucharist into our daily lives. Our conclusion: *The Eucharist* is the battle strategy of the Lamb. *The Eucharist* proclaims the mystery of the gospel; it is the center of the New Covenant Kingdom.

This sacrament strengthens our souls for our battles with the dragon. It proclaims the mystery of the one spiritual Kingdom of Jew and Gentile for the entire world to see. It turns our hearts toward home, our eternal home, by reminding our eye of faith that what we see is not always what we get. It reminds us that there is a home for us that will be everlasting, although it is now unseen. It strengthens us for the pilgrimage. It makes the Truth, which is the Lion's primary weapon, take root in our lives. But most of all, it fulfills the promise of Christ in the seventh letter: "If anyone hears my voice and opens the door, I will come in to him and eat with him, and he with me" (3:20).

The three angels

Now the strategy of the Child starts to unfold. The eucharistic song of these chaste, holy martyrs has stirred three angels. In the midst of the 144,000 singing virgins, an angel announces, "Fear God and give Him glory, for the hour of His judgment has come" (14:7). Perhaps there is more power in this song than the dragon thinks.

The first angel announces the "eternal gospel." What is the eternal gospel? "Fear God and give Him glory. . . . Worship Him who made Heaven and earth" (14:7). The gospel revolves around God and His glory, not our wonderful plans and achievements.

We are to give God glory because "the hour of His judgment has come" (14:7). At this point, the angel is not announcing the final, general judgment that all humanity will undergo at the end of time. That must wait until the vision of From Here to Eternity (ch. 19). The judgment this angel announces will descend on those who persecuted the Church in the first century, in answer to the martyrs under the altar who have been pleading for justice since the seals in the initial vision. This judgment occurred in 70 A.D.

We are confirmed in this assessment when we read a few verses later, "Blessed are the dead who die in the Lord from henceforth" (14:13). If this judgment were the final event of history, there would be no people to die "henceforth." In 21:4 we read that after the last judgment, "death shall be no more." We are not at that point yet. Death will be conquered, but we must keep in mind that death is "the last enemy to be destroyed" (1 Cor. 15:26).

The second angel informs us of the object of God's judgment: "Babylon." And the success of this judgment is assured. The angel announces, "Fallen, fallen is Babylon the great" (14:8 and Isa. 21:9). This is not, then, the final judgment of all humanity.

The identity of this city, "Babylon," is hotly contested. It is certainly not the one in Iraq, which had been a ruin for hundreds of years before The Apocalypse was written. That Babylon had already been judged by God. "Babylon" is a code for another city, a city that has already appeared in the initial vision.

Like "Sodom and Egypt" in the initial vision, "Babylon" is a code name for Jerusalem, a city too politically dangerous for St. John to mention by name. In The Apocalypse, "that great city" always refers to Jerusalem (18:10, 16, 19). We should expect that. After all, the destruction of Jerusalem's Temple is what reveals the mystery of the scroll. These visions are a recapitulation of that initial vision. Because of the tremendous civil turbulence engulfing Jerusalem in 68 A.D., St. John disguises the city's identity to protect his readers from automatic persecution if they were to be discovered reading The Apocalypse.

Why would Babylon be chosen as a symbol of first-century Jerusalem? We examined it already in "Belshazzar's folly" in Daniel. The ruler of Babylon, Belshazzar, had defiled God's holy Temple vessels by a profane use. God struck the city with judgment by the invasion of the Persian army. In code-naming Jerusalem "Babylon," St. John points out another city about to endure the judgment of God because of its disdain for God's holiness. She was guilty of "impure passion," another expression for spiritual harlotry, or idol worship (14:8). St. John anticipated this issue in the seven letters to the churches. Jerusalem's complicity in the worship of the sea-beast is about to bring its consequences.

Babylon was judged by God for blasphemy after a prophetic proclamation. That pronouncement was announced via "the hand from God's presence" (Dan. 5). Yet the instrument of that judgment was the Persian army. God Himself never physically appeared in Babylon (GR6).

In 70 A.D., the new Babylon, Jerusalem, was also judged by God after a prophetic proclamation by the Hand of God. Jesus Himself spoke Jerusalem's doom in the Olivet Discourse and elsewhere. The instrument of that judgment was once again an army, this time from Rome.

Now the third angel appears with an urgent warning for Christians, complementing the message of the first angel, which is the eternal gospel. That angel commanded the worship of God; this angel gives them a choice. If Christians do not resist emperor worship, which is worship of the power of the dragon, they will bear the same consequences as Jerusalem. These consequences are of eternal import: "The smoke of their torment goes up forever and ever; and they have no rest, day or night, these worshipers of the beast and its image, and whoever receives the mark of its name" (14:11).

But those who endure and "keep the commandments of God and the faith of Jesus" will partake of eternal bliss (14:12). "Blessed are the dead who die in the Lord henceforth" (14:13). While the persecuted Christians may find that earthly power and its benefits elude them in this life, when they die, they will "rest from their labors, and their works do follow them" (14:13).

This is our hope. It is also our choice: power now or bliss for eternity. This is the battle strategy of the Lamb, to *tell us the Truth about eternity*. There is no better vehicle for this Truth than the Eucharist. While the dragon promises the earthly perks of success through power, the Lamb assures us that we will reap our just reward in eternity. The benefits of following the Lamb flow for all eternity.

Make no mistake: this vision is not about boring theology. The application of these principles is new and fresh for every generation. Our culture is very "dragonish," tempting us to use deceit and power to obtain wealth and pleasure now. In countless decisions every day, we each must choose to worship the power of the dragon or to answer the "call for the endurance and faith of the saints" (13:10; 14:12).

St. John knows it is not an easy choice. But God will not tinker with our free will as the dragon would. The dragon will trick us with deceit and coerce us with power. God's strategy is simply to show the world the Truth. Christ is pictured in The Apocalypse with a sharp sword coming from His mouth. That is Christ's weapon, the Truth of God. You will live for all eternity with the consequences of your choices.

The three messages of the three angels reflect the message of Jesus. First, Christians must fear and obey God. Second, Jerusalem will fall in order to vindicate the eternal power of the risen Christ. Third, all men will be eternally judged in the end for their deeds.

Two more angels

Can you hear the dragon snickering at all this? "Sure, sure," he laughs. "But how do you really *know* that an eternal reward awaits you? I promise you rewards in *this* life. You cannot be *certain* Christ can keep His promises until it is too late. You will be already dead!"

That is a very good question. *How do we know?*

That brings us to the second half of the Child's strategy. Christ anticipated Satan's deception. The early Church taught that one reason we could trust Jesus for our eternal reward is that He kept His promises concerning the Temple in the Olivet Discourse. We know He is capable of an eternal judgment at the final eschaton because He judged His executioners within the generation that He predicted He would. Anyone who can reach back from the other side of the grave to keep His promises and judge His enemies must be God. The judgment upon the Temple is the proof of Christ's claim that we will be judged in eternity!

Two more angels appear to illustrate this. The first angel urges Christ to gather His followers from the land before judgment strikes. "One like a Son of man" reaches with a sharp sickle into the land because "the harvest of the land is fully ripe" (14:14-15). We have been waiting for just this announcement. Earlier, God had been waiting for more martyrs and Jewish believers before He would answer their pleas for justice (6:11; 7:3). The pleas came from the souls under the altar in the initial vision. Now the angel tells the "Son of man" that the sheaves are ripe and the time for judgment is ready. But before the judgment strikes Jerusalem, Christ Himself will remove His followers from harm's way. As we saw in the Olivet Discourse, Jesus met this responsibility: He warned them, they fled, and they were spared.

The second angel gathers, not wheat for protection, but grapes for crushing in the "winepress of the wrath of God" (14:19). The judgment on the Sanhedrin is about to commence. When it comes, it substantiates the claims of Christ. He has the right to promise His faithful an eternal reward because He really is the "Son of man." He rose from the dead and judged His accusers. "The treading of the winepress is the retribution" (COA, XIV). As the Son of man, He first protects His own. Then He proceeds with the judgment promised to His accusers.

This imagery of both angels is taken directly from the prophet Joel: "Put in the sickle, for the harvest is ripe. Go in, tread, for the winepress is full. The vats overflow, for their wickedness is great" (3:13). In the winepress imagery, St. John also includes the truth asserted by Ezekiel: "As I live, says the Lord God, I will prepare you for blood, and blood shall pursue you; because you are guilty of blood" (35:6).

The winepress of God's wrath

The second angel harvests the grapes, unbelieving Jerusalem, for crushing; and the crushing is horrible: "The winepress was trodden outside the city, and blood flowed from the winepress, as high as a horse's bridle, for one thousand six hundred stadia" (14:20).

One thousand six hundred stadia is approximately 180 miles. It is no coincidence that this is the length of ancient Israel. When the Roman army under Vespasian and then Titus marched through ancient Israel to conquer Jerusalem, the toll was horrific.

Rapture

What do you see when you imagine the winepress of God? If you are like most Christians, nothing specific comes to mind. But imagine the city of Jerusalem surrounded by crosses. So many crosses ring the city walls that the Romans run out of trees to cut down. When the Romans catch a Jew, they whip him and nail him to a cross. Beaten and bloody captives are lying about, awaiting their crucifixion when crosses becomes available. As the blood pours down from the crosses encircling Jerusalem, it looks like the very life of Judea is being crushed out of it.

Because of the Passover, it has been estimated that 2,700,200 people were trapped inside Jerusalem by the Romans. During the last five months of the siege, a million were killed (Apoc. 9:5; *WJ*, VI, 9:3; *AEV*, 96; *RKC*, 27). That is about seven thousand victims every day without rest for a full five months! These crucified Jews were elevated within sight of the city walls to instill fear in Jerusalem. The wounds of the crucified were approximately at the height of a horse's bridle.

St. John mentions the horse's bridle to anticipate the next visions, in which the ancient plagues of Egypt revisit Jerusalem. The horse's bridle brings to mind the first exodus from Egypt, when the Hebrews passed through the Red Sea. When the Egyptian persecutors tried to pursue them with horse and chariot, the Red Sea surged and drowned the Egyptians and their horses. God later judged Egypt for its treatment of His people. Ezekiel painted a rather grotesque picture of this judgment of Egypt: "I will drench the land even to the mountains with your flowing blood; and the watercourses will be full of you" (32:6).

Just so, the new people of God were to pass through a red sea to obtain deliverance from the new Egypt, which was the Old Jerusalem. This sea would not be of salt water this time, but of the blood of those Jews who had attempted to keep Christians in bondage. The sea of red ringed Jerusalem and drenched the hills around it with blood, like a "great winepress . . . outside the city" (14:19-20).

The winepress image also recalls Isaiah's beautiful love song about the vineyard of God that "yielded wild grapes" (5:1-7). As a result, the owner had to abandon his vineyard (cf. Ps. 80). Jesus borrowed this Old Testament analogy when He spoke of Jerusalem as a vineyard in Matthew. Because the tenants of the vineyard beat the owner's servants, and ultimately killed the owner's son, the parable ends with the tenants of the vineyard being put "to a miserable death" (21:33-46). Jesus was saying that the unfaithfulness of the priests and the Sanhedrin's rejection of the Messiah would result in their downfall. The chief priests understood Jesus perfectly, so they "tried to arrest Him" (21:46). But within a generation, these leaders met the "miserable death" that Jesus had predicted. It may not always be pleasant or easy, but one thing remains: Jesus tells the Truth.

SECTION III:C: THE BATTLE STRATEGY OF GOD'S PEOPLE

Now we know the battle strategy of the Lamb — namely, the Truth as told best in the Eucharist. But what of the Lamb's Church? What is their strategy? This question is answered in Chapter 15.

This vision begins in the same place as the one we just examined, and as the initial vision of the scroll: in the throne room of God. We encounter the same "sea of glass" (15:2). This should reinforce our belief that these visions recapitulate each other. This vision does not break new ground chronologically.

At first blush, it seems as if the Church's strategy is just as filled with singing as the Lamb's. We clearly see that the Church in Heaven has already conquered the dragon and his beasts. Yet there has been no mention of the saints fighting! What kind of battle strategy is this? All singing and no fighting?

The strategy of the Lamb and the strategy of God's People hearken back to Daniel, who, when forbidden by the government to pray to God, opened his window and worshiped as always, in defiance of the state (Dan. 6).

This was also the battle strategy of Daniel's three friends under attack by a government hostile to their faith. Hananiah, Azariah, and Mishael refused to worship a statue of the king, so they were thrown into a fiery furnace. The deuterocanonical portions of Daniel include the Prayer of Azariah and the Song of the Three Holy Children. The three prayed and sang in the midst of their persecution (Dan. 3).

St. John calls Christians to hold to the truth of Christ in the same manner. This parallel is a small hint that scholars are correct when they claim that St. John used a copy of Daniel that included the deuterocanonical portions. This may be one minor reason rapturists have trouble understanding this book. They use a truncated Old Testament!

The Church, too, has a strategy of prayer in the face of a beastly government. Her prayer involves joining herself to the eucharistic celebration of Heaven. The Eucharist is the Church's highest prayer.

The battle strategy of the Old Testament people of God was enunciated in the vision of the seventy weeks. If they would build the Temple of God, the Messiah would come shortly thereafter. It would involve work and much prayer, but that was their strategy. In much the same way, the battle strategy of the New Testament people of God is to build the new Temple of God, Christ's Church. The prayer of the Eucharist does it best.

Here in The Apocalypse, St. John has twice paused to say, "Here is a call for the endurance and faith of the saints" (13:10; 14:12). The first time, this call immediately follows an admonition about the futility of armed conflict against the beast. "If anyone slays with the sword, with the sword must he be slain" (13:10). The second time follows a warning not to accept the mark of the beast; in other words, do not "worship the beast." We must "fear God and give Him glory" (14:7).

This is how the battle is won! When faithful Christians refuse idolatry and immorality, when they endure even to the point of death, then the dragon and his beasts are defeated. Instead of worshiping the beast, the Church worships Christ. We see the same "singing of an ode" in this vision that we noticed in the Child's strategy. The highest worship we can give the Lamb is in the Mass.

Keep in mind: this defeat of the dragon may not be immediately apparent here on earth. We must raise our line of sight from earthly events and comprehend that the victory that counts is the victory in *eternity*. The dragon will win his interim skirmishes here on earth through his strategy of raw power and deceit. But he will lose the *war* for all eternity. In fact, he already has lost. The dragon aims for a finish line that ends with our earthly death. The Church understands the Truth of a deeper reality: this world is not all there is. We are made for eternity. That is the strategy of the Church, flowing directly from the strategy of the Lamb that was slain.

So the singing in Heaven makes sense. It is a part of the Eucharist. The victors sing "the song of Moses" and "the song of the Lamb." The song of Moses was first sung by the Hebrews when God parted the Red Sea for them and destroyed their enemies in the flood of its returning waters. Its inclusion anticipates the exodus theme of the next vision: the Church is the New Israel of God being freed from the tyranny of spiritual Egypt — physical Jerusalem. The song of the Lamb makes it clear that these are the citizens of the New Jerusalem: Christians on a spiritual exodus from the Old Covenant of Old Jerusalem. The mere mention of the Lamb should recall His Passion. This song of the Lamb is eucharistic.

Just as in the strategy of the Child, the singing of the Church in Heaven stirs angels to action. This time there are seven of them, bringing seven bowls of plagues that proceed from God's Temple. St. John tells us that these "seven plagues . . . are the last, for with them the wrath of God is ended" (15:1). "The wrath of God always strikes the obstinate people with seven plagues, that is, perfectly, as it is said in Leviticus" (COA, XV). The seven bowls of plagues are enough to exhaust God's wrath over the treatment of His Son.

This is an important point. "The wrath of God is ended" with these seven plagues. Therefore, just as the ancient Roman Empire cannot be reconstructed and then held responsible for the events of two millennia ago, neither can the modern Jews of Jerusalem be made responsible for the actions of the first-century Sanhedrin. Anti-Semitism is a twisted sort of Winkle Warp that ignores the history it finds inconvenient.

Present-day anti-Semites may try to hide behind religious reasons, but it is my experience that they have other motives. We must not be fooled into anti-Semitism; God's wrath with Judaism was ended in the winepress of 70 A.D. — period.

Vision III:D: The Great Battle

Now that we know the strategies of the three personalities in Daniel's seventieth week, a question remains: When it comes to pitched battle, which strategy will win out?

The vision of the Great Battle recapitulates the events of the earlier visions, with a new emphasis. Old earthly Jerusalem is cast in the role of Egypt, seeking to keep God's New Covenant people in slavery to the Law. As we have noted, St. John anticipated this theme for us in the two prior visions.

Jerusalem's judgment has been the overarching theme throughout The Apocalypse. Now we encounter new symbolism in that regard: "Come, I will show you the judgment of the great harlot" (17:1). We know these visions are recapitulating, and we know that "the great" refers to Jerusalem, so we should suspect that this "harlot" is none other than Jerusalem.

In this vision, the object of God's judgment is the city that "shed the blood of saints and prophets" (16:6; 18:24). This echoes the words of Jesus, when He spoke of Jerusalem. In Matthew, Jesus announced seven woes upon the religious leadership of Jerusalem. At the end of these woes, Jesus says, "O Jerusalem, Jerusalem, killing the prophets and stoning those who are sent to you! . . . Behold, your house is forsaken and desolate" (Matt. 23:37-38). St. John will subtly reflect these seven woes of Jesus in the seven bowls of the Great Battle.

As if that were not enough to designate Jerusalem as the harlot, St. John links the harlot with Babylon. We already know that Babylon symbolizes Jerusalem: "Babylon the great, mother of harlots and of earth's abominations" (17:5-6).

So we see that harlot is another code name for Jerusalem. This should not surprise us if we have read the Old Testament. The prophet Isaiah accused Jerusalem of harlotry: "How the faithful city has become a harlot, she that was full of justice! Righteousness lodged in her, but now murderers" (1:21).

So the names for Jerusalem thus far include the great city, Sodom, Egypt, Babylon, and the harlot. In addition, Jerusalem was the land-beast that cooperated with the sea-beast and will soon appear as the false prophet. Jerusalem's judgment as the new Egypt is the focus of this vision. But the events are the same as when "the kings of the earth . . . and everyone, slave and free, hid in the caves" in the sixth seal (6:15). They are the same events as when "the four angels were released, who had been held . . . to kill a third of mankind" at the end of the trumpets (9:15). The seven seals examined these events from the King's perspective; the seven trumpets examined them from the Sanhedrin's perspective. The seven bowls examine the destruction of Jerusalem from the Church's perspective.

The battle is waged by the Lamb against the beasts of the dragon for the benefit of the Church. The battle is placed in the context of the plagues that God visited upon Old Egypt in the time of Moses' exodus. Now the "plagues" of Egypt start to work against

Rapture

Old Jerusalem, the symbolic Egypt, to the benefit of the New Jerusalem, the Church.

The first six plagues

In the vivid imagery of apocalyptic literature, we see Jerusalem subjected to the same plagues as ancient Egypt had been: "foul and evil sores . . . blood . . . fierce heat . . . darkness . . . frogs . . . earthquakes . . . and great hailstones." Since these are apocalyptic descriptions, we need not expect literal fulfillment in every detail (GR5, 6). The point of this vision is that the Church, the New Jerusalem, is being led in exodus from the slavery of Old Jerusalem, which is now the new Egypt (GR3).

There are interesting parallels between Jerusalem's leadership and Egypt's Pharaoh Ramses. They both wanted to keep the children of God, His *ekklesia*, in slavery to their law. God in His grace wanted to free His children, so both Pharaoh and the religious leadership of Jerusalem "cursed the name of God who had power over these plagues, and they did not repent and give Him glory" (16:9).

Everything will not be identical, however. In the first exodus, the Egyptian army attempted to cross the dry Red Sea to keep the Jews in slavery. This time the army that crosses the river is there to judge the "Egypt" that refuses to liberate the Christians. "The great river Euphrates . . . was dried up, to prepare the way for the kings from the east" (16:12). That was the direction over which Titus led his troops — drawn from all provinces of the empire, including "from the east." The invasion of the sixth bowl precisely parallels the invasion of the sixth trumpet: they are one and the same event.

Yet another Winkle Warp

Rapturists looking for a literal, modern fulfillment miss the main message of The Apocalypse. The famous rapturist preacher

Harry Ironside exhibited a rather severe case of Winkle Warp in 1938: "Who are these kings? It is not necessary to guess, as the word for *east* is simply *sun-rising*. The kings of the sun-rising! Japan has been known as the empire of the rising sun for a millennium. . . . There you have the kings of the sun-rising, all in readiness for . . . the Armageddon conflict. . . . The yellow peril becomes more and more ominous. The preparation of the day of the Lord goes on apace" (*TKB*, January 1938).

Rather than engage in this type of nonsense, it is better to understand the river Euphrates being dried up as an allusion to the Red Sea. The Red Sea protected the Hebrews on the original exodus. The Euphrates had always stood as a protective barrier to invasion of Israel from the north. No more. It would not stop the Roman army and its allies.

The place called Armageddon

As the kings of the east pour *en masse* over the dried-up Euphrates in the sixth plague, we encounter the name of a new location: "They assembled them [the armies] at the place which is called in Hebrew 'Armageddon.' " This was a famous military spot in ancient times. In fact, some military histories begin with a description of the battle between Syria and Egypt (commanded by Thutmose III) on this very spot. That famous battle occurred at the Mount of Megiddo, also know as "Armageddon."

This mount controlled the pass between the plain of Jezreel and the plain of Sharon; in Scripture, this area was the scene of many battles. Deborah and Barak slew Sisera on this plain (Judg. 4-5). Gideon defeated the Midianites (Judg. 6-7) and the Philistines slew King Saul here (1 Sam. 29-31). By bringing up the Mount of Megiddo, St. John reminded his Jewish readers of all these events.

But by far the most pertinent previous battle of Armageddon was the battle of the Judean King Josiah against the Egyptian Pharaoh Necho. King Josiah was a great spiritual reformer in Judah.

He did battle with Egypt and was killed (2 Kings 23:29; Zech. 12:10-11). History records that a short time later, Pharaoh and Egypt were defeated by a third country, Babylon. The holy city was destroyed, and Israel was sent into its seventy-year captivity in Babylon. The mention of Armageddon would bring to memory all the events that led to the fall of Jerusalem and the destruction of Solomon's Temple by the Babylonians.

This parallel would have been evident to St. John's initial readers. The great spiritual reformer (Jesus) was killed by the leaders of the city that St. John code-names "Egypt." But then in 70 A.D., this new Egypt (Old Jerusalem) is defeated and the holy city destroyed by Rome (GR3).

At this point, we must take serious exception with the teachings of many popular rapturists. They speak continually about the "Battle of Armageddon," but there is not the slightest mention anywhere in The Apocalypse of a battle near the Mount of Megiddo, which is west of the Jordan River in the plain of Jezreel.

Read the passage again: "They assembled them at the place which is called in the Hebrew 'Armageddon.' " It describes only the gathering of the army there, and that is precisely what occurred in the Jewish-Roman War. General Titus gathered his troops in this area between ancient Samaria and Galilee. From there he pushed into the siege that eventually destroyed Jerusalem and its Temple. There is no future Battle of Armageddon awaiting the world. This prophecy was completely fulfilled by Titus.

The seventh plague

With the seventh bowl, "the great city was split into three parts" (16:19). We have encountered this symbolism of thirds twice already. They were both in anticipation of this more developed treatment.

This symbolisim was undoubtedly included by St. John to bring to mind the prophecy of Ezekiel: "O son of man, take a sharp sword; use it as a barber's razor and pass it over your head and your beard; then take balances for weighing, and divide the hair. A third part you shall burn in the fire in the midst of the city, when the days of the siege are completed; and a third part you shall take and strike with the sword round about the city; and a third part you shall scatter to the wind, and I will unsheathe the sword after them" (5:1-2). Thus, Jerusalem was to suffer in three ways: death within the city by pestilence, death outside the city by sword, and the living death of exile. All three occurred when Rome defeated Jerusalem, just as Jesus had predicted in the Olivet Discourse.

The seventh plague, the hailstones, has an interesting fulfillment. The Roman army set up catapults to heave great stones into Jerusalem during the siege. Josephus tells us that each stone weighed about a talent, or approximately a hundred pounds. This was just what St. John predicted: "Great hailstones, heavy as a hundredweight, dropped on men from Heaven, till men cursed God for the plague" (16:21). Who could ask for a more historical fulfillment?

But Josephus adds a little irony in his narrative. When an incoming hailstone was spotted by the watchmen of Jerusalem, they would cry "out aloud, in their own country language, 'The Son cometh'; so those that were in its way stood off . . . but the Romans contrived how to prevent that by blacking the stone" (WJ, V, 6:3). The irony is in the way Josephus translates the warning of the watchmen. In Hebrew the words for *son* and *stone* are *ben* and *eben*. These words could easily have been confused when the watchmen shouted their warning. But Josephus chose to record this misunderstanding in his book, which was not written in Hebrew, but in Chaldee or possibly Greek. In neither of these languages can the word for *stone* be misunderstood as the word for *son*.

Why would Josephus insert this ironic twist? He probably figured his Roman readers would get a good chuckle out of the irony of Jerusalem's watchmen announcing the arrival of Caesar Titus, the son of Caesar Vespasian.

Of course, the Christian reader would discern an even deeper meaning. The coming of the stone was really a sign of the coming of the Son of man in judgment as predicted in Daniel and in the Olivet Discourse. Just as God came to judge Egypt in the army of the Assyrians, and just as God came to judge Babylon in the army of the Persians, so Christ came to judge Jerusalem in the army of the Romans (GR6).

The harlot and the beast

The angel of the last bowl reveals Jerusalem just as the Church would perceive her: a harlot riding a scarlet beast. Remember, the Church is the Bride of Christ. We have already determined the identity of the harlot. The imagery surrounding the harlot reflects the Old Testament prophets' denunciations of Jerusalem. The first three of the Major Prophets are emphatic in their denunciations of the harlotry of Jerusalem (Isa. 1:21, 57:8; Jer. 2:20, 3:1-25; Ezek. 16:15-39, 23:1-21). Hosea went a major step further. He married an unfaithful woman to illustrate dramatically the anguish and charity of God toward Israel, the harlot (Hos. 1:2ff).

The harlot (earthly Jerusalem) is the alter-ego of the Woman (the Church) who fled into the wilderness to escape the dragon. This contrast between these two women sets up a perfectly mirrored image of the battle in St. John's visions. Christ joins battle on behalf of the Woman, New Jerusalem. He does battle with the harlot, old Jerusalem, who acts as the mouthpiece of the dragon. The description of this harlot dovetails with everything we have read about Jerusalem thus far in The Apocalypse.

The reference to the harlot's being "seated upon many waters" is a reflection of Jeremiah's description of the original Babylon, whose destruction was a type of Jerusalem's destruction (51:13; GR3). But it is also true that Jerusalem was well known for its abundant source of spring water. This was one of the reasons Jerusalem was a difficult city to conquer. It could endure a long siege.

In this vision, the harlot sits on "a scarlet beast" that "had seven heads and ten horns" (17:3). We also know who this beast is from an earlier vision: none other than the sea-beast that symbolized Rome in the vision of the dragon's strategy (III:A). Even rapturists admit this. The dragon's ten horns are the ten kings of the provinces of the Roman Empire: Italy, Achaia, Asia, Syria, Egypt, Africa, Spain, Gaul, Britain, and Germany.

The harlot is "drunk with the blood of the saints and the blood of the martyrs of Jesus" (17:6). In the early days of the Church, Jerusalem's religious leaders were the major persecutors of Christians. The book of Acts makes this quite clear. The harlot rides the scarlet beast; symbolizing Jerusalem's use of pagan, idolatrous Rome to implement their persecution of the Christian Church. It took her three decades to get Rome to initiate the Great Tribulation, but she eventually succeeded in 64 A.D.

Jerusalem enjoyed tremendous influence within the ancient Roman Empire. Her influence was such that it would not be an exaggeration to say of ancient Jerusalem that she exercised "dominion over the kings" (17:18). Josephus tells his readers that "the royal city Jerusalem was supreme, and presided over all neighboring countries as the head does over the body" (WJ, III, 3:5). The fact that the city was defeated and destroyed can obscure for us the vast influence and power it held before it fell from favor.

This harlot also possesses vast wealth. "The woman was arrayed in purple and scarlet, and bedecked with gold and jewels and pearls" (17:4). Jerusalem straddled a major trade route in the ancient world. These merchants brought tremendous wealth into Jerusalem.

Seated on seven hills
Just to be certain we do not misunderstand him, St. John points to the Woman's identity by giving us a geographical clue related to the seven heads of the beast: "The seven heads are seven hills on which the woman is seated" (17:9).

Rapture

The interesting twist from our twenty-first-century perspective is that there were two ancient cities surrounded by seven hills. Almost every modern student of ancient civilizations is aware that Rome is surrounded by seven hills. Many modern students do not know, however, that Jerusalem is also built upon seven hills. Josephus even records the names of these hills: "Zion, Acra, Moriah, Bezetha, Millo, Ophel, and Antonio" (WJ, V, 5:8). The Apocalypse was written for Jewish Christians. They would undoubtedly have thought of Jerusalem as the city on seven hills. Many of them would have actually been there and walked through those hills.

We can be sure that the city symbolized by the harlot could not have been Rome, as many rapturists teach. Besides the intertwined code names and images that we have already discussed, there is a simple reason right in this vision. St. John may have used vivid imagery. He may seem extravagant in his verbiage to a modern reader. He may be accused of being long-winded and repetitive. But St. John has not once been contradictory or illogical in these visions. And that is what he would have been if he had used the harlot to signify Rome.

The sea-beast on which the harlot has been riding will change its mind about this evil woman and ultimately "will hate the harlot . . . will make her desolate and naked, and devour her flesh and burn her up with fire" (17:16). It is illogical to make Rome the object of Rome's hatred and destruction. It makes much better sense to see the sea-beast as Rome and the harlot as Jerusalem. This understanding also has the advantage of consistency with the rest of The Apocalypse.

There could be no clearer fulfillment of these verses than in the events of the decade leading up to 70 A.D. Jerusalem's Sanhedrin had sought to repress the Christians from the very first beating they administered to Peter and John (Acts 4). Three decades later, in 64 A.D., they finally convinced the Roman authorities to help them in their pursuit and persecution of the

Christians. The harlot Jerusalem then rode the beast Rome into the Church's Great Tribulation. But in 66 A.D., Jerusalem revolted. The Roman Empire turned on the city of the seven hills in rage at this treachery and utterly destroyed Jerusalem and its Temple. The beast Rome did indeed "hate the harlot . . . make her desolate . . . and burn her up with fire."

Seven emperors, plus one

St. John informs us that the seven heads of the beast have a double meaning (GR4): "The seven heads are seven hills on which the woman is seated; they are also seven kings" (17:9-10). Throughout our examination of The Apocalypse, we have often noted a dual symbolism. The witnesses symbolize the Law and the Prophets, and also Moses and Elijah. The Woman symbolizes the Church and also Mary. The sea-beast symbolizes Rome and also her Caesars, whether Nero, Vespasian, or Titus. Here St. John explains that the seven heads symbolize not only the seven hills of Jerusalem, but also the seven kings who ruled the beast.

The seven horns "are also seven kings, five of whom have fallen, one is, the other has not yet come, and when he comes he must remain only a little while" (17:10). As we discussed in the vision of the battle strategy of the dragon, the Julio-Claudio lineage of Roman emperors began with Julius Caesar; then came Augustus, Tiberius, Caligula, and Claudius I. This would correspond to the method used by ancient Jews when counting emperors. These are the "five [who] have fallen." Nero reigned after these five. Therefore, at the time of St. John's vision, Nero is the who "is." A seventh Caesar is spoken of as "the other [king who] has not yet come." This would be Vespasian. He would not be emperor until mid to late 69 A.D. John predicts his reign before it is established (GR1). Vespasian came to attack Jerusalem, but "when he comes he must remain only a little while." Vespasian actually led three campaigns against the Jews. The first one was in 67 A.D., the second in 68 A.D. When Nero died, Vespasian stopped fighting. He eventually went to Alexandria to intercept the grain shipments headed to Rome. He returned for a third short campaign in midsummer of 69 A.D. Since St. John's perspective is that of 68 A.D., this short campaign is the one predicted here (GR1). When he left Judea after "a little while," it was to return to Rome to claim the throne.

Nero (emperor number six) was the Caesar when The Apocalypse was penned. It was ultimately under the rule of Vespasian (emperor number seven) that Jerusalem was sacked and the Temple destroyed. That is why the beast has seven heads (GR2).

Here the humanity of John, the son of thunder (Mark 3:17), shines through. Although St. John has already given us an explanation of the seven heads, he cannot resist designating an eighth emperor. The mere mention of an eighth emperor illustrates John's awareness of the nature of God's Kingdom. Although the eternal Kingdom of Christ has been established, there will still be earthly governments here on earth, in this case another Roman emperor.

"As for the beast that was and is not, it is an eighth but it belongs to the seven, and it goes to perdition" (17:11). This is the same beast that "ascend[ed] from the bottomless pit" earlier in this vision (17:8). The beast that ascended is a clear reference to the "king . . . the angel of the bottomless pit . . . Abaddon," who appeared at the head of the locust/scorpion army of the fifth trumpet! These visions really do review the same events again and again.

We have already determined that Abaddon was General Titus, the son of Vespasian. This would explain how he "belongs to the seven[th]" — by blood relation. How is it that Titus "was and is not" (17:11)? As of 68 A.D., Titus had been in Judea with his father for the war in 67 and 68 A.D. He was there, twice. But when Nero committed suicide, Vespasian sent Titus to Rome. This would explain the phrase "is not." At this time, General Titus is not in Judea.

But Titus would return, to the consternation of Jerusalem. Considering his role in the winepress, is it any wonder that he would "go to perdition" (17:11)?

So once again we see one symbol, the sea-beast, serving as a sign for more than one reality. At times the beast is most clearly Nero; here it is most evidently Titus. In either case, however, the individual represents the Roman Empire, which is the primary reality that the beast symbolizes. But notice that these realities are all related in their fulfillment. They complement one another, just as Mary complements the Church, just as Moses complements the Law, and just as Elijah complements the Prophets.

A new Roman Empire?

Rip Van Winkle would be proud. Rapturists totally ignore the minute details already fulfilled by the harlot and the scarlet beast she rides. The shear number of details that fit the eight kings makes it outrageous for rapturists to ignore their clear fulfillment. They expect a future reformulation of the Roman Empire to fulfill these prophecies. They look to ten nations of the European Union as the ten kings. (This idea is much less ballyhooed about now that there are fifteen nations and counting in the European Union.) But why look for something in the future that has already been fulfilled, and in such detail? At the risk of sounding harsh, may I suggest that this is almost akin to what the Sanhedrin did? They, too, refused to see the detailed fulfillment of the Messianic prophecies in their own day. They, too, looked elsewhere for a fulfillment. They, too, wanted that fulfillment to be more physical and less spiritual. They, too, were wrong, trapped in their own kind of Winkle Warp.

Ten future kings

Just as the seven heads have a double meaning, so do the ten horns of the sea-beast (GR4). We have seen that they were the ten

provinces of the Roman Empire. Now St. John uses them to signify ten future kings, or emperors, who "have not yet received
royal power, but they are to receive authority as kings for one hour,
together with the beast" (17:12). This is obviously not a reference
to the provincial kings who crossed the dry Euphrates with Titus
to gather at Armageddon. This description clearly says they are
future kings.

Their opponent is different as well. The beast and the ten provincial kings are presently at war with the harlot, Jerusalem. But
these future emperors "will make war on *the Lamb*" (17:14). The
object of their hatred will be Christ and His Church, rather than
Jerusalem. It must have been sobering reading for Christians reel-
ing from the Great Tribulation. St. John makes it very clear that
even after the victory of Rome over Jerusalem, they will still have
emperors of Rome eager to persecute them.

Nero is identified by the early Church Fathers as the first to use
the official authority of the Roman empire to persecute Christians. But there would be "ten" more persecuting emperors who
followed in his wake (*TBR*, 372), ten being the number of com-
pleteness (GR2).

The persecution ebbed and flowed and finally reached a climax around 303 A.D., during the reign of Emperor Diocletian.
Entire towns of the empire, such as Phrygia, were executed down
to the last person when they refused to sacrifice to the emperor.
Tertullian wrote in the early third century: "If the Tiber reaches
the walls, if the Nile does not rise to the fields, if the sky doesn't
move or the earth does, if there is famine, if there is plague, the cry
is at once: 'The Christians to the lions!' " (*APO*, 40:2). As St.
John writes elsewhere in The Apocalypse, "Here is a call for the
endurance and faith of the saints."

Civil war raged in the empire after the death of Diocletian,
and the next uncontested emperor of Rome was Constantine
the Great in 324 A.D. He legalized Christianity, so that people

would not be persecuted simply because they were members of the Church.

The Apocalypse had promised the struggling Church that this future persecution would be temporary. These persecutors would be "kings for one hour." The short reign of these ten persecuting kings is contrasted with the Christ. Although the kings of the dragon appear invincible, they are not. They are only speed bumps on the road to eternity.

This is meant to draw a sharp contrast between the forces of the dragon and the forces of the Lamb. The ten kings "receive[d] authority *for one hour.*" With all its power, even the beast "was and *is not.*" Christ is a superior King. We learned at the beginning of The Apocalypse that Christ is He "who is and who was and who is to come" (1:4, 8). He is "the firstborn of the dead . . . the Alpha and the Omega" (1:5, 8). He states, "I am the first and the last, and the living one; I died, and behold I am alive forevermore" (1:17-18).

This is the essence of the Truth that the Rider on the white horse proclaims: live for the dragon, and enjoy yourself now. Live for God now, and be rewarded for all eternity.

The fall of Babylon

After the plagues have run their course, another angel announces the results: "Fallen, fallen is Babylon the great!" (18:2). This should not surprise us, as this was declared by the second angel in the battle strategy of the Lamb.

We have finally found an article of fact on which the dragon and the Lamb can agree: Jerusalem should be nicknamed Babylon. The allies of the dragon, with their emphasis on power, would view this as the supreme compliment. The allies of the Lamb would understand this name as St. John intends it: it is a harbinger of this city's doom because of its prideful disregard for God and His holiness.

Rapture

An angel from Heaven warns the Christians, "Come out of her, my people" (18:4). The message is clear: get out of Jerusalem. Two reasons are given.

First, "lest you take part in her sins" (18:4). This hearkens back to the message of the letters to the churches and the oft-repeated admonition to endure and keep faith. It also reflects the admonitions in Hebrews, which we examined earlier. Given the environment of "Babylon" (Jerusalem) at the time of St. John's visions, the holiness of the Christians was a major concern. Josephus describes the activities going on at the time in Jerusalem, but I will not detail them; they would make for very uncomfortable reading.

But the biggest sin of "Babylon" is mentioned toward the end of this vision: "All nations were deceived by thy sorcery" (18:23). Under the Davidic covenant, Jerusalem (Zion) was to be a light to the nations, a beacon that would point them to the true God of Abraham, Isaac, and Jacob. The Minor Prophets illustrate this clearly with their message to the nations. But instead of telling the Truth to the nations, as the Lamb did, Jerusalem "deceived" them in accord with the battle strategy of the dragon. This was her greatest sin. She did not live up to the covenantal responsibilities of David's heirs. In fact, she killed those who tried to: "In her was found the blood of prophets and of saints" (18:24).

There is a second reason given for Christians to come out of Jerusalem, though. Leave, "lest you share in her plagues" (18:4). This echoes the warnings of the Olivet Discourse, but put into the context of the Great Battle that St. John is describing. We can hear the words of Jesus: "Flee to the mountains. . . . Let him who is on the housetop not go down. . . . Let him who is in the field not turn back. . . . For then there will be great tribulation" (Matt. 24:16-21). Judgment was coming upon "Babylon." The message is clear: if you are there, you will share in its pain.

But even as her destruction unfolds, Jerusalem remains in complete denial. "Since in her heart she says, 'A queen I sit, I am no widow, mourning I shall never see' " (18:7). This passage is lifted almost verbatim from Isaiah's description of the original Babylon before her destruction (47:7-9). The Babylon of old grew complacent in her impregnability. In fact, Belshazzar was throwing a party at the very moment the Persian army was entering his stronghold. The old Babylon was mistaken in her complacency, and so was Jerusalem, the new Babylon. We have already noted the jeering of the inhabitants of Jerusalem, even after Titus had breached some of her defenses.

Jerusalem had been "widowed" before this. When Jerusalem was conquered by Babylon, it was described as "widowhood" because God her "husband" had forsaken her (Isa. 54:4-5).

She did not realize it in time, but now it was happening again half a millennium later. God turned His back on the Old Covenant when she rejected His Son, the Messiah. Zechariah made this clear when he broke his two staffs. The Old Covenant was being supplanted, never to be revisited again (Appendix Three). Jerusalem had traded the love of a faithful Husband for the powerful thrill of a scarlet beast, and now she would be required to face the consequences of her spiritual harlotry.

A millstone into the sea

An angel announces that the city warranted this judgment: "A mighty angel took up a stone like a great millstone and threw it into the sea" (18:21). Once again St. John reminds his readers of the destruction of the original Babylon, this time by referencing a story from Jeremiah.

Before the destruction of the first Babylon, God had instructed Jeremiah to act out a drama to drive home his prophecy of defeat and captivity. Jeremiah wrote down the prophecies concerning the fall of Babylon. He instructed one of the Jewish prisoners to take these prophecies with him into captivity in Babylon. The Jew was to "read all these words, and say, 'O Lord, Thou hast said concerning this place that Thou wilt cut it off, so that nothing shall dwell in it, neither man nor beast, and it shall be desolate forever.' When you finish reading this book, bind a stone to it, and cast it into the midst of the Euphrates, and say, 'Thus shall Babylon sink, to rise no more, because of the evil that I am bringing upon her' " (Jer. 51:61-64). The old Babylon was judged for its treatment of God's holy people and vessels. Her fate was analogous to that of a stone sinking into a river. St. John draws a parallel to the sinking destruction of the new Babylon, Jerusalem (GR3).

The angel closes his statement with the phrase that reminds us, once again, that this is the ancient city of Jerusalem: "In her was found the blood of prophets and of saints, and of all who have been slain on earth." That is why Jerusalem is being judged. Ever since God had chosen and loved His Old Covenant People, they had disregarded His messages. Their rejection had culminated in the Crucifixion of His Son.

Indeed, the millstone was an apt illustration. Jerusalem's destruction was complete. First, the Temple was destroyed by the Romans in 70 A.D. It took the Romans three years to dismantle the city defenses and eventually erect a pagan shrine on the Temple site. Almost seventy years later, in 132 A.D., the Jewish leaders felt that perhaps their exile had been completed. The chief rabbi in Israel proclaimed Simon bar Kochba to be the Messiah. By 136 A.D., Roman soldiers stood once more victorious within Jerusalem. This time, the Romans completely leveled the city and expelled all Jews from Jerusalem. "Babylon the great . . . has become . . . a haunt of every foul spirit, a haunt of every foul and hateful bird" (18:2). Roman law made it punishable by death for a Jew to be caught within the boundaries of Jerusalem.

Reaction of the dragon's allies

When the destruction finally takes place, the allies of Jerusalem's secularized leadership are dismayed at its destruction. Three times this vision mentions that "in one hour has the judgment come." This lament is taken up by the kings (18:10), then the merchants (18:17), and finally the sailors (18:19). All of these mourned the destruction of a powerful, wealthy, sophisticated trading center. "No one buys their cargo anymore, cargo of gold, silver, jewels and pearls, fine linen, purple, silks and scarlet . . . spice, incense, myrrh, frankincense, wine, oil . . . cattle and sheep" (18:11-13). Many of these expensive items were used in Temple worship at Jerusalem. Notice that there is no mourning over her spiritual demise. That had happened long before.

Reaction of the Lamb's allies

But there is another reaction to the destruction of Jerusalem and its Temple. In contrast to the three allies of Jerusalem (kings, merchants, and sailors), the three victims of the Jerusalem's savage and relentless persecutions are told by the angel with the millstone to rejoice: "Rejoice over her, O Heaven, O saints and apostles and prophets, for God has given judgment for you against her!" (18:20).

The "saints" include those martyrs who met death during the Great Tribulation of 64 to 67 A.D. We first encountered these saints in Daniel's vision of the strategy of the beasts (Dan. 7:21, 22, 25). In Daniel, we learned that Nero, the little horn, would persecute them. In The Apocalypse, we first encountered them under the altar in the throne room of God in the fifth seal of the initial vision (Apoc. 6:9-11).

There is joy in Heaven that the cry for justice from the martyrs under the altar has finally been answered. Now thrones have been provided for them. Justice is finally being served. "Praise our God, all you His servants. . . . Hallelujah! For the Lord our God, the Almighty, reigns" (19:5-6). God does answer prayer when we endure and remain faithful.

Immediately after the angel's announcement, all Heaven bursts forth in rejoicing at God's righteous judgment: "Hallelujah! . . .

Hallelujah! . . . Amen. Hallelujah! . . . Praise our God, all you His servants, you who fear Him, small and great" (19:1-5). "A great multitude in Heaven" praises God because "He has judged the great harlot who corrupted the land with her fornication" (19:2). Notice that Babylon's primary sin is idolatry, also known in the Old Testament as harlotry. The Sanhedrin compromised with Rome's emperor worship, but the Church would not.

The scene of rejoicing in Heaven is outside the constraints of earthly time. As a result, the multitude continues its praises in anticipation of the "marriage of the Lamb" (19:7). The Bride of the Lamb is "clothed with fine linen . . . the righteous deeds of the saints" (19:8) for the marriage. We will come to the marriage next, in the final vision of The Apocalypse. This is another illustration of John's repeated use of anticipation. We will soon encounter in depth "the Bride, the wife of the Lamb."

Although the actual marriage of the Lamb is in the next vision, the marriage supper has been an underlying theme throughout The Apocalypse. This celebration began in the initial vision of the scroll with seven seals (Apoc. 4-5) and has been just below the surface ever since. It came into clear focus in the battle strategies of the Lamb and of God's People, both of which centered on the Eucharist (Apoc. 14-15). We have noticed the similarity to the Mass as the four living creatures sang, "Holy, holy, holy is the Lord God Almighty, who was and is and is to come!"

Here the angel tells St. John, "Blessed are those who are invited to the marriage supper of the Lamb" (19:9): the Eucharist! This is not a common phrase in the Bible, but the concept is. The Eucharist is referred to as "the Lord's supper" (1 Cor. 11:20). In Matthew 22, Jesus used the marriage feast to illustrate the invitation to join His Kingdom. Indeed, those who are invited are "blessed." They are part of the Kingdom and will one day witness the "Bride" in all her splendor. In our present celebration of the Eucharist, we partake in the celebration that eternally continues in Heaven.

But we must keep in mind the warning of Jesus: "A man who had no wedding garment . . . [will be] cast into the outer darkness" (Matt. 22:11-13). The vision of The Apocalypse reminds us that the Bride is clothed in linen, and "the fine linen is the righteous deeds of the saints" (19:8). To attend the marriage feast, we must have the mark of God on our forehead, signifying loyalty, and on our hand, signifying righteous deeds.

So we have seen the three battle strategies played out. The dragon, with his emphasis on deceit and earthly power, was defeated by the eternal Truth that the Lamb speaks. Nowhere is this Truth more apparent or effective than in the Eucharist of the Lamb that was slain.

The Lamb has won the first round. In the next and last vision, we will see this strategy work for the Church again. Our faith in the Lamb should be strengthened because of this first victory. He has kept His promise, and He can be trusted to keep future promises.

SECTION III:E: FROM HERE TO ETERNITY

St. John's final vision transports us from here (70 A.D.) to eternity (GR9). As in Daniel's last vision, St. John begins with the events of Daniel's seventieth week and then extends his outlook to include the final eschaton.

As the visions of St. John have progressed, we have observed repeatedly the use of anticipation. We noticed it with the seals and trumpets, the dragon, the tabernacle and the Woman, the beast, the horse's bridle, the marriage of the Lamb, and even Babylon. This device has tied the many visions of the book together into a cohesive whole.

The first time St. John used the technique of anticipation was in the first seal during the initial vision. A rider on a white horse appeared who, like the marriage supper of the Lamb, was a promise of a later hope. The rider on a white horse now reappears: "I saw

Heaven opened, and behold, a white horse! He who sat upon it is called Faithful and True, and in righteousness He judges and makes war. . . . The name by which He is called is The Word of God. . . . On His robe and on His thigh He has a name inscribed, King of kings and Lord of lords" (19:11, 13, 16).

The picture St. John paints dovetails perfectly with the words of Jesus in the Olivet Discourse: "Then will appear the sign of the Son of man in Heaven, and then all the tribes of the land will mourn, and they will see the Son of man coming on the clouds of Heaven with power and great glory" (Matt. 24:30). We have already examined this passage and found that it undoubtedly refers to 70 A.D.

This rider symbolizes Christ's victory over the Sanhedrin. Remember, this is apocalyptic literature, so we must not expect to see our Lord upon a literal white stallion at His coming into His Kingdom, nor must we believe that horses will suddenly learn to fly. The sword coming out of His mouth (19:15) is not made of tempered steel.

The sword is a symbol of the eternal Truth He embodies and speaks. That is the battle strategy of the Lamb. The Truth of the Word of God is so powerful that it conquers the physical kingdoms of this world and breaks the dragon's power over people's minds. This is the "stone" of Daniel that crushes the statue (Dan. 2:45). This is the "Son of man" coming to judge (Dan. 7:13; Matt. 24:30). This is the breaker of the scroll's "seven seals" (Apoc. 5:9). This is the Child who will "rule with a rod of iron" (Apoc. 12:5). This is the treader of the "winepress of the fury of the wrath of God" (Apoc. 14:20). This is the nemesis of the dragon and its two beasts.

Here is the hope of The Apocalypse: Christ's victory is inexorable because His weapon is Truth.

St. John makes clear that this is not a new battle. This rider on the white horse "will tread the winepress of the fury of the wrath of

God the Almighty" (19:15). This is a recapitulation of the battle described earlier in the battle strategy of the Lamb (14:17-20).

These verses are a word picture of the moment when Christ's prediction in Matthew 24 was fulfilled. It is a snapshot of the earthly evidence that Daniel's prophecy was fulfilled in Heaven. The Son of man "came to the Ancient of Days and was presented before Him. And to Him [the Son of man] was given dominion and glory and kingdom, that all peoples, nations, and languages should serve Him; His dominion is an everlasting dominion, which shall not pass away, and His kingdom one that shall not be destroyed" (Dan. 7:13-14).

Remember, Jesus Himself applied this prophecy of Daniel to Himself in His trial before the Sanhedrin (Matt. 26:64). Jesus told the priests who were conducting His trial that they would see this occur. He promised that "this generation will not pass away till all these things take place. Heaven and earth will pass away, but my words will not pass away" (Matt. 24:34-35). This is not the second advent; it is His predicted coming on the clouds to judge the Sanhedrin. St. John wants his readers to be absolutely certain that Christ kept His promise. Because Christ kept that promise, we can endure in the assurance that Christ really will return! Rest assured, a major reason St. John wrote The Apocalypse was to point out that the judgment upon the Sanhedrin stands as a proof that the eternal judgment will come (GR3).

The great supper of God

We now encounter a highly symbolic picture that, to be honest, is rather disturbing to twenty-first-century sensibilities. An angel "called to all the birds that fly in midheaven, 'Come, gather for the great supper of God, to eat the flesh of kings . . . and the flesh of all men' " (19:17-18). Like so many other details of the visions of St. John, the meaning of this gruesome imagery becomes clearer after looking to the Old Testament.

In prophesying the victory over the original Babylon, Ezekiel painted a vivid picture of a sacrificial meal in celebration of victory (39:17-24). Although there is in both instances some literal fulfillment, this is not the main point of either passage. In Ezekiel, God states that this victory feast is proof to the entire world that "I am the Lord" (39:7). When the enemies of God are defeated, then "all the nations shall see my judgment which I have executed" (39:21). That is the main point. It is the same point that is made in the "Son of man" passage in Daniel. This is the implied threat that we noticed when Jesus responded to the High Priest at His trial (Matt. 26:64). By predicting and then judging the Temple, Christ proved to the entire world that God had coronated Jesus Christ as victor.

This is also precisely what Jesus claimed in the Olivet Discourse. He would use the Roman army to punish Jerusalem for its sins, and "the tribes of the land . . . will see the Son of man coming on the clouds of Heaven with power and great glory" (Matt. 24:30). In the destruction of Jerusalem, the world would finally understand the kingship of Christ. When we understand the Old Testament milieu from which St. John draws, it is clear that this is the description of the fulfillment of the Olivet Discourse. That fulfillment within a generation stands as proof of Christ's promised return at the final eschaton.

The victorious Christ now metes out justice on behalf of His martyrs. The false prophet, also known as the land-beast Jerusalem, is "thrown alive into the lake of fire" along with the sea-beast. The lake of fire is the place of complete and final punishment. There is no return from its depths.

The false prophet is Jerusalem's leadership, and this is an accurate picture of what happened to biblical Judaism in 70 A.D. It was utterly destroyed. The Jews returned from the Babylonian captivity to resurrect their sacrificial system, but biblical Judaism can never be validly reinstated after Rome's destruction. The priestly line is lost, and the Temple site is desecrated, but most important, the unique relationship that Jerusalem had enjoyed with Yahweh has been superseded by another Bride. There is a marriage supper already in progress in the heavenly Jerusalem. The Messiah came, was rejected, and founded His new people, His *ekklesia* (Matt. 16:18). New olive branches have been grafted onto the old stump (Rom. 11). Christians should take no pleasure in the destruction of Jerusalem and biblical Judaism, but neither should we deny its irrevocability. The Old Covenant religion of Jerusalem's Temple is history. Modern Rabbinic Judaism is not the same thing. Even if the Temple were rebuilt in Jerusalem, the Old Covenant cannot be revived.

Some have suggested that Christ's judgment of the beast (Rome) and the false prophet (the Sanhedrin) is too severe, but they fail to understand the relationships involved. Christ's bride, the Church, has been subjected by both the beast (the sea-beast) and the false prophet (the land-beast) to persecution, torment, and injustice. Their purpose has actually been the destruction of the Bride. Would not any loving bridegroom do what Christ does here? He says, "Get your hands off my Bride!"

The defeat of the sea-beast is most certainly a reference to the revolt of Rome against Nero, and his subsequent suicide. The imagery is lifted directly from Daniel's vision of the four beasts: "The beast was slain, and its body destroyed and given over to be burned with fire" (Dan. 7:11). The beast has symbolized Nero elsewhere in The Apocalypse as the head of the Roman Empire. In this instance, he is identified as the one who "gathered to make war against Him who sits upon the horse and against His army" (19:19). This is a reference to the Great Tribulation: that intense, government-sponsored persecution of the Christian Church from 64 to 67 A.D., initiated at Nero's direction. Clement of Alexandria identified Nero as the very first emperor to persecute the Christian Church (STO). In punishment for this persecution, Nero and his dynasty were destroyed forever. In fact, history tells us that the dynasty of Vespasian and Titus did not survive either. Any and all "beastly" actors in this drama perished forever.

The leftover *loipos*

But in addition to the religious leaders of Jerusalem and the Caesars of the Roman Empire, there was another group of evil men active in this drama. These men are *loipos*, "the rest [who] were slain by the sword" (19:21). In the initial vision, during the sixth trumpet, there is described a group of men of Jerusalem "who were not killed by these plagues, did not repent of the works of their hands nor give up worshiping demons and idols of gold and silver and bronze and stone and wood . . . nor did they repent of their murders or their sorceries or the immorality of their thefts" (9:20). These were the Zealots.

Josephus describes the lawless Zealots within Jerusalem: "Nor did any age ever breed a generation more fruitful in wickedness than this was, from the beginning of the world. . . . They were the slaves, the scum, and the spurious and abortive offspring of our nation, while they overthrew the city themselves . . . and did almost draw that fire upon the Temple. . . . When they saw that Temple burning from the upper city, they were neither troubled at it, nor did they shed any tears on that account" (WJ, V, 10:5).

Josephus goes on to suggest that "had the Romans made any longer delay in coming against these villains, that the city would either have been swallowed up by the ground opening upon them, or been overflowed by water, or else been destroyed by such thunder as the country of Sodom perished by, for it had brought forth a generation of men much more atheistical than were those that suffered such punishments; for by their madness it was that all the people came to be destroyed" (WJ, V, 13:6).

This remnant, *loipos*, remained defiant to the very end. Josephus tells us that, yes, "all the birds were gorged with their flesh" (19:21).

Present benefits of Daniel's six blessings

With this description of the judgment of Christ's enemies in 70 A.D., St. John has completed all the events surrounding that year. In the timetable, we referred to these as past events. In Chapter 20, we leave the past (70 A.D.) and enter the present (the time from the destruction of biblical Judaism until the eschatological end of time). Verses 1 through 6 describe the situation in the present, from Jerusalem's destruction until Christ returns in glory.

We are still within the timeframe of Daniel's final vision, which also starts with the victory of Christ in 70 A.D. and ends in eternity with Daniel's final judgment. We live today between those two points; this is a description of our time. Daniel's week (seven decades) of covenantal transition are over. The six blessings that the Messiah gained for us during Daniel's seventy weeks are being bestowed. Remember them? Daniel predicted that Christ was coming in His first advent "to finish the transgression, to put an end to sin, and to atone for iniquity, to bring in everlasting righteousness, to seal both vision and prophet, and to anoint a most holy" (Dan. 9:24).

The Millennium

This time of Church blessing is also known as the Millennium:

Then I saw an angel coming down from Heaven, holding in his hand the key of the bottomless pit and a great chain. And he seized the dragon, that ancient serpent, who is the Devil and Satan, and bound him for a thousand years, and threw him into the pit and shut it and sealed it over him, that he should deceive the nations no more, till the thousand years were ended. After that he must be loosed for a little while. Then I saw thrones, and seated on them were those to whom judgment was committed. Also I saw the souls of those who had been beheaded for their testimony to

Jesus and for the word of God, and who had not worshiped the beast or its image and had not received its mark on their foreheads or their hands. They came to life, and reigned with Christ a thousand years. The rest of the dead did not come to life until the thousand years were ended. This is the first resurrection. Blessed and holy is he who shares in the first resurrection! Over such the second death has no power, but they shall be priests of God and of Christ, and they shall reign with Him a thousand years (20:1-6).

The highly symbolic language in this particular vision is striking. St. John continues the symbolism borrowed from Ezekiel that we witnessed in "the great supper of God" (19:17). That context should never be ignored.

Intractable problems arise when we attempt to interpret this vision too literally. First of all, what kind of chain would be able to hold an entirely nonphysical spirit such as Satan? What kind of seal would hold Satan in a pit? Can a pit really be bottomless?

St. John is clearly using symbolic language to describe a spiritual reality, but for some reason, people forget the nature of apocalyptic literature when they approach this vision (GR5, 6). This vision continues the story of the victory of Christ begun with "the great supper of God." Not only will the beast, the false prophet, and the remnant of evil men be cast into the lake of fire; the dragon behind it all will not have free reign to deceive as he has up until this point. But this is not a permanent situation. After one thousand years, "he must be loosed for a little while" (20:7).

The "thousand years" is mentioned six times in seven verses. Remember, St. John is writing at the end of an apocalyptic book filled with visions that are not chronological. His repetition of a time reference should catch our attention. For at least these few verses, chronology is on the author's mind. Obviously, he is now addressing a long period that follows on the heels of the previous visions of Jerusalem's destruction. After many chapters of recapitulating visions, he is breaking new ground chronologically. Then, after these six verses, he makes clear that he is discussing a time *after* the thousand years are ended. "When the thousand years are ended . . . " (20:7). These six verses stand alone chronologically.

This raises the question: What does St. John mean by this thousand-year period? Does he mean there will be a future, earthly Kingdom distinct from the present Church age? More than one devout Catholic or Protestant has told me, "God said it. I believe it. That settles it." This principle has a certain ring and a strong emotional appeal to it. And it sounds very holy. But unfortunately it begs the very question under consideration.

The question is not what is written: we can all read. The question is, what does it mean? Did St. John mean literal, 365-day years, or was he pointing to something symbolic (GR3)? I suggest the immediate context is highly symbolic.

So is the number itself. *One thousand* is ten cubed, a very complete number. Ten cubed has a reflection in the physical reality that ten to the fourth or fifth power does not have. Ten cubed is a reflection of an object with ten for its height, length, and depth.

One thousand is repeatedly used in the Bible to imply a large, but symbolic amount. For example, God owns the "cattle on a thousand hills" (Ps. 50:10). No one thinks to ask which hills are a part of the thousand, nor should we assume that God does not own the cattle on the hills not included in that thousand. He owns all the cattle on all the hills (and in all the valleys), which number far more than a thousand.

One thousand cubits is used symbolically four times as the depth of water flowing from below the threshold of the Temple (Ezek. 47:3-6). This chapter of Ezekiel is very important as a basis for the last three chapters of The Apocalypse (as we will see shortly). It is not at all a stretch to assume that the thousand years reflect the thousand cubits of water in Ezekiel. We will encounter this thousand cubits of water toward the end of this vision.

In addition to these two references, there are many more symbolic uses of *one thousand* in the Old Testament (Deut. 7:9 and Ps. 84:10; 90:4; 91:7; 105:8). The Davidic kingdom itself was said to last a thousand years, signifying a number too large to warrant counting.

St. John certainly understood this symbolism. To claim that this passage teaches that the kingdom of Christ must exist for exactly one thousand years makes no more sense than to ask how a chain could bind Satan. Numbers have a different role to play in apocalyptic literature (GR2). St. John uses a thousand years to signify a large, complete time. The time will extend past the lifetime of even someone's great-grandchild's great-grandchild. Christ's Kingdom will endure on earth at least as long as even King David's.

So what do we know so far? Following the public vindication of Christ, Satan is kept from "deceiv[ing] the nations" for an extremely long period, figuratively spoken of as a thousand years. At present, he is restrained by God's power; "after that he must be loosed for a little while." This is the same chronology as St. Paul noted, although he told us specifically that the Church was living during the time of the "restraining" of Satan (2 Thess. 2:6).

St. John includes a description of the activities of Christ and His Church during the Millennium. The Church "*reigned* with Christ a thousand years" (20:4). Lo and behold! This is a description of the Kingdom that was established as a result of Christ's Passion and Resurrection. This Kingdom was mentioned all the way back in the initial vision before any of the seals. "Thou wast slain and by Thy blood didst ransom men for God from every tribe and tongue and people and nation, and hast made them a *kingdom* and priests to our God" (5:9-10). This Kingdom was won on the Cross, was proclaimed at Pentecost when the Holy Spirit came, and was vindicated when Christ judged the Sanhedrin by destroying their Temple.

Refuting three key rapturist claims

Rapturists disagree. They claim that these six verses are the clearest enunciation of a still-future Millennium in the Bible. This paragraph is not only their clearest hope of a biblical basis for their theology; it is their only hope. This concept, so important in American Protestantism, is mentioned nowhere else in Scripture!

In these few short verses, rapturists claim to find the cornerstone for their belief in premillennialism. They believe that at this time the Church will have been secretly raptured. (Even though this event is never mentioned, they insert it at the beginning of The Apocalypse.) Then the Jewish people will endure the Great Tribulation and finally recognize their Messiah. Then there will be a thousand-year reign of Christ here on earth, the Millennium. They cite these brief verses as support for this scenario, claiming that they teach:

1. All Christians will have a reigning role in Christ's future earthly Kingdom.

2. All Christians will be resurrected in their glorified bodies at the start of this thousand years.

3. Christ will be physically present on earth, reigning from the throne of David in Israel.

But look at these verses carefully. Not one of these three statements is actually taught in this vision. By looking at what is *not* taught here, we should get closer to a clear understanding of what *is* taught in this part of the vision of the end.

• *Point 1: All Christians will reign.* "All Christians will have a reigning role in this future Kingdom." Actually, two groups of people are mentioned as ruling in this Kingdom. First, those for whom thrones had been "committed" (20:4). This seems to be an obvious reference to the Apostles, who had been promised this role by Jesus Christ before His Passion: "Truly, I say to you, in the new world, when the Son of man shall sit on His glorious throne, you who have followed me will also sit on twelve thrones" (Matt. 19:28).

The other group who rule are those martyrs who died during the battles with the beast, those "who had not worshiped the beast" (20:4). We know these people! They have already been mentioned in The Apocalypse. Most notably, they were under the altar in the initial vision (6:9-10). In that passage, they petitioned for justice to be served on their oppressors. They are not only given justice now, but also participate in dispensing it. They are given the opportunity to reign with Christ, alongside the Apostles.

Notice that it is "souls" who are mentioned as ruling (20:4). Nowhere are we given the slightest justification for assuming these are souls with bodies. They are not. The resurrection of all people for their final judgment has not occurred yet. Not until the resurrection of all humanity will souls be given their glorified bodies like Christ (20:12).

These martyrs are the saints who rejoiced at the defeat of "Babylon" (18:20). They do reign. They are given the opportunity to affect history. We saw that already. The prayers of the martyrs affect events on earth. This is not sometime in the future; this occurs right now. These reigning souls are the saints in Heaven right now, the Church Triumphant. Catholics make requests of saints in Heaven for just this reason: they are present with Christ in a ruling role. If they take up our cause before Christ, it will more likely be accomplished (James 5:16). This Millennium is a present reality with benefits bestowed through the victory of the Lamb during the week of covenantal transition.

We would be remiss not to note how these Christians reign: "They shall be priests of God and of Christ." Rapturists adamantly maintain that there is no role for the sacerdotal duties of the priest in the New Covenant. But St. John states simply that this is their primary function. The Millennial Kingdom is the present ecclesiastical one. The fact that St. John feels no need to justify the statement makes it all the more significant. He assumes that, although his readers may need to have the meaning of the first resurrection explained (as we will see in a moment), they certainly would not question the need for and role of the Church's priesthood in ruling with Christ. The reason is simple: St. John was a priest himself.

Nowhere does this passage teach that all Christians will be involved in ruling during this thousand-year Kingdom of Christ. Actually, the very fact that two distinct groups are mentioned specifically implies that *not* all Christians will be given the opportunity to rule during this time.

Of course, a well-informed Catholic already knows that, during this period, there are two groups of Christians not ruling from Heaven. The Church Militant is a name for the Christians on earth during this time. You and I find our place with this group, sometimes also called the Pilgrim Church. The other group of Christians during this time is the Church Suffering, who are in the process of purification in a place traditionally known as Purgatory (CCC, pars. 1030-1032).

So, the best understanding of these six verses is that they describe the present state of affairs, what some call "the Church age." The Church Triumphant in Heaven assists the Church Militant on earth through prayer. The Church Militant, in turn, can help the Church Suffering through prayer.

• *Point 2: Resurrection precedes the Millennium.* We now turn to the second rapturist claim: "Christians will be resurrected in their glorified bodies at the start of these thousand years." Here we must not forget that we are reading apocalyptic literature that uses the imagery of physical resurrection to describe the spiritual reconstitution, renewal, or rejuvenation of God's people. This is not something new; it runs throughout the Bible (GR7).

Even our entry into the Church is designated as "regeneration," a resurrection of the spiritually dead. The sacrament of Baptism is imbued with this resurrection symbolism. Let's take the example of a new convert in the early Church. He would have been placed under water by the baptizer three times. The baptizer would have said, "I baptize you in the name of the Father, and the name of the Son, and the name of the Holy Spirit." Going into the water symbolizes death to this world and its appetites. Coming out of the water symbolizes the new life to which a Christian is called via the power of the Holy Spirit. The new Christian has been resurrected to a new life in Christ.

The "first resurrection" that John mentions here is not a physical one, but the taking of a soul to Heaven by God. Upon death, these Christian saints join the Church Triumphant. It is the ultimate renewal and reconstitution of God's people! To the casual reader, it may not seem like much of a resurrection at all. So St. John specifically tells the reader what it is: "This is the first resurrection" (20:5).

The first resurrection is experienced only by Christian saints, including the martyrs of the Neronian persecution. Upon death, they are bestowed with a ruling role in the Kingdom. Only Christian saints experience this immediate "first resurrection." "The rest of the dead did not come to life until the thousand years were ended" (20:5).

Those who experience the first resurrection will never experience "the second death, the lake of fire" (20:15). The letter to Smyrna anticipated this idea with significant detail: "He who conquers shall not be hurt by the second death" (2:11). The Christians in Smyrna were fighting the temptation of those in the "synagogue of Satan." The Jewish leaders were using persecution to entice Christians to forsake their faith in Christ and return to the Old Covenant sacrifices. The Apocalypse assures the Church in Smyrna that those who die in the Faith will not be hurt by the second death: eternal separation from God in the lake of fire after the final judgment.

Let us now apply this insight. "Blessed and holy is he who shares in the first resurrection! Over such the second death has no power" (20:6). See the parallel? A group of people are described, over whom the second death (damnation) has no power. They are described as those who conquer (keep the Faith to the death) in Chapter 2, and then they are described as those who experience the first resurrection in Chapter 20. These are Christian saints who die and immediately go to rule with Christ in Heaven.

St. Paul expounds the same teaching in his letter to the Corinthian Church: "We know that while we are at home in the body, we are away from the Lord . . . and we would rather be away from the body [first death] and at home with the Lord [first resurrection]" (2 Cor. 5:6, 8).

Let us sum it all up:

1. First death is when any human dies.

2. First resurrection is when the soul of the Christian saint goes to Heaven at the first death.

3. Second resurrection is when all are raised to be judged at the final judgment.

4. Second death is damnation, judgment in the lake of fire at the great white throne.

There is no indication in this vision that all Christians will be physically resurrected at some future point to rule for a thousand years. The first resurrection has been occurring throughout the

Church age, as Christian saints have died and their souls have entered Heaven.

- *Point 3: Christ will reign on earth physically.* In examining the rapturists' third claim, we need only look at the language of the passage. Nowhere does it say that "Christ will be physically present on earth, reigning from the throne of David in Israel." Nowhere does this passage even *imply* a physical, earthly kingdom in Jerusalem, Israel. It seems almost blasphemous to picture Christ seated on a throne doing administrative tasks, involved in ruling the day-to-day affairs of the earth. Rather, His Kingdom is spiritual. His Kingdom is universal. His Kingdom is ecclesiastical.

Thrones *are* mentioned, as is Christ. But locating these events on earth rather than in Heaven reads something into the passage. The souls of the martyrs are specifically mentioned as being in Heaven under the altar (6:9). Since those souls are also reigning, it is more consistent to understand them as still being in Heaven. Nowhere do we have reason to deduce that these are embodied souls. They are ruling with Christ, who in this vision is ruling from Heaven.

These are all spiritual realities. It makes no sense to try to plant Christ on a physical throne in Jerusalem (GR6).

Summary of the Millennium

St. John describes the "Church age" in this passage (20:1-6). This age started with the birth of the Church at Christ's Passion. Satan was then definitively defeated, but his public "chaining" occurred when the Temple in Jerusalem fell. From this point, Christ reigns with His saints over a worldwide spiritual Kingdom. The blessings of Daniel are being bestowed via the "strong covenant" he predicted (Dan. 9:27). The forces of evil are hampered by God's restraining of Satan. The saints of the Church Triumphant in Heaven have undergone the first resurrection. By their prayers, they are active in the affairs of the earthbound Church Militant during the entire Millennium. The reign of Christ and His Church will extend for a very long time, until the Father's plan is complete. At that point, Christ will again physically enter human history at the second advent.

Some rapturists maintain that the majority of the early Church Fathers believed in a literal, physical, future thousand-year reign of Christ on earth. I believe that this is a misunderstanding of the record. Yet it is a claim worth examining.

Throughout our examination, we have repeatedly referred to the *Commentary on The Apocalypse*, written by Victorinus in 270 A.D. This earliest extant explanation of The Apocalypse speaks of the Millennium clearly: "Those years wherein Satan is bound are in *the first advent of Christ, even to the end of the age;* and they are called a thousand, according to that mode of speaking, wherein a part is signified by the whole, just as is that passage, 'the word which He commanded for a thousand generations,' although they are not a thousand. . . . [During this time] the Devil [is] excluded from the hearts of believers. . . . That is, [God] forbade and restrained his seducing those who belong to Christ" (COA, XX).

Eusebius is known as the father of Church history. He makes it clear that those who believed in a future, literal, physical reign of Christ were a fringe element of the Church, whose beliefs were odd in other ways as well. They accepted questionable, noncanonical teachings of Christ (perhaps now lost), as well as some of the more unbelievable apocryphal stories about Christ. Although they appeared early in Church history, and were at times even numerous, worldwide they were always in the minority.

This is how Eusebius describes them: "This same historian [Papias] also gives other accounts, which he says he adds as received by him from unwritten tradition, likewise certain strange parables of our Lord, and of His doctrine and some other matters rather too fabulous. In these he says there would be *a certain millennium after the resurrection*, and that there would be a *corporeal reign* of Christ on this very earth; which things he appears to have imagined, as if they were authorized by the apostolic narrations, not understanding correctly those matters which they propounded mystically in their representations. For he was very limited in his comprehension, as is evident from his discourses; yet he was the cause why most of the ecclesiastical writers, urging the antiquity of man, were carried away by a similar opinion; as, for instance, Irenaeus, or any other that adopted such sentiments" (*EH*, III:39).

Some try to draft St. Jerome into the premillennialist camp. Yet he clearly taught that "the Holy City denote[s] the present world" (*REV*, 65).

Justin Martyr, too, is supposed by some rapturists to have been an early example of premillennialism. But listen to his words: "The Spirit of prophecy speaks . . . in this way: 'For out of Zion shall go forth the law. . . . And He shall judge among the nations . . . and *they shall beat their swords into ploughshares*, and their spears into pruning-hooks: nation shall not lift up sword against nation, neither shall they learn war anymore.' *And it did so come to pass, we can convince you.* For out of Jerusalem there went out into the world, men, twelve in number, and these illiterate, of no ability in speaking: but by the power of God they proclaimed to every race of men that they were sent by Christ to teach to all the word of God" (*ACR*, XXXIX). Justin Martyr makes it clear that he believed the peace promises of the Old Testament were a present reality.

How do we reconcile this very amillennial (Catholic) statement of Justin Martyr with his supposed reputation as a premillennialist? Actually, I think he was being inconsistent. His basic view is definitely amillennial, because he clearly believed the Kingdom's benefits were readily available in the Church. Yet the idea that the Messiah would "reign on earth for one thousand years . . . is rooted deeply in early Jewish apocalyptic tradition" (*NCE*, IX, 852). He adopted the prevailing mindset of the Jewish apocalyptic tradition without thoroughly Christianizing it. As a result, he ended up with a belief system that at points contradicted itself. But regardless of that, Justin Martyr did see the benefits of the Millennium as already a present reality. He cannot be regarded as a justification for the rapturist viewpoint by any means.

Ultimately, the key issue is not what certain writers of the early Church believed. The crucial issue for Catholics revolves around the beliefs held by the successors to the Apostles, the bishops of the early Church. As a whole, they vehemently repudiated pre-millennial notions of a corporeal kingdom on earth distinct from the Church. We need not count heads. It is enough to remember that the Eastern part of the early Church refused to recognize the canonicity of The Apocalypse because some perceived it as premillennialist. It was only when the Western part of the early Church succeeded in convincing the East that premillennialism was *not* integral to this book that it was universally accepted as canonical.

Of course, that is the view of this book that we have been expounding. But we must not miss the point. The Church was willing to reject as inspired any book that *did* teach premillennialism. Why? The bishops were overwhelmingly *not* premillennial. They believed the Millennium had begun at Christ's first advent and would end at His second advent. They believed in a thoroughly spiritual Kingdom, the Church. During the first few centuries of the Church, a thousand years was "further than the eye could see."

I grew up as a rapturist. I was convinced of the truth of these beliefs for much of my adult life, and I know how most rapturists would respond. They would say something like this: "David, the world today just does not fit the description of what the Millennium is supposed to be like. Where is the lion lying down with the lamb? Where is worldwide peace?"

Rapture

It may surprise these rapturists to know that the early Church did believe that the world had changed in *precisely* this way, due to the preaching of the gospel. This includes even those they try to claim as premillennialists, such as Justin Martyr. Reread his quotation six paragraphs above. He wrote, " ' . . . neither shall they learn war anymore.' And *it did so come to pass, we can convince you.*"

From our perspective two millennia later, we perhaps do not fully appreciate the impact the gospel had on humankind in the first century. St. Athanasius certainly saw his fair share of strife. Yet like Justin Martyr, he firmly believed that the peace promised in the Millennium had already arrived. "Who is He that has *united in peace* men that hated one another, save the beloved Son of the Father? . . . It was prophesied of the peace He was to usher in, where the Scripture says: 'They shall beat their swords into ploughshares, and their pikes into sickles, and nation shall not take the sword against nation, neither shall they learn war anymore.' . . . Even now those barbarians cannot endure to be a single hour without weapons: but when they hear the teaching of Christ, straightway . . . instead of arming their hands with weapons, they raise them in prayer" (*INC*, LII).

Unlike these early Church Fathers, it seems that present-day rapturists want to see a smithy on television hammering someone's sword into a farm implement. But is not this the same problem that plagued the Sanhedrin? They would not accept John the Baptist as the new Elijah, nor Jesus as the Messiah, because the fulfillment was not tangible enough for their standards.

Origen would say that rapturists are looking for too literal a fulfillment; that a careful reading of Scripture leads one to believe that God never envisioned a physical, political kingdom. "Many, not understanding the Scriptures . . . have fallen into heresies. . . . They think, also, that it has been predicted that the wolf, that four-footed animal, is, at the coming of Christ, to feed with the lambs . . . and the bull to pasture with lions, and that they are to be led by a little child to the pasture . . . that lions also will . . . feed on straw. . . . Some have not believed in our Lord and Savior, judging that those statements which were uttered respecting Him ought to be understood literally . . . that He ought also to eat butter and honey, in order to choose the good before He should come to know how to bring forth evil. . . . Now, the cause, in all the points previously enumerated, of the false opinions, and of the impious statements or ignorant assertions about God, appears to be nothing else than not understanding the Scripture . . . but [understanding] the interpretation of it agreeably to the mere letter" (*TPR*, IV:1:7-8).

I can almost hear the rapturist sighing and admitting, "Okay, maybe the early Church did interpret Scripture differently from the way we do. But say what you will, there still does not seem to be a Millennial Kingdom of Christ evident in the world today. Christ and His morality have just as many enemies as friends in the world in this age — maybe more."

To which I say: *Dealing with enemies is what reigning entails.* Christ does not wait to reign until after complete and total victory. That is how we, the Church Militant, are active in cooperating with the Church Triumphant. Christ "must reign *until* He has put all His enemies under His feet" (1 Cor. 15:25). St. Paul assumed that the *overcoming* of Christ's enemies was the main focus of ruling the Kingdom! The battle can be exhilarating when you already know who will win. We are sure Christ will be victor in the end, because He kept His appointment with the Sanhedrin: He judged them within the generation He had predicted.

Future benefits of Daniel's strong covenant

Although visions in apocalyptic literature do not necessarily follow chronological order (GR8), St. John clearly and specifically places the next events immediately at the conclusion of Christ's Kingdom: "And when the thousand years are ended"

(20:7). This is a time statement. St. John announces his intention to be specific about the order of events. He started this vision with Christ's vindication in 70 A.D. and continued it into the Millennium that signifies the present Church age, in which we live. What he is about to describe comes at the end of the Millennium, at the end of the spiritual Kingdom over which Christ has ruled; at the final eschaton. This is the first time in all of these visions that the final events of history are in focus (GR3).

Do you feel as if all you ever do is fight a battle with evil? Well, the best is yet to come! After the extremely long and complete kingdom age — "the thousand years" — there will be one final confrontation between good and evil: "When the thousand years are ended, Satan will be loosed from his prison, and will come out to deceive the nations . . . Gog and Magog, to gather them for battle. And they marched up over the broad earth . . . but fire came down from Heaven and consumed them, and the Devil . . . was thrown into the lake of fire and brimstone where the beast and the false prophet were, and they will be tormented day and night forever and ever" (20:7-10).

This description begins at the moment described by St. Paul: "He who now restrains it will do so until he is out of the way" (2 Thess. 2:7). St. Paul is not speaking in apocalyptic language, however, so he makes it clear this is at the end of the Church age.

Notice that there is no reference to a revival of the beast (sea-beast) or the false prophet (land-beast). This is a common rapturist premise, that the beast and the false prophet will be active at the final battle. But they have already been defeated and destroyed in the first century. Since the antichrist is still in the future, there will have been at least two millennia between the defeat of the beasts and the defeat of Satan and his antichrist. That gap is not presumptuous; it is right in the text. After his defeat, Satan is cast into "the lake of fire" to join the beast and the false prophet. They are already there, awaiting the reunion with their dragon.

What are Gog and Magog?

The reference to "Gog and Magog" gives us further evidence that this is the final battle. Originally Gog was the king of Magog. In the Old Testament, Gog and Magog ultimately took on the aura of a mythical people, representing the entire heathen world as it opposed Yahweh. Gog and Magog were the subject of Ezekiel in Chapters 38 and 39. The battle language here and in Ezekiel have the same sense of finality. God states, "I will not let my holy name be profaned *anymore*" (39:7).

In Ezekiel, the evil Gog and Magog are condemned for plotting war against God's people when they are least expecting it. They "devise an evil scheme and say, 'I will . . . fall upon the quiet people who dwell securely . . . to assail the . . . people who were gathered from the nations'" (38:10-12). This mirrors the words of Jesus when He described the world situation immediately before the final battle and His return. In His answer to the second question of the Olivet Discourse, Jesus predicted that, at His second coming, people would be living their normal, everyday lives in peace and security, without any expectation of the flood about to encompass them (Matt. 24:37-39).

The Apocalypse gives few details about the final battle. But it is certainly different from any battle envisioned so far in The Apocalypse. The army is as numerous as "the sand of the sea" (20:8). God promised Abraham that his children of faith would one day be as numerous as "the sand of the sea" (Gen. 32:12). The use of this phrase is meant to show the immense breadth and depth of Satan's influence with mankind once he is released. As always, his forces appear at least as numerous and powerful as Christ's.

The army of Gog and Magog "marched over the broad earth and surrounded the camp of the saints and the beloved city." "The beloved city" has not been mentioned yet in The Apocalypse. This Greek word *agapao* is used commonly in the New Testament in reference to Christians. This final confrontation will be between Satan with his followers and Christ with His faithful. Whether that city is an actual location on earth is doubtful. This seems to be another method of referring to the Church Militant. The new people of God will be savagely assaulted by Satan and all the evil forces he can muster.

Amazingly, there are no details of a battle. When Gog and Magog surround the saints, when prospects for the Church are at their blackest, "fire came down from Heaven and consumed them" (20:9). That is it. Divine judgment is administered quickly. "And the Devil . . . was thrown into the lake of fire" (20:10). The "Battle of Armageddon" that so many rapturists foresee will probably not resemble the final battle at all. As we have already determined, the events of Armageddon actually occurred two millennia ago (and The Apocalypse never tells of a battle at Armageddon anyway). The final battle of Gog and Magog will be primarily a *spiritual* assault on the Church.

Many Christians wish to have more details about this final battle between Satan and God. But we need not fear. Although few details are related, the end of this final conflict is certain. These verses witness "God's victory over the final unleashing of evil, which will cause His Bride [the Church] to come down from Heaven" (CCC, 677). That is as we would expect. After all, Christ won the Great Battle of the prior vision partially to give us assurance that He will emerge as the victorious Judge in the end.

The great white throne

The battle of Gog and Magog will end with the utter defeat of Satan and his forces. Immediately after the victory of Christ over Satan, "a great white throne" is set up for judgment (20:11). The second resurrection occurs, which is the bodily resurrection of all people for judgment on the basis of "what they had done" (20:12). Remember the strategy of the Child? "Blessed are the dead who die in the Lord henceforth . . . for their deeds follow them" (14:13).

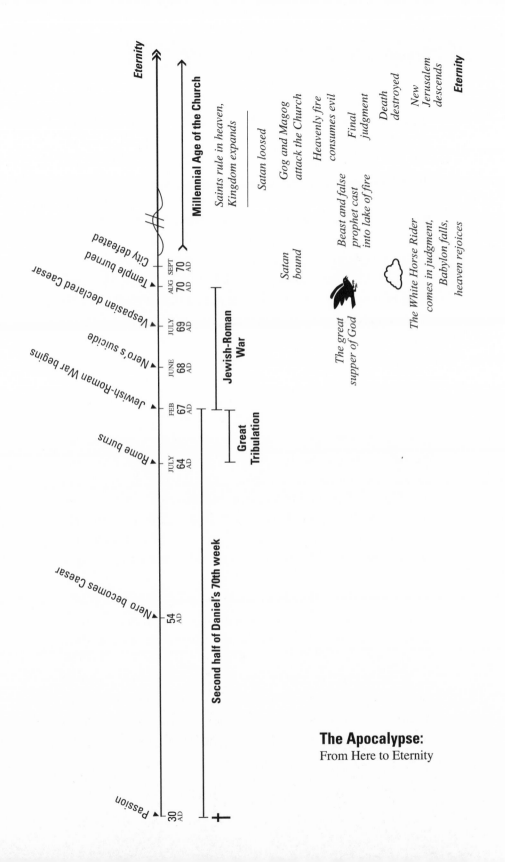

The Apocalypse:
From Here to Eternity

The battle strategy of the Lamb involved telling us the Truth about reality: that what we do here and now will be accounted for at the final, general judgment.

At the end of the Olivet Discourse, Jesus told His disciples this would happen. Not only is what we believe important, but also what we do. Jesus specifically mentions the corporal works of mercy: "I was hungry and you gave me food; I was thirsty and you gave me drink; I was a stranger and you welcomed me; I was naked and you clothed me; I was sick and you visited me; I was in prison and you came to me" (Matt. 25:35-36).

Rapturists postulate a total of two, three, or four judgments still in the future. (Part of this is based on their faulty view of the Church, which we have already discussed.) But this one great-white-throne judgment is really the only general, universal judgment contained in Scripture. (The only other one we face is our own particular judgment, which follows our own death.)

Those "not found written in the book of life" join Satan, Death, and Hades in their eternal destruction in the "lake of fire." This is "the second death" (20:14-15).

A new Heaven and a new earth

We are at the very end, when time dissolves into the more substantive reality of eternity. One way we know this is that Death is "thrown into the lake of fire" (20:14). And we know from St. Paul that death is the last enemy to be conquered (1 Cor. 15:26).

In perhaps his last use of anticipation, St. John uses this destruction of death to unite the great-white-throne judgment to the "new Heaven and ... earth." He has mentioned the death of Death and now links it to our heavenly encounter with God: "God himself will be with them [His People]; and He will wipe away every tear from their eyes, and *death shall be no more*" (21:4). The destruction of death is accomplished. The consequences of Adam's choice have finally been reversed by Christ.

Another indication that we are at the very end of time is that our Heaven and earth have been destroyed: "I saw a new Heaven and a new earth; for the first Heaven and the first earth had passed away" (21:1). This is reflective of the language of St. Peter: "The day of the Lord will come like a thief, and then the heavens will pass away with a loud noise" (2 Pet. 3:10).

St. John tells us this new Heaven and new earth will have no sea (21:1). What a seemingly strange attribute! But this doesn't necessarily mean there won't be large bodies of water. Remember, in the Old Testament, the sea was commonly a reference to the Gentiles, the outsiders of God's kingdom, the unbelievers. There are no more unbelievers at this point. All the evil and faithless have already been cast into the "lake of fire," and all those left are followers of Christ. History and time melt away, and eternity asserts itself (20:15).

The wonderful eternity in store for these followers of Christ is now St. John's final topic. We approach the climax of all biblical events since Genesis (GR3). In the first three chapters of Genesis, God creates the earth, and then Adam and Eve defile it through sin. Now history and the Scriptures culminate in "a new Heaven and a new earth."

The New Jerusalem

The Church Militant and the Church Suffering are subsumed into the Church Triumphant: "I saw the holy city, New Jerusalem, coming down out of Heaven from God prepared as a bride adorned for her husband. . . . 'Behold, the dwelling of God is with men'" (21:2-3). This is the "marriage of the Lamb" for which "the marriage supper of the Lamb" makes our hearts yearn (19:7, 9). The joy of the Eucharist becomes ever present. The people of God now enjoy God's presence forever.

This is not a new theme in Scripture. It is contained within the Old Testament prophets: "The new heavens and the new earth which I will make shall remain before me, says the Lord" (Isa. 66:22).

Who does this? God alone is mighty enough to destroy the world and remake it in perfection. He proclaims, "Behold, I make all things new" (21:5). Here stands the pinnacle of The Apocalypse. These are the first words in the whole book spoken by God from His throne in Heaven.

It is a fitting finale. God really was in control. It may not have seemed possible, but He was the mover behind it all. He ushered His Bride into eternity for the marriage of the Lamb. He was the One to "make all things new."

SECTION V: THEMATIC SUMMARY

Congratulations are once again in order! With verse 21:5a, we have completed the visions of The Apocalypse that describe the casting out of the Old Covenant in favor of the New Covenant, along with the final extension of our vision all the way to eternity. Three times St. John has examined the Jewish-Roman War, repeatedly giving us new insights into many of the key characters involved in that drama. Along the way, he has helped us to develop a much clearer view of Christ's Bride, the Church.

We are now at the end of St. John's visions of The Apocalypse. Beginning in 21:5b, we start a summary of the themes of these visions. Notice that St. John is still reflecting Daniel's outline: Daniel 13 and 14 are a thematic summary of Daniel's message. St. John tells us when he is ready to give us *his* thematic summary of The Apocalypse by deliberately repeating a unique phrase found in Daniel.

In Daniel's initial vision, where the mystery of the Messianic Kingdom was first revealed, King Nebuchadnezzar gave his assessment of the vision by praising God and promoting Daniel and his friends. But to signal the end of the vision and interpretation, and to introduce the assessment of the king, Daniel says, "The dream is *true* and the interpretation is *trustworthy*" (Dan. 2:45, NIV). We know that St. John would have studied this passage in the Septuagint or a similar Greek translation. The English word *true* is from the Greek *alethinos*, and *trustworthy* is from the Greek *pistos*. St. John uses this unique pair of Greek words, when, like Daniel, he ends his visions and introduces the assessment of the King.

Christ the King "who sat upon the throne" now speaks: "These words are *trustworthy* and *true*" (21:5) — *alethinos* and *pistos*. Just as we did in Daniel's vision, we now will get the assessment of the King. In this case, the King is Christ.

St. John takes Daniel one step further, using this phrase to signal the *end* of his thematic summary. When the angel speaks the words *alethinos* and *pistos*, we know that the thematic summary has been completed (22:6). After that, the book ends with concluding remarks, a blessing and a warning (22:7b-21).

In this last segment of The Apocalypse, it is as if St. John were put into an armchair and told to relax for the rest of the book. In the previous sections of The Apocalypse, we were given the perspectives of Heaven, of the Sanhedrin, of the Church, of friends of Jerusalem, and of the martyrs. Now we will be treated to God's thematic summary. This is actually an overview of the Church itself. It has three parts: the Church's gospel message, the Church's nature, and the Church's mission. This emphasis on the Church should not surprise us. Remember that the battle strategy of God's People was to build the Temple (the Church) of God.

The Church's gospel

In summarizing the Church's message to the world, God states that there are two groups of people. Those who do not respond to Him with upright lives will be subjected eternally to "the lake that burns with fire and brimstone" (21:8). In contrast, "he who conquers shall have this heritage, and I will be his God and he shall be my son" (21:7). Have we heard this so often that its novelty has worn off? Remain faithful to God, and you will be God's *son!* This is the divine filiation, the divination of humanity, of which the early Church Fathers spoke so often. God does not desire slaves, but true "heirs of God and fellow heirs with Christ" (Rom. 8:17; Gal. 4:7; James 2:5).

The grace of God in making this possible is almost beyond comprehension. It is a gift from Him. "To the thirsty I will give water without price from the fountain of the water of life" (21:6). This grace that starts us in the Christian pilgrimage is free and undeserved. Jesus promised this same "free water" of the Holy Spirit when He was talking to the Samaritan woman: "Whoever drinks of the water that I shall give him will never thirst; the water that I shall give him will become in him a spring of water welling up to eternal life" (John 4:13-14).

What is this free water? Why, it is nothing other than the life of God Himself. God enlivens us with the Holy Spirit through no merit of our own. The sacrament of Baptism is both the symbol and the enabling substance of the Holy Spirit's work in a new Christian. In love, God makes us His very own children.

Yet God's free gift requires a loyal response, and that response is undeniably more than just mental assent. "He who conquers shall have this heritage." Although the initial grace to begin the journey is free and undeserved, God expects much of His children. By enduring under trial, we become true sons and daughters of God. That is "conquering." The "eternal gospel" proclaimed by the first angel in the strategy of the Lamb has not changed (14:6-7); the Truth coming from the rider's mouth as a sword is ever the same: the gift is free, but never cheap. It is our responsibility to obey the gospel that never changes: "Fear God . . . and worship Him" (14:7). Our response will determine our everlasting fate.

The Church's mission

The mission of the Bride is to bring the Truth of Christ to the world, and it revolves around the twin images of light and water.

The light of the Church has been a central theme of The Apocalypse under a different symbol: the sword of Truth that Christ wields. As we on earth wait for the second advent, we are to shine the light of Truth into every aspect of reality. It will cut like a sword. "By its *light* shall the nations walk; and the kings of the earth shall bring their glory into it, and its gates shall never be shut by day — and there shall be no night there; they shall bring into it the glory and the honor of the nations" (21:24-26).

The unbelieving world finds Christ's Truth most clearly displayed in the lives of faithful Christians. Elsewhere, St. John wrote that God is light, and we walk in that light when we live without sin: "*God is light* . . . if we say we have fellowship with Him while we walk in darkness, we lie . . . but if *we walk in the light, as He is in the light,* we have fellowship with one another, and the blood of Jesus, His Son, cleanses us from all sin. If we say we have no sin . . . *the truth* is not in us. If we confess our sins, He is faithful and just, and will forgive our sins and cleanse us from all unrighteousness" (1 John 1:5-9).

But the light of Truth is not the only aspect of the Church's mission. It also involves water. There is a "river of the water of life . . . flowing from the throne of God" (22:1). God says, "I am the Alpha and the Omega, the beginning and the end. To the thirsty I will give water without price from the fountain of the water of life. He who conquers shall have this heritage" (21:6-7).

This is the fulfillment of the thousand cubits of water that Ezekiel saw flowing from under the Temple (47:6-12). This abundant source of water brings to mind the words of Jesus: " 'Whoever drinks of the water that I shall give him will never thirst. . . . If anyone thirst, let him come to me and drink'. . . . Now this He said about the Spirit, which those who believed in Him were to receive" (John 4:14; 7:37, 39). The water symbolizes the gift of the Holy Spirit to the Church and, through the Church, to the world: the sacrament of Baptism.

To sum it all up: the Bride's mission is to proclaim the light of Truth and to make available the water — the powerful, transforming love — of the Holy Spirit. Light symbolizes the sword of the Rider, the Truth of Christ. Love without Truth leads to rottenness, just as water without light does. Conversely, Truth without Love begets harsh dryness, as does light without water. But together, water and light foster life, "the tree of life" (22:2).

When Love and Truth are offered in balance by the Church, the world will be able to taste of the tree of life. The people of God will have lived up to her mission. This is the same tree of God's presence and fellowship that was available to Adam and Eve in the Garden of Eden (Gen. 2:9). When we live as Christ wants His Bride to live, we enjoy God and His gifts. Our eternal life starts here and now. This is why we hope and wait for the second coming of our great God and Savior, Jesus Christ. His coming will bring all the fruits of the tree of life to abundant fruition.

The Church's nature

Now an angel offers us an introduction to "the Bride, the wife of the Lamb." She was the mystery whose nature was revealed in the initial vision of the scroll. She was the Woman with offspring. She was the object of the dragon's everlasting hatred. She was the celebrant of the Eucharist, a sacramental community. She was the New Israel being liberated through the plagues of the great battle. We have just seen her as the New Jerusalem descending from Heaven. She is the Church, "the Bride, the wife of the Lamb."

We are truly privileged. This is the mystery that Daniel could not fully understand in his final vision. This is what Jesus said the Old Covenant prophets longed to see, but could not (Matt. 13:17). This is the spiritual Kingdom of the Messiah. This is the everlasting Kingdom that accepts Jew and Gentile on an equal footing as long as they are willing to eat together at His Supper as one People. This is the Church, redeemed with His Blood.

Even a cursory reading of this passage immediately reveals one aspect of the Church's nature. She is somehow intimately tied to the number *twelve*: "[The Bride had] twelve gates, and at the gates twelve angels, and on the gates the names of the twelve tribes. . . . The city had twelve foundations and on them the twelve names of the twelve Apostles. . . . Its length [was] twelve thousand stadia . . . its wall [was] 144 cubits . . . adorned with . . . [twelve] jewels. . . . The twelve gates were twelve pearls (21:12, 13, 16-17, 19, 21). Once again, we are seeing the importance of symbolic numbers (GR2).

The most important appearance of *twelve* in the Old Covenant had to do with God's chosen people, His *ekklesia*. There were twelve sons of Israel, and they headed the twelve tribes of the household of God. With his symbolic use of the number *twelve*, St. John makes it crystal clear that this new Bride has superseded the tribes of Israel. She contains the twelve tribes' names, but is built on the foundation of the twelve Apostles. The new people of God have sprung historically from the old, but the leadership is new.

There is no going back to the Old Covenant. The New Covenant replaced the Old, as Zechariah had predicted when he broke his two staffs (Appendix Two). This is the strong covenant of Daniel, made with the Church, rather than with ethnic Israel. The Church's message is the gospel we have just examined. Her eternal dignity stems from her choice as the Bride of the Lamb. That is the reason for her creation and existence. The Old Covenant's time is over, due to unfaithfulness. That is a central message of the Great Battle vision we just examined.

We must not make the all-too-common mistake of spiritualizing this Bride altogether, so that we have only "an invisible Church." She has a founder (Christ), as did the Old Covenant (Moses). The New is built upon a foundation of Her Apostles, just as the Old had its prophets. She has a priesthood, just as the Old Covenant did. She has initiation rites (Baptism), as did the Old

Rapture

(circumcision). She has essential ceremonies (the Eucharist), as did the Old (animal sacrifices). Perhaps most essential to remember, she has human leadership (bishops), just as it did the Old (kings and high priests). In a word, she is a visible institution, just like the Old. Because Old Covenant Israel was composed of humans, it looked imperfect from the outside; but it was still the Chosen People of God. Just so, the Church may appear fraught with human frailties on the surface. Yet the new people of God on earth *is* this visible institution — not merely an invisible network of spiritually attuned converts who are "born again." The world must be able to see this institution as an organization here on earth, for "a city set on a hill cannot be hid" (Matt. 5:14).

In addition to this, what else have we learned of the nature of this Bride during The Apocalypse? After all, that is the meaning of Apocalypse in Greek: *apokalupsis* means "revelation." The nature of the Church has been a mystery since time immemorial, but with the opening of the scroll, she is now revealed. What do we find?

In The Apocalypse, there are four clear characteristics of the Bride revealed for us.

• *One*. First, Christ's Bride is *one* Church. This was the crucial message of the initial scroll vision. Jew and Gentile can join together as equals in the Bride's marriage supper. Identification as a Christian supersedes the old ethnic categories of Jew and Gentile. Spiritually, the distinction of Jew and Gentile no longer exists! This is obvious from the way the seven churches were all addressed by St. John. They were geographically diverse, yet institutionally and spiritually one Body of Christ. They were in communion with one another and obedient to the same Christ. When their martyrs died, they all joined together under one altar, with no distinction among nationalities. We expect nothing less when we understand the mystery of this Church, where Jew and Gentile eat at one Table.

• *Apostolic.* Second, it is obvious that these geographically scattered churches were also faithful to the same teaching — that of St. John. There is one and only one gospel preached in The Apocalypse. The beliefs they held and the Eucharist they celebrated were those of the one Christ, as they were passed down through *the Apostles*. Their battle strategy of remaining faithful to the Truth of the Eucharist was the same, because they got it from the same source: the Apostles. Their destiny was that which was promised to them by Christ through St. John, because they were part of the apostolic tradition. This is all integral to the manner in which they were addressed by St. John.

• *Holy.* Third, this Bride is undeniably *holy*. We read that she exudes "the glory of God" Himself (21:11). We have seen evidence of this holiness from the very beginning of the visions. The martyrs under the altar in the fifth seal of the scroll vision were holy. The 144,000 chaste were "spotless." One of the major admonitions of The Apocalypse is the call to holiness. We could summarize much of the book thus: "Do not take the mark of the beast by worshiping idols. That unholy compromise will exclude you from the New Jerusalem." Speaking of the New Jerusalem, St. John states, "Nothing unclean shall enter it . . . but only those who are written in the Lamb's book of life" (21:27). Make no mistake, this Bride is holy.

• *Catholic.* Fourth, this Bride of the Lamb is *catholic*, meaning "universal." This universality exhibits itself in two forms. First, the Church is catholic because Christ is present in her. As St. Ignatius of Antioch said, "Where there is Christ Jesus, there is the Catholic Church" (*EPS*, VII:2). That is her gift and treasure. Second, the Church is catholic because of her mission to the whole world (CCC, pars. 830-831). The City of God contains the "144,000" ethnic Jews, but it also encompasses "every nation and tribe and tongue and people" (14:6). All are welcome, and all meet Christ when they come.

Rapture

So what do we have when we add it all together? St. John's Bride is none other than the one, holy, catholic, and apostolic Church that celebrates the Eucharist and waits in hope for the second advent. She is both institutionally visible and innately supernatural. Is there a name for this Church of St. John? One thing is certain: this is not a snapshot of the independent rapturist church that has sprouted up in your neighborhood within the last couple of generations. Today, the only Church that even approaches these qualifications is known worldwide as the Roman Catholic Church. She is the Bride of Christ by nature.

It is done!

Now that we have analyzed the thematic summary that God gives us of the Lamb's Bride, let us go back to the future for just a moment. With the descent of the New Jerusalem (which occurs at the final eschaton), God declares, "It is done!" (21:6). During creation, God repeatedly found that His work deserved the label, "It is good" (Gen. 1). But now that we are at the end of time, and eternity has begun, God states, "It is done." All of time — in fact, the very purpose of time's creation — was necessary for the epitome of God's plan to be done. The Church has entered eternity!

Just what is God referring to as being "done"? Since we are at the summit of the entire book, I believe God is referring to the complete thrust of these visions. The mystery of the Kingdom has been revealed, the final battle between the Woman's offspring and the dragon has been completed, the final judgment has occurred, and the New Jerusalem has come down from Heaven. The final and complete victory of Christ on earth causes the Church Triumphant to descend in glory. This is what is "done": God's plan for His Church, God's plan for the world, the mystery of the gospel.

This culmination of God's plan for His Kingdom is something for which we pray every day. When we pray the Our Father, we say,

Our Father, who art in Heaven,
    Hallowed be Thy name.
    Thy kingdom come.
    Thy will be done,
    On earth as it is in Heaven. . . .

The Apocalypse makes it clear that Christ's Kingdom is already here on earth. If that is true, why do we still pray for its coming?

Notice what Jesus actually taught us to pray. We pray that God's "will be done, on earth as it is in Heaven." God's will is already imperfectly accomplished here on earth, and we pray that it may be done perfectly here on earth, just as it is presently done perfectly in Heaven. In a similar way, God's Kingdom has already incompletely come here on earth. We pray for it to come in its fullness "on earth as it is in Heaven." We desire the New Jerusalem in all its glory, just as she is in Heaven already. The prayer that the Lord taught His disciples fits in perfectly with the Church's understanding of the present, limited reality of the Kingdom of God.

Here in this vision at the end of time, we witness the answer to our prayers. "It is done!" God's Kingdom has finally come here on earth as it already is in Heaven. The New Jerusalem has descended in all its fullness. This New Jerusalem is "the Bride, the wife of the Lamb" (21:9).

Notice how we ask God to accomplish His will here on earth via the same means He uses in Heaven. Think about this for a moment. All through this book, God's will has been done through the obedience of a Son. The willingness of the Son to live the Truth of the gospel, to put love for God and others before His own physical welfare, enabled the strategy of the Lamb to be victorious. That is how God wants to accomplish His will on earth as well: through the obedience of His children, through our endurance and faith.

CONCLUDING REMARKS

The Apocalypse concludes with a note of encouragement. We have seen that, in the end, the goodness of God overcomes the evil of Satan and his forces. Jesus concludes by telling us, "Surely I am coming soon" (22:20).

This statement primarily refers to His coming in 70 A.D. Since this vision was recorded in 68 A.D., He did come soon in His judgment of Jerusalem. He had predicted this judgment before His Passion forty years ahead of time, and He came as promised.

Yet this statement has an application for us in the twenty-first century as well (GR3). Christ is coming for you and me in our generation. It may be at the final eschaton. It may not. It may be at our own death. Surely, though, one way or another, we will experience the coming of Christ as Judge in our generation: at our own final moment. That final moment will be no later than when we die.

Christ can be trusted to keep His promises. The events of 70 A.D. stand as a promissory note that assures us that Christ is capable of coming again as promised. He will come as Judge at our death and at the final eschaton as well. Christ speaks Truth.

TWO QUESTIONS IN SUMMARY

We must now ask ourselves two straightforward questions.

First, *Where in the Bible is there a passage that teaches a two-stage coming, including both a secret rapture and then a glorious second coming?* We have examined all the relevant passages, and the answer remains the same. *There is no passage anywhere that teaches both a rapture and a second advent.*

This seems to be the least that rapturists should provide. But the passage does not exist, and they know it, which is why they are forced to pick and shuffle passages between these two events, in an attempt to shoehorn their theology into Scripture. In so doing, they leave the true meaning of the Bible behind. For a movement that vocally espouses *sola Scriptura*, this is a fatal flaw.

The second question has two parts: *Is there anything in these twenty-two chapters of The Apocalypse that necessitates a secret rapture before a future seven-year Great Tribulation? Is there anything in The Apocalypse that clearly predicts a future physical reign of Christ, centered in the Middle East for a thousand years?*

I have spent a great deal of time with you in The Apocalypse. Some might say I have been too thorough. But I wanted to be thorough enough to answer this second question.

The answer should be obvious. No, there is not. There is nothing anywhere in The Apocalypse that demands a rapture or a seven-year Great Tribulation or an earthly Millennium in the future. There is not even a shred of justification for these teachings. Some of the misinterpretation fails to take into account the apocalyptic nature of the book. Much of it ignores precedents within the Old and New Testaments. A fair share is a result of sleeping through ancient-history class and developing Winkle Warp.

Even more disturbing, rapturist teaching turns The Apocalypse into a virtual maze of symbols and events that confuse Christians to the point of exasperation. The average Christian decides that this book is not understandable and so decides not to study it. In so doing, he misses out on a blessing: "Blessed is he who keeps the words of the prophecy of this book" (22:7). How can Christians hope to adhere to this book's prophetic message when they quail at even opening it? In the process, they lose the opportunity to hear St. John's vision of the Church's message, nature, and mission.

We are now ready to answer the original question of this book. Will you, or I, be "left behind" the next time Jesus comes? The only biblical answer is an unequivocal no. Christ *will* come again, but all of us will experience it, believer and unbeliever alike. It will be glorious. It will be final. It will be accompanied by the final judgment. When it happens, some might want to be left behind, but all will be included: some to everlasting life and bliss, and some not.

Rapture

This is a message of hope for the Church. From our perspective, the first nineteen chapters of The Apocalypse have already been historically fulfilled. This should give us solid assurance that the one chapter still future really will take place. The ninety-five-percent down payment has already been fulfilled as predicted. This should give us confidence in the five-percent promise yet to come.

"Amen. Maranatha! Come, Lord Jesus" (22:20).

Part IV

Wrapping Up the Rapture

Chapter Nine

Why the Rapture Is Appealing

If you have stuck with our investigation thus far, you may have come to the same conclusion as I have: although the rapturist position here in the United States has many adherents, it has no adequate biblical basis. Why, then, does this position continue to enjoy such wide popularity?

Granted, some people believe in a secret rapture because they have been misled about what the Bible actually teaches. They are committed to something that they have been taught to be true, but have never objectively examined. But I believe there are other reasons that explain some believers' unshakable adherence to this system of theology. Here are a few that I have observed in my experience.

THREE PSYCHOLOGICAL REASONS
Three of the factors that makes rapturist theology appealing to Americans are more psychological than theological.

Comfortable pessimism
Rapturism allows for "comfortable pessimism"; that is, it gives people a positive response to the evil we witness in the world today. Belief in an imminent rapture is a very simple, comforting filter through which to view life. It lends meaning to current events.

Rapture

For example, when the World Trade Center was destroyed on September 11, 2001, a close rapturist friend informed me that this was a fulfillment of Chapter 18 of The Apocalypse, when Babylon is to be burned in an hour and its destruction mourned by the merchants. Another rapturist pointed to that horrific event and implied that I should take comfort that the end was near.

When anything bad happens, the rapturist can say, "Well, we all know that things will get worse and worse just before Christ raptures us away. It is obvious the end is near, but at least we won't be here to suffer through it." The belief system of rapturists allows them to take a certain comfort in the face of evil. For when things really deteriorate into chaos, they expect to be safely tucked away in Heaven.

There is a problem with this approach to life, however. It may comfort the person witnessing suffering, but it does absolutely nothing positive for the person *experiencing* the suffering. This theology is appealing only as long as the pain is someone else's.

Some observers have linked the attraction of comfortable pessimism to the Great Depression and to the horrors of World War II. These events turned many Americans of that generation into latent pessimists. The idea that they would be the ones to witness the apocalyptic end of this world seemed completely in line, on a cosmic level, with their experience of evil. Many of the institutions that promote rapturist theology today were founded and expanded by this generation.

The system continues to appeal to new generations of Americans because of the despair that is so prevalent in our culture. Rapturism is a natural spiritual home for those who think the world is careening out of control. To a large extent, they can keep their basic outlook of despair, but remain able to cope on a daily basis.

This basic pessimism also helps explain the relative political inactivity of this group of Christians. Darby himself understood that his new theology left no room for political involvement. He claimed that "it is absolutely necessary that we should renounce everything." He believed that this world and its governmental systems are evil.

Darby taught that this world is irrelevant to the future of committed Christians, because they will be raptured out of its problems. He told his followers, "We do not mix in politics; we are not of the world" (*WRI*, II:44). Early rapturists even refused to vote. Although this has certainly changed, modern rapturist preachers emphasize the imminent judgment of this world by asking, "Why polish the brass on a sinking ship?" They do not believe this world is worth improving. They believe that a Christian's goal is to hang on until Christ raptures him away, while attempting to take as many with him as possible.

This mindset may explain a peculiar phenomenon that has puzzled some political commentators here in the United States. Fundamentalist Protestants have been unable to keep any political institution viable and active for any extended period. Jerry Falwell's Moral Majority was a dynamic force on the political scene for a decade, and then it virtually disappeared. Pat Robertson and Ralph Reed were connected with the Christian Coalition, which was a force to be reckoned with for another decade. Yet no Fundamentalist organization has been able to remain a force for much longer, even during the heyday of rapturist theology in the last quarter of the twentieth century. Is it because the theology that lies beneath these organizations cannot sustain political activity? This seems at least possible.

At the same time, the freedom — even the command — to reject political responsibility can be appealing. If you are tired of hearing sermons on social justice or on the Christian community's responsibility to change the culture for Christ, then a rapturist Church can seem like paradise — although a pessimists' paradise to be sure.

"Health and wealth" gospel

There is a serious problem underlying all of this, however. While the hope of a rapture allows rapturists to cope with tragedy, it also saddles them with a non-Christian view of the world. Quite simply, the rapturist system contains no Cross. Although some rapturists do not hold to it, by its very nature this theology is closely allied to the "health and wealth" gospel. This is the idea that, since Christ suffered on the Cross for us, Christians need never suffer again. These Christians believe that God wants our lives on earth to be free from any hardship and overflowing with material goods. The presence of these material blessings is evidence of one's high spiritual estate, and the absence of them is evidence of a lack of faith.

While the appeal of this idea is obvious, it is absolutely antithetical to the teaching of our Savior. Jesus never promised us a rose garden because of His suffering. In fact, He promised us our own Gethsemane. Jesus taught that any follower of His must "deny himself and take up his cross daily" (Luke 9:23). He called us to His Cross, and then showed us how to carry our own crosses for God.

Jesus further said, "Whoever does not bear his own cross . . . cannot be my disciple" (Luke 14:27). The choice presented by Christ is quite stark. Later in His ministry, Jesus warned His followers that "in the world you [will] have tribulation" (John 16:33). In Christ's prayer for His disciples and future Church, Jesus never once prayed that His followers would be exempted from suffering. Even less did He intimate that they would be secretly raptured away from this world's sufferings. He prayed that His followers would have the strength to *endure* the trials He knew would be coming: "I do not pray that Thou shouldst take them out of the world, but that Thou shouldst keep them from the evil one" (John 17:15). Meditation on this verse undermines the assumptions behind the purpose of a secret rapture.

Endurance in suffering was the constant message of The Apocalypse, as well. Christians must expect suffering and endure it for the sake of salvation. This was the teaching of the early Church without exception. In the first century, the Pastor of Hermas reminded Christians, "Those who continue steadfast and are put through the fire will be purified by means of it . . . wherefore cease not speaking these things into the ears of the saints" (*TSV, IV*). Suffering is to be expected in the Christian pilgrimage because it is a means to holiness.

Many committed rapturists believe they will be exempted even from the suffering of death. They take great comfort in their belief that Christ must rapture away this generation, the "generation of the fig tree," the one that has witnessed the founding of Israel. As we have seen, however, there is actually no biblical basis for this false comfort.

I have known some committed rapturists as friends and have seen some of these friends meet death. They — and everyone in this generation and in generations to come — will continue to die until Christ returns in all His glory, and there is no guarantee that it will occur within this generation any more than during the generation of Montanis or of Joseph Smith. Remember them? They, too, were certain that Christ would return before their generation died.

Inside knowledge

The same human instinct that causes people to visit palmreaders and fortune-tellers makes rapturist theology so popular. When world events seem to spin out of control, the rapturist can sit comfortably in the knowledge that he has the inside scoop on the future. This appeals to anyone's innate sense of curiosity and promotes a sense of security.

Unfortunately, pride is a very natural result of this thinking. I do not say this with pleasure. I myself was an integral part of the rapturist movement for most of my life. Just like all the other "end of the world" sects that have sprouted since the Montanists ruined the Church picnic almost two millennia ago, we are supposed to believe that we are the final generation, that we have the blueprint for all of history in our back pockets. This puts us, and the leaders of this movement, at the apex of history. Nothing in history is as important as what is happening now. Our generation is involved in the final battle of good and evil, and no other generation has a more important role to play than ours. And not only do we know all of history; we know the important events of the next few years before they even happen. This can be a tremendous ego-booster!

In contrast, the Catholic Church teaches that we may or may not be in the final confrontation between God and Satan. God took at least two or three millennia to get the world ready for His greatest creation, which is Christ's Bride, the Church. Why should God now end the work of the Church after a mere two millennia? There is no scriptural basis for believing that the Church will not continue growing here on earth for ten thousand years or more.

This perspective need not make our present generation feel unimportant just because we will not consummate the entire plan for the last days. In fact, it should do just the opposite. Everything we do now will have repercussions for generations to come. Our actions today — good and evil — can lead to consequences in five hundred years that we can hardly imagine!

The pride engendered by claiming to have the blueprint to history is the original "hook" that gets many Catholics interested in rapturist beliefs. The Catholic Church tells us how this world will end, but it often seems to be so far in the future. In contrast, rapturists promise to clue us in to events that are unfolding before our very eyes. At first, their system seems to answer to the biblical data, give meaning to the daily news, and satisfy our curiosity, all at the same time. Why go to a palm-reader when the local preacher at the corner church will answer many of your questions about the immediate future?

Believe me, this appeal of the rapture and the Great Tribulation is not lost on rapturists, who use their premillennial system as a wedge for pulling people out of the Church. Most Catholics do not understand rapturist theology. After all, it is not even two hundred years old! It is so far afield from the traditional understanding of the Church throughout the ages, that even Catholic leaders are sometimes caught flat-footed when asked to respond. I have gotten letters from Catholic pastors at a total loss as to how to respond to rapturists.

As a result, the most anti-Catholic of the Protestant groups find that when they teach about an imminent secret rapture and the ensuing Great Tribulation, they have an extremely effective method of drawing Catholics away from the Church. Many former Catholics admit that they first considered leaving the Church after being introduced to this doctrine. By the time a faithful Catholic family figures out what this teaching is all about, they have lost a child, a brother, or a spouse to the local Fundamentalist group down the street.

TWO THEOLOGICAL REASONS

Although I believe that these psychological reasons are an important aspect of rapturism's appeal, there are two important theological reasons as well. They rely on opposite, extreme views of Scripture.

Too "high" a view

The first view is *sola Scriptura*, which seeks to place the Bible on a pedestal that the Bible itself flatly rejects. Rapturists stand firmly in the tradition of the radical, Anabaptist Protestant Reformation. They accept no other authority than the Bible. They do not accept bishops or any type of spiritual authority vested in any man. They firmly believe that if a person approaches Scripture with a pure heart, the Holy Spirit will unerringly lead him to the truth. Their faith is completely individualistic.

This approach leads to a problem. What would happen if one of these Christians were to admit that a Bible passage was symbolic or figurative? Well, then whoever had the authority to determine what was symbolic, and what was not, would really be more authoritative than the Bible itself. At least, that is the way they view the situation. They do not want to open that Pandora's box.

As a result, they take everything in the Bible as literally as possible (except for the clear teaching on the Eucharist, of course). Rapturists naturally tend to the belief that the universe was created in six literal, twenty-four hour days. Because of the genealogies in Genesis, many of them would hold that the world is less than ten thousand years old. They must understand all passages of the Bible literally because they think that otherwise they will have left the barn door open for the horses to escape: once any passage is declared to be figurative, where do they stop, without an accepted authority as a guide? Rapturists choose to be literalistic in their interpretation of apocalyptic literature because they think that anything else is just too dangerous. Literal Scripture interpretation is their only anchor of stable spiritual authority.

Given their assumptions, they may be justified in their fear. Ultimately, mainline liberal Protestantism has shown that in the absence of any central teaching authority, even the Virgin Birth and the Resurrection will be allegorically interpreted. Yet the Bible itself makes clear that a literal meaning is not intended for many apocalyptic passages. *Sola Scriptura* itself is never taught in the Bible, and is actually antibiblical (*BFB*, 3). That is why I have labeled it as "too high" a view of Scripture.

Of course, the Catholic has an advantage in interpreting Scripture. As Catholics, we have a three-legged stool to support our faith: the Church's Tradition, the Church's Magisterium, and the Church's Scripture. The great fourth-century Bible scholar, St. Jerome, wrote, "We do not attempt to prove either the advent of Christ or the falsehood of antichrist from . . . the passages of Scripture. Because our authority is more secure [and biblical], we have the liberty to understand certain passages as symbolic when warranted, without the fear that even the Incarnation might eventually be taken as a 'myth' " (*CID*, 11:45). St. Jerome illustrates that the mainline liberal Protestants' problem that the Fundamentalist worries about is not all that modern after all!

So, *sola Scriptura* actually prevents the rapturist from understanding the Bible as clearly as the Catholic can. This is true not only concerning the symbolic nature of some passages, but also concerning events that occurred after the last historical book of the New Testament ends. That book is The Acts of the Apostles, and its story ends with St. Paul imprisoned in Rome. Since St. Paul died in the Great Tribulation of 64 to 67 A.D., there is no mention of that event or of the fall of Jerusalem. Although many rapturists may not be consciously aware of this, as a group they tend to work under the assumption that events not recorded in Scripture are not essential for the understanding of their faith.

Since the fall of Jerusalem is not recorded in Scripture as history, rapturists start with a distrust of any attempt to understand the prophecies of The Apocalypse, the Olivet Discourse, and Daniel through the lens of that event. Especially in the pews, many rapturists hold to a version of *sola Scriptura* that is indefensible even among many Protestant scholars. These rapturists refuse even to consider the events of 70 A.D. as a key to understanding any prophecies of the Bible *because the events themselves are not enumerated in Scripture*. It is almost as though these events did not even occur. Therefore, they are left groping for a still-future fulfillment.

Admittedly, this is an extreme application of *sola Scriptura*, but it is nevertheless a reality within rapturist circles. This approach certainly simplifies the amount of data one needs to work with to understand the Bible, but ultimately it clouds the truth.

Too low a view

The second theological appeal of the rapturist system has more to do with Catholics than Protestants. I believe that this one is the most important reason people leave the historical Church that Christ founded two millennia ago to join a rapturist movement founded two centuries ago. The recent ascendancy of *modernist theology* within Catholic biblical studies stands at the center of the issue.

You may have been wondering why, in a book about rapturists, I have spent time dealing with the modernist position. Well, to a large extent, rapturists are a reaction to the emergence, or more accurately the re-emergence, of modern skepticism. Sometimes good people are attracted to premillennialism as an antidote to the modernists' denial of the supernatural.

An important precedent to this phenomenon can be found in the early Church. Bishop Irenaeus developed the theological rationale for premillennialism. There is no clear evidence of premillennialism in the leadership of the Church before him. Why would he experiment with a theology that was more Jewish than Christian, was undoubtedly innovative, and would end up being condemned by his contemporaries and those Church Fathers who read him in later years? It is impossible to understand this good bishop in a vacuum. I believe that Irenaeus was motivated by the desire to protect the Faith of the fathers from the Gnostics.

The Gnostics were practical dualists who predated Christianity and saw the spiritual realm as innately good and physical reality as completely evil. As Christianity spread throughout the Middle East, Gnostics infiltrated and distorted the message of the Church. Their distrust of "the grossness of matter" led them to teach that salvation was obtained exclusively through knowledge, rather than through faith-filled obedience. In fact, the Gnostics were ultimately pessimists: all physical reality was so evil that it was incapable of salvation. This led them to deny the reality of the Incarnation. They could not accept that a spiritual, "pure" God (the Parent-Spirit) could unite with a physical, "evil" body. Their dualistic view of reality also led them to deny the hope of any real, physical return of Christ at the final eschaton. Of course, the true significance of the Eucharist would be anathema to them as well (CE, NCE).

In brief, the Gnostics denied that the supernatural could impinge upon the physical world. To anyone who has studied modern skepticism, that should sound familiar.

Bishop Irenaeus was on the front lines in the Church's battle against this virulent heresy. He decided that the Millennium mentioned in The Apocalypse must actually entail a prophecy of a physical reign of Christ here on earth. He believed that this thousand years of peace on earth would occur after the second advent. He understood that this view of the Millennium would be a forceful argument against the Gnostic's refusal to admit the possibility of the Incarnation. A physical Millennium would be a convincing proof that the physical world was not totally evil and incapable of redemption, as Gnosticism claimed. It could be argued from the Millennium that Christ was pure, even though He was fully divine and fully human at the same time. The orthodox belief has always been that the Incarnation was the salvation of the physical realm. A corporeal Millennium could be strong proof of that.

But the rest of the Church determined that Irenaeus had gone one step too far in his attempt to defend the orthodox view of the Incarnation. In reading The Apocalypse as though it taught the promise of a future corporeal kingdom, he had stepped outside the deposit of Faith that had been handed down from the Apostles. Simply put, this Millennium could not be reconciled with Christ's original teaching. In fact, this view of The Apocalypse led to the rejection of its canonicity in the Eastern Church until it was affirmed that this was not integral to the book's message. The Church continued to affirm its belief in the unity of the physical and spiritual in the God-Man, Jesus Christ. It never hesitated to teach the physical return of Christ at the final eschaton. It lovingly clung to Christ's teaching concerning the Eucharist. But the Church adamantly rejected Irenaeus's novel teaching of a physical Millennium here on earth after the second coming.

What does this have to do with the resurgence of the rapturist movement in twenty-first-century America? Once, while still a Protestant, I made friends with a European theologian. He could not understand why premillennialism was such a potent force in the United States. After all, most of the rest of the Evangelical Protestant world outside the United States found this theological system very unconvincing.

Through that friendship, I came to realize that, just as Irenaeus's premillennialism must be understood in light of his desire to fight the anti-supernatural Gnostics, American Fundamentalist and Evangelical thought cannot be understood apart from its roots as a reaction against modern skepticism in mainline Protestantism. Around the beginning of the twentieth century, modernist theologians in the Protestant pulpits of America started questioning many of the doctrines the Gnostics rejected: the deity of the God-Man, Jesus Christ; the reality of the Resurrection; and the sure hope of Christ's return. In the early twentieth century, Protestants began to hear from the pulpit that maybe Jesus was merely a very holy prophet, and that the Resurrection was more an illusion than a reality. The miracles of Jesus were explained away. Like the Gnostics, *Protestant modernists rejected the supernatural in all its physical expressions.*

Just as in Irenaeus's day, the reaction against this heresy was a movement toward premillennialism. Darby and his followers had already formed a beachhead in America in the latter half of the nineteenth century. Rapturist premillennialism provided an answer to modern skepticism that the average parishioner could understand. The man in the pew knew what he believed about Christ, and he knew that modern skepticism smelled "off." Rapturist premillennialism offered a seemingly orthodox alternative.

The Church recognized the common spirit shared by present-day modernists and ancient Gnostics: "[T]he Rationalists [are the] true children and inheritors of the older heretics" *(PD)*. Unfortunately, Catholics were not immune to this virus of the mind. About the time rapturists were gaining momentum in Protestant circles, American Catholics started to flirt with modernist theology. The flirtation turned into a torrid love affair. Perhaps unwittingly, modernist Catholics flung open the doors to rapturists seeking to woo away Catholics disillusioned by skepticism.

Thankfully, the ancient battle against Gnostic skepticism was eventually won in the early Church. Premillennialism then faded away when there remained nothing against which to react. That can give us hope today. If the Church forcefully reaffirms the traditional truths of the Faith, the appeal of premillennialism will inevitably fade, just as it did in the generations following Irenaeus's time. When the modernist heresy within the American Catholic Church is finally overcome (as it surely will be eventually), rapturism will lose much of its theological appeal to Catholics.

I believe that the first step in the reaffirmation of Christ's Truth against modernism is to recognize modernists' assumptions and strategy. Modernists assume that supernatural events are impossible, and they apply that assumption to the Mass, where they place all emphasis on the symbolic nature of Christ's Body and Blood. Granted, the Eucharist is a symbol, but it is more than just a symbol: it is a sacrament, a sign that *really is* what it symbolizes. When loyal Catholics see the modernist assault on this part of the Mass, they usually rally to protect the deposit of Faith handed down to and through the Church.

Many Catholics, however, do not initially recognize the modernist assault on the other half of the Mass, the Liturgy of the Word. There the modernists' strategy is the same. They deny the supernatural origin of Scripture just as they deny the supernatural nature of the Eucharist. They deny the Church's historical teaching that the original autographs of the Bible are guaranteed to be inerrant by divine inspiration.

Hear me carefully. I am not arguing against understanding the Bible in the light of poetic, symbolic, apocalyptic, mythological, or phenomenological language. These types of language are used in the Bible and must be understood for what they are. I believe this book illustrates that I am not arguing for the Fundamentalists' "wooden" view of inerrancy. I will gladly allow rapturists to argue for that position.

An antidote to the too-low view

What am I proposing, then? Nothing less than a re-emphasis of the historical belief in the "intelligent inerrancy" of the holy Bible. The Church's historical teaching is that there are no errors in what the Bible means to teach on any subject anywhere — period. Modernists deny this because it requires a supernatural understanding of the inspiration of God, and they abhor any whiff of the supernatural.

The Church has been clear and consistent in this teaching. Vatican II clearly stated that Scripture is fundamentally a revelation of God Himself, culminating in the deeds and words of our Lord Jesus Christ. "The books of both the Old and New Testaments *in their entirety, with all their parts*, are written under the inspiration of the Holy Spirit, they have *God as their author*. . . . God chose men . . . so that with Him acting in them and through them, they, as true authors, consigned to writing everything and only those things which He wanted. Therefore, since *everything asserted . . . must be held to be asserted by the Holy Spirit*, it follows that the books of Scripture must be acknowledged as teaching solidly, faithfully, and *without error* that truth which God wanted put into sacred writings for the sake of salvation" (*DV*, 11).

Lest some think this is ambiguous, the council fathers assured us it is a restatement of earlier Church teaching.

What is that teaching? Modernists generally avoid asking, but we need look no further than the ecumenical council immediately before Vatican II — namely, Vatican I (1869-1870). The Fathers of the Church declared that the books of the Bible were canonical, not because "they were afterward approved by her authority, nor *merely* because they contain revelation *without error*, but because, having been written under the inspiration of the Holy Spirit, they have *God for their author*" (*DCF*, II, 7). The fact that revelation in Scripture is error-free is mentioned in an almost off-handed manner, as though no competent Catholic would question it. The inerrant nature of the Bible has a supernatural foundation: God is the *author* of Scripture.

Pius XII's pontificate (1939-1958) helped implement the teaching of Vatican I, and his writings serve as a basis for understanding the fathers of Vatican II. Pope Pius XII chided those who sought to *"restrict the truth of Sacred Scripture solely to matters of faith and morals. . . .* In Scripture divine things are presented to us in the manner which is in common use among men . . . so the words of God, expressed in human language, are made like to human speech in every respect, *except error*" (*DAS*). That effectively closes the door on modernists who try to parse the words of Vatican II (cf. *PDG* and *SPA*)!

The Church makes clear that this teaching does not ignore the use of figurative, poetic, phenomenological, or apocalyptic language. "In demonstrating and proving its immunity from all error, [the commentator] should . . . determine . . . to what extent the manner of expression or the literary mode adopted by the sacred writer may lead to a correct and genuine interpretation. . . .

Rapture

When some persons reproachfully charge the Sacred Writers with some historical error or inaccuracy in the recording of facts, on closer examination it turns out to be nothing else than those customary modes of expression and narration peculiar to the ancients . . . sanctioned by common usage" (DAS). In other words, we must be intelligent in our examination of Scripture and its inerrancy.

In this, Pope Pius XII reiterated a point St. Thomas Aquinas had expounded: "The author of the Scriptures is God. . . . We must not forget that the literal meaning of a parable or figure of speech is not the figure of speech itself but what it is used to say. When Scripture talks of God's arm, it is not literally attributing a bodily limb to God but that which an arm represents: power to act. With this proviso we can say that *the literal meaning of Scripture is never in error*" (SUM, 4).

Modernists often try to use a straw man to attack the Church's historical teaching about inerrancy. They try to interpret a parable or poetic text in woodenly literalistic fashion and then mock this interpretation as untenable, uninformed, and anti-intellectual. Yet the Church has always taught "intelligent inerrancy."

Pope Pius XII offers an enlightening contrast that illustrates what the Church teaches. He states that the Latin Vulgate (a translation) was affirmed by the Church "*to be free from any error whatsoever in matters of faith and morals. . . . Its authenticity is . . . juridical.*" In contrast, when approaching the original autographs of Scripture (which are not translations), it is "absolutely wrong and *forbidden* either to narrow inspiration to certain passages of Holy Scripture or *to admit that the sacred writer has erred*" (DAS). In other words, the Vulgate is trustworthy for faith and morals, but the original texts of the Bible are *without any error whatsoever*. The contrast in the different levels of reliability is clear. Yet modernists persist in their attempts to lower the perception of the Bible's reliability to the level of the Latin Vulgate: "juridical."

THE ROOTS OF MODERNISM

Why do some modernist Catholics persist in claiming errors exist in Scripture if the Church has denied them that avenue? Much of it seems to stem from the desire for scholarly acceptance of one's work by one's peers. The emergence of modernism among Catholic scholars came only after Protestantism had almost entirely been infected with modernist assumptions. The antisupernatural presuppositions within the historical critical method affect all of its related critical methods. These include form criticism, source criticism, and redaction criticism — all grouped as "higher criticism."

There is some credible evidence that the historical critical method originated with Islamic scholars who were attempting to discredit the Bible's miraculous account of the life of Christ. (Islam, of course, views Christ as merely a holy prophet.) Modernist Protestants started to employ the historical critical method in earnest during the end of the nineteenth century and the first half of the twentieth. Catholic scholars eventually succumbed to the *zeitgeist* ("spirit of the times") within academia — learning the method from Protestant scholars.

The Church, however, forcefully resisted the skepticism innate within the historical critical method from its very onset: "There has arisen . . . an *inept method*, dignified by the name of the 'higher criticism,' which pretends to judge of the origin, integrity, and authority of each book from *internal indications alone*" (*PD*).

Of course, some modernists would respond that the Church should simply butt out of this debate. They would claim that they feel hindered by the Magisterium's guidance. They would assert that true scholarship can occur only in the *absence of faith*. But they forget that theological and biblical studies in the absence of the Church's Faith immediately degenerate into a mere study of the philosophy of religion.

A TRADITION OF
AUTHORITATIVE GUIDANCE

Biblical Judaism certainly understood the need to interpret Holy Scripture in harmony with the leadership of God's people. We can see this in Matthew 2:1-12. (We looked at this passage in GR1.) Matthew relates how the Jews predicted the place of Messiah's birth by referencing Micah 5:2. From our perspective, it is relatively obvious that Micah's prophecy was fulfilled in the birth of Jesus.

But at the time the prophecy was actually fulfilled, the situation was a tad more opaque, and even the morally bankrupt Herod understood that the study of the Bible was sometimes complex and beyond the limitations of any single person. Placing great importance on the predicted location of the baby King, he immediately called on the leadership of God's people for the proper interpretation of God's prophecy (Matt. 2:7). Although he was certainly an evil man, he understood that isolated interpreters can easily fall into error.

During the Old Covenant, the chief priests and scribes Herod interviewed held the position of authority in interpretation. Jesus acknowledged as much three decades later when He said, "The scribes and the Pharisees sit on Moses' seat; so practice and observe whatever they tell you" (Matt. 23:2-3).

Of course, Jesus did not leave this authority with the leadership of old Israel. *Ekklesia* is the word that the Old Testament Septuagint used to refer to Israel as the "People of God" (*BFB*, 190). Jesus applied this word to His Church and then put His disciples into the places of leadership over His new people of God (Matt. 16:18-19). His disciples argued over the pecking order of the new Church leadership, but they never seemed to doubt that the leadership itself had been delegated to them. The God-given teaching authority of those men who are successors of the first Apostles is called the Magisterium.

Like Herod in Matthew's account, we need to consult the leadership of God's people when we try to understand Scripture. It is not enough to claim that by being knowledgeable or degreed or studious or holy, we are protected from error in our understanding of the Bible. For we can misunderstand Bible prophecy even when it is being fulfilled right before our eyes. Jesus told His disciples that John the Baptist was the greatest of the Old Testament prophets: "Among those born of women there has risen no one greater than John the Baptist; yet he who is least in the kingdom of Heaven is greater than he." Then He let them in on a secret: John's ministry was the fulfillment of the return of Elijah that had been prophesied in the Old Testament: "If you are willing to accept it, he is Elijah, who is to come" (Matt. 11:11-14).

Jesus tells His disciples much the same thing in Matthew 17:9-13, which follows the Transfiguration. He was referring to the well-known prophecy of Malachi 4:5: "Behold, I will send you Elijah the prophet before the great and terrible day of the Lord comes." The entire Jewish nation of the first century seemed to be holding their breath, waiting for Elijah to come and prepare the way for the Messiah. Jesus said that John the Baptist was this prophet.

Yet some of Jesus' disciples had earlier been disciples of John. They had probably been present when John had answered the questions of the Jewish leaders. "The Jews sent priests and Levites from Jerusalem to ask [John], 'Who are you? . . . Are you Elijah?' He said, 'I am not' " (John 1:19, 21). Although Jesus claimed John was Elijah, John had denied it!

The best way to reconcile these two passages is to admit that John did not have a clear understanding of how the Old Testament prophecies were being fulfilled. The fulfillment was not just happening before his very eyes; he was a central player in the drama! We must never forget that it is very difficult to study Scripture, especially prophecy, in isolation from God's ordained leadership. This was true even for a man as holy as John the Baptist.

THE GOSPELS ARE ALSO RELIABLE HISTORY

Some Catholics seem to think that they can use the historical critical method (higher criticism) on the Old Testament without affecting belief in the Gospel. Modernist Protestants proved the naiveté of that idea long ago. What is used on one part of Scripture will inevitably be used on all. In the case of higher criticism, the result more often than not is the undermining of true faith.

The four Gospels are a special case. Although all of Scripture is without error, the Church defines the nature of the Gospels more specifically. Not only are the Gospels without error whatsoever; they are to be understood as *reliable history*. Thus, the Church emphatically closes the door on the modern idea that there might be a "historical Jesus" who must be unearthed from the Gospel accounts of the "Christ of faith." The Church further defines the authorship of the four Gospels as "apostolic."

Unfortunately, this clear teaching of the Church is too often ignored in America. Let me give you an example. To question the historical reliability of the Gospels stands in direct opposition to what Vatican II specifically teaches. Yet I have heard many Catholic homilies suggesting that the Gospels are historically unreliable for various reasons. One criticized the accuracy of the Gospels because they speak of the "brothers" of Christ.

The obvious conclusion may sound rather harsh. This homilist had received such poor training in the seminary that he did not know what you may already know: that the word *brother* in Hebrew could just as easily mean "uncle" or "cousin." The most elementary search of a Bible concordance will substantiate this. This is why the culture and language of the writer *must* be understood when interpreting Scripture. (My book *Born Fundamentalist, Born Again Catholic* discusses this at some length.)

Yet it seems as if, when this priest was in training, no one explained the Hebrew culture and language to him and his fellow seminarians. My guess is that his professors took the easy way out:

any time they did not understand something in the Bible, they assumed it was an error. But it becomes all too easy to assume that the Bible is mistaken when the real problem is that we are too lazy to work at understanding it. It takes very little work to point out "errors" in the Bible; it makes a person sound so intelligent and sophisticated without any labor. It is hard work to delve below the surface of the text, do some research, and substantiate the Church's historical teaching.

The Church teaches us there are no errors in Scripture. Modern skeptics claim there are errors and inconsistencies. It really boils down to a simple issue: who is more to be trusted? Is my own intellect or the wisdom of modernist scholars to be trusted fully, or should I submit my intellect to the spiritual authority of its Maker? As St. Augustine wrote, "God wished difficulties to be scattered through the Sacred Books inspired by Him, in order that we might be urged to read and scrutinize them more intently, and experiencing in a salutary manner our own limitations, we might be exercised in due *submission of mind*" (EPT).

READING SCRIPTURE WITH THE EYES OF FAITH

Rather than take the easy solution of accusing the Bible of an error, St. Augustine proposed the following in a letter to St. Jerome: "If in these books I meet anything which seems contrary to truth, I shall not hesitate to conclude either that the text is faulty, or that the translator has not expressed the meaning of the passage, or that I myself do not understand" (EPI, 1:3). This threefold admission of human frailty — copyist error, translation error, and personal inability to understand God's thoughts — is an example of true intellectual humility from one of the greatest minds in history.

As students of Scripture, our first goal must be to "clarify the true meaning of Scripture" (SME). As St. Jerome wrote, "The office of a commentator is to set forth, not what he himself would prefer, but what his author says." When that is done, rather than take the easy way out by accusing the Holy Writ of an error, it is our job "to find a satisfactory solution, which will be in full accord with the doctrine of the Church, in particular with the traditional teaching regarding the *inerrancy of Sacred Scripture*" (DAS).

A PIVOTAL ISSUE

Am I making too much of our Catholic view of Scripture? No, I am not. Does this issue really cause people to leave the Church and join the rapturists? Yes, it does.

I speak from experience. Before I became Catholic, I actually encouraged people to leave the Church over just these issues. When I served as a Fundamentalist missionary, my job description included teaching classes on how to get your friends and acquaintances to convert to rapturist Christianity. It is a false dichotomy, but when faced with accepting a reliable Church or a reliable Bible, many will choose the reliable Bible. That false dichotomy has caused Catholics to doubt the Church's authority.

There are many sincere Catholics who have experienced the risen Christ in their lives. Then they have been in the pew when the homilist called the Real Presence into doubt. Or they have heard a theologian explain the miracles of Jesus in simplistic, naturalistic terms. Or they have read an otherwise loyal Catholic catechist call into question the historical reliability of the Gospel narrative. A devout Catholic instinctively understands, even if he is unable to explain why, that a denial of the reliability of the Scriptures undermines the Church's authority. The rapturists' wholehearted belief in the supernatural inspiration and complete reliability of the Bible is a major reason people find rapturist theology so appealing. Remember, that was the lesson we gleaned from St. Irenaeus's arguments with the Gnostics.

The average Catholic in America may be undereducated in his Faith, but he is certainly not stupid. He knows that if the small miracles recorded in the Gospels were made up and inserted by the early Church, there is no compelling reason to believe in big supernatural events, such as the Resurrection. The idea of an Incarnation is much more miraculous than finding a coin in a fish's mouth (Matt. 17:26). The average Catholic knows in his heart that, without the supernatural, apostolic succession and even Catholicism itself is a fraud. When the Catholic teacher, deacon, or priest takes on the role of a modernist skeptic, he drives the devout into the waiting arms of the Protestant rapturists. Believe me, if Catholic modernists open the door, rapturists will gladly put out the welcome mat.

As Catholics, we must recognize the modernist heresy for what it is: an attempt to pervert both halves of the Mass. Modern skepticism is really not all that different from the early heresies that the early saints spilled their blood to refute. Our struggle with modern skepticism will not be easy, but it will be worth it. We must answer the unremitting assault on the Liturgy of the Eucharist and the Liturgy of the Word. Until we do, sincere Catholics who really believe in the supernatural message of Christ will continue to gravitate to places where they can be sure the supernatural will not be denied. Unfortunately for them, they will find less of the supernatural there than they suppose.

Chapter Ten

What Is an Honest Christian to Do?

Where do we go from here? We have looked at passages in the Bible individually, trying to understand them in the way most consistent with historical events, the views of the early Church, the guidance of the Magisterium, and — most important — the context of Scripture itself. In this last chapter, we will take a slightly wider view, in an attempt to summarize the teaching of the Church concerning the end of the ages. Make no mistake: the Church's message is a message of *hope*.

CHRIST WILL RETURN

First, we know that *Christ will return*. Rapturists often imply that because Catholics do not subscribe to an imminent secret rapture of believers only, we do not long for the return of Christ. This is absolute nonsense.

The creed we recite every Sunday makes it abundantly clear that we hope for Christ's return: "He will come again in glory to judge the living and the dead." This hope is also considered part of the mystery of faith we proclaim with the priest when we say, "Christ has died; Christ is risen; Christ will come again."

The Scriptures read during every Mass declare the hope of Christ's return as a central focus of the Catholic Faith. This hope has been central since His first advent. The angels asked the

Rapture

disciples at the time of the Ascension, "Men of Galilee, why do you stand looking into Heaven? This Jesus, who was taken up from you into Heaven, will come in the same way as you saw Him go into Heaven" (Acts 1:11).

Lest Catholics misunderstand the Liturgy and Scripture, the *Catechism* emphasizes the Church's hope in the second coming: "Christ's reign is yet to be fulfilled 'with power and great glory' by the king's return to earth" (CCC, par. 671).

Modern pessimists can learn a lesson from this unchanging hope of the Church. The fifteenth century saw popular fears similar in many ways to the paranoia of our day. Common wisdom held that the world was soon going to be destroyed. In 1459, Pope Pius II tried to allay these fears by clearly stating that "the world should [not] be naturally destroyed" (CUM). Christ is going to come back to a world that is still in existence. He will be the One to replace this old world with a new Heaven and a new earth. Perhaps it is a sign of twenty-first-century egoism that we believe it is possible for us to destroy the earth completely. No fear: we won't. God will.

THE END IS "HERE"

Further, we know that Christ will return *in these last days*. We have already determined that the end of the ages started with the Messiah's first advent, so we will not belabor the point (GR9). But next time you see a cartoon depicting a man with a sandwich board declaring, "The end is near!" remember that the Church declares, "The end is already *here.*" It has been here since the most important event of all history: the coming of the Son of God in the flesh.

This is such a settled issue for the writers of the New Testament that it almost seems superfluous to pick out certain verses. But here are a few of them.

On the day of Pentecost, St. Peter declared in his first apostolic sermon that the promised "last days" had arrived (Acts 2:17-18).

St. Paul agreed with this appraisal: he wrote that his generation was the one "upon whom the end of the ages has come" (1 Cor. 10:11). The writer of Hebrews also perceived the first advent as the beginning of the last days: "In these last days He has spoken to us by a Son" (Heb. 1:2).

The present successor to Peter has also reaffirmed this idea. In his general audience on April 22, 1998, Pope John Paul II stated, "We must not forget that for Christians the '*eschaton*,' that is, the final event, is to be understood not only as a future goal, but as a reality which *has already begun* with the historical coming of Christ. His Passion, death, and Resurrection are the supreme event in the history of mankind, which has now entered its final phase."

I suppose we should not find it surprising, then, that the *Catechism* affirms this principle: "Since the Ascension God's plan has entered into its fulfillment. We are already at 'the last hour.' Already the final age of the world is with us, and the renewal of the world is irrevocably under way. . . . Christ's kingdom already manifests its presence" (CCC, par. 670).

Of course, we ought to face up to the fact that we are all within "one generation" of meeting Christ's judgment. For those of us who do not live long enough to see the second advent, Christ's promise to come in judgment will not be broken. We, too, will suddenly be ushered into eternity to meet Christ — at our death. As even the Old Testament advises, "Remember your *last days*. Remember *death* and decay, and cease from sin!" (Sir. 28:6, NAB).

CHRIST'S RETURN
WILL BE UNMISTAKABLE

When Christ does return in these last days, it will be *not in a hidden manner, but publicly and unmistakably*. All the language of Scripture and the Church is clear on this. The second advent will be gloriously public. There will not be a secret rapture first, because that has never been taught by Scripture or by the Church.

Scripture and the Church have never taught it because Jesus never did.

Jesus *did* teach that "as the lightning comes from the east and shines as far as the west, so will be the coming of the Son of man" (Matt. 24:27). St. Paul taught in 1 Thessalonians 4:16 that "the Lord Himself will descend from Heaven with a cry of command, with the archangel's call, and with the sound of the trumpet of God." Both passages speak of the second advent as unmistakably obvious. There is nothing secret about lightning, cries of command, angel calls, or trumpets.

In the general audience of April 22, 1998, Pope John Paul II reminded the faithful of this teaching: "The second coming of the Son of Man will not take place in the weakness of flesh, but in divine power." This will make it public and obvious to all.

HE IS COMING LIKE A THIEF

Although it is clear in Scripture that the second coming will be public, it will nevertheless burst upon the world *unexpectedly, suddenly, and imminently.* Jesus warned us to be prepared lest "that day come upon you suddenly like a snare" (Luke 21:34).

St. Peter reiterated the warning: "But the day of the Lord will come like a thief, and then the heavens will pass away with a loud noise, and the elements will be dissolved with fire, and the earth and the works that are upon it will be burned up" (2 Pet. 3:10).

St. Paul coined the "thief in the night" verbiage that has been so often misapplied to a secret, private rapture. But as we determined in our examination of the epistles, this passage is speaking of the *second coming.* "The day of the Lord will come like a thief in the night. When people say, 'There is peace and security,' then sudden destruction will come upon them as travail comes upon a woman with child, and there will be no escape" (1 Thess. 5:2-3). The destruction here is not the Great Tribulation, but our eternal judgment.

The Church has always spoken of the *imminent* return of Christ. Historically, that term had always meant that Christ could return during any generation. But rapturists have started to teach that it means Christ would rapture His believers at any moment, perhaps even before you finish reading this paragraph. They teach that there are no other events that must precede that rapture, not even the final confrontation between good and evil.

While they are certainly free to use language in their own manner, the Church uses the word as it always has throughout its two-thousand-year history. Christ may come back in our generation, or He may not. Only the Father knows. As the *Catechism* states, "Since the Ascension Christ's coming in glory has been *imminent*, even though 'it is not for you to know times or seasons.' This eschatological coming could be accomplished at any moment, even if both it and the final trial that will precede it are 'delayed'" (CCC, par. 673).

ONLY THE FATHER KNOWS WHEN

The fact that the second advent will come unexpectedly implies that we do not know its timing. But we have such an innate curiosity about the end times, that we will be explicit: The second coming will occur *at a time which only God the Father knows*. Perhaps the most amazing verse in the entire Bible is found in Mark, where Jesus tells His disciples that even He is not privy to the timing of the second coming! "But of that day or that hour no one knows, not even the angels in Heaven, nor the Son, but only the Father" (13:32).

In Matthew, Jesus emphasizes that this ignorance extends even to committed Christians: "But of that day and hour no one knows, not even the angels of Heaven, nor the Son, but the Father only. Watch therefore, for you do not know on what day your Lord is coming. But know this, that if the householder had known in what part of the night the thief was coming, he would have watched and would not have let his house be broken into. Therefore you also must be ready; for the Son of man is coming at an hour you do not expect" (24:36-44).

The desire to know the timing of God's plans is so irresistible that even the disciples fell prey to its allure. Just before the Ascension, they asked the risen Christ whether He would consummate all things at that time. He replied, "It is not for you to know times or seasons which the Father has fixed by His own authority" (Acts 1:7). That should satisfy us, yet it so often does not. But it should.

That the timing of God's plan is unknown and unknowable to us was an accepted fact in the early Church. Origen wrote, "We speak on this subject very cautiously and diffidently, rather by way of discussion than coming to definite conclusions. The end and consummation of the world will be granted, [but] God alone knows that time" (*TPR*, I, VI, 1-4). Origen had some peculiar beliefs, but in this he was solidly in the mainstream of the early Church Fathers.

GOD'S MERCY DELAYS CHRIST'S RETURN

As we wait for the glorious return of our Lord, we must remember that *any apparent delay in the second coming is a result of God's mercy.*

We must keep in mind that God is in eternity, while we are in time. He sees the end from the beginning constantly, while we experience reality in sequential order. This is what St. Peter is referring to here: "With the Lord one day is as a thousand years, and a thousand years as one day. The Lord is not slow about His promise as some count slowness, but is forbearing toward you, not wishing that any should perish, but that all should reach repentance" (2 Pet. 3:8-9). Throughout history, some have tried to use this verse to determine the date of the second advent. But the thrust of the passage is not that we can mathematically corner God as to His plans, but that our perception of time is irrelevant.

Many unbelievers may find this delay a cause for derision. When Christian sects persist in setting dates that do not pan out, the mockery increases. This happened even in St. Peter's time: "First of all, you must understand this, that scoffers will come in the last days with scoffing, following their own passions and saying, 'Where is the promise of His coming? For ever since the fathers fell asleep, all things have continued as they were from the beginning of creation'" (2 Pet. 3:3-4). Things really have not changed all that much, have they?

There is a very good reason for God's delay: everyone is not ready for Christ's return just yet. After our study of The Apocalypse, we should anticipate this reason. The judgment of Jerusalem was delayed as long as possible, specifically to allow time for more Jewish people to be saved from judgment (Apoc. 7:3; GR3). The *Catechism* tells us, "The glorious Messiah's coming is suspended at every moment of history until His recognition by 'all Israel,' for 'a hardening has come upon part of Israel' in their 'unbelief' toward Jesus. The 'full inclusion' of the Jews in the Messiah's salvation, in the wake of 'the full number of the Gentiles,' will enable the people of God to achieve 'the measure of the stature of the fullness of Christ' in which 'God may be all in all'" (CCC, par. 674).

THE FINAL BATTLE
IS YET TO BE FOUGHT

The very next event on the "end-times agenda" is not a secret rapture, but the final massive assault upon the Church by the forces of Satan (Apoc. 20:7-9). *There is yet to be one final battle between good and evil.* Nowhere does Scripture or the Church teach that there is any event that must precede this final cosmic battle.

The *Catechism* summarizes this by saying, "Before Christ's second coming the Church must pass through a final trial that will shake the faith of many believers. The persecution . . . will unveil the 'mystery of iniquity' in the form of a religious deception offering men an apparent solution to their problems at the price of apostasy from the truth" (CCC, par. 675).

Although there may be thousands of years in which peace and godliness prevail before this final apostasy, that peace will not trigger the second advent. There will not be a gradual ascendancy that elevates the world to righteousness until we are good enough to merit Christ's return.

Indeed, the emergence and ascendancy of *evil* will be the catalyst for the second coming. The *Catechism* states, "The kingdom will be fulfilled, then, not by a historic triumph of the Church through a progressive ascendancy, but only by God's victory over the final unleashing of evil, which will cause His Bride to come down from Heaven" (CCC, par. 677).

True, the assault of evil upon good has been almost without pause since the first advent. Both the New Testament writers and the *Catechism* recognize this. St. John wrote that many antichrists have come (1 John 2:18). The *Catechism* states, "Christ's reign is still under attack by the evil powers, even though they have been defeated definitively by Christ's Passover. . . . The present time is . . . a time still marked by 'distress' and the trial of evil which does not spare the Church. . . . The antichrist's deception already begins to take shape in the world every time the claim is made to realize within history that messianic hope which can only be realized beyond history through the eschatological judgment. The Church has rejected even modified forms of . . . millenarianism, especially the 'intrinsically perverse' political form of a secular messianism" (CCC, pars. 671, 672, 676).

But the final assault of evil will be so intense that many will be in danger of losing their faith. St. Paul's letter to Bishop Timothy records, "Now, the Spirit expressly says that in later times some will depart from the Faith by giving heed to deceitful spirits and doctrines of demons" (1 Tim. 4:1). Satan's ability to deceive humanity is now restrained by God. But during the final distress, Satan will be "released" from this restraint once again to weave his deceptive web with all his cunning (Apoc. 20:1-3, 7-10; 2 Thess. 2:7).

Has that final assault begun? I don't know. But of one thing I am quite certain. If the final trial of evil is upon us, we are in its very early stages. Why do I believe that? There have been times when it was much harder to be a Christian than it is now: during Hitler's Germany, Mao's China, Stalin's Russia, Elizabeth's England, Voltaire's France, Domitian's Rome, and even Arian Egypt.

THE ANTICHRIST WILL
LEAD SATAN'S ASSAULT

This intense assault of evil will be orchestrated by a man commonly referred to as the antichrist, the man of sin, and the son of perdition. St. Paul warns not to let anyone "deceive you in any way; for that day will not come, unless the rebellion comes first, and the man of lawlessness is revealed, the son of perdition" (2 Thess. 2:3).

The early Church fully anticipated the revelation of the antichrist before the second coming. St. Jerome wrote, "I told you that Christ would not come unless antichrist has come before" (*EPS*). St. John Chrysostom preached, "The time of antichrist will be a sign of the coming of Christ" (*HFT*, 9). St. Augustine clearly concurred, "The kingdom of antichrist shall fiercely, though for a short time, assail the Church" (*COG*, XX, 23). It might be nice to be safely tucked away in Heaven when this happens, but all early Christians expected the Church to be party to this struggle.

The antichrist need not be of Middle Eastern descent, as some rapturists have claimed. The final battle against Gog and Magog will be a spiritual struggle — which could very well begin anywhere in the world — and will present all Christians with a choice. The choice will be between God's narrow way and the broad path to destruction, but it will not be presented by Satan's side in those terms. "The supreme religious deception is that of the antichrist, a pseudo-messianism by which man glorifies himself in place of God and of His Messiah come in the flesh" (CCC, par. 675).

The antichrist will attack Truth at its core. He will attempt to replace the true worship of the Church with a counterfeit: "The son of perdition . . . [will take] his seat in the Temple of God, proclaiming himself to be God" (2 Thess. 2:3-4). Exactly how he will insert himself into the worship of the Church is unclear. But it seems likely that he will attempt a victory over the Church's belief from within.

This antichrist will be impossible to resist without God's grace: "The coming of the lawless one by the activity of Satan will be with all power and with pretended signs and wonders, and with all wicked deception for those who are to perish. . . . Therefore God sends upon them a strong delusion, to make them believe what is false" (2 Thess. 2:9-11).

The first-century Church certainly knew what persecution entailed: they endured the Great Tribulation! As a result, this theme of the antichrist loomed large in their faith. The author of the *Epistle of Barnabas* most likely had seen the Great Tribulation firsthand, and he stated, "The final stumbling block approaches. . . . Withstand . . . that the Black One may find no means of entrance."

Yet even early on, the Church knew that the final confrontation would be similar, but worse than their experience. About halfway through the second century, Melito wrote, "With all his strength did the adversary assail us, even then giving *a foretaste* of his activity among us which is to be without restraint" (*DRE*, I, 8).

St. Athanasius fled before the persecution by the Arians. He said of the Church's enemies, "They have not spared Thy servants, but are preparing the way for antichrist" (*HOA*, VIII, 79). This antichrist will do everything in his power to destroy Christ's Church.

CHRIST'S RETURN WILL WIN THE VICTORY

On one point we can agree with rapturists. We know how the battle with the antichrist ends up: "The lawless one will be revealed, and the Lord Jesus will slay him with the breath of His mouth and destroy him by His appearing and His coming" (2 Thess. 2:8).

It will not be a long, drawn-out battle once Christ appears. The antichrist and his forces "surrounded the camp of the saints and the beloved city; but fire came down from Heaven and consumed them" (Apoc. 20:9).

We have finally arrived at the actual second coming of our Lord and Savior, Jesus Christ. While it is certainly our job to resist evil at all times, the final victory cannot be won without Christ's second advent. *The victory will be won at the glorious appearance of Christ.* Our responsibility is to endure and believe the Truth: "Here is a call for the endurance and faith of the saints" (Apoc. 13:10).

THE RESURRECTION WILL FOLLOW

God's mercy — in allowing time for more people to enter His Kingdom — is evident when we survey the series of events that transpire on the heels of the second advent. At the second coming, all people will then be resurrected. In his first letter to the Corinthians, St. Paul outlined a compelling argument refuting those who reject any future resurrection of the body. He completes his argument by saying, "For as in Adam all die, so also in Christ shall all be made alive" (1 Cor. 15:12-22).

Whether we are alive or dead at the second advent, we will be raised. "For God has not destined us for wrath, but to obtain salvation through our Lord Jesus Christ, who died for us so that whether we wake or sleep we might live with Him" (1 Thess. 5:9-10).

This second resurrection is being postponed in mercy to allow more people to experience the first resurrection. Pope John Paul II stated in his April 22, 1998 General Audience, "The resurrection of the dead expected at the end of time already receives its first, decisive realization in spiritual resurrection, the primary objective of the work of salvation. It consists in the new life given by the risen Christ as the fruit of His redemptive work."

THEN COMES THE FINAL JUDGMENT

At the time of our resurrection, *everyone will face the final judgment*. The first-century Churchman Polycarp wrote, "Christ comes as the Judge of the living and the dead" (*EPP*, II). Although rapturists teach that Christians will not be judged at the Great White Throne, the Bible clearly teaches that they will. We examined this in the final vision of The Apocalypse, but first saw it in the Olivet Discourse. In Jesus' parable, the Master rewards the works of His servants: "Well done, good and faithful servant; you have been faithful over a little, I will set you over much; enter into the joy of your master" (Matt. 25:21). These are servants of the Master, not enemies.

The Church's voice has been loud and clear concerning the certitude of judgment: "God's triumph over the revolt of evil will take the form of the Last Judgment after the final cosmic upheaval of this passing world" (CCC, par. 677). This final, general judgment does not negate the *particular* judgment that each of us will undergo immediately after death. As the *Catechism* clearly states, "The New Testament speaks of judgment primarily in its aspect of the final encounter with Christ in His second coming, but also repeatedly affirms that each will be rewarded immediately after death in accordance with his works and faith" (CCC, par. 1021).

THE WICKED WILL BE
SEPARATED FROM GOD FOREVER

Many of us shrink from a discussion of Hell and judgment, but Jesus spoke of Hell more than two dozen times. The wicked will spend *eternity without any good or God*. Rejection of God *now* leads to an *eternity* of anguish at being judged and sent out of God's joyful presence forever. "Behold, the Lord came with His holy myriads, to execute judgment on all, and to convict all the ungodly of all their deeds of ungodliness which they have committed in such an ungodly way" (Jude 14-15). "Those who do not obey the gospel of our Lord Jesus . . . shall suffer the punishment of eternal destruction and exclusion from the presence of the Lord and from the glory of His might, when He comes on that day to be glorified" (2 Thess. 1:8-10).

Hell was not designed for mankind. It was created for rebellious angels such as Lucifer. But "for the cowardly, the faithless, the polluted, the murderers, fornicators, sorcerers, idolaters, and all liars, their lot shall be in the lake that burns with fire and brimstone, which is the second death" (Apoc. 21:8). These will join the demons in Hell forever.

ETERNAL LIFE
FOR THE RIGHTEOUS

On the other side of the final judgment stands eternity. Time has been destroyed along with the old Heaven and earth. Those who have responded to God throughout their lives, *the righteous, will experience no more death.*

This is the consummation of God's plan. In John 3:16, we read, "For God so loved the world that He gave His only Son, that whoever believes in Him should not perish but have eternal life." Jesus offered eternal life to everyone: "Truly, truly, I say to you, he who hears my word and believes Him who sent me, has eternal life" (John 5:24).

With death conquered, sorrow itself will also be overcome. God "will wipe away every tear from their eyes, and death shall be no more, neither shall there be mourning nor crying nor pain anymore, for the former things have passed away" (Apoc. 21:4).

GLORIFIED BODIES

Just as Christ's body was resurrected, *the righteous will now have glorified bodies*. This new body will still be ours, but glorified. The *Catechism* states our belief simply and succinctly: "After the universal judgment, the righteous will reign forever with Christ, glorified in body and soul" (CCC, par. 1042).

St. Paul is very thorough in his treatment of our eternal bodies: "What is sown is perishable; what is raised is imperishable. It is sown in dishonor; it is raised in glory. It is sown in weakness; it is raised in power. It is sown a physical body; it is raised a spiritual body. If there is a physical body, there is also a spiritual body. . . . For this perishable nature must put on the imperishable, and this mortal nature must put on immortality. When the perishable puts on the imperishable, and the mortal puts on immortality, then shall come to pass the saying that is written: 'Death is swallowed up in victory.' 'O death, where is thy victory? O death, where is thy sting?' " (1 Cor. 15:42-44, 53-55).

Catholic theologians have discerned four qualities of the resurrected body described in this passage. If we follow St. Paul's order, our new bodies will have incorruptibility, clarity, agility, and subtlety.

 • *Incorruptibility* is also known as impassability. Our new bodies will not be susceptible to the elements, as are our present bodies. Temperature, food, stress, and pain will no longer affect us. As St. John states, we "shall hunger no more, neither thirst anymore, the sun shall not strike [us], nor any scorching heat" (Apoc. 7:16).

 • *Clarity*. The second glorious aspect of our new bodies has been described as clarity. An example of this quality can be found in the Transfiguration of Christ. Jesus' "face shone like the sun" (Matt. 17:2). It seems that the glorious joy of being with God overflows from the soul into the body. The body brims up with this joy and becomes virtually luminous! This is what awaits those who love God!

• *Agility.* Our new bodies will have agility — that is, they will have powers that at present belong only to the mind. For example, presently we can imagine ourselves in a certain place instantaneously. After the resurrection, the body will accompany the mind at that same lightning speed. To think of being in another location will be no swifter than traveling there in our glorified bodies. The mechanics of this are hard to comprehend, but we know that Jesus moved at will through space in His glorified body. Our abilities will be similar, because our bodies will be like His.

• *Subtlety.* Finally, our glorified bodies will have subtlety; that is, they will be spiritual. This does not mean they will not be physical, but that the physical will be completely controlled by the spiritual. The best illustration of this can be found in the body of the resurrected Christ. His body was able to pass through walls and doors, yet at another time He could eat fish. His body was real and physical, but did exactly what He demanded of it (John 20:19, 26). It might seem like a trivialization, but in a sense it boils down to "mind over matter."

We should remember that it was no easier for the early Church to accept this on faith than it is for us. Irenaeus died around 200 A.D., after a lifelong battle with the Gnostics. Like modernists, the Gnostics rejected any supernatural resurrection of the body. In answering them, Irenaeus wrote, "If men think only of the weakness of the flesh, and do not consider the power of Him who raises it from the dead, they ignore the might of God. We ought to infer God's power in all these things from a consideration of our beginning; God took clay from the earth, and fashioned man. . . . This was a task far harder, far more incredible, than to restore this creature when it had been created and then re-dissolved into the earth. If God gave existence, when He so willed, to those who did not exist, much more will He restore those who have come into being to the life which He gave them, if He so wills" (AG, V, II, 2-3).

It is our present responsibility to treat our body and its appetites in the knowledge of its future total subjection to the spirit. Every committed Christian is in a lifelong struggle to keep his body and its appetites in subjection to his will. As we become more and more like Christ, we should be more and more in control of our earthly appetites. St. Paul expresses this thought like this: "When Christ who is our life appears, then you also will appear with Him in glory. Put to death therefore what is earthly in you" (Col. 3:4-5).

WE WILL BE IN
GOD'S PRESENCE FOREVER

What will happen throughout all eternity? Christians will live without fear of death and will *enjoy the Beatific Vision forever*. It is hard to imagine the joy that God's presence will bring to Christians: "For now we see in a mirror dimly, but then face-to-face. Now I know in part; then I shall understand fully, even as I have been fully understood" (1 Cor. 13:12). But while this joy is ultimately inexpressible, we already know that it will never fade. It is a joy reserved for the purified righteous ones. Jesus said, "Blessed are the pure in heart, for they shall see God" (Matt. 5:8).

The *Catechism* quotes from St. Augustine's *City of God:* "The New Testament uses several expressions to characterize the beatitude to which God calls man: the coming of the Kingdom of God; the vision of God; entering into the joy of the Lord; entering into God's rest. 'There we shall rest and see, we shall see and love, we shall love and praise. Behold what will be at the end without end. For what other end do we have, if not to reach the Kingdom which has no end?' " (CCC, par. 1720).

THE TRUE "BLESSED HOPE"

The prospect of this future joy *should cause us to be hopeful* in the present. In fact, this is the true meaning of the "blessed hope" of the Bible. The blessed hope is not some secret, private rapture designed to rescue believers from a Great Tribulation here on earth. Our hope awaits "the appearing of the glory of our great God and Savior, Jesus Christ" (Titus 2:13). Our joy at His second advent will be evident and eternal; our hope will have been realized. We will see Christ as He is, for we will be like Him and with Him forever.

WATCH AND PREPARE

Not only should we be presently hopeful. *We should also be watchfully prepared.* This is the message of Jesus: "Take heed, watch and pray; for you do not know when the time will come. Watch therefore — for you do not know when the master of the house will come, in the evening, or at midnight, or at cockcrow, or in the morning — lest he come suddenly and find you asleep. And what I say to you I say to all: Watch" (Mark 13:33-37). "Let your loins be girded and your lamps burning, and be like men who are waiting for their master to come home from the marriage feast, so that they may open to him at once when he comes and knocks" (Luke 12:35-36).

Cyril of Jerusalem told catachumens of the fourth century, "The Church declares . . . thou shouldest make thyself ready beforehand" (*CAT*, 15, 9).

The New Testament exhortations to watchfulness are so abundant that perhaps the best strategy would be to cite the *Catechism* in summary: "The present time is . . . a time of waiting and watching" (CCC, 673).

THE EUCHARIST BEST
HELPS US WATCH AND PREPARE

I have often been asked *how* to wait for the blessed hope. Besides living a holy life, how do we demonstrate daily our hopefulness and readiness? There is one method that surpasses all others in its efficacy and involves the battle strategy of the Lamb of The Apocalypse. *We should be faithful in Eucharistic celebration!* When we fully appreciate the hope that we have in our Faith, we will prepare ourselves with the best means available.

The Eucharist is the finest form of faithfulness in watching and waiting for three reasons. First, it is the best way to *proclaim our Faith.* Yes, the best way to tell the world about the mystery of salvation and the Lord's sacrifice for them is not through writing or speaking, but through participation in the celebration of the Eucharist. St. Paul is very clear on this: "For as often as you eat this bread and drink the cup, you *proclaim the Lord's death* until He comes" (1 Cor. 11:26). The Greek word for *proclaim* is *kataggello*, which means to "tell thoroughly." It is more commonly translated as "preach" or "teach" in the New Testament. We should continue our faithful celebration of the Mass until the second coming; doing this thoroughly teaches the gospel to us and to others.

What is this gospel? Remember the strategy of the Lamb and the Church? It involved telling the Truth through the Eucharist: that what you see with your eyes is not all of reality, that humans are eternal beings who will live forever either in Heaven or in Hell, and that the choices we make in this life determine where we will spend eternity. The Eucharist explains this to the world "thoroughly."

The second reason the Eucharist is the finest form of faithfulness is also a major lesson of The Apocalypse. Remember the strategy of the dragon? It promised earthly success to its allies through deceit and earthly power. In response to the lies of Satan, the Eucharist not only preaches the Truth; the celebration of the Eucharist *supernaturally empowers us* to adopt the mindset of the Lamb. Because the Eucharist is a sacrament, it not only symbolizes the sacrifice of the one Man to lead us to eternal life; it *is* Christ: Body, Blood, soul, and divinity. As such, it builds the Truth of the

Eucharist into our daily lives. Once imbedded, that Truth helps us to wait in hope.

Not too long ago, I attended Mass at a conference at which I was a speaker. As it began, I realized anew the gospel message being played out before me. On my left was a Catholic man from the Middle East who had recently converted from Islam. On my right was a Nigerian priest. Next to him was a young Oriental man. In front of me were two little old ladies with white hair. Several rows up knelt a woman who had converted from Judaism a few years earlier. Behind me was a typical Catholic family with five or six young children. As the Mass progressed, I was in Heaven. I really was. Here was the family of God eating the marriage supper of the Lamb as one people. Here was revealed the mystery of the Kingdom, and the Kingdom values exhibited around me were being planted in my soul by Christ.

The third reason the Eucharist is the finest form of faithfulness is closely allied to the second. When we faithfully and hopefully celebrate the Eucharist, we participate in a spiritual adventure that actually hastens the second coming! That's right. We may not know the time of Christ's coming, but we do know that Christ's return can be "hastened" through our worship. We find this truth in the *Catechism:* "The Holy Spirit's transforming power in the Liturgy *hastens the coming of the Kingdom and the consummation* of the mystery of salvation. While we wait in hope He causes us really to anticipate the fullness of communion with the Holy Trinity" (CCC, par. 1107).

Sacraments not only symbolize a Truth; they actually have the supernatural power to accomplish what they symbolize. The joining of our hearts and souls in worship to the heart of the Church Triumphant as they celebrate the marriage supper of the Lamb transforms us. The Church Militant is supernaturally drawn to the Church Triumphant, and the Holy Spirit draws the New Jerusalem closer to that day when it will descend in glory to subsume the

Rapture

Church here on earth. The Eucharist transforms not only my personal inner reality, but the greater reality of the Church as well. As The Apocalypse makes clear, in the Mass, the Church on earth is most closely allied with the Church in Heaven. The Eucharist is the purest foretaste of Heaven on earth.

"The Church celebrates the mystery of her Lord 'until He comes.' Since the apostolic age the Liturgy has been drawn toward its goal by the Spirit's groaning in the Church: Maranatha! The Liturgy thus shares in Jesus' desire: 'I have earnestly desired to eat this Passover with you . . . until it is fulfilled in the Kingdom of God.' *In the sacraments of Christ the Church already receives the guarantee of her inheritance and even now shares in everlasting life, while 'awaiting our blessed hope, the appearing of the glory of our great God and Savior, Christ Jesus'* " (CCC, par. 1130).

"Maranatha! Amen. Come, Lord Jesus!"

Appendixes

Appendix One

Early Church Fathers

BARNABAS

The earliest extrabiblical source we have, the *Epistle of Barnabas*, was written anonymously around the year 100. Although it is certainly not canonical, it stands as an incredibly early documentation of the early Church's beliefs. The apostle John was very possibly alive when it was penned. We will refer to Barnabas as the epistle's author, even though his identity is disputed.

The *Epistle of Barnabas* exhibits the common early Church view that the last week of Daniel was ending as the Church was being born. Barnabas writes, "For it is written, 'And it shall come to pass, when *the week* is completed, the temple of God shall be built in glory in the name of the Lord.' I find . . . that *a temple does exist.* Having received the forgiveness of sins . . . in our habitation God dwells in us. . . . This is the spiritual temple built for the Lord" (*EOB*, 16:6).

It is interesting that Barnabas uses this expression "the week." The reference to Daniel's week does not mention Daniel! Yet scholars agree that this is definitely a reference to Daniel's final seven seasons. Can we infer that the prophecy of Daniel's seventy weeks was so well known and expounded in the early Church that it needed no further explanation? I believe we can. Daniel's prophecy was not avoided by the early Church, as it is today.

In this passage, Barnabas links Daniel's vision of seventy weeks with the prophecy of Haggai 2:7-9. Barnabas states that the purpose of Daniel's seventieth week was the building of a "spiritual temple," the Church. Barnabas obviously believed that Daniel's seventieth week encompassed Christ's first advent. This was when the "spiritual temple" was initially being established. Yet writing in about 100 A.D., he clearly believed that the seventieth week was already completed before he was writing.

It is interesting that Barnabas never justifies his use of Daniel this way. He simply slides it into his argument without a second thought. This implies that in the *very* early Church, it was widely accepted that Daniel's seventieth week contained the events surrounding the incarnation and establishment of the Church and ended within the first century.

So, less than a century after the Passion, it seems that the widespread belief of the Church was that the seventieth week of Daniel was completed. It is certain that Barnabas placed the end of the seventieth week no later than 70 A.D., and his mention of the building of the Church (which was able to grow unimpeded after 70 A.D.) makes it probable that Barnabas saw 67 to 70 A.D. as the specific *terminus ad quem* of Daniel's seventy weeks. He assumes his readers will agree that the events of "the week" led to the building of the Church.

CLEMENT OF ALEXANDRIA AND ORIGEN

Barnabas was by no means alone. Within a century of Barnabas, Clement became bishop of Alexandria until his death in 215 A.D. He clearly taught that the bestowal of the six blessings necessitated the end of biblical Judaism within the seventy weeks (9:24). He referred to the Temple's destruction in the language of Daniel's weeks. He wrote, "Vespasian rose to the supreme power and destroyed Jerusalem, and desolated the holy place" (STO, XXI, 142-143).

Origen (185-254 A.D.) was a student of Clement of Alexandria. It seems quite certain that he agreed with his teacher that the *terminus ad quem* of the seventieth week was the destruction of the Temple. "The weeks of years up to the time of Christ the leader that Daniel the prophet predicted *were fulfilled*" (*TPR*, IV:1:5).

TERTULLIAN

Tertullian wrote the treatise *Against the Jews* in 203 A.D. He, too, held that the seventieth week had been fulfilled in 70 A.D.: "Vespasian vanquished the Jews . . . and so by the date of his storming Jerusalem, the Jews had *completed the seventy weeks foretold by Daniel*" (*AAJ*, VII; *CID*).

ATHANASIUS

Athanasius was bishop of Alexandria from 326 to 373. He clearly taught that the seventieth week culminated in 70 A.D.: "Jerusalem is to stand till His coming, and thenceforth, prophet and vision cease in Israel. This is why Jerusalem stood till then . . . that there they might be exercised in the types as a preparation for the reality . . . but from that time forth all prophecy is sealed and the city and Temple taken" (*INC*, XXXIX:3–XV:8).

Athanasius reflects the view of the entire early Church: once the Messiah had come, the role of the Temple in Jerusalem had been superseded. "Things to be done which belonged to Jerusalem which is beneath . . . were fulfilled, and those which belonged to shadows had passed away" (*FEL*, IV:3-4). Biblical Judaism ended in 70 A.D.

EUSEBIUS

Eusebius, known as the father of Church history, was the bishop of Caesarea from 313 to 340. He understood the seventieth week to have been completed before 70 A.D. In fact, he must have found that belief so universal in his day that he felt compelled to construct a rather unusual framework for the Ascension to accommodate it (*EH*, VIII).

IRENAEUS, HIPPOLYTUS, AND APOLLINARIS

Irenaeus was a contemporary of Clement of Alexandria. He and his pupil Hippolytus are the only two writers from this early in the Church who believed in a still-future fulfillment of Daniel's seventieth week. The priest Hippolytus probably reflected the views of his teacher Irenaeus, so we will not draw sharp distinctions between their thoughts. They both placed the seventieth week at the end of the gospel era and so are the first to postulate a gap between the sixty-ninth and seventieth weeks (*AG*, V). Both predicted a specific date for the second coming that has come and gone.

Their belief in a future seventieth week was never widely accepted. St. Jerome went a step further in his criticism of their system. He specifically pointed out that the numbers of years in their system did not coincide with the historical events they purported to cover. This was certainly a problem (*CID*).

Later, Apollinaris expected the end of Daniel's weeks to be still future. Like Hippolytus, he predicted a specific date for Christ's return. Apollinaris taught that the seventy weeks were a 490-year period between Christ's first and second comings. Counting from the birth of Christ, he expected the second coming in 483 A.D. (*ISW*).

It is widely accepted that Apollinaris was mistaken in his prophecy. About half a century after Apollinaris, Jerome wrote, "If by any chance those of future generations should not see these predictions of his fulfilled at the time he set, then they will be forced to seek for some other solution and to convict the teacher himself of *erroneous interpretation*" (*CID*).

The fact that they were in such a minority should tell us something. The lack of any sizable number of futurists among the early

Church writers is definitely a serious blow to rapturists. As a point of history, the views of Irenaeus did give seed to premillennialism. But this concept was strongly and universally denounced by the other leaders of the Church. The early Church understood the presumptuous-parenthesis theory (see Chapter 5 of this book) that rapturists employ in this vision, but they resoundingly rejected it.

The most prevalent understanding of the early Church leaves no room in Daniel for a future seven-year Great Tribulation, which means Daniel's time line of future events leaves no room for the rapturist system.

Appendix Two

The Masoretic *Silluk* in Daniel

There is a valid objection to our interpretation of Daniel's last vision. We have attached the last phrase of verse 10 — "none of the wicked shall understand; but those who are wise shall understand" — to the first phrase of verse 11 — "from the time that the continual burnt offering is taken away, and the abomination that makes desolate is set up" (12:10-11). Our decision to link these two phrases is justified, because it makes sense of the passage. It explains why the wise will understand at a certain point in the future, whereas Daniel could not understand, even though he was one of the wise.

But there is a traditional Jewish understanding of this passage that instead attaches the phrase, "from the time that the continual burnt offering is taken away, and the abomination that makes desolate is set up" to the phrase that follows it, "there shall be a thousand two hundred and ninety days." This traditional understanding is based on the Masoretic *silluk* between the two phrases we have attached. The trouble with the Masoretic reading is that it makes the passage undecipherable.

Before discussing it further, we need a very short lesson in Hebrew. In its original written form, Hebrew did not include any vowels, punctuation, or accent marks. It was just a series of consonants. The reader supplied the rest as he read. Later, consonants were used as a stand-in for vowels.

Rapture

About five hundred years after Christ's first advent, Jewish scholars called Masoretes took the consonants of the Hebrew language and started to develop vowels and accent marks (for punctuation). They did the bulk of their work from around 700 to 1000 A.D., and the Masoretic text of the Old Testament dates from around this time. The Dead Sea Scrolls have verified that the Masoretic text is still one of the most reliable sources for what the original Hebrew text (made up exclusively of consonants) actually contained.

The Masoretic text contains vowels and accent marks (for punctuation), both inserted into the text by the Masoretic scholars. The *silluk* is the strongest punctuation mark used in Hebrew, analogous to our period. Here is the passage, with a double asterisk (**) placed in the text to show the location of the Masoretic *silluk*.

> Then I said, "O my lord, what shall be the issue of these things?" He said, "Go your way, Daniel, for the words are shut up and sealed until the time of the end. . . . None of the wicked shall understand; but those who are wise shall understand.** And from the time that the continual burnt offering is taken away, and the abomination that makes desolate is set up, there shall be a thousand two hundred and ninety days. Blessed is he who waits and comes to the thousand three hundred and thirty-five days. But go your way till the end; and you shall rest, and shall stand in your allotted place at the end of the days" (12:8-13).

These punctuation decisions were made well after the time of Christ by Jewish scholars during the Middle Ages. Those scholars were undoubtedly closer to the culture and language than we are now. But at the same time, they were not inerrant (Daniel's original autographs were). Their punctuation marks must be given great weight, but they are certainly not part of the original inspired text. We must not forget that the *silluk* was not in the text until more than a millennium after Daniel penned this vision. This punctuation was not there when Jesus read the passage, nor when St. Peter and St. Paul read it, nor even when St. Augustine read it.

What's the point? Punctuation should make a passage more understandable, not more obtuse. The problem with the Masoretic punctuation is that it leaves the passage without any clear message. So we have chosen to attach the phrase "those who are wise shall understand" to the phrase that follows it, "from the time that the continual burnt offering is taken away." We can then make sense of why the wise will one day understand, and why Daniel would never understand, even though he was certainly wise. The wise were witnesses to certain events that would make them understand the mystery of Christ's Kingdom.

While we should never discard Masoretic punctuation without good cause, in this case there is excellent reason to do so.

Appendix Three

Zechariah

Why investigate Zechariah's message? Pound for pound, Zechariah contains more Messianic prophecies than any other Old Testament book. His message is really quite clear: the Messiah will come and renew the faith of God's people. He will accomplish all of this during Daniel's seventieth week: the seven decades of covenantal transition. But rapturists have misunderstood Zechariah.

Most people (and definitely married people!) know that a minor misunderstanding has the potential to lead to mass confusion. You can state your opinion as clearly as you know how, only to have your listener get the wrong message. Sometimes the confusion persists until you re-examine and eliminate the minor misunderstanding that started it all. From His eternal vantage point, the prophet Zechariah knows exactly how this feels.

THE MINOR MISUNDERSTANDING

What is the minor misunderstanding that must vex this holy prophet? Today's rapturists misunderstand the clear prophecies of Christ's first advent and apply much of them to His second. This minor misunderstanding stems from the same motive as does the presumptuous parenthesis in Daniel. In spite of Daniel's clear message, rapturists resist any implication that the kingdom of God might have been successfully established at the first advent.

Rapture

Instead of understanding Zechariah as the clear and consistent prophet of the first advent, rapturists cut and paste this book into total confusion. They repeatedly apply one verse to the second advent, the next verse to the first advent, and then the very next verse to the second advent again. If their understanding is correct, Zechariah was one very confused prophet!

Each rapturist might tweak the details in a slightly different way, but, generally speaking, the chart on the opposite page illustrates their system. I have used the rapturist system to sort the verses into three groups: Zechariah's time, the first advent, and the second advent. The dating in this chart assumes that rapturists are correct in their contention that the second coming must come before the end of the twenty-first century. Notice the confusion that their minor misunderstanding creates. The arrows illustrate the two-thousand-year gaps, both forward and backward, that rapturists insert.

Their system works for the first seven chapters, but then mass confusion develops quickly (as I have tried to show with the arrows). Notice that they understand the passage after 8:20 as future. But right in the middle of this passage, in 9:9 and again in 13:7, two verses pop up that were undeniably fulfilled by Christ in His first advent. It is undeniable because the New Testament applies them to the first advent. In addition, rapturists understand all of Chapter 11 in light of the first advent.

In a way, rapturists insert the same presumptuous parenthesis into Zechariah that they inserted into Daniel. But this time, it causes three round trips of two thousand years in both forward and reverse modes! We need to look at these "interrupting" verses.

Jesus quotes Zechariah 13:7 in Mark 14:27 to describe His experience in the Passion. "Jesus said to them, 'You will all fall away; for it is written, "I will strike the shepherd, and the sheep will be scattered."'" So Zechariah 13:7 was undeniably fulfilled in the first advent. Yet rapturists place at least a chapter on either side of this one verse at least two thousand years later.

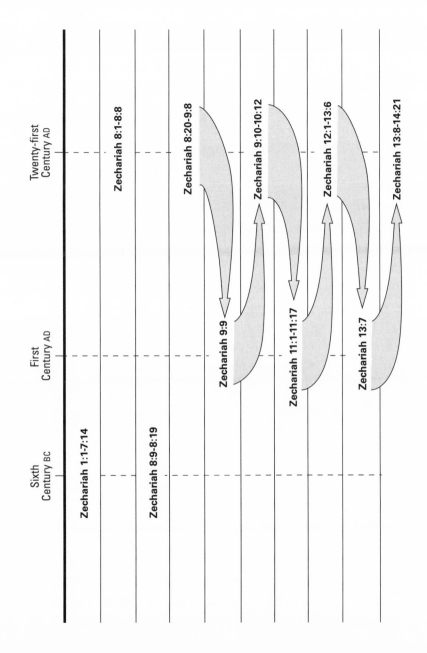

Zechariah

The difficulty in Zechariah 9:9 is even more acute. This verse is part of a single thought that extends at least as far as the tenth verse. To rip it out of its context does violence to Zechariah's meaning. Rapturists believe the entire context around this verse speaks of the second advent, while this *one verse* is about the first advent. That verse is quoted in the Gospels as being fulfilled in the triumphal entry of Christ into Jerusalem: "This took place to fulfill what was spoken by the prophet, saying, 'Tell the daughter of Zion: Behold, your King is coming to you, humble, and mounted on an ass, and on a colt, the foal of an ass' " (Matt. 21:4-5). In spite of this, rapturists claim that all verses preceding and following 9:9 refer to events at least two thousand years later. Of course, the text gives us no hint of any repeated "back to the future" time warps.

In addition to these two verses, the whole of Chapter 11 cannot be taken as applying to anything other than Christ's first advent. Yet rapturists believe that all of Chapters 10 and 12 are a discussion of twenty-first-century events. This interruption of thought goes far beyond the typical disregard of apocalyptic prophecy for time sequence. It makes a muddle of any attempt to understand Zechariah. This system in Zechariah is untenable.

A SIMPLE SOLUTION

If the rapturist system is faulty, what can a loyal Catholic make of Zechariah? The simplest interpretation of Zechariah is to understand it as a prophecy to encourage the Jews of the sixth century B.C. with the promised coming of Messiah. The prophecy starts with that time, but culminates with the events of Christ's first advent. The second coming is not in view anywhere in Zechariah's visions. A careful look at Zechariah substantiates this view.

DANIEL'S SEVENTIETH WEEK

Before we begin, however, we must recall that Zechariah builds on the message of Daniel's seventy weeks. Daniel's seventy weeks viewed the seven decades that began with Christ's conception as a time of covenantal transition. Zechariah follows Daniel's lead, and his prophecy includes all of Daniel's seventieth week. To understand Zechariah properly, we must realize that Zechariah's "day of the Lord" is identical to Daniel's final week. It includes the coming of the Messiah, Christ's judgment on His accusers in the destruction of the Temple, and even the founding of the Church.

This insight, which rapturists miss completely, clears up the minor misunderstanding. Zechariah understands that the Kingdom will be established in the first advent. He does not distinguish between the first and second advents in his prophecies because he has only the first advent in view. There are no two-thousand-year gaps between verses, because everything he prophesied was fulfilled by 70 A.D. Was Zechariah familiar with the oracle of the seventy weeks in Daniel? I believe it is evident that he was.

OUTLINE AND OVERVIEW

There are a variety of opinions among Catholics, but I believe the best understanding of the book is that it was written shortly after Daniel, at the time of the Jews' return from the Babylonian captivity. Although the difference between the first and second half of Zechariah is widely acknowledged, the book's similarity to Daniel is often overlooked. The outline below reflects Daniel's influence on Zechariah the prophet, who imitates the broad outline of Daniel (without the deuterocanonical portions) to a surprising degree.

Introduction	Historical setting, God's people in peril in the sixth century B.C.	1:1-8:23
I	Initial oracle of the day of the Lord	9:1-11:3
II	Key personality, a historical parable	11:4-17
III	Initial oracle recapitulated in a second oracle	12:1-14:21

These similarities cannot be attributed to mere coincidence. Zechariah is conscious of Daniel's book and uses it as a template.

He inserts the key-personality section between the oracles for the same reason Daniel did: otherwise, the later visions make no sense. The key-personality section in Daniel explains what is meant by the "coming" of God in judgment. Here in Zechariah, this section explores the key element in covenantal transition: the establishment of a New Covenantal people of God after the breaking of the old covenantal bond.

THE DAY OF THE LORD

Zechariah uses a phrase to place his prophecy at a specific time in the future. He states that certain events will occur on the "day of the Lord," or "that day," which is equivalent to Daniel's last week. By following this phrase throughout the book, we can understand the full scope of Zechariah's message.

The prophet warms up to this phrase as the book continues. He uses it once in Chapter 2 as the climax to the third vision, once again in Chapter 3 as the climax to the fourth vision, and one more time in Chapter 8 as a climax to the historical setting of Section I.

Zechariah uses the phrase only once in the initial oracle in Chapter 9. Then, as he starts to recapitulate the initial oracle, he uses "that day" a surprising seventeen times (this is after the key-personality section). The book builds to a crescendo in the recapitulating oracle of the final three chapters. At the beginning of the book, Zechariah concentrates on the sixth-century-B.C. historical setting. In the second half, he focuses on the Messiah's coming and the New People He will choose for Himself during "the day of the Lord." These are the recipients of the blessings bestowed during Daniel's final week of covenantal transition.

So what does Zechariah tell us about the "day of the Lord"? The scope of this book does not allow for an in-depth treatment.

But simply following this phrase through the book will reveal much.

I. HISTORICAL SETTING

The first section, Chapters 1 through 8, contains the historical setting of Zechariah's time and eight visions that are designed to encourage the Jews of the sixth century B.C. Those Jews were in peril as they returned to Jerusalem from the Babylonian captivity. They are promised that Jerusalem and its Temple will once again prosper and be the center of God's activity on earth. There are two references to "that day," pointing to the climax of the restoration of Jerusalem that unfolds during Christ's first advent.

The phrase first occurs in 2:11. We learn that the gentile nations will convert and "join themselves to" the true God of Israel. This is a prediction of the mystery of the gospel, which came to fruition in St. Paul's ministry. The mystery of the gospel is a major theme of the entire first vision of The Apocalypse, so we will return to that topic.

At that time, God will literally "dwell in the midst" of His holy people, a reference to the Eucharist. The Apocalypse is an extremely eucharistic book, but even here in the Old Testament we can detect hints of the Mass.

Further, God's people will understand that He has been "sent" in "that day." The phraseology whereby God is being "sent" by God is difficult to decipher without knowledge of the Incarnation. When else was God sent by God?

The prophecy continues by predicting that the Lord will "again" choose Jerusalem. When put into the context of what we find later in Zechariah, this is best understood as the choosing of Christ's *ekklesia*; the New Jerusalem described in the Gospels and The Apocalypse. We will see this theme expanded in the key-personality section, in which Zechariah acts out the drama of Daniel's seventieth week.

The phrase occurs a second time in 3:10. "In that day," guilt will be removed "in a single day." This is reminiscent of Daniel's description of the seventieth week, when atonement was accomplished in a single day, Good Friday. We also learn that a generous love for one's fellowman will be the outgrowth of God's forgiveness.

The third time we see this "day" mentioned is at the end of this section. "In those days" the Gentiles will flock to God through the Jews. If Zechariah's vision is to be taken seriously, the Jews would be quickly outnumbered in the Church: "Ten men from the nations of every tongue shall take hold of the robe of a Jew" (8:23).

The first section is primarily focused on the events of the sixth century B.C., so this is all we learn about the first advent. Yet we already see the general theme of the New Covenant that was established during Daniel's last week.

II. INITIAL ORACLE

The second section encompasses slightly more than the next two chapters. This is the first of two major oracles that focus primarily on Daniel's seventieth week. The message boils down to this: the countries surrounding Jerusalem are strong and hostile, but when the Messiah arrives, He will establish His everlasting dominion. The New Jerusalem will eventually be victorious throughout the earth.

Unlike earlier in the book, "that day" now becomes the major theme of the visions. Zechariah obviously understands "the day of the Lord" in the context of the first advent, as is evidenced in 9:9: "Lo, your King comes to you; triumphant and victorious is He, humble and riding on an ass, on a colt the foal of an ass."

This coming of the King results in "peace to the nations." This is the famous peace of the New Covenant that Ezekiel proclaims: "I will make a *covenant of peace* with them" (37:26). This peace is built on the generous love of the earlier vision. That love was a result of the forgiveness obtained on "a single day," Good Friday.

The Messiah's "dominion shall be from sea to sea." Rapturists who deny the establishment of God's Kingdom during Christ's first advent must explain these verses some other way. But Catholics can take them for what they obviously mean. When Christ came the first time, He rode into Jerusalem on a colt. As a result of what happened during Holy Week (and throughout the rest of Daniel's week), He was recognized as the victorious King with an established Church that stretches into every corner of the world. The Church is the physical representation on earth of the Kingdom of God in Heaven. The Kingdom is essentially ecclesiastical.

"That day" reappears in 9:16. Salvation will come from God at this time. "Yea, how good and how fair it shall be!" (9:17). This exclamation reminds us of the "joy of our salvation" that we sometimes take so much for granted. Would anyone really want to be unregenerate again? It is a privilege to share in the benefits of "the day of the Lord."

III. HISTORICAL PARABLE
OF THE GOOD SHEPHERD

Zechariah 11:4-17 contains an interlude between the two major oracles of the second half of the book. Zechariah is the only key personality examined. His experiences as a shepherd become a living parable of the Messiah during "the day of the Lord" (GR3).

As a true and compassionate shepherd, Zechariah replaces a group of evil shepherds. It becomes crystal clear that these evil shepherds are the crux of the problem, not the sheep themselves. Jesus had harsh words for the chief priests and the scribes. Do you hear an echo of those words here in Zechariah? "My anger is hot against the shepherds, and I will punish the leaders" (10:3).

Zechariah cares for the sheep: "So I became the shepherd of the flock doomed to be slain for those who trafficked in the sheep" (11:7). Here we see the love of Christ for His sheep. This love of

God was the motivating factor in the Passion. Jesus, too, was "doomed to be slain" by His intense love.

But people are not satisfied with Zechariah as the shepherd. He is bought off with thirty shekels of silver: "They weighed out as my wages thirty shekels of silver. Then the Lord said to me, 'Cast it into the treasury' — the lordly price at which I was paid off by them" (11:12-13). It does not take much experience in reading prophecy to see these experiences of Zechariah as pointing to the Messiah (GR3). The connection to the betrayal of Christ by Judas for thirty pieces of silver is striking.

Now the most important event in Zechariah's living parable occurs. Zechariah breaks his two staffs, "Grace" and "Union": "I took my staff Grace, and I broke it, annulling the covenant which I had made with all the peoples" (11:10). How much clearer must Zechariah be? This symbolizes the annulling of the covenant between God and Judah. During Daniel's seventieth week, the Old Covenant was annulled and a New Covenant, a strong, everlasting one of peace, was established.

"Then I broke my second staff Union, annulling the brotherhood between Judah and Israel" (11:14). Judah was the believing remnant of the holy bloodline of Israel. Israel was the unbelieving majority. This symbolizes the breaking of any tie of unity between the believing and unbelieving remnant of God's people. No longer would God concern Himself with a holy bloodline. The New Covenant will be primarily spiritual rather than physical. As Christ Himself stated, from this point on, His family will be those who hear and obey His commandments.

This is a crucial vision for any consistent understanding of Christ's work during Daniel's final week. The annulment of the Old Covenant when it was superseded by the New Covenant is clearly predicted. Zechariah is clear that the Good Shepherd will annul the Old Covenant with Israel and break the staffs, "Grace" and "Union."

Rapturists (along with many modernists) like to claim that there is no basis for our belief that the New Covenant superseded the Old Covenant. They like to claim that we are anti-Semitic for believing that God annulled His Old Covenant in favor of the Church. But the split within Judaism caused by Christ was foreseen in the Old Testament.

Not only is the annulment of the Old Covenant clear here in Zechariah; prophecies of its demise are sprinkled liberally all throughout the Old Testament. For example, in the very next minor prophet, Malachi, we read, "I [God] will put you [the Levitical priesthood] out of my presence. . . . You have corrupted the covenant of Levi. . . . The Lord whom you seek will suddenly come to His Temple. . . . Then I will draw near to you for judgment. . . . Then those who feared the Lord . . . I will spare them as a man spares his son who serves him. . . . Behold, the day comes, burning like an oven, when all the arrogant and all evildoers will be stubble." We know that Malachi uses "the day" as does Zechariah, because he tells us that God "will send you Elijah the prophet before the great and terrible day of the Lord comes" (Mal. 2:3, 8; 3:1, 5, 16-17; 4:1).

In opposition to the clear prophecies of the minor prophets, rapturists believe that during the Great Tribulation and the Millennium, God will reinstate the Old Covenant, along with its ceremonial blood sacrifices. But this does not take into account what Zechariah taught in the drama of the Good Shepherd. Zechariah predicted that the Good Shepherd would annul the Old Covenant during His first advent. This annulling is intimately associated with the death of the Shepherd, sold for thirty pieces of silver. How much more proof do rapturists require?

IV. SECOND RECAPITULATING ORACLE

Zechariah's second oracle (chs. 12-14) clearly recapitulates the first oracle, the events of Daniel's last week. This oracle can seem like a puzzle unless we remain mindful that this vision comes after the shepherd story of Zechariah. In that object lesson, it becomes clear that God will be "annulling the covenant which [He] had made"; so the second oracle will concentrate on the New Covenant made with the New Jerusalem, otherwise known as the "strong" covenant of Daniel's seventy weeks. The Church as the New Jerusalem comes into sharp focus only after Zechariah envisions the Good Shepherd breaking the two staffs, "Grace" and "Union."

"That day" is liberally sprinkled throughout the second oracle because the seven decades of covenantal transition have taken front stage in Zechariah. We discover that at this time "all the nations of the earth will come together against" Jerusalem (12:3). This certainly happened when Titus invaded. His army was made up of soldiers from each of the ten provinces of the empire and even contained mercenaries from outside the empire.

As we noted in Daniel, the Jewish people believed to the bitter end that the Lord would deliver Jerusalem yet one more time. Zechariah also predicts this delusion. They wrongly believed that "the inhabitants of Jerusalem have strength through . . . their God" (12:5). Zechariah predicts that they will believe this even after the rest of Judah has been defeated. In fact, the strategy of Titus was to defeat Judah first, "while Jerusalem shall still be inhabited" (12:6). Only when the surroundings of Judea were subdued did the Roman army turn its attention to Jerusalem. The decision of Titus might very well have been based on the devastating retreat of Cestius a few years earlier, but Zechariah had predicted it.

Zechariah now turns his attention to the New Jerusalem, created when the staffs "Grace" and "Union" were broken. "The Lord will put a shield" around His People. And in fact, as Eusebius records, not a single Christian died when Jerusalem fell. After earthly Jerusalem's defeat, God will not abandon His New Jerusalem. We see in 12:9 that God will take vengeance on all those who come against His people.

The feast of booths

The worship of the New Jerusalem will center on "the feast of booths" (14:16-19). This is the only festival mentioned during "the day of the Lord." One unique feature of this feast was the holy day it observed. Normally, the Old Testament Jews kept the seventh day of the week, Saturday, as the Sabbath. But the day of rest during the feast of booths was the *first* day of the week, Sunday (Lev. 23:33-36).

This is an amazing truth hidden in Zechariah. Rarely is Zechariah 14 used to help Seventh Day Adventists (this group of Christians worships on Saturday) understand why the Church worships on Sunday, the first day of the week. Of course, that is the day Christ rose (Easter) and the Church was born (Pentecost). But the institution of Sunday for "holy convocation" in the New Jerusalem is foretold all the way back in Zechariah.

As if that were not enough, the feast of booths commemorated the exodus of God's people from the slavery of Egypt. This theme of the New Covenant exodus has already appeared in the first oracle: "They shall pass through the sea of Egypt" (10:11). The Apocalypse expands on the connection between the Old Covenant exodus celebrated in the festival of booths, and the New Covenant exodus from spiritual Egypt in 70 A.D.

The pierced One

During "that day," "the inhabitants of Jerusalem . . . when they look on Him whom they have pierced, they shall mourn for Him" (12:10). Rapturists believe this must happen at the end of the Great Tribulation, but the early Church understood this prophecy as being fulfilled during the fall of Jerusalem to Rome. For example, Lactantius, who lived in the second half of the third century, lists a long series of Old Testament prophecies that were fulfilled in the first advent: "Also Zechariah says: '*And they shall look on me whom they pierced.*' Amos thus speaks of the obscuring of the sun:

'In that day, saith the Lord, the sun shall go down at noon, and the clear day shall be dark.' Jeremiah also speaks of the city of Jerusalem, in which He suffered: 'Her sun is gone down while it was yet day; she hath been confounded and reviled, and the residue of them will I deliver to the sword.' *Nor were these things spoken in vain. For after a short time the Emperor Vespasian* subdued the Jews, and laid waste their lands with the sword and fire, besieged and reduced them by famine, overthrew Jerusalem" (*TED*, 46).

When the inhabitants of Jerusalem were defeated, they realized that it was the punishment of God upon them for their treatment of Jesus. They had not been the "wise" who understood and fled. They were of the wicked, and so they mourned (Dan. 12). This understanding of Zechariah is substantiated in the Olivet Discourse.

The second oracle continues in Chapter 13 with more predictions concerning "that day." Zechariah introduces a fountain, which he develops further in 14:8. This fountain of water flows with "living waters" which will "cleanse them from sin and uncleanness" (13:1). Jesus used this "living waters" symbol in the New Testament. Ezekiel describes a thousand cubits of water flowing from the Temple. The Apocalypse uses all of these to symbolize the Holy Spirit and the blessings He bestows on us. What better description of the baptismal font of the New Jerusalem could we expect?

Next, we learn that "on that day" God will definitively defeat the idols that some Jews were worshiping (13:2). The worship of these idols is evidenced by two actions described earlier in Zechariah, lying and stealing: "Everyone who steals shall be cut off henceforth according to it, and everyone who swears falsely shall be cut off henceforth according to it" (5:3). From this it is not too difficult to figure out that the idols were material wealth and comfort, gained through deceit and power. The antidote is to "love truth and peace" (8:19). We see in The Apocalypse that Truth is the primary weapon of the New Jerusalem against the dragon's deceit and power.

Prophecy will also cease, which reminds us again of Daniel's seventy-weeks vision. All Old Testament prophecy has been fulfilled in Christ and His Kingdom.

The spoils of war

A beautiful passage that returns to the theme of the Good Shepherd is inserted at this point. Before Zechariah continues with the last chapter of his book, he re-emphasizes the lessons of the shepherd parable. We read, "Strike the shepherd, that the sheep may be scattered" (13:7). A gruesome fact is pointed out that The Apocalypse will enlarge upon: "Two-thirds shall be cut off and perish, and one-third shall be left alive" (13:8).

This should tip us off. This last chapter will perhaps concentrate on the part of Daniel's seventieth week in which the New Covenant Messiah was vindicated over the Old Covenant leaders. Zechariah 14 is perhaps the most important chapter in this book. It foreshadows a theme we encounter in Galatians and in The Apocalypse. The Old will be cast out in favor of the New when the two staffs are broken during the seven decades of covenantal transition.

Rapturists misunderstand this entire chapter as being in the future, yet there is really no good reason to do this. We have already noted the mass confusion caused by this approach.

There are seven references to "that day," in the last chapter. Every one of them fits the events of 70 A.D. "The spoil taken from you will be divided in the midst of you" (14:1). After Titus defeated Jerusalem, the army regrouped while the residents and goods of the city were sorted, distributed, and sold. "The city shall be taken and the houses plundered and the women ravished; half of the city shall go into exile" (14:2). This certainly has already occurred. The Romans were very thorough in their pillaging.

There is a ray of hope in this black picture: "The Lord will go forth and fight" for His people at this time (14:3). But we must not forget the lessons of the shepherd parable. God will not be fighting for Old Jerusalem, but for the citizens of New Jerusalem.

Historians tell us that not a single Christian was killed in the overthrow of Jerusalem by the Romans and their allies. The focus of God's protection is now on New Jerusalem, since the Old Covenant has been "annulled." God did indeed fight for His People, as we clearly see in The Apocalypse.

The Mount of Olives

There remains one phrase in Zechariah that rapturists are absolutely certain remains unfulfilled. We read that "His feet shall stand on the Mount of Olives which lies before Jerusalem on the east, and the Mount of Olives shall be split in two" (14:4). Rapturists teach that this refers to the second coming. They understand the "split" very literally — the topography of Israel will be suddenly transformed. Mountains will literally be split in two and instantaneously flattened into plains.

But rapturists ignore the other uses of this kind of language in the Old Testament (GR5, 6). We have already encountered this even in Zechariah: "What are you, O great mountain? Before Zerubbabel you shall become a plain" (4:7).

Christ's greatest battle was won during the Passion. Just before that awful weekend, Jesus was on the Mount of Olives with His disciples, sweating great drops of blood while He prayed. This night was the climax of Daniel's last week, the halfway point during which the "strong covenant" would be made with New Israel. The splitting of the topography was understood by the early Church in much the same way as other apocalyptic literature is understood: the great dynasties of the Jewish people were destroyed by the sacrifice of Christ, whom they rejected. Previous categories and loyalties (Jew and Gentile) have been superseded by two new groups of people (Christian and non-Christian). The holy bloodline's two staffs were broken.

Tertullian clearly applies this prophecy to the Agony in the Garden. " 'But at night He went out to the Mount of Olives.' *For thus had Zechariah pointed out:* 'And His feet shall stand in that day on the Mount of Olives' " (AGM, IV, 40).

Eusebius also understood Zechariah 14:1-5 as being fulfilled in the first century. In fact, no Church Father found it necessary to justify this exegesis of Zechariah, leading us to the conclusion that it was probably the common understanding of the entire early Church (POG, VIII, 4:144-6).

Flee for safety

Zechariah continues by predicting that the people of God "shall flee as you fled from the earthquake in the days of Uzziah, king of Judah" (14:5). Perhaps we easily miss the significance of this. Zechariah is predicting that during "that day," people will flee for safety *away from* Jerusalem. This was antithetical to everything the Jews had done throughout their history when invaded by a conquering army. After all, a fortified city is a relatively safe haven during war. Zechariah can come up with only one instance from the past to illustrate their flight during the "day of the Lord": when an earthquake struck the area, and the residents fled out of the city into the open country for safety.

This is exactly what Jesus exhorted His followers to do in the Olivet Discourse. This should assure us that we are on the right track. "That day" is the same period during which the Church was founded and then fled from Jerusalem into the desert. When given the opportunity, the Christians of Judea obeyed and were delivered.

The New Kingdom established on "that day" will be a blessed time with continuous day (14:6). It is interesting to look up every mention of light in the Gospels. Starting with the beautiful passage in John's Gospel, Chapter 1, we see that Christ and His Church are viewed as the source of light in the world. The light of the Church will pierce the darkness of the world. This theme is taken up in The Apocalypse, along with the theme of the living waters.

The theme of the split between the Old Covenant Israel and the New Covenant Church is so important in salvation history that Zechariah revisits it in 14:14: "Even Judah will fight against Jerusalem." No longer will there be a believing and unbelieving portion of the holy bloodline of Israel. The new categories of non-Christians versus Christians is dealt with in depth by St. Paul and St. John in the New Testament.

The Eucharist

As we have noted, rapturists believe that Zechariah 14 describes events that will occur in the future, during a corporeal millennial kingdom of Christ. This minor misunderstanding led to the mass confusion we charted at the beginning of this appendix. Because of their misunderstanding, they understand the last two occurrences of "that day" in the last paragraph of Zechariah 14 as still future. This part of Zechariah has a personal relevance to me because of how it fit into my own reconciliation with the Catholic Church.

When I was a Protestant seminary student at Trinity Evangelical Divinity School, this paragraph became the topic of a discussion I will never forget. It describes the actions of all those "who sacrifice" in Jerusalem during the Millennial Kingdom (14:21). I was visiting with a teacher whose specialty was eschatology and who believed the Millennium was still future. A young man approached us and asked about the verse: "If Jesus' sacrifice is final and complete, why will there be future animal sacrifices needed in Jerusalem during the Kingdom? After all, this is after the death and Resurrection of Jesus." I will always remember what the teacher said: he reluctantly admitted that he knew of no plausible Protestant explanation for this verse!

The problem does not revolve around whether sacrifices will occur. Almost all rapturists believe that the animal sacrifices of the Old Covenant will be reinstituted in the Millennium after the second coming of Christ. That is not the problem for which this teacher had no answer. The question was, and remains, "Why?"

Protestants are emphatic that the Crucifixion of Christ was the last sacrifice ever needed. Why would God even *allow* those endless animal sacrifices to be performed — sacrifices that were only a shadow of our Lord's Passion?

Why? This question and its answer bothered me for more than sixteen years. I found a satisfactory answer shortly before reconciling with the Catholic Church at the age of forty-one. Zechariah was referring, not to the animal sacrifices of the Old Covenant in a future Millennium, but to the *Eucharist* in God's Kingdom here and now. The sacrifice of the Mass is being offered every day in Jerusalem. As Zechariah makes clear, the Eucharist is celebrated without interruption all over the world. I remember realizing with a jolt that the unbloody sacrifices of the Church were foretold in the Old Testament. The sacrifice of the Mass brings God's grace gained at the Passion into our lives. It does this because it is actually the same sacrifice, brought into the present here on earth through the power of the Holy Spirit.

Since the Good Shepherd drama, Zechariah's focus has changed from the earthly Jerusalem to the New Jerusalem, the Church. Given that, we can understand how Zechariah is able to close his book with the assertion that no Philistine, or "trader," shall ever enter "the house of the Lord of hosts on that day" (14:21). On that day, a new House of the Lord will be built that will no longer depend on a physical Temple in Jerusalem: the worldwide, ecclesiastical Kingdom that Christ set up at His first advent, the Kingdom that we participate in through the sacraments. No one who is

Rapture

unworthy because of unbelief will be able to enter this spiritual Kingdom.

SUMMARY

The insights of Zechariah are enough to take our breath away. Our brief treatment of this magnificent book has provided only a whiff of the feast that this prophet prepares for us. Remember, Zechariah lived in the sixth century B.C., yet the themes and predictions within his prophecies ring true throughout the New Testament and in the teachings of the early Church. Zechariah's prophecies expand our knowledge concerning Daniel's final week of covenantal transition. Our previous work in Daniel helped us develop the proper perspective. Zechariah views the seven decades surrounding Jesus' Incarnation as a whole, just as Daniel did.

Authorship and Dating of The Apocalypse

AUTHORSHIP

The Church has traditionally understood the human author of The Apocalypse to be none other than St. John the Apostle. The list of early Church Fathers who accepted St. John's authorship is formidable: Melito, Papias, Justin Martyr, Irenaeus, Hippolytus, Tertullian, Clement of Alexandria, Origen, Cyprian, Athanasius, Cyril of Alexandria, and Basil, to name the most prominent. However, among those who doubted Johanine authorship are Dionysius, Denis of Alexandria, Cyril of Jerusalem, Gregory Nazianzen, and John Chrysostom.

Most of the doubters, however, had one thing in common: they strongly objected to what they perceived to be the book's millenarian slant. They believed that an apostle would never have held the millenarian position that they thought was integral to The Apocalypse.

In that they were right. If The Apocalypse taught a future thousand-year corporeal reign of Christ after the second advent, the book could not have been apostolic in origin. This concept was Jewish in origin, but not a part of the deposit of Faith Christ gave to the Apostles. But since St. Augustine conclusively showed that the book does not have a millenarian slant (unless the reader brings it with him), I believe we can discount that objection.

Rapture

Some modernists claim The Apocalypse was the work of several men: a "visions by committee." That position does not take into account the beautiful unity of the book. Perhaps a reader who is just starting to study the book might find this theory plausible, but not a longtime student. In fact, "Most scholars judge that Apocalypse is the work of one author . . . that actually had a supernatural vision" (NCE). Since there is broad support among scholars that the book was authored by one man, I see no convincing reason to abandon the traditional Church position: St. John is the author.

DATING
Modern opinions

Nonetheless, many modern scholars split the book into parts (usually three) and date each from a different period. They claim that one person then compiled these three parts and made them into a whole.

The first "text" (say modernists) contains the letters to the seven churches that begin the book (chs. 1-3). The authorship of this section is usually dated at the supposed time of compilation, around 96 A.D., during the reign of Domitian.

The major reason this text is dated late is because of the mention of numerous heresies. The modern scholar usually doubts that these heresies could have existed any earlier than the end of the first century, partly because they imagine early Christianity as an undogmatic spiritual movement. Given that presupposition, how could heresy spring up before there was a unity of Church belief against which to define it? Of course they could not, say modernists, so the letters to the Churches must be dated later.

Modernists date the largest text section (chs. 4-14) from the reign of Nero because there exists virtually unanimous agreement that the 666 refers to Nero (Apoc. 13:18). "Scholars . . . believe that the historical background of Apocalypse was the reign of either Nero (54-68) . . . or Vespasian (69-79)" (NCE).

The third text (ch. 15 ff) is believed to have been written after the start of the reign of Vespasian (69 A.D.). Scholars see a reference to him in the list of kings in the final part of Apocalypse (Apoc. 17:9). If you do not believe in prophecy, this section could not have been written *before* Vespasian took the throne. (GR1).

In spite of the accepted thesis that the unity of the book argues strongly for one author, many scholars follow this three-text theory. The French scholar Boismard pioneered some of these ideas (*LAP*, 507-541; *NCE*).

Frame of reference

So where does this leave us? If we are careful, we will notice that we are actually in a similar situation as we were in Daniel. Many scholars hold to a later date of writing, but believe the visions were intended to be read as though they were written in 68 A.D. That is the crucial question for our study: *What is the author's intended frame of reference?*

Scholars accept that the intended setting of the large second section of text is 68 A.D. Yet they reject that date for the first and third texts because, quite frankly, they reject the possibility of the supernatural. We do not have that problem (GR1).

The modernists' presupposition underlying the first text (that there couldn't have been heresy early in the Church) is faulty. The Church was born "whole" on the day of Pentecost precisely because Her birth *was* supernatural. As the *Catechism* states, "The Church was catholic on the day of Pentecost [i.e., having correct and complete confession of faith, full sacramental life, and ordained ministry in apostolic succession]" (CCC, par. 830). If one accepts the supernatural nature of the Church, there is no problem accepting the existence of heresy in 68 A.D. We should keep in mind that Gnosticism was the Church's initial plague. It pre-existed the Church by centuries and pounced upon the Church right from its initial introduction into the non-Jewish intellectual world.

Rapture

We can find ample evidence that other Churches struggled with heresy early. For example, St. Peter wrote his first epistle before 68 A.D., which is the latest reasonable date for his martyrdom. Yet he is worried about the sexual promiscuity of the Nicolaitins, just as St. John was, without referring to the heretics by name. "I beseech you as aliens and exiles to abstain from the passions of the flesh" (1 Pet. 2:11; *AEX*, 50).

Also, Jesus warned His disciples in the Olivet Discourse (Matt. 24) that heresy would crop up in His Church before the fall of the Temple! A close study of The Apocalypse shows that St. John was careful to substantiate the fulfillment of the eight signs of the Olivet Discourse for his readers. Those who try to give the seven letters a late date do not take into account the words of our Savior (or they date the Olivet Discourse later also, and place those words in the mouth of the early Church instead of attributing them to Jesus).

We have already alluded to our reasoning concerning the third section. Because they reject the possibility of true prophecy, many scholars date this third text during the reign of Vespasian. But even granting that the text refers to Vespasian (I argue in the main body of this book that Nero is a much more logical choice), I see no problem with St. John's having written it before Vespasian became emperor in 69 A.D. If one accepts the possibility of the supernatural, there is no compelling reason to date *any* of the book after 68 A.D.

The *New Catholic Encyclopedia* states, "Some scholars believe that the historical background of Apocalypse was the *reign of Nero* (54-68 A.D.). . . . The preparatory vision in Heaven (chs. 4-5) serves as a second prophetic investiture for the revelation of God's interventions *from the Resurrection of Christ to the fall of Jerusalem*. [Some scholars] find apocalyptic allusion to different phases of the Jewish War of 66-70" (*NCE, LAH*).

Regardless of the date of authorship, the crucial issue is that many scholars agree that The Apocalypse describes in apocalyptic language the world events that transpired from 66 to 70 A.D. I go a step further. I believe that St. John the apostle saw the visions and wrote them down around the same date as the frame of reference, 68 A.D.

We must not overemphasize the importance of the date of authorship. As long as we agree with modern scholarship about the author's intended frame of reference, we can clearly understand The Apocalypse. So the discussion concerning the actual date does not directly impinge on the purpose of this book. But if you are curious about the reasons for dating the authorship of The Apocalypse in 68 A.D., then hang with me.

Internal evidence of authorship

The internal evidence within The Apocalypse points to a 68 A.D. date of writing, or at least to that time as a frame of reference for its writing. The evidence I point to in this short summary is not adequately dealt with in the modern three-text theory, nor in rapturist theories.

"Soon"

Of one thing we can be absolutely certain: the book was not primarily written about events that would not transpire until hundreds or even thousands of years later. If it had been, it would be the only book of the Bible that was intentionally meant to be undecipherable to its original readers. God does not pull tricks like that on people who are undergoing intense persecution: this book could not be primarily speaking of events in our own day.

The language St. John uses makes this crystal clear. He includes the repeated assertion that these events must happen "soon." The book starts with this statement: "The revelation of Jesus Christ, which God gave Him to show to His servants what must *soon* take place" (1:1). In verse 3, St. John re-emphasizes that "the time is *near*."

The contrast with Daniel's statement regarding these events is noteworthy. Daniel is told that "the words are shut up and sealed until the end of time" (Dan. 12:9), because the time of its fulfillment was so far away (five centuries). The angel tells St. John, "Do not seal up the words of the prophecy of this book, for the time is near" (22:10). Yet rapturists attempt to place the fulfillment twenty centuries later! No can do. It is not honest interpretation.

Those who try to see current events in The Apocalypse should learn the lesson of Joachim of Fiore. He understood this problem and so used the seven letters to symbolize seven epochs of Church history that stretched from St. John's time to his own thirteenth century. That was the only way he could justify the use of the word *soon*. But his solution was innovative in his day and has been justly discredited since.

As we will see, the events of 70 A.D. fit very well as a fulfillment of many of the events that "must soon take place." However, a later dating (of 96 A.D.) leaves us with nothing of significance that took place anytime "soon." Of course, this is an argument that modernists would use against the earlier dating. They freely admit that the visions of The Apocalypse were fulfilled in 70 A.D., but would want to date it around 96 A.D. to avoid the appearance of supernatural prophecy (GR1). By the modernist view, a later author wrote after 70 A.D. as though he were writing before then. In scholarly circles, this is called "antedating."

Although I disagree with the modernist in his antisupernatural assumptions, I grant that the book can be understood using this assumption. The subject of the book is the overthrow of Jerusalem in 70 A.D. The book is an enlargement on the themes in the Olivet Discourse and in the even-earlier prophecies of Daniel.

People and places disguised

The many instances in which St. John disguises the true characters and events through symbolism argue for authorship during a time of intense persecution. These disguises would protect the Christian community from reprisals if a copy of the book were ever confiscated. While the persecution of Domitian was certainly intense enough to warrant this use of disguise, some of the book will not tolerate that late a dating.

Further, some of the disguised symbols point to Jerusalem in an uncomplimentary light. What would be the purpose of disguising the references to a city that had been sacked twenty-six years earlier? The symbolism pointing to Jerusalem definitely suggests a date of writing *before* Jerusalem lost its influence in 70 A.D.

Only seven churches

In Chapters 2 and 3, there are letters written to seven churches, as though these seven encompass the entire scope of St. John's concern. But by 96 A.D., there would have been many more than seven Churches to address. Opponents of the earlier dating try to claim that these seven were symbolic of all the Churches in 96 A.D., but there is no textual reason for this assertion. The simplest, most logical conclusion is that the failure of John to address any more churches points to an authorship before there were any more, in 68 A.D.

666

We have already mentioned this, but St. John alludes to the man symbolized by 666 (13:18). With the exception of rapturists, the consensus of scholars is that this refers to Nero. This is clear evidence that St. John meant his readers to understand the book as being written no later than 68 A.D., when Nero committed suicide.

The numbering of kings

We have also mentioned the seven kings who are noted in text three (17:9-11). Although other alternatives have been proposed, the only solutions that do justice to history and the text remain Vespasian and Nero. Although I believe Nero is the best interpretation, even the reign of Vespasian does not extend the writing of the book to 96 A.D., as proposed by rapturists.

But besides these seven kings, there are also ten *future* kings mentioned by St. John (17:12). They are specifically mentioned as warring against the Lamb. There were ten persecuting emperors starting with Nero and ending with Diocletian (*TBR*, 372). If we start from 96 A.D., there were not.

St. John's health

In Chapter 10, St. John is told, "You must again prophesy about many peoples and nations and tongues and kings." It is possible that this is a reference to the rest of The Apocalypse, but it seems to refer to something beyond the scope of that book. In 68 A.D., John had another thirty years of life and ministry left, and he certainly could fulfill this directive. But by 96 A.D., John was an invalid who, according to St. Jerome, "was with difficulty carried into the Church, and could speak only a few words to the people." His prophetic ministry was drawing to a close at that point, and it is doubtful he would have had the strength to write The Apocalypse, much less look forward to prophesying "again."

The Temple is standing

St. John writes of Jerusalem and its Temple as though they were still standing and functioning. In Chapter 11, John is instructed to measure the Temple and its altar, but to omit measuring the outer court of the Temple because it will be trampled by the Gentiles. It is not referred to as the former Temple, nor is any reference made to its past destruction or the future rebuilding of a third Temple. Nor is the book referring to the heavenly Temple; both the last chapter of Zechariah and The Apocalypse assure us that no gentile unbelievers will have access to the New Jerusalem. Yet by 96

A.D. the Temple had already been trampled by the Gentiles, and even destroyed. It seems peculiar that there would be no reference to these events unless The Apocalypse was written before them, when everyone knew the Temple was in existence.

Language and grammar

All language develops over time as different events affect its usage and idioms. For example, *mouse* and *bug* took on new meanings after the invention of the computer. In the third century B.C., the translation of the Hebrew Old Testament into the Greek Septuagint introduced Hebraistic elements into the Greek language. Experts tell us that these elements were identifiable in writings before the destruction of Jerusalem, but that they rapidly disappeared after 70 A.D. They are patently evident in the language of The Apocalypse, which necessitates its writing before 70 A.D. (*TBR*, 43-44).

Scholars proficient in this critical analysis claim this evidence is absolutely trustworthy and irrefutable. Some claim that their analysis proves that St. John wrote The Apocalypse first, then his Gospel, and finally his three epistles.

This order would explain the difference in the language between St. John's five books (*BAP*, 255). The Greek grammar in The Apocalypse is certainly defective. For example, in Apocalypse 3:12, 14:12, and 20:2, the author adds an apposition in the nominative to a word in the oblique case. In 68 A.D., St. John's Greek abilities would have been less advanced than when he wrote his Gospel two or three decades later. By this understanding, the Gospel of John could be part of the "further witness" of St. John mentioned earlier.

Coming and mourning

This last piece of internal evidence makes sense only when The Apocalypse is understood in the broader contexts of Daniel and the Olivet Discourse. Since we have been careful in our examination of these two earlier sources, we are able to catch a phrase that many might easily overlook. St. John starts his book by writing, "Behold, He is coming with the clouds, and every eye will see Him, everyone who pierced Him; and all tribes of the earth will wail on account of Him" (1:7).

What event is in view here? This is the same language surrounding Daniel's "Son of man" vision. This is the same language Bertrand Russell misunderstood in the Olivet Discourse. In both instances, we discovered that this language refers to the events of 70 A.D. St. John is letting us in on the secret to understanding his visions. The events of Daniel's final week of covenantal transition will take center stage for the great bulk of this book.

Summary

These nine internal evidences can let us rest assured that if The Apocalypse was not written in 68 A.D., its author certainly planned meticulously for us to think that it was. This has been the conclusion of many scholars, including the eminent scholar Philip Schaff (HCC, I). Because the visions purport to be prophecy, and since we do not reject the possibility of supernatural prophecy, the best understanding of the internal evidence points to a date of authorship around 68 A.D. (GR1).

ANCIENT WITNESSES

"But wait," you may ask. "What about the isle of Patmos?" St. John tells the reader he was on that isle when he saw these visions. Doesn't everyone know that St. John was on the isle of Patmos in 96 A.D.?

Actually, there are two traditions in the very early Church concerning the imprisonment of St. John on the penal isle of Patmos. Irenaeus dated St. John's imprisonment during the reign of Domitian, between 81 and 96 A.D. Since Irenaeus claimed the acquaintance of Polycarp, the disciple of St. John, his testimony is given great weight. Yet Epiphanius states that St. John was first imprisoned under Claudius, who reigned from 41 to 54 A.D. (*HE*, II, 12, 33). Since Claudius was another name used by Nero, Epiphanius is certainly an early witness to the possibility of an earlier, 68 A.D. authorship.

So what do we make of Irenaeus? Irenaeus was the bishop of Lyons until his death in about 200 A.D. Every scholar, whether ancient or modern, who holds to 96 rather than 68 A.D. bases it on Irenaeus's witness. But Irenaeus's testimony is not without its difficulties. Simply stated, we cannot be absolutely sure of what Irenaeus meant!

Here are the details. Speaking of the man behind the 666, Irenaeus wrote, "If it were necessary to have his name distinctly announced at the present time, it would doubtless have been announced by him who saw the apocalypse; for it was not a great while ago that [he/it] was seen, but almost in our own generation, towards the end of the reign of Domitian" (*AG*, V:30:3). I have put the disputed words in brackets.

The dispute centers on what or whom was seen. Was "he" (St. John) seen toward the end of the reign? Or was "it" (the visions) seen by John toward the end of the reign? The grammar of the text gives no clue as to the proper understanding (*BAP*, 256-257). The first would allow an early dating, but the second would not.

The larger context, however, seems to imply the former understanding. Earlier in this passage, Irenaeus refers to "ancient copies" of The Apocalypse. If there were "ancient copies" already in Irenaeus's day, would this not presuppose that the original was even older? That would mean the original could not have been from 96 A.D. The context of Irenaeus's quote turns it into a persuasive argument for an earlier dating of The Apocalypse!

Is there any other evidence to corroborate this understanding of Irenaeus and the unambiguous witness of Epiphanius? Yes. We find more external evidence in a second-century Syriac Version of the New Testament, the *Peshito*. It is the earliest of all the actual translations of the Bible, dating from within a century of The Apocalypse. The title page of The Apocalypse reads, "The Revelation which was made by God to John the Evangelist in the island Patmos, into which he was thrown by *Nero Caesar*." As we have already noted, Nero died in 68 A.D. This is not irrefutable on its own, but when added to Irenaeus and Epiphanius, it is very strong evidence.

Some have tried to translate the last two words of this title page as *Domitian* rather than *Nero*. Dr. Robert Young was a meticulous student of biblical languages who compiled *Young's Analytical Concordance* without a computer. He wrote that the emperor *(Domitianou)* being referred to on the title page was Domitius, another name for Nero *(COR)*. Dr. Young held that the original word *Domitianou* was later "stupidly mistaken" (his words) as *Domitianikos* by Sulpicious and Orosius. *Domitianou* would refer to Nero, who died in 68 A.D., while *Domitianikos* would refer to Domitian, who began his rule in 95 A.D.

But that is not all. Theophylact, Arethas, and other early writers all firmly confirmed that "John saw these visions in the reign of Nero, and that they were written by him during his banishment by that emperor" *(CCO)*. Origen referred to St. John's banishment to Patmos as being decided by the "king of the Romans," a title that was used only of the Julian emperors. Nero was the last of these *(BJF)*. The list goes on and on.

The best solution to all this evidence is to hold confidently to 68 A.D. as the date of authorship. Major objections to an early date come from two sources. The modernist freely admits the subject of the book is the persecution and the Jewish-Roman War of the late 60s, but would like to date the book later to avoid any appearance of true prophecy. The rapturist argues that the book was written after the destruction of Jerusalem so that he can still look for a future fulfillment. But the internal evidence argues persuasively against him. Even Irenaeus wrote in his treatise *Against Heresies* that much of The Apocalypse referred to the first advent of Christ.

I believe that the case for a 68 A.D. authorship by St. John is very strong indeed. However, as in Daniel, it is enough if we settle for what is agreed to by many scholars. Andreas of Cappadocia, who wrote the earliest Greek exposition of The Apocalypse in the middle of the fifth century, stated, "There are not wanting those who apply this passage to the siege and destruction of Jerusalem by Titus" (*ITR*, Apoc. 6:12). He continues, "These things are referred by some to those sufferings which were inflicted by the Romans upon the Jews" (*ITR*, Apoc. 7:1). If we can agree on that, it is enough.

Appendix Five

A Response to Hyperpreterism

Starting with the reformers of the sixteenth century, Protestantism has found it virtually impossible to resist using The Apocalypse against the Catholic Church. They spoke of the Pope as the false prophet, the Catholic Church as the whore of Babylon, and Rome as the great city, Sodom. As a result of this apologetic ploy, they have been forced as a group into some variation of Joachim's historicism when interpreting these visions.

But these methods do not do justice to the original intent of St. John. Recently, Evangelicals have discovered that much of The Apocalypse can be best understood through the lens of the first century. This method of interpretation has been labeled "preterism" (*ZPE*). Evangelical preterists have done valuable work in interpreting The Apocalypse. As we have noted, however, this interpretation of these visions is not recent by any means. Andreas of Cappadocia made it clear that this view was widespread a thousand years before the Protestant Reformation (*ITR*, Apoc. 6:12; Apoc. 7:1). I believe St. John intended us to see the first century in his descriptions, and then apply those lessons to our own times.

As so often happens in Protestantism, however, the valuable rediscovery that preterism makes has recently led to an overreaction. It entails the transformation of a valid hermeneutic (interpretive) tool into a theological system: hyperpreterism, or strict preterism. Hyperpreterism emphasizes the events of the first century to the exclusion of all else that the Bible teaches about the future. They end up denying the future return of Christ at the final eschaton. They believe that even these promises were fulfilled in 70 A.D. Obviously, this is not a valid option for loyal Catholics.

There are two major difficulties with hyperpreterism that are immediately obvious. First, the Church has always cherished those passages that clearly speak of Christ's return at the final eschaton. Second, strict preterism has no adequate explanation for the existence of death in our present experience.

CHRIST'S RETURN

There are certain passages that clearly teach a still-future return of Christ. We see evidence of this in His Olivet Discourse (see Chapter 6). The second half of Christ's answer is awkward for the hyperpreterist. Of course, there are others that predict the second coming as well. The Apocalypse looks to a future consummation of the world order at Christ's second advent.

All of this hints at a problem that makes hyperpreterists squirm. The early Church, without exception, hoped for a physical resurrection and a literal return of Christ. The hyperpreterist tries to separate the beliefs of the early Church from the Bible passages they examine. They believe in *sola Scriptura* on steroids!

In this way, preterists are similar to rapturists. The preterist begins with a theology and then seeks to force all Bible passages and Church belief into conformity with that presupposition. They both try to fit the biblical data into a pre-existing system. As a result, they are left with "problem passages" that do not support their theology and must be explained away.

An example of early Church belief exists in the Didache, written just after 100 A.D. It says, "May your grace come and this world pass away!" The Didache was written after the events surrounding 70 A.D., but still within the generation of people who had known some of the Apostles. The Church was still awaiting the final eschaton: the final consummation had not yet occurred by their generation.

Although we believe that here "on earth, the seed and the beginning of the Kingdom" has begun, we still wait "until there be realized new heavens and a new earth in which justice dwells" (*LUM*, 3:5). "The pilgrim Church, in her sacraments and institutions, which belong to this present age, carries the mark of this world which will pass, and she herself takes her place among the creatures which groan and travail yet and await the revelation of the Son of God" (*LUM*, 48ss3).

The ancient prayer of the Church has always been, "Maranatha! Come, Lord Jesus!" It still is. The second coming is proclaimed in every Mass: "Christ has died, Christ is risen, Christ will come again." Christians have always believed that the Bible teaches there will one day be a second coming.

DEATH

This brings us to a second problem for the hyperpreterists: death. Because they do not anticipate any future, bodily resurrection at Christ's return, they are forced to claim that death has already been destroyed. They know that Scripture tells us that death is the last enemy to be conquered, and it will happen at Christ's return (1 Cor. 15:26). Because the hyperpreterist believes there is no future second advent of Christ, he is forced into the rather foolish argument that death has already been destroyed! Without repeating his claims, let me assure you that they do not match present reality. Death is the separation of our soul from our body, and that event is occurring throughout the world even as you read this page.

Justin Martyr reminds us that "death is a debt which must at all events be paid," even today (*ACR*, XI). Yet, as Catholics, we remind ourselves that death is not final. At death, Catholics point their hearts and minds to Christ's second advent. At funerals, we pray that we will "share in Your glory when every tear will be wiped away. On that day we shall see You, our God, as You are. We shall become like you and praise You forever through Christ our Lord."

If the only victory over death is the present one, with no hope of a future resurrection, then "we are of all men most to be pitied" (1 Cor. 15:19).

THE TEMPLE

Hyperpreterists fail to understand the Bible adequately for several reasons: they hold to a radical sense of *sola Scriptura*, they come to passages with a preset agenda, and they impose a twenty-first-century American mindset on a book written by and for first-century Christians.

For an example of this third failure, we will examine the biblical use of the word *temple*. The Bible uses this word in many ways, but it always signifies a specific physical place where God dwells.

By that definition, of course, the ultimate Temple is the God-Man, Jesus Christ. Of course, the two buildings that stood in Jerusalem are the most obvious Temples. God did dwell in the Old Covenant Temple. When Jesus stood in the Temple courtyard, He used the different understandings of the word *temple*. Speaking of His own physical body, He said, "Destroy this Temple, and in three days I will raise it up" (John 2:19). Later His disciples realized this was a clear reference to His impending Crucifixion and Resurrection. The Jews, however, confused His reference to the Temple of His body with the Temple building that Herod had built of stone (Matt. 26:61).

But Jesus was not the only one whose body was a Temple. Your body is also a temple: "Do you not know that your body is a temple of the Holy Spirit within you, which you have from God? . . . So glorify God in your body" (1 Cor. 6:19-20).

Of course, aside from Jesus, the greatest example of a human temple is Mary, the mother of Jesus. She flawlessly housed God's Spirit in the same manner that you and I do imperfectly. But she experienced much more. Her body was actually the physical home of God the Son for nine months during her pregnancy. This is why Scripture likens her to the new ark of the covenant. In his vision, John records, "God's Temple in Heaven was opened, and the ark of His covenant was seen within His Temple. . . . And a great portent appeared in Heaven, a Woman clothed with the sun. . . . She brought forth a male Child, one who is to rule all the nations with a rod of iron" (Apoc. 11:19; 12:1, 5). Just as the Old Covenant Temple received God's glory, so Mary is said to have been "overshadowed" by the "power of the Most High" (Luke 1:35).

St. John was not making a novel comparison in this passage. John of Damascus writes that, as a group, the original Apostles applied the psalms that speak of the Temple to Mary (Homily I:12). He does not defend this, as though it were a novel idea. He mentions three psalms that the Apostles used to point to Mary as the true Temple: "There is a river whose streams make glad the city of God, the holy habitation of the Most High. God is in the midst of her, she shall not be moved; God will help her right early" (Ps. 46:4-5). "We shall be satisfied with the goodness of thy house, thy holy Temple!" (Ps. 65:4). "Look . . . at the mount which God desired for His abode" (Ps. 68:16).

Without reservation, the early Church continued this tradition of drawing an analogy between the Temple and Mary. Many in the early Church saw in Mary the fulfillment of the new Temple promises in the Old Testament. Tobit implies that certain Jews did not understand the Temple of Herod to fulfill the future Temple promised by God, so Mary fulfilled them (13:10).

There are more Temples than just human ones, though. Christ's Church is also a Temple of God. The Church is made of physical members, but God's Spirit enlivens her. St. Paul repeated this theme often: "You are . . . members of the household of God, built upon the foundation of the Apostles and prophets, Christ Jesus Himself being the cornerstone, in whom the whole structure is joined together and grows into a holy Temple in the Lord" (Eph. 2:19-21). "We are the Temple of the living God; as God said, 'I will live in them and move among them, and I will be their God, and they shall be my people'" (2 Cor. 6:16; Exod. 25:8; Ezek. 37:27).

In Old Covenant times, the Bible was viewed as a Temple. The Pentateuch — the first five books of the Bible — was the inner sanctuary, the Holy of Holies. The prophets were the Holy Place. The writings were the outer court of the Gentiles.

Even Jerusalem was considered a Temple. God dwelt in this city in a unique way, because of the sacrificial Temple.

There is one more Temple the Jews discerned within the Old Testament. The largest Temple of the Bible was the earth (or alternately, the whole universe) (AJ, III, 6, 4, 122-126; III, 7, 7, 180-183). Like the other Temples, it was a physical place that held God's presence. As early as Genesis 1:2, God's Spirit is present interacting within the universe. Isaiah compares the Jewish Temple to the Temple God built for Himself, namely the physical universe. "Thus says the Lord, 'Heaven is my throne, and the earth is my footstool; what is the house which you would build for me?'" (66:1).

The way the Bible uses temple is really an illustration of ground rule 3. Biblical history prophesies the future. The Old Testament foretold that the Temple building must be destroyed and then rebuilt. History confirms that Jerusalem was destroyed and rebuilt. Our bodies are going to be destroyed in death and then resurrected (2 Cor. 4:16). Every temple must be destroyed and reborn. When the Messiah came, even the Temple of Jesus' body would meet the destruction of death on the Cross. While the rebuilding of the Temple foreshadowed the Messiah's Resurrection, Christ's resurrection foreshadows the resurrection of all Christians at the end of history; because Christ is "the first fruits" of all human resurrection (1 Cor. 15:20).

Yet all of these temples point to the future destruction and rebirth of another temple. The final temple to be destroyed at the end of time is the temple of heaven and earth, the physical universe: "The heavens will pass away with a loud noise, and the elements will be dissolved with fire, and the earth and the works that are upon it will be burned up" (2 Pet. 3:15). Some people understand St. Peter as describing the events of 70 A.D. I do not accept that view because of the context of verses 6 and 7, but that is largely irrelevant. If Peter is primarily speaking about the destruction of the Temple, it still points to that final death and resurrection of the temple of the universe at the final eschaton. That new heaven and new earth will be as different from the present one as the resurrected body of Christ is from His old body. (And the old one will be gone, just as Christ's was!) All of the various temples in history point to that final cataclysmic event.

The Church reminds us that even the Bride of Christ must undergo this rebirth. The *Catechism* teaches that "The Church will enter the glory of the Kingdom only through this final Passover, when she will follow her Lord in His death and Resurrection" (CCC, par. 677).

We must keep the mindset of the early Church and its Jewish forebears in mind when we look at various ideas concerning the future. Theological systems that discount the need for a death and rebirth of our bodies, the Church, or the universe should be immediately suspect. Hyperpreterism just does not do justice to the scriptural mindset.

Bibliography

AAJ   *An Answer to the Jews* (c. 200), by Tertullian, in *The Writings of Quintus Sept Florens Tertullianus*, S. Thelwall, trans. (Edinburgh: T. and T. Clark, 1870).

ACR   *Apologies for the Christian Religion* (c. 150), by Justin Martyr, in *St. Justin Martyr: the First and Second Apologies*, Leslie William Barnard, trans. (New York: Paulist Press, 1997).

ADH   *A Door of Hope* (anonymous 1657 tract), in *FMM*.

AEV   *An Eschatology of Victory*, by J. Marcellus Kik (Nutley, New Jersey: Presbyterian and Reformed Publishing Co., 1971).

AEX   *The Apocalypse Explained*, by H. M. Féret, OP, Elizabethe Corathiel, trans. (Fort Collins, Colorado: Roman Catholic Books, 1958).

AG   *Against Heresies* (174), by Irenaeus, in *The Writings of Irenaeus*, Alexander Roberts and W. H. Rambaut, trans. (Edinburgh: T. and T. Clark, 1874).

AGM   *Against Marcion* (c. 200), by Tertullian, in *The Writings of Quintus Sept Florens Tertullianus*, S. Thelwall, trans. (Edinburgh: T. and T. Clark, 1870).

AIR   *Annals of Imperial Rome* (109), by Cornelius Tacitus (New York: Penguin Books, 1989).

AJ *Antiquities of the Jews* (c. 100), by Flavius Josephus, in *The Life and Works of Flavius Josephus*, William Whiston, trans. (Peabody, Massachusetts: Hendrickson Publishers, Inc., 1987).

ANF *The Ante-Nicene Fathers: Translations of the Fathers Down to A.D. 325*, 10 volumes, Alexander Roberts and James Donaldson, eds. (Grand Rapids: Eerdmans Publishing Co., 1989).

APO *Apologetic* (c. 200), Tertullian, in *Works of Tertullian*, C. Dodgson, trans. (Oxford: J. H. Parker, 1842).

ATF *After the Rapture*, by Raymond Schafer and P. H. Johnston (Santa Ana, California: Vision House, 1977).

AWL *Are We Living in the End Times?* by Tim LaHaye (Wheaton, Illinois: Tyndale House, 1999).

BAP *Biblical Apocalyptics: A Study of the Most Notable Revelations of God*, by Milton S. Terry (Eugene, Oregon: Wipf and Stock, 2001).

BET *Beyond the End Times*, by John Noe (Bradford, Pennsylvania: International Preterist Assoc., 2000).

BFB *Born Fundamentalist, Born Again Catholic*, by David B. Currie (San Francisco, Ignatius Press, 1996).

BJF *Before Jerusalem Fell: Dating the book of Revelation*, by Kenneth L. Gentry (Tyler, Texas: Institute for Christian Economics, 1989).

BS *Bibliotheca Sacra Journal* (Dallas, Texas: Dallas Theological Seminary).

CAT *Catecheses, Catechetical Lectures* (348), by Cyril of Jerusalem, in *The Works of Saint Cyril of Jerusalem*, Leo P. McCauley and Anthony A. Stephenson, trans. (Washington, DC: Catholic University of America Press, 1970).

CCC *Catechism of the Catholic Church* (Boston: St. Paul Books and Media, 1994).

CCE   *Contra Celsus* (c. 200), by Origen, in *Origen Against Celsus*, James Bellamy, trans. (London: B. Mills and J. Robinson, 1660).

CCO   *Catechetical Commentary on the New Testament* (1884), by William Hurte, in *TBR*.

CE   *Catholic Encyclopedia*, 18 volumes (New York: The Encyclopedia Press, 1913).

CEC   *Celibacy in the Early Church*, by Stefan Heid (San Francisco: Ignatius Press, 2001).

CH   *Chronologia* (397), by Julias Africanus, in *NPN*.

CHR   *Chronicle* (c. 300), by Eusebius Pamphilius, in *ANF*.

CID   *Commentaria in Danielem* (408), by Jerome, in *Jerome's Commentary on Daniel*, Gleason L. Archer, Jr., trans. (Grand Rapids, Michigan: Baker Book House, 1958).

CLH   *Clementine Homilia* (c. 200), by Titus Flavius Clemens (Clement of Alexandria), in *The Apostolic Father*, 2 volumes, Kirsopp Lake, trans. (Cambridge: Harvard University Press, 1959).

CNT   *Commentary on the New Testament from the Talmud and Hebraica* (1674), by John Lightfoot (Peabody, Massachusetts: Hendrickson Publishers, Inc., 1989).

COA   *Commentary on The Apocalypse* (270), by Victorinus, in *ANF*.

COG   *The City of God* (c. 400), by Augustine (New York: Modern Library, 1950).

COR   *Commentary on Revelation* (1884), by Robert Young, in *TBR*.

CSP   *Clarendon State Papers* (c. 1640), in *FMM*.

CT   *Chicago Tribune* (daily newspaper).

CUM   *Cum sicut* (1459), by Pope Pius II, in *DNZ*.

DAS   *Divino Afflante Spiritu*, by Pope Pius XII (Boston: Daughters of St. Paul, 1943).

DCF   *Dogmatic Constitution on the Catholic Faith*,
      Vatican I, 1870.

DHF   *Apologia de Fuga* (*Defense of His Flight*; 358), by
      Athanasius, in *NPN*.

DID   *Didache* (c. 100), author uncertain, in *The Apostolic
      Father*, 2 volumes, Kirsopp Lake, trans. (Cambridge:
      Harvard University Press, 1959).

DJT   *Dialogue with the Jew Trypho* (c. 150), by Justin
      Martyr, in *ANF*.

DKP   *Daniel, The Key to Prophetic Revelation*, by John
      Walvoord (Chicago: Moody Press, 1989).

DM   *Decision Magazine* (Evangelical Christian periodical).

DNZ   *Enchiridion Symbolorum: The Sources of Catholic Dogma*,
      Henry Denzinger, ed., Roy J. Deferrari, trans. (St. Louis:
      Herder Book Co., 1957).

DRC   *De Resurrectione Carnis, Treatise on the Resurrection*,
      by Quintus Florens Tertullian, Ernest Evans, trans.
      (London: SPCK, 1960).

DRE   *Discourse on the Resurrection* (c. 150), by Melito of
      Sardis, in *On Pascha and Fragments*, Stuart George Hall,
      trans. (Oxford: Clarendon Press, 1979).

DT   *Dispensational Truth* (Fundamentalist Christian
      periodical).

DV   *Dei Verbum*, in *Vatican Council II: The Conciliar and Post
      Conciliar Documents*, Austin Flannery, OP, ed. (North-
      port, New York: Costello Publishing Co., Inc., 1992).

EH   *Ecclesiastical History* (325), by Eusebius Pamphilius,
      Kirsopp Lake, trans. (New York: Harvard University
      Press, 1980).

EOB   *Epistle of Barnabas* (c. 100), author uncertain, in *ANF*.

EP   *Epistle 30 to Paula* (c. 400), by Jerome, in *The Letters
      of Saint Jerome*, James Duff, trans. (Dublin: Brown and
      Nolan Limited, 1942).

EPA   *Epistle of Augustine* (c. 400), by Augustine, in GCC.

EPI   *Epistle 82 to Jerome* (405), by Augustine, in *The Correspondence (394-419) Between Jerome and Augustine of Hippo*, Carolinne White, trans. (Lewiston, New York: Edwin Mellen Press, 1990).

EPJ   *Epistle 121 to Algasiam* (c. 400), by Jerome, in *The Letters of Saint Jerome*, James Duff, trans. (Dublin: Brown and Nolan Limited, 1942).

EPP   *Epistle to the Philippians* (c. 150), by Polycarp, in *ANF*.

EPS   *Epistle 21* (c. 400), by Jerome, in *Certain Selected Epistles of St. Hierome*, Henry Hawkins, ed. (St. Omer: English College Press, 1975).

EPT   *Epistle 149 to Paulinum* (c. 400), by Augustine, in *Letters of Saint Augustine, Bishop of Hippo*, translator: J. G. Cunningham, ed. (Edinburgh: T. and T. Clark, 1872).

ET   *Everyman's Talmud*, Abraham Cohen, ed. (New York: Schocken Books, 1995).

ETS   *Epistula ad Smyrnaeos* (*Epistle to Smyrna*; c. 100), by Ignatius of Antioch, in *ANF*.

ETV   *End Time Visions*, by Richard Abanes (Nashville: Broadman and Holman Publishers, 1999).

FA   *First Apology* (c. 150), by Justin Martyr, in *ANF*.

FEC   *First Epistle of Clement to the Corinthians* (c. 70), by Clement of Rome, in *ANF*.

FEL   *The Festal Letters* (c. 350), by Athanasius, William Cureton, ed. (London: Society for the Publication of Oriental Texts, 1848).

FMM   *Fifth Monarchy Men*, by B. S. Capp (Totowa, New Jersey: Rowman and Littlefield, 1972).

FS   *Future Survival*, by Chuck Smith (New York: Aperture, 1978).

GCC   *Golden Chain*, by Thomas Aquinas (New York: Mowbray, 1956).

GHF   *The Gnostic Heresies of the First and Second Centuries*, by Henry L. Mansel (London: J. Murray, 1875).

GPR   *Global Peace and the Rise of the Antichrist*, by Dave Hunt (Eugene, Oregon: Harvest House Publishers, 1990).

HCC   *History of the Christian Church*, 8 volumes, by Philip Schaff (Grand Rapids, Michigan: Eerdmans, 1950).

HE   *Heresies, The Panarion of St. Epiphanius of Salamis* (375), by Epiphanius, Frank Williams, trans. (New York: E. J. Brill, 1987).

HFT   *Homilies on First Thessalonians* (c. 400), by John Chrysostom, in *The Homilies of Saint John Chrysostom on the Epistles of St. Paul the Apostle to the Philippians, Colossians, and Thessalonians*, H. Walford, ed. (London: W. Smith, 1879).

HOA   *History of the Arians* (c. 350), by Athanasius, in *Historical Writings of St. Athanasius*, William Bright, trans. (Oxford: Clarendon Press, 1881).

HOM   *Homily on Matthew* (c. 400), by John Chrysostom, in *Homilies of Saint John Chrysostom, Archbishop of Constantinople, on the Gospel of St. Matthew* (London: W. Smith, 1885).

IAH   *Is The Antichrist at Hand?* by Oswald J. Smith (Toronto: Tabernacle, 1926).

INC   *Incarnation* (c. 350), by Athanasius, in *The Incarnation of the Word of God* (New York: Macmillan, 1946).

ISW   *Interpretation of Seventy Weeks of Daniel*, by Louis E. Knowles (Chestnut Hill: Westminster Theological Journal, 1948).

ITR   *Interpretation of the Revelation* (c. 450), by Andreas of Cappadocia, in *BJF*.

KJV   *Authorized King James Version of the Bible* (New York: Oxford University Press, 1945).

LAH   *L'Apocalypse et L'Histoire* (1957), by S. Giet, in *NCE*.

LAP   *L'Apocalypse ou les Apocalypses de Saint Jean?* (1949), by M. E. Boismard, in *NCE*.

LB   *Left Behind: A Novel of the Earth's Last Days*, by Tim LaHaye and Jerry B. Jenkins (Wheaton, Illinois: Tyndale House, 1996).

LGP   *The Late Great Planet Earth*, by Hal Lindsey (Grand Rapids, Michigan: Zondervan, 1970).

LUM   *Lumen Gentium*, in *Vatican Council II: The Conciliar and Post Conciliar Documents*, Austin Flannery OP, ed. (Northport, New York: Costello Publishing Co., Inc., 1992).

NAB   *New American Bible* (New York: Catholic Book Publishing Co., 1991).

NCE   *New Catholic Encyclopedia* (New York: McGraw Hill, 1967).

NIV   *The Holy Bible, New International Version* (Grand Rapids, Michigan: Zondervan Bible Publishers, 1978).

NNF   *1994?* by Harold Camping (New York: Vantage Press, 1992).

NPN   *Nicene and Post-Nicene Fathers of the Christian Church*, 14 volumes (New York: The Christian Literature Co., 1890).

NTD   *The New Testament Documents, Are They Reliable?* by Frederick Fyvie Bruce (Downers Grove, Illinois: Intervarsity Press, 1960).

PD   *Providentissimus Deus*, by Pope Leo XIII (Boston: Daughters of St. Paul, 1893).

PDG   *Pascendi Dominica Gregis*, by Pope Pius X (Boston: Daughters of St. Paul, 1907).

PE   *Pentecostal Evangel* (Christian periodical), 1949.

PEN   *Pascal's Pensées* (c. 1656), by Blaise Pascal, W. F. Trotter, trans. (New York: Dutton, 1958).

PEW   *Planet Earth — 2000 A.D.: Will Mankind Survive?* by
       Hal Lindsey (Torrance, California: Western Front
       Ltd., 1994).

POD   "Preterism and the Orthodox Doctrine of Christ's
       Parousia: a Constructive Critique of M. R. King," by
       Richard A. White (Trinity Evangelical Divinity School
       Thesis, 1988).

POG   *The Proof of the Gospel* (c. 300), by Eusebius Pamphilius,
       W. J. Ferrar, trans. (New York: The Macmillan Co.,
       1920).

PSB   *Prophecy Study Bible*, John Hagee, ed. (Nashville:
       Thomas Nelson Publishing, 1997).

REV   *Revelation*, by John Peter Lange, in *Lange's Commentary
       on the Holy Scriptures*, 24 volumes (Grand Rapids,
       Michigan: Zondervan Publishing House, 1960).

RKC   *Revelation: Kingdoms in Conflict*, by Gene Fadeley
       (Waxhaw, North Carolina: Anchor Publishing, 1995).

RLP   *Will Russia Invade Palestine? Russia in the Light of
       Prophecy*, by Dan Gilbert (Los Angeles: Jewish Hope
       Publishing House, 1944).

RSV   *Revised Standard Version of the Bible, Catholic Edition*
       (San Francisco: Ignatius Press, 1966).

SEC   *Second Epistle of Clement to the Corinthians* (c. 70),
       by Clement of Rome, in *The Apostolic Father*, 2 volumes,
       Kirsopp Lake, trans. (Cambridge: Harvard University
       Press, 1959).

SH   *Sacred History* (c. 400), by Sulpicius Severus, in *The
       Western Fathers* (New York: Harper Torchbooks,
       1965).

SLB   *Shattering the Left Behind Delusion*, by John Noe (Bradford,
       Pennsylvania: International Preterist Assoc., 2000).

SME   *Sancta Mater Ecclesia, The Historicity of the Gospels*
       (Boston: Pauline Book and Media, 1964).

SO   *The Sibylline Oracles of Egyptian Judaism* (c. 100),
        author unknown, John Joseph Collins, trans. (Mis-
        soula, Montana: Society of Biblical Literature for
        the Pseudepigrapha Group, 1974).

SOC   "The Signs of His Coming: An Examination of the
        Olivet Discourse," by David J. Palm (Trinity Evan-
        gelical Divinity School Thesis, 1993).

SPA   *Spiritus Paraclitus*, by Pope Benedict XV (Boston:
        Daughters of St. Paul, 1920).

SRB   *The New Scofield Reference Bible*, C. I. Scofield, ed.
        (Oxford: Oxford University Press, 1967).

SSA   *Sermons*, by St. Augustine, in *The Later Christian
        Fathers: A Selection from the Writings of the Fathers
        from St. Cyril of Jerusalem to St. Leo the Great* (Oxford:
        Oxford University Press, 1970).

STO   *Stromata* (c. 200), by Titus Flavius Clemens, in
        Stromateis, Clement of Alexandria, John Ferguson,
        trans. (Washington, DC: Catholic University of
        America Press, 1991).

SUM   *Summa Theologiae: A Concise Translation* (c.1250),
        by Thomas Aquinas, Timothy McDermott, ed.
        (Westminster, Maryland: Christians Classics,
        1989).

TAP   *The Apocalypse*, by André Feuillet, Thomas E.
        Crane, trans. (Staten Island, New York: Alba
        House, 1964).

TBC   *The Bible Code*, by Michael Drosnin (New York:
        Simon and Schuster, 1997).

TBR   *The Book of Revelation*, by Foy E. Wallace (Fort
        Smith, Arkansas: Wallace Jr. Publications, 1997).

TCA   *Treatise on Christ and Antichrist* (c. 200), by Hippolytus
        of Rome, in *Treatise on Antichrist* (Willits, California:
        Eastern Orthodox Books, 1979).

Rapture

TDY   *The Day and Year of Christ's Birth and Crucifixion*,
      by Robert L. Thomas and Stanley N. Gundry
      (Grand Rapids, Michigan: Zondervan, n.d.).

TED   *The Epitome of the Divine Institutes* (310), by Lucius
      Caecilius Firmianius Lactantius, in *The Divine
      Institutes*, Sister M. F. McDonald, trans. (Washington,
      DC: Catholic University of America Press, 1964).

TEL   *The Essential C. S. Lewis*, Lyle W. Dorsett, ed. (New
      York: Simon and Schuster, 1996).

TEM   *The Everlasting Man*, by G. K. Chesterton (San
      Francisco: Ignatius Press, 1993).

THI   *The Annals* (109), Bks. 1-6, by Cornelius Tacitus,
      W. F. Allen, trans. (Boston: Ginn and Co., 1890).

TKB   *The King's Business Magazine* (Fundamentalist
      Christian periodical), 1938.

TMK   *The Millennial Kingdom*, by John F. Walvoord
      (Grand Rapids, Michigan: Zondervan, 1983).

TPR   *De Principiis* (c. 300), by Origen, in *On First
      Principles: Being Koetschau's Text of the de Principiis*,
      G. W. Butterworth, trans. (Gloucester, Massachusetts:
      Peter Smith Publisher, Inc., 1985).

TRB   *The Rise of Babylon: Sign of the End Times*, by
      Charles Dyer (Wheaton, Illinois: Tyndale House,
      1991).

TRQ   *The Rapture Question*, by John Walvoord (Grand
      Rapids, Michigan: Zondervan, 1957).

TSS   *The Search for Salvation*, by David Wells (Downers
      Grove, Illinois: Intervarsity Press, 1978).

TSV   *The Shepherd: First Book of Visions*, by Hermas, in
      The Apostolic Fathers, 6 volumes, Robert A. Kraft, ed.
      (New York: Thomas Nelson, 1964).

TTC   *Things to Come*, by J. Dwight Pentecost (Grand
      Rapids, Michigan: Zondervan, 1965).

TW   *The Way*, by Josemaria Escriva (New York: Scepter, 1992).

TWE   *The Weekly Evangel* (Evangelical Christian periodical).

UBH   *Unger's Bible Handbook*, by Merrill F. Unger (Chicago: Moody Press, 1967).

USN   *U.S. News and World Report* (weekly news periodical).

WD   *Webster's Dictionary*, David B. Guralnik, ed. (Cleveland: World Publishing Co., 1979).

WIN   *Why I Am Not a Christian, and Other Essays on Religion*, by Bertrand Russell (New York: Simon and Schuster, 1977).

WJ   *Wars of the Jews* (c. 100), by Flavius Josephus, in *The Life and Works of Flavius Josephus*, William Whiston, trans. (Peabody, Massachusetts: Hendrickson, n.d.).

WQT   *The Writings of Quintus Sept Florens Tertullianus*, S. Thelwall, trans. (Edinburgh: T. and T. Clark, 1870).

WRI   *The Collected Writings of J. N. Darby*, William Kelly, ed. (London: G. Morrish, 1867).

XGM   *Exercitations upon the Gospel of St. Matthew, Commentary on the New Testament, Matthew — 1 Corinthians* (1658), by John Lightfoot (Peabody, Massachusetts: Hendrickson Publishers, Inc., 1995).

ZPE   *Zondervan Pictorial Encyclopedia of the Bible*, Merrill C. Tenney, ed. (Grand Rapids, Michigan: Zondervan, 1975).

David B. Currie

David B. Currie was raised in a devout, Fundamentalist Christian family. His father was a pastor, and both parents were teachers at Moody Bible Institute, in Chicago, Illinois. As a child, Currie rubbed elbows with many of the leaders of the Fundamentalist movement. His childhood dream was to become a minister himself.

That dream was fulfilled after Currie studied at Trinity College and at Trinity Evangelical Divinity School. He became a Fundamentalist missionary, as did his wife, Colleen, and his primary responsibility was to train Evangelical college students in methods of college campus evangelization.

Although he had been active in the leadership of Fundamentalist and Evangelical churches throughout his life, Currie continued to investigate theological and biblical questions that he thought had no viable answer in any Protestant tradition. After an often painful search for the truth, he, Colleen, and their six children (they have since been blessed with two more) reluctantly found themselves knocking on the door of the Catholic Church, and all eight of them soon embraced the Catholic Faith.

As a lay apologist for his new Faith, Currie wrote the popular book *Born Fundamentalist, Born Again Catholic* (Ignatius Press, 1996) and has written for *Immaculata Magazine*. Currie speaks

Rapture

about the Faith to Catholic groups and parishes and on retreats, and some of his talks, including "The Great Price of Truth," "The Rapture Revealed," "Wheat Among Thistles," and "Rapture: Ruse or Reality?" are available on tape (St. Joseph Communications).

Currie welcomes questions and comments from his readers: david@saintjoe.com.